Introduction to Multicultural Counseling for Helping Professionals

Introduction to Multicultural Counseling for Helping Professionals

second edition

Wanda M.L. Lee ◆ John A. Blando
Nathalie D. Mizelle ◆ Graciela L. Orozco

Routledge
Taylor & Francis Group
New York   London

Routledge
Taylor & Francis Group
270 Madison Avenue
New York, NY 10016

Routledge
Taylor & Francis Group
2 Park Square
Milton Park, Abingdon
Oxon OX14 4RN

© 2007 by Taylor & Francis Group, LLC
Routledge is an imprint of Taylor & Francis Group, an Informa business

Printed in the United States of America on acid-free paper
10 9 8 7 6 5 4 3 2 1

International Standard Book Number-10: 0-415-95702-8 (Softcover)
International Standard Book Number-13: 978-0-415-95702-1 (Softcover)

Library of Congress Cataloging-in-Publication Data

Introduction to multicultural counseling for helping professionals / Wanda M.L. Lee
... [et al.]. -- 2nd ed.
        p. cm.
    Rev. ed. of: An introduction to multicultural counseling / Wanda M.L. Lee. 1999.
    Includes bibliographical references and index.
    ISBN-13: 978-0-415-95702-1 (pb)
        1. Cross-cultural counseling. I. Lee, Wanda M. L. II. Lee, Wanda M. L.
    Introduction to multicultural counseling.

    BF636.7.C76I58 2007
    158'.308--dc22   2006028992

Visit the Taylor & Francis Web site at
http://www.taylorandfrancis.com

and the Routledge Web site at
http://www.routledge.com

To my beloved multicultural family: Ken, my hardworking and supportive husband; Malia, my creative and independent daughter; Logan, my athletic and empathic son; and Minou, the small, shy one who chose us. And to my mother, Annette, for a lifetime of encouragement.

Wanda

To my loving husband, Brian, and my devoted animal companion, Rudi. To my father and mother, Manuel and Beverly (Apollonia). To my brother, sister-in-law, and niece, Albert, Barbara, and Apollonia.

John

To my loving parents Richard and Julye Mizelle who continue to inspire me.

Nathalie

Para mi linda familia: Samuel, Natasha y Tamara.

Graciela

Contents

12   Middle Eastern Americans in Counseling   189

13   Counseling Women   199

18   **Counseling Bicultural/Biracial People**   291

Preface

When culture-specific information is presented or discussed there is always the danger that the information will form the basis of stereotypes; in other words, making generalizations about any cultural group is potentially misleading. More accurate or positive stereotypes may replace those commonly held, but they are still stereotypes. This issue seems unavoidable when attempting to present cultural knowledge in the hopes that it will broaden the range of assessment and treatment planning considerations counselors make with respect to a particular client. It cannot be overstated that regardless of the general knowledge that is available regarding a particular cultural group, every counselor must be open to meeting each client as a unique individual whose background, values, and other characteristics may or may not be similar to those of others within their cultural group(s).

This book is written primarily with respect to information about ethnic and cultural minority groups within the United States. Many of the general issues and recommendations related to counseling may be applicable to counseling cultural minority populations in other countries; however, the reader is cautioned not to overgeneralize from minority experiences in one country to members of the same cultural group in another country.

It was impossible to include all the relevant cultural groups in the United States. Many specific ethnic groups have not been included or are included only within the context of a broader ethnic group, often due to a lack of research on these groups. The concerns of all groups are significant, but unfortunately there has been comparatively little available research or published writing about some groups. New to this edition are chapters on Middle Eastern Americans and biracial/bicultural people. The most coverage has been given to groups who are numerically or politically most salient and where there is substantial existing counseling or psychology literature.

This book is part of the evolution of teaching a course on multicultural counseling since 1981. Over the years, the first author became increasingly dissatisfied with existing books on the subject because they tended to focus only on ethnicity and there were several other dimensions of cultural diversity that needed to be included in the class to meet curriculum and accreditation requirements, including gender, sexual orientation, physical disability, and aging. Eventually, she developed a course reader that sampled from existing texts and current journal articles. The drawback of this approach was that each writer had a different voice and often covered the material from a somewhat different approach, which was sometimes confusing to students new to the topic. In the end, it seemed that the best way to cover the topic of multicultural counseling, in the manner she felt necessary, with (1) a balance of etic and emic issues, (2) an emphasis on and respect for indigenous treatments, and (3) recognition of the complexity of multiple minority status (e.g., female and ethnic minority, ethnic minority person with a disability, etc.) was to write a book herself. Years later, you are now reading the results of that initial effort, which has now been revised and updated.

New to this edition, in addition to dedicated chapters on counseling Middle Eastern Americans and counseling biracial/bicultural people previously mentioned, are (1) the themes of social class considerations and spirituality have been infused consistently throughout the book, (2) case vignettes with thought questions and multiple reflections by the authors, (3) expanded cultural resource sections with annotations, (4) over 300 new references, and (5) additional coauthors who are diverse in ethnicity, culture, and areas of professional expertise.

The authorship of this edition was expanded to include a multicultural group of authors. We ourselves are a diverse group: a heterosexual Asian American woman, a gay European American man, a heterosexual African American woman, and a heterosexual Latina. We also bring a diversity of counseling expertise to our task with backgrounds in college counseling, community mental health, rehabilitation counseling, and school counseling. You may note some differences in our reflections to the case vignettes, which we feel is a good thing.

It continues to be our sincere hope that this book will be of some help to you along your own path toward multicultural competence.

☐ A Note to Instructors and Training Directors

This book is envisioned as a primer, a general introduction to counseling issues for helping professionals. Ideally, students or trainees would read one chapter each week as an overview of background, cultural, and clinical issues of importance. Each topic can then be supplemented by current specific readings either chosen by the instructor or the learners themselves. Many of the chapters list recommended resources for further cultural education. The case vignettes are provided with several questions to help focus discussions. Multiple reflections from the authors are included to convey different points of view and the message that there is no one correct way to counsel a client. The book is tailored to a college semester format, but can be adapted to a shorter term by assigning more than one chapter per week as needed. In a human service agency, school, or other clinical setting, this book can be used for staff and intern training as well as reference.

Acknowledgments

Many thanks to our students, whose interest and questions over the years motivated the first author to begin and continue the development of this book. In particular, thanks to former student Bita Shooshani, who helped with locating relevant resources about Middle Eastern people. Thanks also to Tamara Orozco and Samuel Orozco, whose expertise on Latino history contributed to our work as well.

Multicultural Counseling: Past, Present, and Future

Who decides what is margin and what is text? Who decides where the borders of the homeland run? Absences and silences are potent. It is the eloquent margins which frame the history of the land.

Janette Turner Hospital (Biggs, 1996, p. 82)

The population of the United States is becoming more and more diverse. Thirty-one percent of the current population is African American, Latino, Asian/Pacific Islander American, or American Indian (U.S. Census Bureau, 2001), yet the vast majority of counselors are European American by ethnicity and all of the major theoretical approaches to counseling were developed by Europeans (Freud, Jung, Adler, Perls, etc.) or Americans of European descent (Rogers, Skinner, Ellis, etc.). The counseling profession is basically a product of European American culture (Das, 1995). As the field of counseling moves into the 21st century, cultural differences in addition to ethnicity have increasingly gained recognition as important considerations in the counseling process: gender roles, sexual orientation, aging, and physical disability. Understanding the complex social and cultural background of each client is integral to successful counseling. This book is written for beginning counselors, practicing counselors, and other helping professionals who have not had previous formal training in working with multicultural clients.

☐ **Culture**

To begin the journey toward becoming a culturally competent counselor, you must first ask yourself, "What is culture?" Haviland (1975) defines culture as "a set of shared assumptions where people can predict each other's actions in a given circumstance and react accordingly" (p. 6). When the client and counselor come from different cultural backgrounds, whether it be in terms of ethnicity, sex, sexual orientation, disability, or age, they may not share the same assumptions about many things, including the counseling process, and counseling may be an uncomfortable unpredictable interaction for both parties. Then the likelihood of a second session, let alone productive change, becomes low.

Culture can be defined in many ways. According to *Merriam-Webster* (2006), it is "the customary beliefs, social forms, and material traits of a racial, religious, or social group." In this definition, what is customary or normative for a particular group is key. In order to understand a client's culture, the counselor must understand what is normative of that client's cultural group(s). In this context, the client's own behavior can then be evaluated as it compares to how others in her or his group would typically behave. Behavior that is abnormal in one culture may be adaptive in another.

Encyclopedia Britannica (2006) defines culture as an

> Integrated pattern of human knowledge, belief, and behaviour that is both a result of and integral to the human capacity for learning and transmitting knowledge to succeeding generations. Culture thus consists of language, ideas, beliefs, customs, taboos, codes, institutions, tools, techniques, works of art, rituals, ceremonies, and symbols.... An individual's attitudes, values, ideals, and beliefs are greatly influenced by the culture (or cultures) in which he or she lives.

There are many facets of culture and many of them, such as language, customs, values, beliefs, spirituality, sex roles, sociopolitical history, and so on, may have an impact in counseling.

There are several ways that culture is important in counseling. First, counseling occurs in a cultural context, within an office, school, college, or other organization, and, beyond this, within a larger community or society. If the client must seek treatment within an environment that is culturally foreign, she or he may be reluctant even to initiate counseling. Second, as briefly mentioned above, appropriate assessment of a client's problems should take into consideration the client's culture. Third, counseling itself is culturally based. Counseling as it has been tradition-ally taught in most English-speaking countries developed from histori-cal and social influences most relevant to White, straight, able-bodied, young clients. There are many cultures that do not have a word for coun-seling and the ways people ordinarily seek help within their culture may not include going to a counselor. Finally, culture itself may be the focus of counseling. When a client is going through cultural transition, when there are cultural differences interfering with intimate relationships, when a client has been the victim of cultural racism, sexism, homopho-bia, ablism, or ageism, when a client's personal culture is so different from that of the surrounding society that the stress is unbearable, then culture itself may become the center of the counseling process.

☐ Ethnicity

McGoldrick, Pearce, and Giordano (1982) described ethnicity as a sense of commonality that is more than race, religion, national, or geographic origin. Conscious and unconscious processes contribute to a sense of identity and historical continuity. Another way to look at ethnicity is as a perceived common ancestry, whether real or fictitious (Shibutani & Kwan, 1965). In this respect there are several broad ethnic groups within the United States: Native Americans, African Americans, Latinos and Latinas, Asian Americans, and European Americans. Some of these eth-nic groups may have persons of several races grouped within them, for example, Latinos. What is salient in the United States is that members of these groups are perceived by others as having a common ancestry even though there is much cultural diversity within each of these groups.

☐ Race

"Race divides human beings into categories that loom in our psyches" (Jones, 1997, p. 339). Common definitions tend to include physical or genetic grouping and a biological underpinning. Current research, how-ever, indicates that there is often more diversity within a racial group than between racial groups. The term actually has more of a socially defined connotation. It is used on a limited basis in this book, primarily when the social aspects of such grouping are the focus of discussion.

☐ Minority Group

Corey, Corey, and Callanan (1988) defined a minority group as people who have been discriminated against or subjected to unequal treatment. All of the ethnic groups mentioned above are minority groups within the United States except some European American subgroups who have historically been afforded the political, social, and economic power to discriminate against others. Using this definition of minority group would also include women, gays and lesbians, the elderly, and persons with disabilities because all these groups have also been subjected to unequal treatment in the history of this nation.

A broad view of cultural differences in counseling and other helping professions includes the need to become aware of and learn about many specific cultural minority groups who may differ from the counselor in a variety of ways, not limited to ethnicity, gender, sexual orientation or identity, age, or disability.

☐ Early Issues

Historically, there have been many ways of looking at cultural differences between people. How differences are viewed has been a reflection of the sociopolitical climate of the time. In the 1800s England was at the height of its colonization of other lands. Sir Francis Galton, a member of the ruling class and relative of Charles Darwin (who proposed the biological concept of natural selection), began to look at differences between people and concluded that they were a result of genetic deficiency. In this case, social science could help justify the social and economic policies that would keep the upper classes in a superior position. This sort of genetic interpretation of cultural differences is still held by more recent writers such as Jensen (1969) in the 1960s, Shockley (1971) in the 1970s, and Murray and Hernstein in the 1990s (Morganthau, 1994).

Another view of cultural differences was a more anthropological one. As anthropology developed into a social science, some may have been drawn to studying different cultures as primitive and interesting scientific curiosities and others wanted to observe and record other cultures before they were destroyed by modern influences. The term "cross-cultural" in psychological literature originally referred to comparisons of behavior in different cultures, particularly different countries.

The next view of cultural differences became popular in the 1960s along with government programs such as the Peace Corps and Vista. Although those who selflessly volunteered in these programs brought increased goodwill and understanding between cultures, an implicit metamessage of these programs was that other cultures were in some ways deficient or deprived and in need of assistance. These sincere efforts should be viewed in contrast to the centuries of slavery, colonization, and commercial exploitation of non-European peoples for centuries that continue today.

In the 1960s, persons of color were described as "culturally disadvantaged" or "culturally different" (Jackson, 1995). Many sources of cultural deprivation were assumed. Nutritional deprivation (i.e., poor diet) contributed to mental retardation and physical susceptibility to illness. Environmental deprivation included crowding, noise, and lack of stimulation, all factors that have negative psychological effects. Sociocultural deprivation included factors such as a lack of role models or parental encouragement. Linguistic deprivation meant a lack of exposure to "proper" English. A person from a cultural minority background might be considered disadvantaged in many of these areas and many social programs were funded to address these possible sources of deprivation. However, the underlying message was still the implication that a minority person's culture was in some way inferior to that of the majority.

The most recent way to view cultural difference is to make the assumption that no culture is more desirable than another and to explore the legitimacy and benefits of any differences between cultures. This implies a valuing of diversity. This view of cultural differences is particularly timely in today's global economy where countries and peoples must increasingly learn to understand and respect each other for their mutual survival. What this means for counseling is that cultural differences between counselor and client are potentially beneficial if accepted and included in the counseling process. This is the viewpoint from which the current field of multicultural counseling has developed.

The study of multiculturalism is a relatively new emphasis within the field of counseling. Much of the professional literature on the mental health needs of ethnic minorities has only been written in the last 30 years (Das, 1995). One of the first books on the subject was Paul Pedersen and colleagues' *Counseling Across Cultures* (Pedersen, Lonner, & Draguns), written in 1976, and now in its fifth edition (Pedersen, Draguns, Lonner, & Trimble, 2002).

Some of the major theoretical developments in the field of multicultural counseling are (1) the triad model, (2) research on culture shock and the acculturation process, (3) multiple developmental stage approaches conceptualizing cultural identity development, and (4) the concept of multicultural competency. The triad model was developed by Pedersen for use in training (1977). The roles of counselor, client, and "anti-counselor," or embodiment of the problem, are used to simulate a counseling session and increase awareness and skills. Years of research on culture shock (Furnham & Bochner, 1986) have yielded models of cultural transition that can be applied to the experiences of foreign students, immigrants, and refugees in counseling. Also, many models of cultural identity development have been proposed and refined to apply to many specific ethnic and other cultural groups. Multicultural competency as a professional focus and theoretical construct has led to the development of many assessment instruments. Each of these conceptual developments is discussed in detail in later chapters. The field of multicultural counseling is growing in maturity and some substantial accomplishments have been made; however, there is still much room for theoretical development and later research substantiation.

☐ Current Issues and Controversies

Is Multiculturalism an Exclusive or an Inclusive Concept?

The issue here is whether multiculturalism should exclusively involve the study of ethnic differences as they affect the counseling process. Proponents of an exclusive viewpoint are concerned that the influence of racism will be ignored or diluted if other cultural differences such as sex, age, sexual orientation, or disability are also included (Jackson, 1995). Proponents of a more inclusive viewpoint recognize that discrimination and unequal treatment for reasons other than race are also widespread and also affect clients, counselors, and the counseling process in important ways that should be studied. Other cultural minorities experience discrimination, as do ethnic minorities, based on a permanent aspect of themselves that cannot be changed. In this book, an inclusive view of multicultural counseling is taken. Some chapters (e.g., Chapter 3, "Understanding and Appreciating Difference") focus on individual differences and prejudice from a broad psychological perspective as they affect all people, and other chapters emphasize the experiences of different ethnic and other cultural groups.

Do the Same Basic Counseling Principles and Techniques Apply to Everyone Regardless of Cultural Background?

The controversy here is between taking an "etic" or an "emic" perspective (Berry, 1969). The etic approach emphasizes the universal elements of counseling that all cultural groups are assumed to share. Examples are: discrimination, identity development, validation and empowerment, communication, social class differences, acculturation, transference, and counter-transference (Das, 1995; Lee, 1994). The emic approach emphasizes the indigenous or specific characteristics of each cultural group that may have an impact on the counseling process. The comparison is between a group (in-depth coverage of specific cultures) versus a conceptual approach to multicultural counseling. Many books on multicultural counseling have tended to take a more emic perspective; however, the best approach is a blend of etic and emic perspectives (Das, 1995). This book adopts a blended approach. The first section covers etic themes that are more universal across cultures (e.g., discrimination, assessment, acculturation, identity development) and the next two sections focus on ethnic groupings (e.g., Native Americans, African Americans, Latinos and Latinas, Asian Americans, European Americans, and Arab Americans) and some specific cultural minorities (e.g., women, gay men and lesbians, older people, and people with a disability). New to this edition, two more etic influences, spirituality and social class considerations, are discussed in the chapters that focus on a broad cultural group.

Should We Be Adapting Traditional Counseling to Meet the Needs of Nontraditional Clients or Examining Nontraditional Counseling to Enlighten Traditional Approaches?

Inasmuch as traditional counseling developed from a European perspective for use with persons of European cultural background, professionals now agree that it is important to modify traditional counseling techniques to fit persons of various cultural backgrounds. One way to do this is to study traditional counseling skills and see how well they apply to each specific cultural group. Some research has been done in this area, but much more remains to be studied, especially because there are myriad counseling techniques and specific cultural groups. Another approach is to study the indigenous helping traditions within a specific cultural group and either work concurrently with traditional healers or learn from them and develop new counseling techniques appropriate to the client's cultural group. This approach calls on the counselor to become somewhat of a cultural anthropologist, to learn about other cultures through travel, film, reading, and personal relationships. This approach is more challenging and requires the counselor to be continually open to new ways of viewing the world and new techniques. Eventually this approach should prove more successful as it makes use of the client's own worldview and values, but there has been, and continues to be, relatively little research that has focused on indigenous counseling techniques. In this book, "indigenous counseling techniques" refers to counseling methods that have been developed by and for the cultural group and, where available, these techniques are described.

Should Multicultural Training Be Required for Licensure or Certification in Counseling?

At present there is no general requirement that a counselor be trained in multicultural counseling before becoming licensed or certified, although the state of Massachusetts requires some training in multicultural issues for psychologists (DeAngelis, 1994a).

The American Psychological Association has adopted Guidelines on Multicultural Education, Training, Research, Practice, and Organizational Change for Psychologists (APA, 2003a), Guidelines for Psychological Practice with Older Adults (APA, 2003b), and Guidelines for Psychotherapy with Lesbian, Gay, and Bisexual Clients (APA, 2000). The Ethical Principles of Psychologists and Code of Conduct (APA, 2002) explicitly includes cultural diversity (see box on page 9). Similarly, the Code of Ethics of the American Counseling Association (ACA, 2005) includes many multicultural tenets in the areas of competency boundaries, discrimination, assessment, training programs, and research (see box on page 11).

There are efforts to make multicultural training a necessary part of a counselor's expertise. The Council for Accreditation of Counseling and Related Educational Programs requires counselor education programs to include content on the social and cultural diversity within the counseling curriculum as an accreditation standard (CACREP, 2006). Among counselor education programs, 90% include specific coursework on multicultural counseling (Das, 1995). Similarly, of 17 model school psychology training programs surveyed, 94% required a diversity issues

Ethical Principles and Standards
Related to Multiculturalism
of the American Psychological Association

Principle E: Respect for People's Rights and Dignity

Psychologists are aware of and respect cultural, individual, and role differences, including those based on age, gender, gender identity, race, ethnicity, culture, national origin, religion, sexual orientation, disability, language, and socioeconomic status and consider these factors when working with members of such groups. Psychologists try to eliminate the effect on their work of biases based on those factors, and they do not knowingly participate in or condone activities of others based upon such prejudices.

2.01 Boundaries of Competence

(b) Where scientific or professional knowledge in the discipline of psychology establishes that an understanding of factors associated with age, gender, gender identity, race, ethnicity, culture, national origin, religion, sexual orientation, disability, language, or socioeconomic status is essential for effective implementation of their services or research, psychologists have or obtain the training, experience, consultation, or supervision necessary to ensure the competence of their services, or they make appropriate referrals, except as provided in Standard 2.02, Providing Services in Emergencies.

3.01 Unfair Discrimination

In their work-related activities, psychologists do not engage in unfair discrimination based on age, gender, gender identity, race, ethnicity, culture, national origin, religion, sexual orientation, disability, socioeconomic status, or any basis proscribed by law.

continued on next page

Ethical Principles and Standards
Related to Multiculturalism
of the American Psychological Association
continued from previous page

3.02 Sexual Harassment

Psychologists do not engage in sexual harassment. Sexual harassment is sexual solicitation, physical advances, or verbal or nonverbal conduct that is sexual in nature, that occurs in connection with the psychologist's activities or roles as a psychologist, and that either (1) is unwelcome, is offensive, or creates a hostile workplace or educational environment, and the psychologist knows or is told this or (2) is sufficiently severe or intense to be abusive to a reasonable person in the context. Sexual harassment can consist of a single intense or severe act or of multiple persistent or pervasive acts.

3.03 Other Harassment

"Psychologists do not knowingly engage in behavior that is harassing or demeaning to persons with whom they interact in their work based on factors such as those persons' age, gender, gender identity, race, ethnicity, culture, national origin, religion, sexual orientation, disability, language, or socioeconomic status."

9.02 Use of Assessments

(a) Psychologists administer, adapt, score, interpret, or use assessment techniques, interviews, tests, or instruments in a manner and for purposes that are appropriate in light of the research on or evidence of the usefulness and proper application of the techniques.

(b) Psychologists use assessment instruments whose validity and reliability have been established for use with members of the population tested. When such validity or reliability has not been established, psychologists describe the strengths and limitations of test results and interpretation.

continued on next page

**Ethical Principles and Standards
Related to Multiculturalism
of the American Psychological Association**
continued from previous page

(c)   Psychologists use assessment methods that are appropriate to an individual's language preference and competence, unless the use of an alternative language is relevant to the assessment issues.

Adapted from the Ethical principles and code of conduct (American Psychological Association, 2002).

**Ethical Principles Related to Multiculturalism
from the ACA Code of Ethics**

A.2.c. Developmental and Cultural Sensitivity

Couselors communicate information in ways that are both developmentally and culturally appropriate. Counselors use clear and understandable language when discussing issues related to informed consent. When clients have difficulty understanding the language used by counselors, they provide necessary services (e.g., arranging for an interpreter or translator) to ensure comprehension by clients. In collaboration with clients, counselors consider cultural implications of informed consent procedures and, where possible, counselors adjust their practices accordingly.

B.1.a. Multicultural/Diversity Considerations

Counselors maintain awareness and sensitivity regarding cultural meanings of confidentiality and privacy. Counselors respect differing views toward disclosure of information....

continued on next page

Ethical Principles Related to Multiculturalism
from the ACA Code of Ethics
continued from previous page

C.2.a. Boundaries of Competence

Counselors practice only within the boundaries of their competence, based on their education, training, supervised experience, state and national professional credentials, and appropriate professional experience. Counselors gain knowledge, personal awareness, sensitivity, and skills pertinent to working with a diverse client population.

C.5. Nondiscrimination

Counselors do not condone or engage in discrimination based on age, culture, disability, ethnicity, race, religion/spirituality, gender, gender identity, sexual orientation, marital status/partnership, language preference, socioeconomic status, or any basis proscribed by law....

E.5.b. Cultural Sensitivity

Counselors recognize that culture affects the manner in which clients' problems are defined. Clients' socioeconomic and cultural experiences are considered when diagnosing mental disorders.

E.5.c. Historical and Social Prejudices in the Diagnosis of Pathology

Counselors recognize historical and social prejudices in the misdiagnosis and pathologizing of certain individuals and groups and the role of mental health professionals in perpetuating these prejudices through diagnosis and treatment.

E.6.c. Culturally Diverse Populations

Counselors are cautious when selecting assessments for culturally diverse populations to avoid the use of instruments that lack appropriate psychometric properties for the client population.

continued on next page

Ethical Principles Related to Multiculturalism
from the ACA Code of Ethics
continued from previous page

E.8. Multicultural Issues/Diversity in Assessment

Counselors use with caution assessment techniques that were normed on populations other than that of the client. Counselors recognize the effects of age, color, culture, disability, ethnic group, gender, race, language preference, religion, spirituality, sexual orientation, and socioeconomic status on test administration and interpretation, and place test results in proper perspective with other relevant factors.

F.2.b. Multicultural Issues/Diversity in Supervision

Counseling supervisors are aware of and address the role of multiculturalism/diversity in the supervisory relationship.

F.3.c. Sexual Harassment

Counseling supervisors do not condone or subject supervisees to sexual harassment.

F.6.b. Infusing Multicultural Issues/Diversity

Counselor educators infuse material related to multiculturalism/diversity into all courses and workshops for the development of professional counselors.

F.10.b. Sexual Harassment

Counselor educators do not condone or subject students to sexual harassment.

F.11. Multicultural/Diversity Competence in Counselor Education and Training Programs

F.11.a. Faculty Diversity

Counselor educators are committed to recruiting and retaining a diverse faculty.

continued on next page

Ethical Principles Related to Multiculturalism from the ACA Code of Ethics

continued from previous page

F.11.b. Student Diversity

Counselor educators actively attempt to recruit and retain a diverse student body. Counselor educators demonstrate commitment to multicultural/diversity competence by recognizing and valuing diverse cultures and types of abilities students bring to the training experience. Counselor educators provide appropriate accommodations that enhance and support diverse student well-being and academic performance.

F.11.c. Multicultural/Diversity Competence

Couselor educators actively infuse multicultural/diversity competency in their training and supervision practices. They actively train students to gain awareness, knowledge, and skills in the competencies of multicultural practice. Counselor educators include case examples, role-plays, discussion questions, and other classroom activities that promote and represent various cultural perspectives.

G.1.g. Multicultural/Diversity Considerations in Research

When appropriate to research goals, counselors are sensitive to incorporating research procedures that take into account cultural considerations. They seek consultation when appropriate.

G.3.c. Sexual Harassment and Research Participants

Researchers do not condone or subject research participants to sexual harassment.

Adapted from the Code of ethics (American Counseling Association, 2005).

---

course (Rogers, 2006). In 1995 the Association for Multicultural Counseling and Development (AMCD) approved a document describing and explaining multicultural counseling competencies (Sue, Arredondo, & McDavis, 1992b). These competencies are accessible to counselors from http://www.counseling.org/Counselors/. Multicultural competencies are becoming widely recognized as needed areas of training.

☐ Emerging Issues and Future Needs

Spirituality

The Association for Spiritual, Ethical, and Religious Value Issues in Counseling (ASERVIC) has recently defined spirituality as "the animating force in life, represented by such images as breath, wind, vigor and courage. Spirituality is the infusion and drawing out of spirit in one's life" ("Summit Results," 1995, p. 30). Spirituality is further described as both an active and passive process, innate and unique to all persons, that moves the individual toward knowledge, love, meaning, hope, transcendence, connectedness, and compassion, encompassing the religious, spiritual, and transpersonal.

Spiritual differences, only one facet of culture, are often confused with ethnic differences, or ancestry. For example, one study of Italian Americans frequently compared them to "Protestants," rather than to another specific ethnic group(s) (C.L. Johnson, 1985a). The differences between the groups might be more related to differences between Catholics and Protestants than between Italians and other ethnic groups. When counseling European Americans, the spiritual differences within these ethnic groups are particularly diverse and relevant to counseling. A client from one ethnic group, German American, for example, might be Catholic, Protestant, Jewish, or have other spiritual beliefs.

It is important for the counselor to assess the client's individual views of spirituality and not assume that membership in a particular cultural group implies religious convictions common to that group. In this book, issues of spirituality are included for each ethnic or cultural group.

Social Class Considerations

Social class is more than the amount of money a person has or earns. It is also a culture.

As a result of the class you are born into and raised in, class is your understanding of the world and where you fit in; it's composed of ideas, behavior, attitudes, values, and language; class is how you think, feel, act, look, dress, talk, move, walk; class is what stores you shop at, restaurants you eat in; class is the schools you attend, the education you attain; class

is the very jobs you will work at throughout your adult life.... class is who
our friends are, where we live and work even what kind of car we drive, if
we own one, and what kind of health care we receive, if any. (Langston,
1998, pp. 127–128)

Class differences are becoming more important as the economic gap
between rich and poor in the United States is widening. The wealthi-
est 1% of the population owned 19% of U.S. assets in 1975, but by 1995
they owned 40% of all personal assets, more than the combined assets
of 90% of the population. At the same time, more than 30% of families in the United States have negative wealth, that is, more debts than
assets (Yeskel & Leondar-Wright, 1997). Also, 26% of the U.S. workforce
is low-paid, that is, earning less than two-thirds of the country's median
annual earnings, a percentage higher than in Canada and European
countries (Wong, 2006).

The effects of social class and ethnicity within counseling are deeply
entangled. Typically, counseling research does not report or control for
differences in income, a marker of social class, when cultural differences
are studied. The effects of poverty are comingled with those of ethnicity
for low-income clients. Where available, social class considerations are
included for each ethnic or cultural group discussed in this book.

Research

There are substantial areas within the field of multicultural counseling that have received significant research interest and development, as
noted earlier. However, there are several areas in need of much additional research. Primary is the need for a broad conceptual framework
for the process of multicultural counseling itself that goes beyond training, identity development, or cultural adaptation. Such a framework
would do well to take into account the counselor's own level of cultural
awareness, individually tailored assessment of the client's cultural background, the sociopolitical influences on both client and counselor, the
use of both traditional and indigenous counseling techniques, and the
complex interaction among client, counselor, and the societal context
surrounding them.

Another need is that of research including within-group differences. There has previously been much focus on differences between
broad ethnic groups, particularly comparing a particular minority group
to the White European American majority. Scholars in the field are now

calling for more sophisticated analyses of variations within an ethnic group, for example, among Chinese, Japanese, Vietnamese, Koreans, and Filipinos or among Mexicans, Puerto Ricans, and Cubans. Examining within-group differences would not only yield more specifically applicable knowledge, it would also tend to counteract the tendency to stereotype people from a similar group.

Culture conflict and its resolution, on a family or small group level, is another area that has had little counseling research to date. In other words, how can the counselor address conflicts between cultures within the counseling setting? For example, physical punishment may be an acceptable form of discipline within the client's own culture, but this comes into conflict with the dominant culture when the behavior is labeled child abuse. Another example is in family counseling where intercultural marriages face many areas of potential conflict.

Developing Multicultural Counseling Competency

… becoming culturally skilled is an active process, that … is ongoing, and that … is a process that never reaches an end point.

(Sue & Sue, 1990, p. 146)

The purpose of this book is to introduce the reader to basic issues and concepts related to multicultural counseling and to develop awareness and appreciation for the need for culture-specific knowledge in the counseling process. As multicultural awareness and knowledge increase, multicultural counseling skills may grow. Practical experience and ongoing interaction with diverse clients are crucial to the development of multicultural skills. Developing multicultural counseling skills is an ongoing continuing education need for counselors in the 21st century as the population of the United States continues to diversify, especially in terms of ethnicity and age. This chapter includes a review of current multicultural theory, the status of the movement toward multicultural counseling competencies for all counselors, training issues with respect to multicultural counseling, and issues of multiculturalism within the counseling profession.

☐ Multicultural Theory

As noted in Chapter 1, there is great need for more comprehensive theoretical development about the nature of multicultural counseling. The most substantial contributions to multicultural theory so far have been more limited in scope: cultural adaptation theories, identity development theories, application of internal/external locus of control theory to multicultural counseling (Sue & Sue, 1990), triad training models (Pedersen, 1977, 1978, 1994), and so on. The field would be unified by a broad conceptual framework for the process of multicultural counseling that incorporates the counselor's own level of cultural awareness, individually tailored assessment of the client's cultural background, cultural adaptation processes, cultural identity development, the sociopolitical influences on both client and counselor, the use of both traditional and indigenous counseling techniques, and the complex interaction among client, counselor, and the societal context surrounding them.

The most highly developed attempt at creating a comprehensive theory of multicultural counseling to date has been the book, *A Theory of Multicultural Counseling and Therapy*, edited by Derald Sue, Allen Ivey, and Paul Pedersen (1996). These scholars, who have themselves made substantial contributions to the field of multicultural counseling (Wehrly, 1991) have criticized the narrow focus of earlier counseling theories on either feelings, thoughts, behaviors, or social systems and ignoring biological, spiritual, political, and cultural influences. The broad metatheory of multicultural counseling and therapy (MCT) that they propose has as a base six propositions and many ensuing corollaries. The first proposition states that MCT is a theory about theories and offers an organizational framework or alternative worldview. The second proposition recognizes the multiple levels of experience (individual, group, and universal) and contexts (individual, family, and cultural milieu) that affect both counselor and client and whose many interrelationships need to be central in treatment. Proposition 3 recognizes the importance of cultural identity development. The fourth proposition calls for utilizing treatment goals and modalities that are culturally consistent for the client. According to Lee (1996), proposition numbers 5 and 6 are the most radical in comparison to traditional theories of counseling. Proposition 5 expands the counselor's role beyond direct treatment of the individual, family, or group to incorporate prevention and system intervention and Proposition 6 refocuses the basic goal of counseling to be the "liberation of consciousness" within context, utilizing both Western and non-European modes of helping.

Such efforts to elaborate and refine the nature of the multicultural counseling process may be part of a cataclysmic transformation that lies ahead for the entire field of counseling (Lee, 1996). The nature of the counseling process and what it means to be a counselor need to be transformed in order for the field of counseling to stay current and relevant to assist the changing demographic makeup of the United States and other countries.

☐ Multicultural Competencies

Much work has been done toward specifying the competencies any counselor would need in order to function adequately in a multicultural counseling relationship. The seminal article on the topic was a position paper prepared by a group of counseling psychologists within the American Psychological Association (Sue et al., 1982). The paper described 11 characteristics of culturally skilled counseling psychologists in the broad areas of beliefs and attitudes, knowledge, and skills. This initial work was further developed by the Association for Multicultural Counseling and Development (1986; Sue, Arredondo, & McDavis, 1992a & b). There are currently 31 stated cross-cultural competencies and objectives in the broad areas of counselor awareness of their own cultural values and biases (9 competencies), their awareness of the client's worldview (7 competencies), and culturally appropriate intervention strategies (15 competencies). These competencies have been endorsed by several APA and ACA divisions. However, there has been little validation of these competencies with research into process, outcomes, consumer surveys, or expert studies (Atkinson & Israel, 2003).

There have been several instruments developed that attempt to measure multicultural competency. The four existing measures of multicultural counseling competency all were developed with respect to the Sue et al. (1982) position paper (Ponterotto, Rieger, Barrett, & Sparks, 1994; Pope-Davis & Dings, 1995).

The Cross-Cultural Counseling Inventory—Revised (CCCI-R) (LaFromboise, Coleman, & Hernandez, 1991) is the only measure that is not a self-report scale. It is filled out by a supervisor or other professional who rates the counselor on 20 Likert scale items. Coefficient alpha reliability of 0.95 and interrater reliability in the 0.78–0.84 range have been reported for the CCCI-R and it appears to measure one unidimensional factor (Ponterotto et al., 1994).

The other three measures are all self-report, Likert scale ratings. The first measure, The Multicultural Awareness-Knowledge-Skills Survey (MAKSS) (D'Andrea, Daniels, & Heck, 1991), consists of three

20-item scales designed to measure Awareness, Knowledge, and Skills. There are reasonably high reliabilities, measured by Cronbach's alpha, for the three scales (0.75, 0.90, 0.96 for Awareness, Knowledge, and Skills, respectively) and some evidence of criterion validity in that post-test MAKSS scores for a group given multicultural training rose significantly (D'Andrea et al., 1991; Pope-Davis & Dings, 1995).

The second measure, The Multicultural Counseling Knowledge and Awareness Scale (MCKAS) (Ponterotto et al., 2002) contains two sub-scales, the 12-item Awareness scale and the 20-item Knowledge scale. As with the MAKSS, the Awareness scale has a lower coefficient alpha reliability of 0.78 compared to the Knowledge scale at 0.90. Research with an earlier version of the MCKAS indicated Knowledge/Skills scale differences among those who have taken a workshop, seminar, or course and those without such multicultural training, non-White and White test takers, and those with doctoral- compared to master's- and bachelor's-level educations (Pope-Davis & Dings, 1995). No differences on the Awareness scale were found for these same samples. These results suggest that the two scales do seem to be measuring different aspects of multicultural competency, providing limited support for a two-factor multicultural competency model.

The third measure, The Multicultural Counseling Inventory (MCI) (Sodowsky et al., 1994) was developed with the use of factor analysis. It measures four factors: Multicultural Counseling Skills (11 items), Multi-cultural Awareness (10 items), Multicultural Counseling Knowledge (11 items), and Multicultural Counseling Relationship (8 items). Cron-bach's alpha reliability coefficients range from 0.67 (Relationship) to 0.80 or 0.81 for each of the other three scales (Pope-Davis & Dings, 1995). After taking a multicultural course significant increases were found on all except the Relationship scale. The strength of the MCI is that its items are more descriptive of behaviors whereas the other two instruments tend to focus more on attitudes. Another strength is its inclusion of a Relationship scale (Ponterotto et al., 1994).

In their detailed review of self-report multicultural competency measures, Pope-Davis and Dings (1995) concluded that the MCI has the most convincing evidence to support its use. However, Ponterotto et al. (1994) recommend that none of these measures of multicultural com-petency currently have any practical utility due to a lack of systematic, longitudinal validation data. They concluded that factor analyses have provided little validation for a three-dimensional (awareness, knowl-edge, skill) conceptualization of multicultural competency. They also assert that more study is needed of the relationship between scores on these measures and behavioral measures of counseling performance and counseling outcome measures.

Following on the development of multicultural competency measures related to ethnicity, Bidell (2005) introduced a Sexual Orientation Counselor Competency Scale (SOCCS) consisting of 42 items tapping counselor attitudes, knowledge, and skills. For the three scales, the overall coefficient alpha was 0.90 and the one-week test–retest reliability correlation coefficient was 0.84. Correlations between this measure and others suggest a relationship between ethnic and sexual orientation minority competency. Similar concerns about relationship to treatment outcome, supervisor ratings, and client satisfaction as have been reported for the other self-report measures of ethnic multicultural competency measures were also noted.

In addition to the three-dimensional conceptualization of multicultural competency, at least nine other models have been proposed. Little empirical research has been done on most (Mollen, Ridley, & Hill, 2003). One model (Sue, 2001) proposes two additional facets for developing cultural competence in addition to the original three components (awareness, knowledge, and skills). The two other dimensions are the focus of competence (individual, professional, organizational, societal) and the race- and culture-specific attributes (African American, Asian American, Latino/Hispanic American, Native American, European American). Altogether, this 3 × 4 × 5 matrix describes a possible 60 specific components and foci of multicultural competence. Again, however, research validation is not readily available for this model.

Stan Sue (1998) concluded that there has not been a single scientifically rigorous research study examining the efficacy of treatment for any ethnic minority population. He suggested that this may be due to the potentially controversial nature of ethnic minority research or the practical, methodological, and conceptual problems in undertaking such research that may discourage investigators from multicultural studies. In any case, it is difficult to propose specific competencies on other than theoretical or ideological grounds without more research.

S. Sue (1998) proposed an alternative model also consisting of three general aspects of cultural competency needed for counseling and psychotherapy. The first dimension, *scientific mindedness,* refers to the counselor's ability to carry out clinical hypothesis testing with respect to cultural and other client data. The second dimension, *dynamic sizing,* refers to a counselor's ability to know when to generalize and be inclusive and when to individualize and be exclusive with respect to a particular client. This quality allows a counselor to make use of cultural issues when relevant and not overgeneralize or stereotype a client. The third dimension, *culture-specific expertise,* is similar to the cultural knowledge dimension included in the ACA multicultural counseling competencies and standards proposals and assessment measures. There is some research evidence that treating ethnic minority clients in ethnic-specific programs, which may include modifying therapeutic practices in consideration of cultural customs, employing bicultural–bilingual staff, culture-friendly agency procedures, and so on, has been related to less frequent dropout rates and longer lengths of treatment (Takeuchi, Sue, & Yeh, 1995; Yeh, Takeuchi, & Sue, 1994). However, effects on treatment outcome were unclear. This alternative model also requires further research support before it can be validated.

☐ Multicultural Training

Training Models

Several models have been suggested for programmatic multicultural counseling training. Ridley, Mendoza, and Kanitz (1994) describe five different frameworks for approaching multicultural counseling:

a. A generic or etic framework assumes that counseling is universally applicable without empirical justification or cultural modification.

b. An emic framework may teach a general process for gathering and integrating culture-specific information at the risk of promoting stereotypes.

c. An idiographic framework uses the client as the primary data source and stresses client individuality in cultural matters.

d. An autoplastic approach requires that clients change themselves in order to fit into their cultural environment.

e. An alloplastic approach emphasizes the influences of the client's political, social, and economic environment in contributing to her or his problems and focuses on empowerment and advocacy for clients at the risk of victimization.

Counselor training programs have often taken an etic, idiographic, or autoplastic approach to multicultural counseling training, whereas the current emphasis in the field is toward more emic and alloplastic approaches. The former blur the need for specific curricula related to multicultural counseling inasmuch as cultural influences are viewed as no different from any other specific problem in living that an individual may face. Research evidence over time has documented specific positive changes resulting from multicultural training (Smith et al., 2006).

Wehrly (1991) describes a five-stage developmental model for multicultural counselor preparation that builds on the work of Carney and Kahn (1984) and Sabnani, Ponterotto, and Borodovsky (1991). The first stage calls for a structured and supportive training environment to reduce student anxiety, encourages self-awareness through keeping a journal, and initiates cultural knowledge learning through ethnic/cultural novels and book reports. The second stage emphasizes seeking information about the student's own cultural origins and predominant values as well as researching a different ethnic culture, including circumstances of the group's entry into the United States, treatment (as immigrants, slaves, etc.), and historical help providers throughout their history in this country. The third stage incorporates a deeper understanding of the student's personal involvement in the racism pervasive in the United States and stresses the importance of the counselor addressing racial/cultural differences between counselor and client during the first counseling session. The fourth and fifth stages involve direct experience working with culturally different clients in practicum and internship settings under trained supervisors.

Training Format

The two primary formats that counselor education programs have utilized for multicultural training are the single course and the curriculum infusion (Fouad, Manese, & Casas, 1992) approaches. One national survery revealed that 89% of doctoral programs in counseling require at least one multicultural course and 58% infuse multicultural content throughout their coursework (Ponterotto, 1997). However, another study of school psychology training programs indicated that 40% had neither multicultural content in core courses nor had specific multicultural courses (Rogers, Ponterotto, Conoley, & Wiese, 1992). Even less promising, another survey of psychologists who received their degrees between 1985 and 1987 reported that only 34% of the respondents indicated that a course on diverse populations was available in their doctoral programs, only 25% had actually taken such a course during graduate school, and 46.3% felt that their graduate coursework had "infrequently" or "never" covered diversity (Allison, Crawford, Echemendia, Robinson, & Knepp, 1994).

A single course related to multicultural counseling, although the most common format for multicultural training, is often criticized. It is only a starting point for graduate students and lacks the depth needed in order to foster a high level of awareness, knowledge, or skill; has a potential for stereotyping; and does not allow for integration of awareness, knowledge, and skills (D'Andrea et al., 1991; Reynolds, 1995; Rooney, Flores, & Mercier, 1998; Vasquez & Garcia-Vasquez, 2003). Instructors of single multicultural courses are advised to include issues of power and discrimination, histories of oppression, and to reframe resistance to multicultural training as resolving ethical dilemmas (Alvarez & Miville, 2003; Vasquez & Garcia-Vasquez, 2003).

On the other hand, comprehensive infusion of multicultural content into course work and field experience requires institutional commitment and resource allocation that many counselor training programs are either not willing or able to make (D'Andrea et al., 1991). Assistant and adjunct faculty members are likely to be responsible for implementing multicultural training efforts (Bell, Washington, Weinstein, & Love, 1997; Hills & Strozier, 1992). Faculty at lower ranks generally have less knowledge of the institution, less power, and less influence in bringing about curricular change.

Even when a program has made a stated commitment to include multicultural training in all its coursework, real compliance and outcomes are difficult to monitor. It is one thing to include some multicultural topics and references in course syllabi and another to truly integrate multicultural issues and perspectives into all lectures and discussions.

There are other ways to obtain multicultural training aside from formal coursework. In addition to training in cultural awareness, knowledge, and skills, Preli and Bernard (1993) include contact with cultural minority people and counseling practica with minority clients. However, only 5.7% of university counseling center predoctoral internship programs studied required interns to have ethnic clients (Murphy, Wright, & Bellamy, 1995). Enns (1993) noted that although feminist therapists over the past 20 years have educated themselves by taking courses on counseling women or on feminist therapy, more learning took place from personal study and research, professional workshops, informal conversations and study groups, and actual counseling experience with women clients. Multicultural training is a multifaceted, lifelong process.

In addition to the direct potential benefits in more effective treatment for multicultural clients that may result from multicultural training in counseling, other benefits are that students become more aware of multicultural issues in general, students come to believe that it is less desirable to ignore cultural differences, and students have a place to deal with their own feelings about racial issues instead of during the counseling process as counter-transference reactions (Jordan, 1993). Ethnic minority counselors benefit from multicultural training as well inasmuch as it should not be assumed that counselors from cultural minority groups are automatically able to relate to clients from the dominant culture (Brown, 1996). Training in multicultural counseling is also a professional licensure requirement for independent practice in at least one state (DeAngelis, 1994). Pre–post testing with multicultural counseling competency assessment measures suggests that single course and workshop format multicultural counseling training results in perceived changes by participants (D'Andrea et al., 1991; Pope-Davis & Dings, 1995). However, research into the long-term effects of multicultural training is needed (Jordan, 1993).

A Model Training Curriculum

Although there is great variability among multicultural training programs, a model curriculum outlined in terms of awareness, knowledge, and skills is offered here that combines recommendations from several sources (Das, 1995; Enns, 1993; Fouad et al., 1992; Preli & Bernard, 1993; Ridley et al., 1994) as well as those of the authors. Elements of a model curriculum are outlined in the box on page 28, Multicultural Training Curriculum Content.

Some elements of this model curriculum are currently part of most counselor education programs (e.g., ethical knowledge, handling client resistance), many are not (e.g., second language fluency, indigenous healing practices), and others expand the counselor's role (e.g., prevention issues, advocacy) in nontraditional directions. There are substantial resources written in the area of cultural self-awareness (Katz, 2003; McIntosh, 1988) and the vast preponderance of multicultural counseling literature concerns culture-specific knowledge and its potential impact in counseling. However, the greatest challenge in multicultural counselor training currently is in the area of skills: "The pinpointing of specific counseling skills that would assist the counselor in making their work with an individual client culturally effective" (Lee, 1996, p. 2).

A model multicultural training program would put the content described above into practice by providing opportunities for contact within the program and in the surrounding community with people from cultural minority backgrounds and requiring practicum experience with cultural minority populations (McRae & Johnson, 1991;

Multicultural Training Curriculum Content

Awareness	Consciousness raising with respect to issues of racism, sexism, homophobia, transgenderphobia, ageism, and ablism Cultural self-awareness of the counselor's own ethnic background(s) and potential reactions of clients and other implications for counseling Cultural self-awareness of the counselor's own gender, sexual orientation, gender identity, age, and social class and potential reactions of clients and other implications for counseling Cultural self-awareness of the counselor's own physical and mental disabilities and potential reactions of clients and other implications for counseling Respecting cultural differences
Knowledge	Sociopolitical context of counseling, including oppression, discrimination, and racism, barriers to service, and social causes of psychological distress Cultural and racial bias in testing issues Cultural identity development models Acculturation issues Cultural variations in family make-up, developmental patterns, client expectations, views of health and illness Ability to critique existing theories for cultural relevance (worldview) Second language fluency Cultural knowledge of normative characteristics of specific cultural groups Cultural knowledge of within-group differences Indigenous healing practices Immigration regulations

continued on next page

Multicultural Training Curriculum Content
continued from previous page

	Laws regarding sexual harassment, hate crimes, housing and employment discrimination Ethical knowledge and practice (e.g., ethical guidelines for use of indigenous techniques) Prevention issues
Skills	Interview skills for talking about cultural differences Assessment of cultural background and issues Development of an individualized theoretical orientation Displaying culturally responsive behaviors Communicating empathy in a manner culturally recognized by the client Handling client resistance Consultation skills for communication with indigenous healers Case management skills Advocacy skills for influencing organizations Community outreach/organizational skills Group conflict resolution skills Teaching skills for community education

Preli & Bernard, 1993). Access to supervision and internship experiences relevant to diverse cases have been rated as the most effective multicultural training experiences (Allison et al., 1994). Unfortunately, only 35% of counseling doctoral programs offered opportunities to engage in multicultural fieldwork (Ponterotto, 1997) and 46% of psychologists surveyed felt that the supervision they received in graduate school "never" or "infrequently" addressed cultural issues (Allison et al., 1994). In school psychology training programs, nearly 30% of the students received little or no experience with culturally diverse children in their fieldwork (Rogers et al., 1992).

Training Methods and Process

A variety of instructional strategies has been used in multicultural training (Pedersen, 1977; Preli & Bernard, 1993; Ridley et al., 1994), including experiential self-awareness exercises (see Chapter 3 for several examples) and games as well as didactic methods, videotape viewing, readings, written assignments, modeling/observational learning, technology-assisted training (e.g., videotaping and reviewing counseling sessions), and supervised practica and internships. The multicultural training technique that has perhaps received the most attention is the triad role play model developed by Pedersen (1977, 1978, 1994). In this role play exercise, participants take the roles of counselor, client, and problem/anti-counselor and simulate a counseling session that may help in articulating cultural problems, anticipating resistance, diminishing counselor defensiveness, and teaching recovery skills. A modification of this exercise which substitutes a pro-counselor for the anti-counselor role gives the counselor a supportive ally and may be more helpful with beginning counselors (Neimeyer, Fukuyama, Bingham, Hall, & Mussenden, 1986) and to develop knowledge and skills (Sue, 1979, cited in McRae & Johnson, 1991). The original anti-counselor version seems more effective for developing sensitivity and awareness (Sue, 1979, cited in McRae & Johnson, 1991). Another training technique is a multicultural genogram including at least three generations of family history, cultural labels, and experiences, and perceptions of diversity (Vasquez & Garcia-Vasquez, 2003).

Multicultural counselor training is a complex process that combines personal growth with content learning and skill development. According to Das (1995, p. 47), "The cognitive distance between the mental health service providers and the lower class and minority consumers can be bridged through didactic instruction, but the social and emotional distance can be reduced only through an intensive program of reeducation of the counselors, one aimed at changing their attitudes." Effective multicultural trainers need to do more than convey information, they need to balance cognitive and emotional learning strategies and create a safe environment that nurtures personal risk-taking (Ponterotto, 1998). Effective multicultural training requires the trainer to possess many of the qualities of a good counselor as well as a good teacher. Trainer ability to self-disclose her or his own developmental experiences with multicultural awareness has been stressed as an important characteristic of effective training (Ponterotto, 1998; Rooney et al., 1998). In addition, trainers must be cognizant of the individual cultural developmental backgrounds of their students, as each student's level of cultural identity development may vary with respect to race, gender, sexual orientation, aging, or disability dimensions (Rooney et al., 1998).

Reynolds (1995) recommends training counseling faculty in cultural diversity content regarding specific cultural groups, how oppression works, group work, how multicultural issues affect counseling, and so on. There are good reasons for more White faculty to become multicultural trainers (Kiselica, 1998). White faculty who have developed multicultural expertise can be role models for White counselors who are grappling with their own cultural identity development. Lark and Paul (1988) assert that some ethnic or cultural similarity to the trainer is important for both credibility and modeling.

☐ Multiculturalism Within the Counseling Profession

Current Status

Although people of color make up more than one-third of the U.S. workforce and more than one-fourth of college students, they represent only 18% of all bachelor's degree recipients and 14% of all doctoral recipients (Abraham & Jacobs, 1999; American Council on Education, 2006). In psychology, ethnic minority students represent 20% of undergraduate psychology majors, 18% of entering graduate students, and 9% of those with doctorates, eventually resulting in only 5.5% of the nation's psychologists from ethnic minority backgrounds (APA Presidential Task Force on Enhancing Diversity, 2005; Pate, 2001; Youngstrom, 1992). In counselor education programs, Black and Hispanic students have long been underrepresented (Atkinson, 1983). Even when ethnic minority students are enrolled in counselor education programs, they are less likely to be full-time students or in doctoral-level programs (Atkinson, 1983).

Underrepresentation of ethnic minority people among psychology and counseling faculty is also evident. Nationally, 5% of all higher education faculty are Black, 4% Asian, 3% Hispanic, and 0.4% American Indian/Alaskan Native (Murray, 1998). Ethnic minority faculty made up only 11% of psychology doctoral faculty nationwide (Pate, 2001). Ethnic minority representation is consistently higher among part-time faculty and ethnic minority representation is also greater in master's-level departments as compared to doctoral-level psychology departments

(Norcross, Hanych, & Terranova, 1996). Bernal (1990) noted that the level of ethnic minority faculty in psychology graduate departments has remained relatively stable even though graduate student enrollment and doctorate recipient figures have increased.

Among faculty who train service providers, ethnic minorities make up 8% of full-time clinical, counseling, and school psychology faculty (Kohout, Wicherski, & Cooney, 1992) and 8.2% of clinical psychology and 9.9% of counseling psychology faculty (Quintana & Bernal, 1995). Non-White representation among APA-approved counseling psychology faculty was noted at 11% in one survey, with ethnic minority representation higher at lower faculty ranks (Hills & Strozier, 1992). The profession has apparently not changed dramatically since Atkinson's 1983 report indicating that ethnic minority faculty in counselor education programs are more likely to be part-time, nontenured instructors and that Asian Americans, Hispanic Americans, and Blacks were underrepresented (Atkinson, 1983). Ponterotto (1997) noted that only 29% of counseling doctoral programs reported having at least 30% faculty of color.

Representation issues for women have changed somewhat. The majority of psychologists are now female as the proportion of female psychologists increased to 52% in 2004 (APA Presidential Task Force on Enhancing Diversity, 2005). Although 70% of entering doctoral psychology program students are female, only 36% of doctoral psychology faculty are women (Pate, 2001). In psychology, more full-time faculty women are employed in master's-level than doctoral-level psychology departments and representation of women is consistently higher among part-time faculty than full-time faculty (Norcross et al., 1996). Although statistics regarding representation of gay, lesbian, or bisexual faculty and faculty with disabilities are often not collected, informal observation suggests that issues of underrepresentation are apparent for these cultural groups as well. Currently 6.3% of American Psychological Association members surveyed identified themselves as gay, lesbian, or bisexual and only 2.1% reported experiencing sensory or motor impairment (Allison et al., 1994; APA Presidential Task Force on Enhancing Diversity, 2005). The number of older psychologists is growing and currently 25% are over age 60 (APA Presidential Task Force on Enhancing Diversity, 2005). The underrepresentation of cultural minority faculty is particularly detrimental in that an important contribution to multicultural training is facilitated by multicultural mentoring over time (Lark & Paul, 1998).

Barriers to Participation

Barriers that prevent cultural minorities from becoming counselors begin early in life and are continued throughout graduate training. These barriers are economic, social, and cultural.

Finances are a real barrier to ethnic minority graduate students. A NSF survey of doctoral recipients in psychology indicated that White students relied more on their families and teaching assistantships for financial support, Asian students relied most on teaching assistantships, and Black and Hispanic students on university fellowships (Moses, 1992).

A higher proportion of ethnic minority psychology graduate students enroll in doctoral-level as compared to master's-level programs, perhaps due to a greater availability of scholarships, teaching and research assistantships, and other sources of financial assistance in doctoral programs. Brazziel (1987/1988) asserted that the university itself is the most important source of money for graduate students in general, but that jobs on campus seem to be more available to White graduate students. Indeed, most ethnic minority graduate students enroll on a part-time basis (Nettles, 1987) and financial constraints are a likely cause. In the 1980s an increase in loans and decrease in grants as sources of funding began to affect minority graduate enrollment (Nettles, 1987). Extended family responsibilities may be an extra financial stress. Counselors of color reported feeling more stress in graduate school from contributing to the financial support of family not living in their household than did White counselors (Lee, 1995).

Social isolation is also a barrier to more cultural minority students becoming counselors. Research has indicated that the number of ethnic minority students in a graduate department and contact with ethnic minority faculty outside of class are important variables and ethnic minority students in more integrated departments had higher grades, better adjustment, and self-perceptions that they were making good progress (DeFour & Hirsch, 1990). However, only 33% of counseling doctoral programs report having a critical mass of at least 30% ethnic minority students (Ponterotto, 1997) and even school psychology programs noted for their multicultural training perspective had only 25% of their faculty being representative of racial–ethnic minority groups (Rogers, 2006). The majority of ethnic minority graduate students feel isolated from much of their academic environment, have few faculty mentors, and, when they have mentors, those mentors are White and mostly male (DeFour & Hirsch, 1990; Leal & Menjivar, 1992). Among ethnic minority graduate students there also may be feelings of alienation from one another, little networking between cultural groups (e.g., Latinas and Latin American women) (Leal & Menjivar, 1992), and few incentives for intergroup communication or cooperation.

Cultural barriers to minority graduate students are formidable. Learning the language of academia and acclimating to professional jargon was a noted barrier to Native American women in graduate school (Macias, 1989). According to Sedlacek (cited in Foster, 1996), African American students on White campuses may experience verbal racial stereotyping, graffiti with racial slurs, and threats or violence in residence halls, fraternities, interracial dating, or campus athletics. The effects of institutional racism should not be underestimated. Counselors of color reported significantly more stress in graduate school from having personal experience with racial prejudice on campus and from contacts with White faculty and graduate students (Lee, 1995). Similar social and cultural barriers may confront graduate students who are gay, lesbian, or bisexual, older, or have a disability.

Remedies

Many remedies to alleviate these barriers have been suggested on an individual level, including financial help, increased program flexibility, multimodal learning, strategies for study organizing, and mentoring (Macias, 1989; Youngstrom, 1992). Other suggestions have been made at the institutional level. To increase ethnic minority enrollment, Ponterotto (1998) recommended that admissions criteria include experience with minority populations, multicultural research interest, experience with extensive travel or living abroad, second language linguistic competence, and the like. Establishing campus training institutes to offer basic, advanced, and topic-specific courses, establishing a clearinghouse or registry of diversity consultants, collegewide multicultural curriculum committees, and an institutional multicultural awareness education program for faculty and staff are other organization-level remedies (D'Andrea & Daniels, 1991; Foster, 1996). Multicultural competency can be included in tenure, reappointment, promotion, merit pay, and chair selection criteria and in evaluation instruments for all courses and practica (Ponterotto, 1998).

CHAPTER

Understanding and Appreciating Difference

I know that people will say, "Look, African Americans just hang out with their radio." So, as an African American, I'm always afraid that when I walk into a class, people are not going to see me as a serious student....

African-American female student, 24 years old
(Woodlief, Thomas, & Orozco, 2003, p. 83)

Counselors can begin to develop an understanding of the potential impact of cultural minority status on the psychological experience of their clients by turning to the work of social psychologists who have long been interested in examining the roots of prejudice and the effects of discrimination, stereotyping, and racism on individuals.

The word "prejudice" comes from the Latin words *prae*, meaning before and *judicium*, meaning judgment. In other words, prejudice occurs, for example, when someone is prejudged before any real knowledge of that person is known. Gordon Allport (1954) defined prejudice as a negative attitude or dislike based on faulty and inflexible generalization.

According to social comparison theory (Festinger, 1954), people tend to make judgments about themselves by comparing themselves to a similar group of people, or "reference group." If the comparisons are positive, they feel better about themselves. "Prejudice" occurs when a person takes her or his own group as the positive reference point from which to judge other people negatively. "Discrimination" takes place when actions occur that favor one group at the expense of a comparison group. An example of this would be if a person thinks of her or his own ethnic group as her or his primary reference group. To the extent that he or she feels he or she is succeeding, in comparison to others in the reference group, her or his self-esteem may increase. However, if he or she judges people from other groups as unfit or inadequate compared to her or his ethnic group, he or she is exercising prejudice. If he or she then takes actions to favor her or his ethnic group at the expense of another group, for example, to pass laws that do not allow members of another group to own property, vote, and so on, this constitutes discrimination.

One definition of a "stereotype" (Ho, 1990) is a generalized description of a group of people that has usually developed over time based upon cross-cultural interactions. In this media-rich age of television, DVDs, and CDs, it is easy to take media exposure as true cross-cultural interaction. Someone who has never met another person from a particular ethnic background may have a stereotype, that is, a limited or inflexible cognitive view (Abreu, 2001) of that culture based on what they have heard, seen, or read, but not based on real personal interaction with others of that ethnicity.

Stereotypes can be psychologically useful. They can assist memory by providing a device for chunking several pieces of information together under one label. This can seem helpful to an individual because it makes the world less complicated, more predictable, and as a result, more comfortable. When counselors see a client's age, sex, or ethnic background on an intake form, they may feel more at ease meeting their new client because they use the information as a stereotype in recalling all their previous experience with persons of a similar age, sex, or ethnicity. However, there are also drawbacks to stereotypes. If a counselor puts too much emphasis on stereotypes of a new client, the counselor may assume that he or she already knows a lot about the person and may neglect to consider ways in which the client does not fit the stereotypes. This can result in faulty assessment and treatment planning.

There are also potential negative effects of a client's own stereotypes. Such stereotypes may contribute to increased mistrust and unwillingness to self-disclose with a counselor who is different from him- or herself. If the client has incorporated negative stereotypes into her or his own self-image, this may contribute to low self-esteem and limited optimism for change. This process has been called "internalized oppression" or "internalized racism." According to Jones (2000), internalized racism occurs when members of a stigmatized group accept negative images about themselves. They may reject their own culture and embrace "whiteness" by changing their hair texture or using bleaching creams. For example, in one study, African American children pointed to a drawing of a White child more often than an African American child when asked which of the two is more beautiful or smarter (cited in Pine & Hilliard, 1990). One interpretation of the data is that the African American children had internalized the negative societal messages they had been exposed to regarding their ethnicity. A competing interpretation is that the children responded in what they might have perceived to be a socially desirable or "correct" manner and that they do not necessarily believe the negative stereotypes of African Americans.

Claude Steele has studied the concept of "stereotype vulnerability," an effect that may occur when a person tries to do well in an atmosphere in which he or she is aware that others of a similar cultural background have had difficulty and that can detract from her or his performance ("How Affirmative," 1995; Watters, 1995). Stereotype vulnerability operates as an extra burden on the person to disconfirm a negative stereotype. To date, evidence for this phenomenon has been found with African Americans tested with verbal Graduate Record Exam (GRE) questions and women tested with math problems (Watters, 1995).

☐ Racism

One definition of "racism" requires two components: first, the assumption that traits and abilities are biologically determined by race and second, the belief in the inherent superiority of one race and its right to dominate other races (*New Oxford American Dictionary*, 2005). Given this definition, which combines an assumption and an ensuing belief, it is not surprising that racism is so prevalent. The assumption that abilities are biologically determined is very controversial (see discussion of IQ and culture in Chapter 4, "Cultural Aspects of Psychological Assessment"). However, even the concept of race is itself very questionable. Race is usually associated with physical features, especially skin color and type of hair (Ho, 1990), yet there is no anthropological standard as to the physical definition of one race versus another. Indeed, the American Association of Physical Anthropologists has asserted that race is not a legitimate scientific concept, as genetically homogeneous populations do not exist in the human species (Scott-Jones, 1995). Zuckerman (1990) noted large amounts of variability within one race compared to the degree of variability between races when examining psychological traits, supporting the notion that the biological distinctiveness of various racial groups is also an illusion when it comes to examining traits and abilities. "The major component of genetic diversity is between individuals in the same tribe or nation" (Zuckerman, 1990, p. 1300), as this accounts for 84% of the total variance in a large, well-conducted, multicultural, multinational study.

Another definition of racism involves unjustified negative treatment resulting from individual prejudice and discrimination or institutional policies and procedures (Pine & Hilliard, 1990). This second definition includes "institutionalized racism" or the use of established laws, customs, and practices or norms that produce racial inequities (Baratz & Baratz, 1970). These established norms create differential access to material conditions and most importantly, to positions of power (Jones, 2000; Niemann, 2001).

Institutionalized racism may manifest itself as differential access to information, which results in less power or less voice. For example, equal access to a college education is more difficult for students of color. School counselors may have a tendency to counsel or track ethnic minority students toward classes that are not college preparatory courses in high school, which then results in a disadvantage when applying to college. The use of written essays as a college admissions criterion can result in Asian Americans with equal grades and test scores being subsequently accepted at a lower rate than European Americans. The practice of using standardized test scores as a selection criterion for graduate admissions (when past grades or other factors may be a better predictor of graduate performance) works against students from many ethnic groups who tend to, as a group, score lower on either the verbal, quantitative, or both sections of the GRE. The lack of information on the contributions of minority groups to the history of the United States in the schools is another area that reflects the devaluing and exclusion of certain groups.

Institutionalized racism can be very subtle and difficult to detect because it can be done under the guise of customs, norms, policies, or practices that are not illegal but do result in inequities. For example, locating a counseling center in an area that is inaccessible to public transportation, having no evening hours, no sliding fee scale, and staff who speak only English can easily contribute to a restricted ethnic diversity of clientele, even before a client ever meets a counselor. Note that none of these practices is illegal in that they do not exclude a specific ethnic group, yet they can result in inequitable service provision to ethnic minority clients. Jones (2000) refers to institutionalized racism as the most important type of racism to address before stigmatized groups can overcome internalized forms of racism and believe in themselves.

"Cultural racism" occurs when one cultural group believes that another group is inferior in some way and possesses the power to impose its standards on the other group. This broadens the definition of racism beyond just ethnicity. If men believe that women are too emotional or fragile to hold positions of responsibility and have the power to make such judgments in not hiring women for managerial posts, cultural racism is occurring. A more specific term for this form of cultural racism is "sexism." When cultural racism occurs based on age, it might be called "ageism." "Heterosexism" is cultural racism based on sexual orientation and "ablism" is cultural racism based on physical disability. What all these cultural groups share is that they may experience discrimination based on an aspect of their culture that they cannot themselves change. A milder, but no less harmful, version of cultural racism is the assumption that there is no specific uniqueness to another culture. This failure to acknowledge the cultural differences of the group carries with it an implicit failure to acknowledge discrimination that the group may experience.

It may be very difficult for someone who is part of the cultural majority in power to acknowledge her or his cultural racism. According to psychologist Leon Festinger's *A Theory of Cognitive Dissonance* (1957), when an individual is confronted with a discrepancy between her or his own professed attitudes and her or his actual behavior, this creates an uncomfortable state of disequilibrium or "cognitive dissonance" that can be resolved by rationalizing or justifying the discrepant behavior. A White person who does not believe others should be treated inequitably and who also receives benefits or privileges in a society that discriminates against ethnic minorities can rationalize the cognitive dissonance he or she experiences by denying her or his participation in a racist system by not perceiving him- or herself as "White" or identifying with any ethnic group. Unfortunately, this denial of one's own ethnicity can by itself result in identity confusion, discomfort, and unconsciously perpetuate racism. If someone of European American ethnicity is not White, or European, or English, and so on, then what is he or she and with whom can he or she identify? And why are other people so overly focused on their ethnicity?

☐ Barriers in Counseling

From the first use of slaves during the early colonization of North America in the 1600s through modern legal battles over the use of affirmative action in educational and employment settings, racist beliefs have been ingrained in U.S. society. American psychologists, as a part of that society, have been greatly affected, either consciously or unconsciously, by racism and, through them, the field of psychology in general. Several fascinating examples of this have been documented by Leon Kamin in his book, *The Science and Politics of I.Q.* (1974). Three eminent psychologists,

Lewis Terman from Stanford University, Henry Goddard of the Vineland Training School, and Robert Yerkes at Harvard, were responsible for developing the Army Alpha and Beta group intelligence tests. Both Terman and Yerkes served as president of the American Psychological Association at one time. The same three men were also members of societies and organizations, such as the Eugenics Research Association and the Galton Society, that interpreted scientific data to promote political beliefs in the genetic inferiority of some races. These organizations supported practices such as sterilization of prisoners and persons on welfare and limiting immigration by persons who were members of ethnic groups that were considered to be intellectually inferior.

These psychologists' work assisted in the passage of a 1917 immigration law that severely restricted the number of immigrants from southern European countries. For example, Goddard, as described in *The Science and Politics of I.Q.*, tested immigrants at Ellis Island and found that 83% of the Jews, 80% of the Hungarians, 79% of the Italians, and 87% of the Russians were mentally retarded. Psychologists who were part of the movement to promote the testing of mental abilities "pressed upon the Congress scientific I.Q. data to demonstrate that the 'New Immigration' from southeastern Europe was genetically inferior. That contribution permanently transformed American society." (Kamin, 1974, p. 12). Issues of cultural bias in testing (discussed in Chapter 4), such as a lack of familiarity with the language in which the test is given or lack of comfort with the test administrator, were ignored. Another noted psychologist of the era, Carl Brigham, credited with the development of the Scholastic Aptitude Test (SAT), interpreted the relationship of length of time in the United States with higher I.Q. scores as supportive of the intellectual superiority of Nordic races, who had immigrated earlier, rather than the effect of acculturation.

Counselors are at great risk to behave in a racist manner without being aware of it. This problem was first described by Wrenn (1962) as the "culturally encapsulated counselor." It follows from Wrenn's prophetic entreaty that counselors be open to change, that the encapsulated counselor is so completely engrossed by the traditional approaches and attitudes of Western counselor training that they have no awareness that cultural differences might be important within the counseling process. These encapsulated counselors may be proud of the notion that they treat all their clients equally and that they are "color blind." They may assert that color makes no difference to them at all in their assessment, goals, treatment planning, client communication, or selection of counseling skills. These counselors assume that cultural modifications are not needed or are unwilling or unable to make them. In practice, however, failure to acknowledge or appreciate differences may instead communicate disrespect for the client's cultural background and lead to inappropriate or ineffective treatment. One qualitative study found that acknowledgment of racial differences was a key strategy for effectively processing racial differences in the counseling relationship (Hernandez Morales, 2005). Counselors may be surprised if a client who is culturally different from themselves drops out of counseling and they may attribute lack of progress as due to resistance or client unreadiness as opposed to a mismatch between their knowledge and skills and what the client actually needs.

Ridley (1989, 2005) expanded upon the influence of racism in counseling to include seven counseling process qualities. In addition to (a) color blindness, (b) "color consciousness" involves attributing all the client's problems to her or his cultural background, (c) "cultural transference" refers to client reactions to the counselor that arise from the therapist's cultural background alone, whereas (d) "cultural countertransference" refers to counselor reactions toward the client based on the counselor's past experience with others of a cultural background similar to that of the client. (e) "Cultural ambivalence" is related to counselor paternalism, "The Great White Father Syndrome" (Vontress, 1981). (f) "Pseudotransference" involves labeling the client's defensive reactions to racist behavior by the counselor as pathology. Finally, (g) the counselor may misinterpret client nondisclosure as paranoid behavior, rather than as healthy cultural skepticism. These characteristics are indicative of unintentional covert racism on the counselor's part. Ridley asserted that unintentional racism is the most insidious form of racism because people are unaware of it.

From another perspective on cultural barriers in counseling, Sue and Sue (2003) grouped the generic aspects of counseling, developed from a European perspective, into three major categories that counselors need to consider. In the first category, culture-bound values include focusing on the individual; valuing client expressiveness toward the counselor; openness; a linear, cause-and-effect approach; and a mind–body dichotomy. The second category, class-bound values, includes adherence to time schedules, unstructured, exploratory problem solving, and long-term goals. Social class differences influence many aspects of clients' lives, including diet, discipline, and child-rearing practices (Havinghurst & Neugarten, 1968) as well as how counselors may react to the clients (Lorion, 1974). The third category, language variables, includes dependence on standard English and verbal communication skills. These values and communication styles differ among various ethnic groups within the United States and, in a multicultural counseling context, many of these aspects may come into sharp contrast.

☐ Developing Cultural Awareness

All counseling is cross-cultural (Arredondo, 1999; Sue, Arredondo, & McDavis, 1992a). Counseling does not occur in a vacuum. The relationship that emerges between counselor and client is a reflection of larger values within society. The worldview of each participant in the counseling process is shaped by historical and current sociopolitical realities of the United States. Acknowledging the experiences of racism and discrimination as well as circumstances of privilege and power in the counseling relationship is considered essential to the process. For the counselor, a beginning and ongoing task involves examining one's assumptions, values, and biases (Ivey & Ivey, 2007; Pengra, 2000; Sue & Sue, 2003).

Unlearning racism is the first step that a counselor must take in the path of developing cultural awareness. This involves first acknowledging the prevalence of cultural racism in the United States and then beginning to understand one's own prejudices toward those who are in some way culturally different. Wilkins (1995) asserted that, "Denial of racism is much like the denials that accompany addictions to alcohol, drugs or gambling" (p. 412). The first step is breaking through the denial. This is an emotional as well as cognitive process and is often facilitated by experiential exercises to increase self-awareness. Several such exercises are included in this chapter to give you a sample from which to choose. Several handbooks are available that are collections of multicultural awareness exercises (California Tomorrow, 2004; Ho, 1990; Katz, 1989; McGrath & Axelson, 1993).

When counselors come face to face with their own cultural racism, it may be a very unsettling experience. Most people do not intentionally discriminate against others. Feelings of anger, guilt, sadness,

---

Exercise 1: The Color of Fear

Arrange to see the documentary film, *The Color of Fear* (Lee, 1994). This is a 90-minute film about a weekend group experience about racism and how it affects the Asian American, African American, European American, and Latino men who are participants in the group. Viewing this film brings up many personal and emotional feelings for those watching it. Discuss the film afterward with others. DelVecchio (1995) reviews the film.

Exercise 2: Questions About Culture

Answer the following questions for yourself.

• What are some of the prejudices of your ethnic group, your religion, your gender group, or other subcultures to which you belong?

• In what ways are these prejudices expressed?

• What are your personal prejudices?

• How does your socioeconomic level affect your attitude toward people of other economic groups?

• How might your cultural prejudice give you difficulty in connecting with others in your professional role?

• How would you describe your own state of mental health, culturally speaking?

• Have you ever gone through a period of confusion and uncertainty about any of the values and practices with which you were raised?

• Have you borrowed any practices from other groups or cultures to help you live a better life? List all of them, and what they have done for you.

Note: Adapted from D. S. Murphy (1994) and L. Ho (1990).

or confusion about personal participation in cultural racism may be temporarily overwhelming. However, these feelings are a positive sign in many ways. First, they are an indication that the counselor is not in denial of the effects of cultural racism, that her or his learning includes her or his whole being, and that emotional as well as cognitive change is occurring. Second, the counselor may be able to use her or his own feelings as a source of new or renewed empathy for the client. Third, the effects of cultural racism, ideally, are experienced by the counselor in a

---

Exercise 3: Sharing About Culture and Class

With a partner (preferably someone you don't know well who is culturally different from you), spend about 10 minutes sharing your ethnicity and social class and the advantages and disadvantages of each in your life. Then discuss your cultures and find some similarities and some differences between your experiences.

Exercise 4: Institutionalized Cultural Racism

In a small group, develop policies and procedures for your own counseling center. For purposes of the exercise, pick a group to discriminate against and build this legitimately into your plans. For example, it is illegal to put up a sign that says "No persons of X cultural group allowed," but it is easy to discourage clients from X cultural background by the location, physical layout of the office, reading materials and decor of the waiting room, intake procedures, fee structure, availability of hours, languages of counseling available, choice of therapeutic orientations offered, and so on. When you are finished, share your plans with another group and see if they can determine which cultural group you are trying to exclude. Discuss together how institutionalized cultural racism can be subtly and legally incorporated into counseling and other institutions.

---

more controlled setting, such as a workshop, class, or training session, outside the counseling interaction, ensuring that the client is not burdened by having to deal with the counselor's feelings.

The second step in developing cultural awareness is when the counselor begins to increase her or his appreciation of cultural differences. Allport (1954) contended that contacts with members of minority groups that result in increased knowledge and understanding lead to more accurate and stable beliefs about minority groups and eventually reduce prejudice. A counselor may seek out people and experiences in her or his personal life that increase her or his exposure to other cultures. Arredondo (1999) recommends that counselors become active participants outside the counseling setting to broaden their perspective of minorities. This could involve a whole spectrum of behavior, such as going to movies and restaurants, being part of community events and celebrations, reading novels, increasing travel, and developing new friendships. This is a time of personal change and exploration for the counselor and care should be taken that the counselor does not bring this newly awakened interest into her or his counseling sessions as a matter of countertransference. The culturally different client is in counseling to receive help, not to increase the counselor's knowledge and experience. More appropriate at this time is for the counselor to seek out professional development activities, courses, and workshops with a cultural focus, and to consult colleagues with different cultural backgrounds for professional stimulation. A hallmark of a counselor engrossed with this level of cultural awareness is that multicultural experiences become welcomed as opposed to forced or merely tolerated. This implies that counselors at this stage can accept other worldviews as legitimate, even while not subscribing to the particular worldview.

☐ Counseling Clients Who Have Been Subject to Discrimination

Clients who become aware that they have been subjected to racial discrimination, sexual harassment, or cultural racism in other forms may be referred to or seek assistance from a counselor. Discrimination has many effects on individuals. The client may experience feelings of helplessness or anger. Sexual harassment is one example of discrimination and because it is an abuse of power and humiliating, victims may tend not to report it (Hamilton, Alagna, King, & Lloyd, 1987). The same may be true for other forms of discrimination. Koss (1985) reported that victims often do not perceive themselves as victims. They may not want to acknowledge the loss of control and self-esteem, and other negative experiences, and they may not want to compare themselves with other stigmatized individuals (Taylor, Wood, & Lichtman, 1983).

Recommendations for treating victims of discrimination may be generalized from those for treating women who have been sexually harassed described by Koss (1990):

1. Validate the victim's feelings.

2. Provide information. Discrimination may be frequent given the current norms of American society and the distribution of power.

3. Express anger safely.

4. Monitor the effects of discrimination, including maladaptive coping patterns by the victim or impact on the victim's family.

5. Provide a place to mourn losses (e.g., loss of a belief in a fair world), build new beliefs, and develop support systems.

6. Offer hope. Filing a complaint with a pertinent agency or bureau may eventually have beneficial effects. The counselor need not press for legal justice, but offering options, including legal remedies, helps empower the victim.

Even if a client is not aware that he or she has been subjected to discrimination, the results can have great psychological impact. Boden (1992) has noted, in working with disabled lesbians, that "When difference is experienced as a defect, it results in shame, self-loathing, and fear of exposure. These shame-based feelings become the central themes that color self-organization" (p. 158). She asserted that it is crucial for the counselor to welcome and understand difference in order for shame-laden material to be revealed and worked through, leading to increased self-esteem. These considerations may be relevant for any client who experiences difference from any source, among them ethnicity, gender, sexual orientation, age, or disability.

Thus, to develop as a culturally skilled counselor (Abreu, 2001; Arredondo & Arciniega, 2001), one must actively embrace a never-ending process of becoming aware of one's assumptions about human behavior, values, and biases as a way of understanding how our worldview has been shaped by social, cultural, and political forces. Secondly, the culturally skilled counselor actively attempts to understand the worldviews of culturally different clients with respect and appreciation, realizing the legitimacy of such viewpoints. Lastly, the culturally skilled counselor actively engages in a counseling process that incorporates intervention strategies that are relevant and sensitive to the goals, life experiences, and cultural values of their clients (Sue & Sue, 2003).

☐ Case Vignette

Tenisha is a 22-year-old African American heterosexual woman who chose to go to counseling after her first semester in college when she failed a history class. She is experiencing sadness, frustration, and anger about having failed the class. Tenisha questions whether college is for her. She is particularly upset because at an early age, she learned that she had to work hard to get good grades. After studying hard in this course, she cannot seem to learn the material well enough to score passing grades. She has had a difficult time relating to the history professor, a White male in his 50s dressed in an impeccable suit and tie, who regularly lectured at the podium. An only child, Tenisha's working-class parents worked two jobs to send her to private elementary and secondary Catholic schools. Often the only Black person in her classes, she feels as if people, particularly teachers, question her with the attitude of "What are you doing here?" For example, one time when she finally found enough strength to ask a question in her history class, she felt as if the professor barely acknowledged her question. Yet, knowing that her parents have sacrificed a lot to give her a quality education, Tenisha has tried to ignore the fact that she doesn't always feel welcome in classes. Having failed a class, however, has put her at an all-time low and she is seriously questioning why she is in college.

Questions

1. What are some reasons why Tenisha may be having difficulty relating to her professor?

2. If you were Tenisha's counselor, how would you address racist aspects of educational institutions that may be affecting her success in college?

3. What kinds of issues might a White, middle-class counselor bring up with Tenisha in order to build trust and rapport?

Reflection 1

Tenisha is attending college and feels she has to do well because her parents sacrificed working more than two jobs and giving her a quality education. If I were Tenisha's counselor, I would begin by trying to develop trust with her. I would want to explore more about her sadness and disappointment in failing the history class. I would reiterate that she does well in other classes and point out that her grade point average may not be in jeopardy. I would also want to help her discover extracurricular activities and organizations, both on and off campus, to strengthen her sense of community by bringing her into contact with people with whom she could identify and feel comfortable. I would begin to ask questions about why she thinks that the professor ignores her questions and makes her feel upset. As a counselor we would work on how discrimination affects stress levels.

Reflection 2

Class, race, cultural, and gender differences may make it difficult for Tenisha to relate to her professor. If she is seeing a White counselor, it would be particularly important to talk about how Tenisha feels about being counseled by a White person, especially considering that she is having difficulty relating to a White professor. It would be beneficial for a counselor of any ethnicity to explore class, race, gender, and cultural differences with Tenisha in order to help her understand her discomfort in the educational system. A counselor would also want to explore Tenisha's cultural values (e.g., family), the history of African Americans in this country, as well as the current status of this group in society. Finally, helping Tenisha see her many strengths will help her overcome her feelings of failure.

☐ Recommended Cultural Resources

Print Media

Anaya, R. (1972). *Bless me, Ultima*. Berkeley, CA: Tonatiuh International. A fictionalized account of a young boy from New Mexico who learns about the healing powers of the natural world through Ultima, on old curandera.

Angelou, M. (1970). *I know why the caged bird sings*. New York: Random House. Autobiography describing the author's coming of age as a Black girl in the South in the 1930s and later in California in the 1940s.

Thomas, P. (1967). *Down these mean streets*. New York: Vintage Books. A memoir of Piri Thomas's coming-of-age on the streets of Spanish Harlem.

West, C. (1993). *Race matters*. Boston: Beacon. Considered a contemporary classic and intense analysis of racism in America.

Multimedia

Gomez-Peña, G., & Artenstein, I. (1990). *Border brujo* [Videorecording and DVD]. San Diego, CA: Cinewest Productions. An indictment of U.S. colonial attitudes toward Mexican culture and history.

Kasdan, L., Okun, C., & Grillo, M. (Producers). (1991). *Grand Canyon* [Videorecording]. Beverly Hills, CA: Twentieth Century Fox Home Entertainment. The lives of six residents from different backgrounds interwine in Los Angeles.

Lee, M. W. (Producer). (1994). *The color of fear* [Film]. Oakland, CA: Stir-Fry Productions. A powerful and emotional discussion of racism by eight North American men of diverse ethnic backgrounds.

Reid, F. (Director and Producer). (1996). *Skin deep* [Videorecording]. Berkeley, CA: Iris Films. A diverse group of college students reveal their feelings and attitudes toward race and racism.

Cultural Aspects of Psychological Assessment

If we are to achieve a richer culture, rich in contrasting values, we must recognize the whole gamut of human potentialities, and so weave a less arbitrary social fabric, one in which each diverse human gift will find a fitting place.

Margaret Mead, anthropologist (Bartlett, 1992, p. 707)

☐ Historical and Sociopolitical Influences on Testing

IQ and Culture

Almost from its inception, intelligence testing has had a long history of use as a pseudoscientific tool to promote cultural racism. The overlap between prominent psychologists in the development of intelligence testing and the membership of influential political organizations that supported social policies limiting immigration, sterilizing the "feeble-minded," and other repressive practices in the 1900s was described in Chapter 3. In the 1960s, Jensen (1969) cited the lower average IQ scores of Negroes compared to Whites as evidence that IQ is innate and cannot be altered by environmental enrichment and therefore that compensatory education programs are doomed to failure. In 1979, the *Larry P. v. Riles* class-action suit in the state of California banned the use of standardized intelligence tests as a primary selection criterion for placing children into classes for the mentally retarded because it erroneously overselected African American children (Lambert, 1981; White, 1984). The political forces behind the use of testing for discriminatory purposes were so potent that the suit took seven years to litigate, and to the present day it continues to be challenged in the judicial appeals process. Herrnstein and Murray's (1994) book, *The Bell Curve,* which describes correlations between IQ, as a measure of intelligence, and many social problems, has again brought attention to the use of science to promote political agendas.

Objections to the use of intelligence testing have been made on both sociopolitical and scientific grounds. When used for selection purposes in educational programs, college admissions, and employment, intelligence or aptitude testing often has the prejudicial effect of putting more Blacks, Latinos, Native Americans, and other ethnic minority people into stigmatizing programs or denying them access to higher education or jobs. From a scientific standpoint, there is considerable controversy about what the tests really measure and how to control for the effects of social class and cultural differences. For example, social class is correlated with IQ in the 0.35–0.40 range (Jensen, 1969). Zuckerman (1990, p. 1301) summed up the issue:

> Generalizations about the innate intelligence or social responsibility of large and genetically diverse segments of the species are open to criticism on the grounds that they serve no important scientific purpose, given the present ambiguities in definition of the independent variable and immense sampling problems.

However, most states continue to use intelligence tests, perhaps in conjunction with other information, to make important decisions that affect the lives of ethnic minority people (Williams, 1987).

Assessment Concerns

In order to establish treatment goals, there are a number of ways to assess client treatment issues. First, it is essential to assess the individual's racial/ethnic identity stage, attitudes, and behaviors and how each of these variables is relevant to the current status of the client (Helms, 1990). In addition, assessing the client's level of acculturation will provide important information on how the person currently functions in society.

In addition to assessing the level of acculturation, it is also important to utilize other assessment procedures that take an emic perspective (see Chapter 1). The emic approach demands that the assessor must be particularly knowledgeable about cultural factors (Dana, 1993). An example of an emic technique is the life history/case study approach. The use of the life history/case study approach (Dana, 1993) provides an opportunity for the client to tell her or his story to the counselor. The life history/case study will also provide a way for the client to begin to feel comfortable talking in therapy to the counselor. This technique is entirely consistent with the move toward narrative approaches to counseling (see, e.g., Brown & Augusta-Scott, 2006; Payne, 2006). (For an extensive review of assessment concerns in multicultural counseling, see Suzuki, Ponterotto, & Meller, 2001.)

Affirmative Action and Testing

Affirmative action programs are aimed at making positive efforts to remedy past discrimination toward minority groups. Ever since the 1964 Civil Rights Act (see box on page 54 for a brief history of affirmative action), which outlawed disparate treatment of different racial groups, there has been continuing controversy over how to implement programs that seek to remedy past discrimination without in turn discriminating against any other groups (i.e., reverse discrimination).

However, the continuing need for affirmative action is unequivocal. Blacks and Latinos are still denied jobs that are offered to similarly qualified Whites 15–20% of the time (Fendel, Hurtado, Long, & Giraldo, 1996). Asian Americans are admitted to top universities such as Harvard, Yale, Berkeley, Brown, and Princeton at a lower rate than Whites although their academic qualifications may not warrant lower admission rates (Raspberry, 1990).

Additional efforts to increase the employment of minority group members are generally accepted by the public, especially when this entails broadening the pool of applicants. Difficulties arise when affirmative action is applied to the use of tests for selecting one person over another and especially when used to screen out people at early stages of a selection process. Affirmative action selection procedures that have the appearance of giving minority group members preference over others are the center of controversy (Sackett & Wilk, 1994). There are many

A Brief History of Affirmative Action

1964 — Title VII of the Civil Rights Act outlaws disparate treatment based on race.

1970 — Federal regulations require that all government contractors implement written, result-oriented, affirmative action compliance programs with specific goals and timetables for minority hiring.

1971 — *Griggs v. Duke Power Company* Supreme Court ruling decrees that disparate effects are prima facie evidence of employment discrimination and that testing is deemed unlawful if it results in racial differences in selection and the test is not job related.

1978 — Federal guidelines establish the "four-fifths" rule: If the pass rate for any group is less than four-fifths of the group with the highest passing rate, then the test is regarded as having an adverse impact on a particular group.

1991 — Civil Rights Act outlaws race-norming (establishing separate normative groups for different races).

1997 — California Proposition 209 bans all discrimination or preferential treatment related to ethnicity or gender in employment, education, or public contracts. Washington and Florida follow with similar laws.

2003 — *Grutter v. Bollinger* Supreme Court decision upholds the use of race in admissions decisions because it furthers "a compelling interest in obtaining the educational benefits that flow from a diverse student body."

Note: Adapted from Brunner (2006), Gottfredson (1994), and Sackett and Wilk (1994).

methods of using tests that take into consideration group membership. Some of these are assigning bonus points, developing separate within-group norms, establishing separate cutoff scores, creating separate rating lists, banding (treating as equal two individuals whose scores are not statistically significantly different), empirical keying by group, and eliminating test items. There are philosophical and scientific advantages and disadvantages to each of these methods, and no method has been established as widely acceptable. In fact, the use of separate within-group norms, often referred to as *race-norming*, as a means of affirmative action, was banned by Congress in 1991 (Gottfredson, 1994) and the use of bonus points has also been challenged (Brunner, 2006).

☐ Bias in Testing

Using the same test with different cultural groups is problematic, because a test may be biased with respect to one of the groups. Test bias may occur when a test does not select the same proportion of the group that would be selected by the criterion: in other words, if fewer people pass the test than would be successful at the real task for which performance is estimated by the test. A test may be culturally biased in many ways. Some of these sources of bias have to do with the cultural nature of the testing process itself, and others have to do with aspects of test development such as item content, standardization sample, and issues of differential construct or predictive validity (Dent, 1995).

Use of a test often makes the implicit assumption that the person being tested understands the presuppositions of the testing situation itself as well as the language of testing (Rogoff & Chavajzy, 1995). With respect to cognitive testing, Rogoff and Chavajzy (1995), in their excellent review of the cultural issues involved, concluded that one cannot assume "that a cognitive test reveals a general ability across tasks unrelated to people's experience" (p. 863). A person growing up in a nonliterate culture may have different premises about her or his world and may refuse to answer hypothetical questions because her or his worldview is to interact with what she or he has directly experienced. For some recent Southeast Asian immigrants or refugees, many questions typically used for assessment of mental status and cognitive functioning are either inappropriate or senseless because they depend on either an understanding of abstract concepts or school learning. Some examples are: "What is the thing to do if you find an envelope on the street, that is sealed, addressed, and has a brand new stamp?" or "If you had three wishes, what would they be?" (W. M. Lee & Nakagawa, 1996). In addition, people without formal schooling have difficulty memorizing unrelated items and often do not use organizing strategies spontaneously (Rogoff & Chavajzy, 1995), and even a nonverbal task such as matching patterns may seem strange (W. M. Lee & Nakagawa, 1996). These difficulties with testing may also apply to people whose formal education experiences have been lacking in quality.

Many Western cultures value speed and associate intelligence with performing quickly (Rogoff & Chavajzy, 1995). Timed tests may place people from some cultural groups at a disadvantage. For example, the SAT performance of Latinos and Latinas has been shown to be negatively influenced by the demand for speed (Dent, 1995).

Language issues may make test scores unrepresentative of a person's performance. Instructions may be unclear to a person whose first language is not English. Immigrants to the United States have been inappropriately given intelligence and personality tests requiring familiarity with English (Vernon, 1995). Even among native speakers of English there are cultural differences. Some common words are known to have different meanings for Blacks than for Whites (Samuda, 1975). Some tests, such as the Vocabulary subtest of the Wechsler Adult Intelligence Scale (WAIS), tend to unwittingly stress how well a person can articulate her or his ideas regardless of her or his level of understanding. People from cultural backgrounds that do not stress oral dialogue, especially with people in positions of authority, may not elaborate on their answers sufficiently to attain full scoring credit.

Another source of potential bias is the lack of culturally representative standardization groups during test construction. Even frequently used tests may have few ethnic minority people included in the standardization group.

In addition, the test administrator may be an unconscious source of cultural bias, although the research related to this issue is inconclusive. An individual's performance may differ when tested by someone with whom he or she feels more comfortable, perhaps someone from her or his own ethnic background. Similarly, a counselor working with a client from a cultural background different from her or his own may not notice or may misinterpret nonverbal or verbal cues (Takushi & Uomoto, 2001).

Given the many sources of potential test bias (see box on facing page), some of which have been discussed above, it is not surprising that there are group differences on many well-known assessment devices. A review of the literature by Sackett and Wilk (1994) concluded that physical ability and personality test differences have been found to be related to gender, and cognitive and personality test differences have been found to be related to ethnicity.

Culturally Relevant Sources of Test Bias

1. Illiteracy

2. Language differences

3. Emic communication styles (e.g., somatization as an expression of psychological distress)

4. Unfamiliarity with testing procedures

5. Inappropriate item content or test tasks

6. Nondependence on abstract concepts or speed

7. Lack of appropriate normative data

8. Interpreter error

9. Test administrator variance

Note: Adapted from Lee and Nakagawa (1996).

Social Class Considerations

The meaning of group differences in test performance may be linked to inequitable social and environmental conditions. Thus, group differences may be more reflective of systemic problems in U.S. society than of individual deficits. For example, standardized IQ measure scores for Black children tend to be 1 standard deviation below those of White children, and similar differences have been found for Hispanic and American Indian groups. However, when samples are comparable in terms of age, educational level, socioeconomic status, and other demographics, differences between groups on personality and intellectual measures decrease (Suzuki & Kugler, 1995).

Race Issues

On the Minnesota Multiphasic Personality Inventory (MMPI), perhaps the most widely used and well-researched personality assessment test, and its revision, the MMPI-2, Blacks score differently on the Schizophrenia, Paranoia, Mania, and F subscales (Williams, 1987), whereas Asian Americans report more somatic complaints (S. Sue & Sue, 1974). These group differences coincide with general differences in cultural values and experiences. Although the MMPI/MMPI-2 was designed as an etic measure (i.e., with the expectation that it would identify universal qualities; Nagayama, Hall & Phung, 2001), group differences actually support Dana's (1988) assertion that the MMPI/MMPI-2 is an emic instrument, relevant primarily to one particular cultural group for whom it was developed. Thus, the Black alienation syndrome that may turn up on the MMPI/MMPI-2 is not necessarily an indication of individual pathology but rather of cultural group alienation in the United States. One possibly ameliorating recommendation is to carefully explore the life situation of the person being tested whenever the MMPI profile is markedly deviant (Dahlstrom, Lachar, & Dahlstrom, 1986).

Differences among Native American, African American, Mexican American, and Caucasian groups on another widely used personality test, the Meyers–Briggs Type Indicator (MBTI), also have been noted (Oxford & Nuby, 1998). The MBTI, though, has been widely accepted as useful in most of the cultures in which it has been utilized (McCaulley & Moody, 2001).

The Strong Interest Inventory, a widely used vocational interest test, also yields ethnic group differences. Blacks tend to score higher in business and social service occupations, lower in physical science occupations, lower on the Realistic scale, and higher on the Social and Conventional scales on earlier versions of the Strong (e.g., SVIB), and no studies have been reported on the current version of the test with any visibly racial–ethnic group members (Carter & Swanson, 1990). Carter and Swanson (1990) concluded that "Little evidence exists for the psychometric validity of the Strong with Blacks" and that "This lack of research attention is appalling, particularly for an instrument with such widespread use" (p. 206). According to Carter and Swanson, in 1952 Strong himself, the developer of the test, concluded that there was a need for a Black norm group, but no such norms are as yet widely available. It is recommended that counselors explore with Black and other ethnic minority clients the extent to which various occupations may be open to them and the influence of cultural variables in the selection of their college majors and careers (Carter & Swanson, 1990). A more individualized test, such as

Holland's Self-Directed Search (Sweetland & Keyser, 1983), may be more useful with ethnic minority clients.

One survey of 332 vocational rehabilitation counselors found that only 27% rated psychological and vocational evaluation results as often or almost always culturally relevant for Native American clients living on a reservation, and only 35% rated them as relevant for off-reservation clients (W. E. Martin, Frank, Minkler, & Johnson, 1988). Such results also suggest that, for ethnic minority clients, individualized work samples, situational assessment, and on-the-job evaluations should be weighted more heavily than standardized testing.

Other Cultural Issues

People with disabilities also may be misrepresented by traditional assessment devices. For example, hearing-impaired people in the early 1900s were given oral intelligence and personality tests, and even now there is a lack of appropriate instrumentation for properly assessing mental health, educational, and rehabilitation needs of people who are deaf (Vernon, 1995). Bracken and McCallum (2001) indicated that hearing-impaired individuals could be identified as of lower cognitive ability if their intelligence is measured by traditional language-loaded tests. Pollard (1996) noted that unusual diagnostic trends in samples of deaf people appear to be related to testing biases rather than clinical reality.

Older people are yet another group for whom appropriate testing is difficult. Myers and Schwiebert (1996) noted several specific concerns and recommendations relevant to the testing of older people.

1. Use short sessions, as older people may tire more easily.

2. Use of large type and double spacing is helpful.

3. Monitor the reading level demanded by instructions and items.

4. Timed tests may be frustrating and inaccurate because of slower reaction times.

5. Older people may be unfamiliar with standardized testing procedures and lack test-taking behaviors.

6. Guard against lower examiner expectations of test performance as well as low motivation to take tests on the part of the older person being tested.

Many attempts have been made to develop more appropriate, culture-fair tests that have content equally familiar or unfamiliar to all groups and minimize speed and verbal content. Cattell's Culture-Fair Series, Davis-Eells Games, Letter's International Performance Scale, and Raven's Standard Progressive Matrices all de-emphasize verbal content (Sweetland & Keyser, 1983; Williams, 1987). The System of Multicultural Pluralistic Assessment (SOMPA) (Mercer, 1979) incorporates the content of the Wechsler for children (WISC-R) within a broader format including measures of "urban acculturation, socioeconomic status, family structure and family size" (Padilla, 2001).

The work of Reuven Feuerstein (Chance, 1981) is promising in that the Learning Potential Assessment Device (LPAD) does not depend on prior knowledge and focuses instead on finding out what a child can learn. Unfortunately, the LPAD may take from 9 to 15 hours to administer, much longer than conventional aptitude tests. Feuerstein's work has been translated into at least 17 languages and has been used in more than 30 countries.

The Joint Committee on Testing Practices has developed a *Code of Fair Testing Practices in Education* (2004) which makes several excellent recommendations that are relevant to the multicultural use of testing in general (see box on facing page). All in all, however, it is important for counselors to remember that there is general agreement that no test is truly free of culture (Williams, 1987), because it is not possible to remove from a test all references to language, abstract concepts, and prior knowledge.

☐ Culture-Specific Testing

Tests have been developed that incorporate the influence of culture in three specific areas: worldview, acculturation, and identity development. Other tests, such as the Latin American Stress Inventory (Salgado de Snyder, 1987), have been developed to measure a psychological concept (e.g., stress) from a more emic perspective.

One measure developed to assess differences in worldview is the Scale to Assess World Views (Ibrahim & Kahn, 1984). This measure incorporates Kluckhohn and Strodtbeck's (1961) five dimensions of culture: the nature of humans (good–bad), the relationship of humans to nature (harmony with–power over–all powerful), time orientation (past–present–future), the essence of human activity (being–being in becoming–doing), and social relationships (hierarchical–mutual–individualistic). Research and utility in counseling for this instrument are as yet limited.

Code of Fair Testing Practices in Education

Recommendations relevant to multicultural use of tests:

Test Developers

A.7. Avoid potentially offensive content or language when developing test questions and related materials.

A.8. Make appropriately modified forms of tests or administration procedures available for test takers with disabilities who need special accommodations.

A.9. Obtain and provide evidence on the performance of test takers of diverse subgroups, making significant efforts to obtain sample sizes that are adequate for subgroup analyses. Evaluate the evidence to ensure that differences in performance are related to the skills being assessed.

B.2. Provide guidelines on reasonable procedures for assessing persons with disabilities who need special accommodations or those with diverse linguistic backgrounds.

C.2. Provide guidance regarding the interpretations of results for tests administered with modifications. Inform test users of potential problems in interpreting test results when tests or test administration procedures are modified.

C.6. Provide information to enable test users to accurately interpret and report test results for groups of test takers, including information about who were and who were not included in the different groups being compared and information about factors that might influence the interpretation of test results.

continued on next page

Code of Fair Testing Practices in Education
continued from previous page

Test Users

A.7. Evaluate procedures and materials used by test developers, as well as the resulting test, to ensure that potentially offensive content or language is avoided.

A.8. Select tests with appropriately modified forms or administration procedures for test takers with disabilities who need special accommodations.

A.9. Evaluate the available evidence on the performance of test takers of diverse subgroups. Determine to the extent feasible which performance differences may have been caused by factors unrelated to the skills being assessed.

B.2. Provide and document appropriate procedures for test takers with disabilities who need special accommodations or those with diverse linguistic backgrounds. Some accommodations may be required by law or regulation.

C.1. Interpret the meaning of the test results, taking into account the nature of the content, norms, or comparison groups, other technical evidence, and benefits and limitations of test results.

C.2. Interpret test results from modified test or test administration procedures in view of the impact those modifications may have had on test results.

C.6. State the intended interpretation and use of test results from groups of test takers. Avoid grouping test results for purposes not specifically recommended by the test developer unless evidence is obtained to support the intended use. Report procedures that were followed in determining who were and who were not included in the groups being compared and describe factors that might influence the interpretation of results.

Note: Excerpted from: *Code of fair testing practices in education.* (2004). Washington, D.C.: Joint Committee on Testing Practices. (Mailing Address: Joint Committee on Testing Practices, American Psychological Association, 1200 17th Street, NW, Washington, D.C. 20036.)

Measures of acculturation try to assess the extent to which the respondents retain their ethnic group behaviors, whereas measures of ethnic identity development assess the extent to which individuals perceive themselves to be part of their ethnic group and how positively this group membership is experienced. Dana (1993) suggested that to assess a client's degree of acculturation, the counselor may inquire about language preference, primary language spoken in the home, place of birth, community and social relationships, and food and clothing preferences. Even more important, but more difficult to assess, are the client's own values and level of comfort living in U.S. society. For example, Zuniga (1988) suggested asking a client with a Mexican American background to identify Mexican traits that he or she feels characterize her or his family lifestyle, if any, and how the client was affected by these traits. Discussing cultural role expectations and acknowledging cultural preferences also are recommended. Thus, acculturation assessment could be a means of addressing potential culture conflicts in a problem-solving fashion that the client can learn to apply to other situations as well.

It has been estimated that there are 50 specific measures that have been developed to examine either ethnic identity development or acculturation (Grieger & Ponterotto, 1995), and most of these focus on a specific cultural group (Lai & Sodowsky, 1992). Several examples are listed in the box on page 64. These measures vary in terms of their reliability, validity, and how extensively they have been researched. Refer to Dana (1993) for an excellent review of many of these measures.

The White Racial Identity Attitude Scale (WRIAS; Helms & Carter, 1990) provides a good example of the issues involved. The WRIAS was developed to measure five different White racial identity ego statuses and has been widely used. This five-point Likert scale, 50-item instrument reveals that men are more uncomfortable and confused about race than women are and are less accepting of racial differences (Pope-Davis & Ottavi, 1994). However, there has been considerable recent debate about the reliability and factorial aspects of the WRIAS (Behrens, 1997; Behrens & Rowe, 1997; Helms, 1997; Row, Behrens, & Leach, 1995).

The Multigroup Ethnic Identity Measure (MEIM; Phinney, 1992), which takes a broader, more etic view of ethnic identity, has reasonably high reported reliability: 0.81 and 0.90 in samples of high school and college students, respectively. The MEIM is a 20-item, four-point Likert scale instrument that yields a single factor, Ethnic Identity. MEIM Ethnic Identity has a low positive correlation with self-esteem in the 0.25–0.31 range.

Some Group-Specific Measures of
Acculturation or Ethnic Identity

- Native Americans

  Indian Assimilation Scale (Howe Chief, 1940)

  Native American Value-Attitude Scale (Plas & Bellet, 1983)

  Rosebud Personal Opinion Survey (T. Hoffman, Dana, & Bolton, 1985)

- Latinos/Latinas

  Acculturation Rating Scale for Mexican Americans (Cuellar, Harris, & Jasso, 1980)

  Acculturation Rating Scale for Puerto Ricans (Pomales & Williams, 1989)

  Bicultural-Multicultural Experience Inventory (Ramirez, 1984)

  Children's Hispanic Background Scale (Martinez, Norman, & Delaney, 1984)

  Cuban Behavioral Identity Questionnaire (Garcia & Lega, 1979)

  Hispanic Acculturation Scale (Marin, Sabogal, VanOss Marin, Otero-Sabogal, & Perez-Stable, 1987)

- African Americans

  African Self-Consciousness Scale (Baldwin & Bell, 1985)

  Developmental Inventory of Black Consciousness (Milliones, 1980)

  Black Racial Identity Attitude Scale (Parham & Helms, 1981)

- Asian Americans

  Ethnic Identity Questionnaire (Masuda, Matsumoto, & Meredith, 1970)

  Suinn-Lew Asian Self-Identity Acculturation Scale (Suinn, Rickard-Figueroa, Lew, & Vigil, 1987)

- European Americans

  White Racial Identity Attitude Scale (Helms & Carter, 1990)

☐ Recommendations for Multicultural Assessment

Given the many sources of bias in testing and difficulties in developing culture-fair tests, the use of standardized testing should be minimized unless the content is culturally appropriate and relevant norms are available. Even the use of translated tests is questionable, because there are many concerns about their validity and interpretive comparability, and there is no regulating body or ethical code regarding test translation (Suzuki & Kugler, 1995; Dana, 2001). If the purpose of testing is for selection or diagnostic purposes, testing should be scrutinized even more cautiously. Instead, counselors can allocate more time to idiographic and nontraditional assessment, using testing for exploration rather than decision making.

Clinical diagnosis of cultural minority clients is a difficult task. Interviewer bias is hard to avoid and may take many forms. Lopez (1988) noted that the client may be viewed as more disturbed than he or she truly is, some symptoms may be inappropriately viewed as normative for certain groups, and certain diagnostic categories may either be avoided or overapplied as a function of group membership.

Another problem is the diagnostic classification system itself. Even though some attempts have been made to include specific, culturally bound disorders in the most recent edition of the *Diagnostic and Statistical Manual of Mental Disorders (DSM–IV–TR)* fourth edition (text revision; American Psychiatric Association, 2000), it is highly prone to *category fallacy,* which is the use of a category developed for a particular population applied to members of another culture without establishing its validity (Good & Good, 1985). For example, Dana (1993) noted that ethnic minority clients are vulnerable to misdiagnoses of dependent personality disorder or paranoid personality disorder related to differences in population values and experiences.

The many complexities involved in diagnosing Southeast Asian refugees are a good illustration of the cultural problems involved in assessment. Many Southeast Asian refugees consider headaches and nightmares to be a normal part of life and may not even mention them because they are so common among the refugee population (Tien, 1994). Response styles that from a Western perspective may seem like exaggeration or malingering may be related to cultural differences and difficulties in discussing things in a psychological manner (W. M. Lee & Nakagawa, 1996). In addition, post-traumatic stress disorder may be erroneously diagnosed as schizophrenia among refugees (Gong-Guy, Cravens, & Patterson, 1991).

Such difficulties underscore the need to take more time and carry out an assessment interview in a more individualized fashion with a client who is from an ethnic or cultural minority background (W. M. Lee & Nakagawa, 1996). Repeating the same question in a variety of ways may be needed to obtain adequate information. Increased emphasis on exploring gender roles and expectations, childbearing or other reproductive events, and sexual behavior may prove helpful. Also important is the client's perception of the helping process (Dana, 1993). In addition to traditional areas of assessment, culture-specific information should be obtained. The counselor could begin addressing this topic with the question, "What do you call yourself when asked about your ethnicity?" (Zuniga, 1988). Comas-Diaz and Jacobsen (1987) recommended inquiring about the cultures and countries of origin of the client's mother and father, circumstances of the client's immigration, the client's perceptions of her or his family's cultural identity, and the client's own cultural adjustment.

The use of an interpreter may be needed with clients who are not fluent in English. There are many problems with the use of interpreters (Gong-Guy et al., 1991; W. M. Lee & Nakagawa, 1996; Padilla, 2001; D. Sue & Sue, 1987; Tien, 1994):

1. One language may lack the words to fully correspond to the meaning of a word in another language.

2. The interpreter may unintentionally change, embellish, or distort information.

3. The interpreter's own cultural norms and values may interfere.

4. The interpreter may lack an understanding of what is important from a psychological perspective.

5. Confidentiality issues may cause the client to provide more limited information when the interpreter is a friend or family member.

It is difficult to have access to an expert interpreter who is fluent in English and in the client's primary language, and who is trained to accurately represent the content expressed. For example, an interpreter unfamiliar with the counseling process might leave out information that he or she might consider embarrassing or unimportant, such as reproductive or sexual history information (W. M. Lee & Nakagawa, 1996; Padilla, 2001). To minimize some of the problems inherent in the use of interpreters, Marcos (1979) suggested meeting beforehand with the interpreter to discuss the goals of the interview, the areas to be assessed, and potentially sensitive topics as well as the interpreter's level of competence in both languages. Counselors can anticipate potential language difficulties and prepare themselves to use an interpreter effectively.

☐ Case Vignette

Robert, a 10-year-old African American boy, was referred by his teacher due to problems in maintaining attention in class when the teacher or students are talking. The teacher, a 23-year-old Portuguese-American female, mentioned that Robert would stare out the window at times. She stated that she thinks he has attention deficit disorder (ADD) and should be retained. He was referred to the school counselor who, based on meeting with Robert and observing him in class, believes that he needs to take some assessment tests to have documentation of "attention deficit disorder." Robert lives with his mother, father, younger brother, and younger sister in the southern United States. He attended three different schools in three years and had good attendance and very good grades. He wears glasses and is very active. His hearing test results indicate he has some hearing loss in both ears due to the many ear infections he has had all his life.

Questions

1. How might Robert's racial-ethnic and gender identity influence the perception of attention-deficit problems? How might the teacher's racial-ethnic and gender identity influence the perception of attention-deficit problems?

2. How might Robert's visual and hearing limitations potentially affect his performance on assessment measures? What diagnosis would you give Robert?

3. If you were the counselor, what would you recommend? Would you include Robert's family in the counseling and, if so, how and why?

Reflection 1

The difference in his current school situation and his previous school success makes it important to assess Robert carefully. Perhaps there are current environmental issues that are affecting his performance. He may not be stimulated by the teacher's style of teaching. There may be racial prejudices coloring the perceptions of school personnel. Diagnosis of ADD is not appropriate without a comprehensive assessment by the psychologist, including a general clinical interview and a medical exam. It might be helpful to bring Robert's family in to ask about the family's current environment, perceptions of Robert at home, and their thoughts about what might be going on with Robert.

Reflection 2

This type of case may be relatively common in school settings. The teacher notices that a student does not attend during class and assumes that he or she suffers from an attention-deficit disorder. Given the teacher's responsibility for many, many students, I commend her for noticing a difficulty with one of her students and wanting to resolve the difficulty. It seems appropriate that she make a referral to a professional for further assessment. The professional, a school counselor in this case, should conduct a thorough assessment including reviewing a comprehensive, family, social, and medical history. In this review, the student's hearing loss should be identified, as well as his frequent moves from community to community and from school to school. This clearly may have an impact on the observed behaviors of the student. If, after reviewing this information, the counselor still suspects an attention-deficit problem, further testing or referral may be logical. From the limited knowledge we have of the student at this point, further testing and an assumption of attention-deficit problems is premature.

☐ Recommended Cultural Resources

Print Media

Helms, J. E. (2004). Fair and valid use of educational tests. In J. Wall & G. R. Walz (Eds.) *Measuring up: Assessment issues for teachers, counselors, and administrators.* Greensboro, NC: ERIC Counseling and Student Services Clearinghouse.

Nuby, J., & Oixford, R. (1996). *Learning style preferences of Native American and African-American secondary students as measured by the MBTI.* (ERIC Document Reproduction Service No. ED 406-422).

Suzuki, L. A., Ponterotto, J. G., & Meller, P. J. (Eds.). (2001). *Handbook of multicultural assessment: Clinical, psychological, and educational applications* (2nd ed.), NetLibrary Version. San Francisco, CA: Jossey-Bass. This thorough analysis of multicultural assessment covers significant issues, including the major instruments and procedures, cognitive and educational assessment, and cross-cultural sensitivity and ethics.

Multimedia

The Center for Multicultural and Gender Studies.http://www.txstate.edu/mcgs/mc_trans.html. This site includes links, projects, and syllabus transformation that incorporate multicultural assessment issues.

KQED (Producer). (1999). *Making the grade* [PBS television broadcast]. San Francisco: KQED. Retrieved August 22, 2006, from http://www.kqed.org/tv/productions/baywindow/makingthegrade/. Fascinating documentary about two high school seniors who apply to the University of California at Berkeley and the possible effect of changes in affirmative action policies banning race as an admissions factor.

5

CHAPTER

Cultural Transition

All changes, even the most longed for, have their melancholy; for what we leave behind us is a part of ourselves; we must die to one life before we can enter into another!

Anatole France (Ehrlich & DeBruhl, 1996, p. 79)

Always I have this experience, everywhere I go, that other students won't choose to be in a group with me. If you're immigrant, you are either in the group or not in the group. I once thought it was just the English language—because of my accent and because my name is hard for people to say. But then I learn it (English), but it's still going on. It's not only language but culture, what it's like to be a foreigner in another country. It is painful….

Iranian female student, 50 years of age, applying for
an MA program, who has lived over 20 years in the
United States (Woodlief, Thomas, & Orozco, 2003, p. 178)

Many people have experienced the process of cultural transition if they have physically moved from one culture to another. Anyone who has visited another country, moved from one region of the United States to another, or moved from one country to another has experienced this process to some extent. There are many changes that occur in the life of someone who moves into a new culture, and change, even positively anticipated change, can be stressful. Studies of life stress using the Social Readjustment Rating Scale (Table 5.1; Holmes & Rahe, 1967) have found

TABLE 5.1. Social Readjustment Rating Scale

Life event	Scale of impact
Death of spouse	100
Divorce	73
Marital separation	65
Jail term	63
Death of close family member	63
Personal injury or illness	53
Marriage	50
Loss of job	47
Marital reconciliation	45
Retirement	45
Health problems in family	44
Pregnancy	40
Sexual difficulties	39
Gain of new family member	39
Business readjustment	39
Change in finances	38
Death of close friend	37
Change in line of work	36
More/fewer arguments with spouse	35
Large mortgage taken out	32
Foreclosure of mortgage/loan	30
Change in work responsibilities	29
Son or daughter leaving home	29
Trouble with in-laws	29
Major personal achievement	28
Change in spouse's work	26
Starting or leaving school	26
Change in living conditions	25
Revision of personal habits	24
Trouble with boss	23
Change in work hours/conditions	20

Table 5.1 continues on page 73.

TABLE 5.1. *Continued*

Life event	Scale of impact
Change in residence	20
Change in schools	20
Change in recreation	19
Change in church activities	19
Change in social activities	18
Small loan taken out	17
Change in sleeping habits	16
More/fewer family reunions	15
Change in eating habits	15
Vacation	13
Christmas	12
Minor violations of the law	11

Note: Adapted from Holmes and Rahe (1967).

that the cumulative change involved when moving from one culture to another is often so great that it puts a person at risk for serious illness or depression.

A score of 150 on the Social Readjustment Rating Scale in the previous six months can be indicative of stress, 200–300 in one year has been associated with a 50% risk of serious illness or depression, and 300 or more in one year has been associated with an 80% probability of illness or depression. These levels are easily reached during cultural transition when the many changes in place of employment, school, living situation, family, friendships, recreation, and religious activities are added.

The changes are most dramatic when a person moves from one country to another. Immigrants, refugees, international students, military personnel, business assignees, and Peace Corps volunteers are all affected by this process. It is estimated that 2–10% of business people on foreign assignments have adjustment difficulties and 33% of their families return to the United States earlier than planned (Church, 1982). Similarly 15–25% of international students have been reported to experience significant adjustment difficulties and as many as 35–40% of Peace Corps volunteers in some years terminate prematurely (Church, 1982).

☐ Acculturation

Although difficult to define, the term "acculturation" in general refers to the process of cultural change that takes place when two or more cultures come into contact with each other. This process, for an individual, involves acquiring the cultural values, norms, language, and behavior of the dominant society (Atkinson, 2004). The melting pot approach was an early theory of acculturation which posited that immigrant groups completely assimilate to mainstream U.S. culture after putting elements of their own cultures into the pot. Critics of the melting pot theory have pointed out how total assimilation has only been accessible to European immigrants, whereas immigrants of color have been expected to adopt the ways of the dominant culture without being allowed to bring in elements from their indigenous cultures. Early models are also criticized for their assumption that acculturation is a unilinear or monocultural process. In other words, that the cultural values of the indigenous culture are gradually lost and the cultural values of the dominant society are gradually adopted, discounting possible changes in the dominant society that may occur through contact with other cultures.

More and more, researchers are recognizing that immigrants can retain values and behavior from their cultures of origin while simultaneously adopting values and behavior from the new culture. For example, the health and psychological well-being of recent Latino immigrants has been associated with maintenance of language and culture (Alderete, Vega, Kolody, & Aguilar-Gaxiola, 2000; Delgado, 1997; National Coalition of Hispanic Health and Human Services Organizations, 1999). Although greater assimilation to an American lifestyle was considered to be superior in earlier models, studies of Latino mental health suggest that recent Latino immigrants have a healthier mental outlook than second- and third-generation Latinos (Alderete et al., 2000) and that high acculturation to life in the United States increases the likelihood that a person will suffer lifetime psychiatric disorders (Vega, Kolody, Aguilar-Gaxiola, & Catalano, 1999).

Berry's (1997) extensive research on psychological acculturation led him to identify two basic phenomena: (1) behavior shift, the general process whereby individuals move away from behavioral patterns learned in the indigenous culture and move toward behavioral patterns found in the host culture; and (2) acculturative stress, or what some authors term "culture shock" (Oberg, 1960) to describe the state of anxiety that arises from not knowing how to behave in a new culture. Pedersen (1995) elaborated on several characteristics of culture shock:

1. Familiar cues about how to behave are missing.

2. Personal values may not seem to be respected by host nationals.

3. Feelings of disorientation may lead to anxiety, depression, or hostility.

4. Dissatisfaction with the new culture may simultaneously be experienced while idealizing the way things used to be in the home culture.

5. Coping skills may no longer work.

6. There may be a sense that the situation is permanent and will not improve.

Several models have been proposed for the stages that a person may go through in the cultural adjustment process (Adler, 1975; Fontaine, 1983; Oberg, 1960; Pedersen, 1995). Most describe four or five stages with the first being a "honeymoon" stage lasting anywhere from a few days to six months. During this initial stage there are positive feelings of excitement and curiosity about the new culture. Short-term tourists may only experience this phase, which lasts an average of three months (Oberg, 1960).

The second phase, characterized by dissatisfaction and feelings of inadequacy, may last approximately two to three months (Fontaine, 1983). The person in a new culture begins to confront cultural differences that are problematic: language difficulties make it hard to make friends and keep up with current events, legal barriers to employment may become stressful, and dealing with the phone company, post office, or other basic services may be different in the new culture. The world as the person has known it seems to be disintegrating and the person may blame him- or herself for not being able to cope with the differences in the new culture.

The next phase may involve feelings of depression and the person may want to return to her or his home culture, if that is an option. Feelings of grief and bereavement upon losing familiar family, friends, and culture also may be present (Furnham & Bochner, 1986). With time, as a person's language facility and coping skills improve, the feelings of depression may begin to subside. Feelings of anger and active dislike of the new culture may surface. Eventually, however, the person reaches a stage where he or she may cherish differences of the new culture. He or she begins to have a more balanced view of the positives and negatives of both her or his home and new cultures.

A final stage, when the person is truly comfortable in both cultures, is controversial. Adler (1975) posits that it may not really be possible to be truly bicultural, as the person risks losing a stable sense of identity in continually adapting to two cultures. In contrast, the bicultural process model of acculturation (Kim & Abreu, 2001) posits that the bicultural individual is committed to both cultures and selectively chooses aspects of each culture.

Berry (1997) states that the degree of acculturative stress experienced by an individual depends on several factors. One important factor has to do with the level of tolerance for ethnic diversity present in the dominant society. Pluralistic societies that encourage cultural diversity would be expected to subject an individual to less acculturative stress. Policy makers and health professionals also affect the acculturation process. Bilingual education policies and bilingual mental health services can help to reduce acculturative stress for immigrants.

Berry (1997) and Berry, Kim, Power, Young, and Bujaki (1989) refer to four modes or acculturation strategies taken on by individuals as they acculturate. Some individuals will adopt an assimilationist strategy whereby they give up their own identity, attitudes, and behaviors in favor of the identity, attitudes, and behaviors observed in the dominant society. Other individuals may choose a separatist strategy by maintaining their identity and cultural values while rejecting the values of the dominant society. Another strategy is that of the marginalized individual who gives up her or his own cultural values while also rejecting the values of the dominant society. A fourth strategy is an integrated or bicultural option whereby the individual chooses to maintain her or his identity and culture while at the same time identifying with and adopting the attitudes and behaviors of the new culture. Marginalized individuals experience the greatest degree of acculturative stress, those who prefer to assimilate experience intermediate levels of stress, and those individuals who seek to integrate the two cultures experience the least amount of stress. Perhaps those who stay separate attempt to avoid stress. According to Berry (1997), the acculturation strategy that has been found to have more positive adaptations for all types of acculturating groups is that of biculturality or integration. One explanation for this finding is that the integration strategy is based on a willingness and flexibility to accommodate two cultures; positive attitudes exist on the part of the individual who seeks to integrate as well as from the host culture; and involvement in two cultural communities provides two social support systems.

The overall pattern of cultural adjustment was described as a U-shaped curve initially by Lysgaard (1955), but empirical support for this is mixed at best (Church, 1982). Research has not verified that most persons go through a period of excitement and later depression. The time it takes to go through the various stages also varies widely among models. It is important to note that not all people may experience changes or difficulties in cultural adjustment. However, the stress of acculturation can produce feelings of anxiety, depression, marginality and alienation, psychosomatic symptoms, and identity confusion (Berry, Kim, Minde, & Mok, 1987). If a client is experiencing culture shock, the stages of adjustment and U-curve just described may be useful ideas to introduce as a way to help increase client understanding of what he or she is experiencing.

A major point to remember is that there is a lot of individual variation in how well someone will adjust to a new culture. People's experiences may be different depending on the degree of difference between the home and new culture. In addition, sex differences in cultural adjustment are an important consideration (Rogler, Cortes, & Malgady, 1991). There is evidence suggesting that the cultural adjustment process is different and often more difficult for women (Bowler, 1980; Church, 1982; Sjogren, 1988; Useem, 1966), particularly if they are not employed in the new culture. An alternative explanation is that cultural adjustment is equally difficult for both men and women, but women are more likely to seek counseling for their difficulties whereas men may cope by making job or other situational changes (Bowler, 1980). Hopkins (1982) identified some individual qualities that predicted effective adaptation to a new culture for adolescent exchange students: self-confidence, interpersonal interest, low level of ethnocentrism, and educational background match to the new school. Additional variables to consider for anyone going through cultural transition are attitudes toward acculturation, degree of prior knowledge of the new language and culture, previous intercultural encounters, voluntary versus involuntary reason for entering the new culture, and level of education and employment (Williams & Berry, 1991).

☐ Counseling Individuals and Families in Cultural Transition

Treatment for acculturative stress or culture shock may be helpful for many individuals and families in transition from one culture to another. If possible, preventive education is advisable prior to or just after the move. Clients can be taught that the feelings they may experience are part of a normal natural process and that adjustment may take time and be difficult (Boyer & Sedlacek, 1989). One recurrent finding in the research on cultural adjustment is that congruity between expectations and actualities when encountering a new culture affects mental health (Williams & Berry, 1991). Therefore, learning about the new culture should be encouraged. Observing behavior by viewing television and movies of the new culture is one potential source of cultural information. Cultural orientation workshops or counseling sessions also would be helpful for developing realistic expectations and anticipatory problem solving. Use of the new culture's language is an important component of acculturation and accounts for much of the variance in individual adjustment (Rogler et al., 1991). Language training is highly recommended, and it is especially useful to include specific business communication practices, day-to-day conversational dialogue, and idiomatic expressions (Donnelly, 1994).

Once the individual or family has moved to the new culture, it is helpful for them to have interpersonal support to help maintain a positive self-image. Having other people who will listen to them and developing networking skills to make new friends is desirable. A counselor may be useful in this process, and at this point a counselor who is "native" to the new culture is often preferable (Jones, 1975).

Specific issues may arise that are relevant to the particular circumstances of cultural transition, for example, temporary versus permanent transition. Two transitional groups that counselors are likely to encounter are discussed separately: international students and immigrants.

International Students

There were over 565,000 international students studying at American universities in the 2004–2005 academic year. India is the leading sending country, followed by China in second place, the Republic of Korea in third place, Japan in fourth place, and Canada in fifth place. California is the leading host state for international students. The most popular fields of study for international students in the United States are business and management (18% of total), engineering (16.5%), and mathematics and computer science (9%), although other fields such as physical and life science, health professions, intensive English language, and agriculture are experiencing growth (Institute of International Education, 2006).

International students are a high-risk population because most of their home countries do not have a history of providing or encouraging counseling and many international students seek help only as a last resort (Boyer & Sedlacek, 1989; Sandhu, 1993). Although as many as one-fourth of international students may experience cultural adjustment difficulties (Church, 1982), one study revealed that only 13% of them made use of some sort of counseling services (Boyer & Sedlacek, 1989).

When international students do seek help, they tend to view their difficulties as medical as opposed to psychological (Boyer & Sedlacek, 1989). Yeh and Inose (2003) found that social support satisfaction and social connectedness, as well as English language fluency, help to predict lower levels of acculturative stress. International students tend to be more satisfied with their academic than their social adjustment (Church, 1982). They may like American sports, foods, freedom of dress, and openness. In contrast, they may have difficulty with English; living in a different climate; homesickness; discrimination; feelings of depression, irritability, and tiredness; and visa and employment issues. Isolation, negative attitudes toward international students, and lack of cultural sensitivity by Americans are also barriers to their cultural adjustment (Pedersen, 1991). Lee, Koeske, and Sales (2004) reported that social support, particularly as measured by high acculturation to the English language and interpersonal relationships, served to buffer the effect of stress in their study of 74 Korean international students.

The international students who have more understanding and ability to deal with racism, a preference for long-term goals, and an openness to nontraditional ways of seeking knowledge are the ones more likely to seek counseling. It is interesting that these same three qualities also predict better outcomes in terms of grades and retention for international students (Boyer & Sedlacek, 1989). In other words, the students with the best coping skills are the ones more likely to seek counseling and the students who may have the most difficulty may not seek treatment. Orientation workshops that address basic life and safety information for living in the United States, colloquial English, and the nature and availability of counseling at American schools and colleges have been suggested as a way to reach some of these high-risk students (Sandhu, 1993).

Another possibility is group counseling of a "cross-cultural discussion group" nature. The first author of this book co-led such groups in an international student dormitory with good results. Each group session focused on a different educational topic or theme—for example, music, friendship, holiday celebrations—while giving members an opportunity to socialize with and support one another. When international students seek help for difficulties with their academic progress, brief behavioral therapy as opposed to longer-term personality reorganization-focused treatment has been recommended (Thomas & Althen, 1989).

Immigrants and Refugees

Unlike international students, who plan on staying temporarily in the United States, immigrants and refugees often become permanent members of their new culture. The immigrant population in the United States is growing: from 10 million in 1970 to 14 million in 1980 and 20 million in 1990. In March 1999, the estimated foreign-born population in the United States was 26 million (U.S. Census Bureau, 2001) or, roughly speaking, one-tenth of the U.S. population had been born in another country (Portes & Rumbaut, 2001). During this same period between 1970 and 1999, the number of foreign-born U.S. residents from Europe dropped from 62% to 16%; the foreign-born population from Asia increased from 9% to 27%; and the foreign-born population from Latin America grew from 19% to 51%. In 1999, two-thirds of foreign-born Latin Americans were from Central America and Mexico (U.S. Census Bureau, 2001).

One of the major changes immigrants experience is the economic, social, and psychological stress of job loss. It is very difficult for an individual to retain her or his former occupation on entering the new culture. Socioeconomic entry status in the new culture is often lower than status on departure from the home culture (Williams & Berry, 1991). The loss of a job is a multiple loss: The job itself may be mourned, economic stress may develop, especially if a new job is not found or is found at a lower income level, and there may be a loss of personal identity involved if the old job was lucrative, a professional career, or both. It may be helpful for the individual to develop or maintain some sort of personal or professional interest to focus her or his sense of self-worth while transitioning to a new job in the new culture.

Undocumented status may be an additional source of stress for some immigrants (Lefley, 1989). Although immigrants bring energy, talents, and a strong work ethic in their quest to find the American dream, once in America, some of them will feel pressure to conform as they encounter racism, discrimination, and job exploitation, all of which will affect their sense of self-esteem (Suárez-Orozco & Suárez-Orozco, 1995). An undocumented client may be initially reluctant to seek counseling and once in counseling, he or she may be less self-disclosing.

Another more subtle, but growing, issue of concern is cultural racism. Prior to 1970 most immigrants were Europeans, and from 1970 on they have been primarily Latinos and Asians (Kitano, 1989). From 1965 to 1993 the number of Americans who express the belief that immigration should be decreased rose from 33% to 61%. The lack of cultural sensitivity of Americans toward people from other cultures has been notable (Pedersen, 1991; Sandhu, 1993).

One study of immigrant and refugee college students at a large university suggests that their concerns are very similar to those of international students: unfamiliarity with American society and institutions, problems relating to students, teaching assistants, and professors, and difficulties making friends, feeling that they belong, and getting involved with campus organizations (J. McKay, personal communication, October 20, 1980). Most of the immigrant and refugee students were majoring in engineering or computer science and their grades were comparable to other students. However, fewer of them had attended pre-college orientation sessions. More information about student services, additional advising and orientation efforts, bilingual peer advisors, and student or faculty mentors were suggested remedies.

Refugees are particularly at risk for psychological problems because they come to their new culture not voluntarily but because they are forced to leave their homes, fleeing persecution for their beliefs, politics, or ethnicity. Most people who are displaced from their homes stay in their home country, yet in 1995, 14.4 million refugees worldwide left their home countries ("In-Country Refugees," 1995). Based on data from Census 2000, the Current Population Survey, and the U.S. Immigration and Naturalization Service, researchers at The Urban Institute (Capps, Passel, Perez-Lopez, & Fix, 2003) estimate that on average about 70,000–125,000 refugees and asylees entered the United States per year in the 1990s. Fourteen percent of legal immigrants to the United States are refugees, primarily from the Soviet Union and Vietnam (Morrisey, 1995). Many refugees may have experienced traumas such as sexual abuse, physical torture, internment in a refugee camp, or the loss of one or more family members prior to coming to the United States. In this respect, refugees are similar to disaster victims and similar counseling strategies may be applicable (Lefley, 1989). For example, the most frequent diagnoses for Southeast Asian refugees in psychological treatment are depression and post-traumatic stress disorder (Kroll et al., 1989; Mollica, Wyshak, & Lavelle, 1987). The frequent experience of trauma coupled with the involuntary nature of their move makes cultural transition especially difficult for refugees.

Morrisey (1995) has proposed a Multi-Level Model (MLM) for counseling refugees. The MLM involves simultaneously working with the client on four levels:

1. Mental education: educating the client about the counseling process,

2. Western individual, group, and family counseling: applying traditional Western counseling techniques as appropriate,

3. Cultural empowerment: serving as the client's resource guide, culture broker, and advocate, and

4. Indigenous healing: working with traditional healers from the client's culture.

This model may be useful in planning treatment that takes into consideration cultural differences not only for refugees, but for other cultural groups as well.

☐ Re-Entry Shock

Re-entry shock (Fontaine, 1983) is reverse culture shock that an individual may experience upon returning to her or his home culture. Gullahorn and Gullahorn (1963) suggested modifying the U-curve previously proposed to describe the cultural adjustment process to be more of a W-curve instead, to include the re-entry process. Re-entry shock can be as strong as or stronger than the initial culture shock and may be even more difficult for several reasons (Adler, 1981). The individual may not expect to encounter difficulties upon returning home. Also, the initial culture shock may be positively rationalized by the individual as "developmental" whereas returning re-entry shock may feel "regressive" (Harvey, 1970).

People who spend less time living in another culture seem to have an easier time readjusting (Mattox, Sanchez, Ulsh, & Valero, 1982) and some people do not experience re-entry shock at all because psychologically they have never left their home culture (Sobie, 1986). In contrast, people who adjusted most successfully to the new culture may find going home the most difficult (Sobie, 1986). Once a few years have passed in a new culture, the individual may have developed friends and intimate relationships in her or his new culture and may have adopted aspects of the new culture that he or she particularly likes, for example, American music or openness of expression. The prospect of returning to the home culture at this point may be stressful, as the loss of new relationships, experiences, and freedoms becomes a reality. International students and people on temporary military, business, or humanitarian assignments may find the process of returning home to be more distressing than they had initially imagined.

Family and friends in the home culture may not express more than superficial interest in their overseas experiences while at the same time the people themselves may be missing their overseas friends. As a reaction to initial culture shock, they may have come to idealize their home country and upon their return may be surprised to find themselves feeling politically, economically, and socially estranged by the natural changes that have taken place (Koehler, 1980). The individual's values and perspectives may have changed, he or she may think more globally (Scott, 1984), and the individual may find him- or herself drawn to others who have had similar expatriate experiences. Sometimes, there may be a loss of a sense of "specialness" in her or his identity or the realities of shrinking job responsibilities upon returning home to contend with as well (Sobie, 1986). Two examples of problems that may bring someone in to see a counselor at this time are the East Indian or Arab woman who does not want to return to her home country to the prospect of an arranged marriage or the military serviceperson who has a close intimate relationship with a local national in the new culture whom he or she must either leave or marry.

People experiencing re-entry shock may require six months to a year to readjust, and some may need more than two years (Sobie, 1986). Harvey (1970) reported that over 50% of business assignees needed over a year to readjust. Recommendations for minimizing re-entry shock have included pre-return training and education that re-entry shock is normal (Adler, 1981; Dunbar, 1993; Koehler, 1980), continued contact with the home culture while away (Adler, 1981), talking within the immediate family about re-entry experiences as they occur, and talking with others who are also returning (Sobie, 1986). In general, time and support seem to alleviate the accompanying stresses of this natural adjustment process (Koehler, 1980).

☐ Generational Effects of Acculturation

Acculturation continues to affect the descendants of immigrants in future generations. These generational effects can be so notable that, for example, Japanese Americans have specific terms to describe the first through fourth generations in the United States: "issei," "nissei," "sansei," and "yonsei," respectively. Although there may be many cultural variations, often the first-generation immigrants in the United States are grappling with economic and other initial adjustment issues. If they have chosen to immigrate to achieve a better life for their family, they may strongly value their children's success in the new culture.

Second-generation immigrants grow up with U.S. culture, education, and media all around them. They may want to be "American" although they may speak a language other than English at home. They learn to speak English in school and often have superior language proficiency compared to their parents. As a result, they may be placed in the position of translator for the family, upending traditional family structure. They may be embarrassed at their parents' lack of ability to communicate and negotiate American institutions and procedures and thereby lose respect for their parents' authority. Lefley (1989) described intergenerational conflict and the ensuing erosion of family structure as the major problem facing refugees.

One excellent example of this is the case study of the Vietnamese family in family therapy described by Lappin and Scott (1982). Having the mother teach her children about the Vietnamese language and culture was a successful technique used by the counselor as a way for the mother to retain her position of expertise in the family and restore family stability. Second-generation immigrants are often sandwiched between two cultures. One second-generation Chinese American college student described his social circumstances: "I don't mix with new immigrants, yet I know I am not part of the third- and fourth-generation families either. Sometimes I feel caught in the middle" (Scott-Blair, 1986, p. A10).

The third- and later-generation immigrants grow up American in terms of their culture and sense of identity. However, they may find that no matter how "American" they feel, they continue to face discrimination based on their ethnicity. It is at this point that many descendants of immigrants rediscover their grandparents' culture, perhaps developing an interest in what is now a "foreign" language, taking ethnic studies classes, and in other ways learning about their history and cultural roots. This phenomenon of the third generation trying to recapture what the second generation has lost has been called the *Hansen effect* (Kitano, 1989).

Many aspects of the home culture remain even after many generations in the new culture. Sandy Dornbusch and colleagues (cited in O'Toole, 1988) found that in six of the seven ethnic groups they studied, high school grades and the amount of homework done decreased for second-generation and even more for third-generation immigrants. However, the parents of the third-generation students still retained a more authoritarian parenting style when compared to middle-class White American parents. Johnson and Marsella (1978) found that even third-generation Japanese American college students had less aggressive, less assertive, and less egalitarian speech tendencies than European Americans. Similarly, third- and fourth-generation Asian Americans continue to be reluctant to admit to psychological problems (Yamamoto & Acosta, 1982).

In summary, acculturation is a powerful process with many potential effects on individuals and families. Counselors need to be aware of the ramifications of cultural transition on their clients, even if unspoken by them. The process of "becoming American" varies widely across individuals: Some may transition smoothly whereas others may experience trauma. Much will depend on the characteristics that immigrants and refugees bring with them as well as the social context and setting of the host areas. Counselors would do well to inquire about the cultural transition experiences of their clients regardless of whether they seem directly related to the presenting problem.

☐ Case Vignette

Paul Gomez is an 18-year-old Latino high school student who was born in the United States to immigrant parents who earned money from doing seasonal work in three states. School was not easy for Paul as he typically went to at least two, if not three, different schools each year where he often sat at the back of the room, ignored by teachers and classmates. It didn't help that he was also one of the older children in his class. Very few people knew that he served as translator for his monolingual Spanish parents. Nor did they know that he often had to work in the fields after school helping his parents. He, however, did know that school was important and he paid attention in class and did as much as he could. During his ninth-grade year, his father found stable work as a farm laborer in a rural area of California. For the first time, Paul attended the same school the entire year. He began to make friends and to do well academically. The school counselor took special notice of Paul and began to work with him. She encouraged Paul to take college prep classes. By his junior year, Paul was invited by one of the school counselors to consider going to an out-of-state college that was actively recruiting students of color. Paul, however, was not sure that he wanted to attend a college where he believed that people of his background are not easily accepted. Having gone to so many schools across three states brought back memories of when he did not always feel accepted in those schools. If you were Paul's counselor, what might you advise him in terms of college?

Questions

1. How would you help Paul reach a decision about where to go to college?

2. How could Paul's schooling experiences in three states shed light on his current dilemma?

3. How important would it be to include Paul's parents in this conversation about college options inasmuch as they do not truly understand the school system of the United States?

Reflection 1

Paul's college decision needs to be a broad discussion of his talents and resources as well as his fears and concerns. One of his resources is the adaptability he has gained from going to school in so many places. What has he learned about how to adapt that will help him if he were to go out of state to college? Which schools did he like best and why (e.g., knew two other students already, more Latinos, more teachers who were of color, smaller school, located in a rural area, etc.)? These qualities might also help him select a college in which he will thrive. An overview of the higher education system in the United States (private vs. public, community colleges, financial aid, etc.) would be very important to go over with Paul's parents and himself.

Reflection 2

A number of things could be discussed with Paul in order to help him decide on where he wants to go to college. It could be important to explore Paul's level of acculturation to "mainstream American culture" as compared to the culture of his family and community of origin. Does he identify with his family's background? What are the values that are important to Paul and how do those fit in with the values of his family? What do his parents understand about the educational system of the United States and how supportive are they of Paul's wishes to go to college? Because his parents do not have the experience of formal schooling in their country or the United States, informational sessions or one-on-one counseling sessions would help them understand what is involved and how they could be supportive of their son's college experience. A strengths-based approach focusing on the talents of this young man who has learned much from having been at so many schools, his ability to understand and speak more than one language, and his academic skills despite his having moved frequently, would be very beneficial. At a more general level, all students at Paul's school could profit from the opportunity to safely talk about cultural differences, racism, prejudice, and stereotypes, in addition to other multicultural issues, with culturally competent teachers and counselors.

☐ Recommended Cultural Resources

Print Media

Alvarez, J. (1991). *How the García girls lost their accents*. Chapel Hill, NC: Algonquin Books. The coming-of-age story of four sisters in America whose family had to leave the Dominican Republic. In their quest for acceptance, the four sisters rebel against their elders and strive to fit in to their new surroundings.

Fadiman, A. (1997). *The spirit catches you and you fall down*. New York: Farrar, Straus & Giroux. A deeply moving story of the cultural clash between the Western doctors who treated a Hmong child born to recent immigrants who developed symptoms of epilepsy and the spiritual beliefs of her family and community.

Galarza, E. (1971). *Barrio boy*. Notre Dame, IN: University of Notre Dame Press. The acculturation experiences of a young boy and his family beginning with their life in a small Mexican village to their new life in Sacramento, CA, in the early 20th century.

Tan, A. (1989). *The joy luck club*. New York: Ballantine. A best-selling novel that focuses on four Chinese American immigrant families.

Multimedia

Dolguin, G., & Franco, V. (Producers). (2002). *Daughter from DaNang* [Video-recording]. A documentary about an "Americanized" woman and her Vietnamese mother who are reunited after being separated at the end of the Vietnam War.

Nava, G. (Director), Thomas, A. (Producer). (1984). *El norte* [Videorecording]. Farmington Hills, MI: CBS/Fox Video. Portrays the plight of Central American political refugees in a remarkable fusion of documentary realism and visual poetry.

Olmos, E. J. (Director). (1992). *American me* [Videorecording]. Universal City, CA: Universal Studios Home Entertainment. This epic depiction of 30 years of Chicano gang life in Los Angeles focuses on a teen named Santana.

Wenders, W. (Director), Felsberg, U., & Cooder, R. (Producers). (1998). *The Buena Vista social club* [Videorecording]. Berlin, Germany: A Road Movies Production. A documentary about aging Cuban musicians whose talents had been virtually forgotten following Castro's takeover of Cuba.

Cultural Identity Development

I went from being ashamed, to being accepting, to being proud. Really, honestly, I guess that would be the best way to present it. I didn't want to be Black. There was a time period when you can see in my writing: "Oh my goodness, this is the curse of my life." Then, "Well, I'm Black, so (sigh) deal." To the point now where, "I'm Black! Hey I'm glad." I wouldn't change it.

18-year-old African American female (Tatum, 1993, p. 15)

Tajfel (1981) described ethnic identity as part of an individual's self-concept that comes from knowledge of membership in a social group(s) and the value or emotional significance attached to that membership. Similarly, Phinney (1990) defines ethnic identity as consisting of self-identification as a group member, a sense of belonging, and one's attitudes toward one's group. These definitions can easily be broadened and extended to include other aspects of social status, in addition to ethnicity, such as gender, sexual orientation, or disability status, to constitute an individual's cultural identity.

Of the many topics relevant to multicultural counseling, developmental models of cultural identity have perhaps received the most theoretical interest. Many stage models have been proposed to account for the incorporation of culture into an individual's sense of identity. As with other stage models of development, these models are based on the assumptions that (1) progression from one stage to another is desirable, and (2) the order, but not the rate of progression through the various stages, is similar across individuals.

Caution should be taken in applying stage models of cultural identity development, in part due to their commonalities with other stage models. Although the persons developing a particular stage model may not have intended for it to be linear, such that a person may be in more than one stage simultaneously or return to a previous stage without it being perceived as negative (Helms, 1995; Zera, 1992), in application, however, stage models typically are perceived as inherently implying linearity (Weinberg cited in Zera, 1992). Indeed, Hoffman (1991) offered two valid criticisms that apply to most cultural identity development models. From a feminist perspective, such models are hierarchical reflections of a masculine worldview, that progression through stages is likened to tasks to be completed rather than increasing the contextual range of responses available to an individual. Also, with few exceptions (Gutierrez, 1985), cultural identity development models have generally not been compared to other well-established developmental models.

Even given the assumptions and criticisms just mentioned, stage models of cultural identity development may be useful for counselors wanting to understand the cultural context of their clients. These models help explain how individuals may shape their attitudes about themselves, other individuals within their same ethnic/cultural group, and individuals from the majority group. These models also help to dispel the myth that all members of a given cultural group have similar attitudes and preferences (Baruth & Manning, 2003). This chapter explores some of the many stage models of identity development that have been described in the multicultural literature.

☐ Racial/Ethnic Identity Development

Many identity development models have been proposed and elaborated over the past two decades to describe the process that individuals may experience in becoming aware, accepting, and positive in their attitudes about their own or others' racial/ethnic background. Some of these models are more specific to individuals of a particular ethnic minority group, for example, Blacks (Cross, 1995) and Chicanos/Latinos (Ruiz, 1990), and others are described as applicable to a broad range of ethnic minority groups (Atkinson, Morten, & Sue, 1989; Helms, 1995). Some describe the experiences of persons who belong to the dominant racial/ethnic group (Christensen, 1989; Helms, 1995) and some describe the experiences of those who are biracial, belonging to two different racial/ethnic groups (Poston, 1990). Three representative examples of racial/ethnic identity development models are outlined and compared.

One of the oldest and most widely known developmental models relevant to persons of an ethnic minority cultural background is the one developed by Atkinson, Morten, and Sue (1989), currently entitled the Racial/Cultural Identity Development (R/CID) model. This model was first proposed in 1979 and has since undergone some revision. It includes five stages: Conformity, Dissonance, Resistance and Immersion, Introspection, and Integrative Awareness.

In the Conformity stage, an ethnic minority individual holds the same values as those of persons in the dominant cultural group and tends to devalue him- or herself and other ethnic minority people. Such a client would probably prefer a counselor who is a member of the dominant cultural group and might be particularly amenable to a problem-solving approach to counseling. A client in the next stage, Dissonance, is in a state of psychological conflict. The client in Dissonance is beginning to question her or his cultural identity and sense of self-esteem as he or she comes to realize the impact of culture in her or his own life. Here, a counselor who is knowledgeable about the cultural background of the client may be especially helpful. The third stage, Resistance and Immersion, involves a new sense of self and cultural group appreciation and a rejection of the dominant cultural group. A client in this stage may distrust persons of the dominant cultural group and prefer an ethnic minority counselor. Clients may put much of their energy into group action and efforts to combat oppression. Trust issues, racism, and feelings of guilt, shame, and anger may be important in counseling a client at this stage of cultural identity development. The fourth stage, Introspection, involves a growing concern over the basis of self-appreciation and a questioning of ethnocentrism as a premise for judging others. A client in this stage may benefit the most from a counselor with a broad worldview who can assist the client in a process of self-exploration to differentiate her or his individual views from those of others. The last stage, Integrative Awareness, involves a capacity to appreciate oneself as well as others. A client at this stage may have an ongoing desire and commitment to eliminate oppression and a counselor with a broad worldview would again be desired. One might expect that clients at this stage feel secure with who they are and can appreciate not only their culture, but the cultures of others as well (Sue & Sue, 2003).

There is a growing body of research evidence relevant to the R/CID model. For example, Pang, Mizokawa, Moishima, and Olstad (1985) found that Asian American children felt less positive about their physical characteristics than did White children. These children may be in the Conformity stage, deprecating themselves and preferring the characteristics of the White cultural group. Similarly, Tatum (1993) found that half of the African American college students who had been raised in White communities did not consider attending a historically Black college because they were afraid that they would be labeled by other students as "too White." These students might be in the Dissonance stage, aware but uncomfortable with their cultural identity. Interestingly, Kohatsu (1996) found that among Asian Americans, racial mistrust of another ethnic minority group was positively related to levels of Resistance and Immersion attitudes and negatively related to Integrative Awareness attitudes. However, racial identity attitudes were less predictive for Latinos. More research into the validity and utility of the R/CID model is needed. In the meantime, counselors may be able to apply the model on an individual basis as a way to understand some of the potentially contradictory and confusing feelings and actions that an ethnic minority client may experience over time with respect to her or his cultural identity.

Cross's (1995) Nigrescence model of Black identity development is very similar to the R/CID model. First described in 1971 and generally considered to be the first model of Black racial identity development, it encompasses five stages: Pre-Encounter, Encounter, Immersion-Emersion, Internalization, and Internalization-Commitment. The nature of the issues and psychological stresses and attitudes at each stage are generally comparable to those of the R/CID model. Research on the Cross model has yielded two themes: (1) at the Pre-Encounter stage, individuals' views of race vary broadly from race neutrality to anti-Black (Atkinson, 2004); (2) at later stages, individuals might express themselves via a range of ideological preferences, from Black nationalism to multiculturalism.

Ruiz (1990) proposed a Chicano/Latino ethnic identity model also consisting of five stages similar to those in the R/CID model: Causal, Cognitive, and Consequence stages of identity conflict; the Working-Through stage of intervention where the client is ready to discuss ethnic identity concerns, increase ethnic consciousness, and reintegrate disowned parts of her or his ethnic identity; and the Successful Resolution stage characterized by greater self-esteem and cultural/ethnic appreciation. Because this model was developed from the point of view of a practitioner, little empirical validation is available. Ruiz's recommended counseling interventions include cultural assessment, cognitive restructuring of internalized negative injunctions and faulty beliefs related to ethnicity, and recognition of the client's cultural beliefs, values, and behaviors.

Several models have also been proposed to account for the identity development of people who are members of the dominant racial group, which in the United States is White. The experience of being White is developmentally different from that of belonging to an ethnic minority group because Whites in the United States learn that they are entitled to privileges associated with being White (McIntosh, 1988) and learn to deny or distort race-related reality in order to protect the status quo (Helms,

1995). According to Helms (1995, p. 184), "The general developmental issue for Whites is abandonment of entitlement, whereas the general developmental issue for people of color is surmounting internalized racism in its various manifestations."

Christensen (1989) described a Cross-Cultural Awareness Development Model that included five stages for both majority and minority individuals. In the Unawareness stage a majority individual may deny being "White," assert that racial differences are not important, and avoid any personal responsibility for a racist society. In the Transition stage there may be feelings of shame, guilt, anger, or depression as the individual begins to acknowledge what it means to be White. Individuals may suffer impaired relationships with White relatives, friends, or colleagues if they make their feelings known. The third stage, Conscious Awareness, may involve racial self-hatred as the person perhaps overidentifies with people of color. The person may attempt to participate in minority group organizations and activities and be surprisingly rejected and perceived as insincere. In the Consolidated Awareness stage, the individual recognizes her or his Whiteness and negative feelings of guilt and anger begin to subside. In the final Transcendent Awareness stage, the individual has an increased appreciation for cultural diversity and an increased commitment to societal change. Christensen notes that underlying this model are assumptions that racism is an integral part of life in the United States and that all Whites are racist whether they are aware of it or not.

Helms (1984, 1995) proposed a six-status (i.e., stage) White racial identity model that differs from the Christensen model primarily in that the third stage, Reintegration, involves an idealization of things perceived to be White as opposed to a fascination with non-White culture(s) as in the Christensen model. In addition, stage models for racial consciousness development among White counselor trainees (Ponterotto, 1988) and for White racial identity development in counselor training (Sabnani, Ponterotto, & Borodovsky, 1991) have been proposed. The level or stage of White racial identity development affects the process and outcome of a cross-cultural counseling encounter and thus it is recommended that graduate training programs assess the phase of identity development of its White trainees (Sue & Sue, 2003).

Biracial Identity Development

There is a growing segment of the population that is biracial. According to the 1990 census, 1.9 million children in the United States live in homes with parents of different races and now estimates suggest that there are upward of 7 million mixed heritage people of all ages in the country (U.S. Census Bureau, 2001, 2005). Several identity development models that account for the unique needs of biracial or bicultural persons have been developed (Gutierrez, 1985; Poston, 1990).

Poston (1990) proposed a five-stage Biracial Identity Development model. In the first stage, the biracial person is independent of group identity as he or she develops within the context of the family. During the second stage, Choice of Group Categorization, the biracial person is compelled to choose a specific identification group (e.g., White, Black, etc.). For example, children of White–Asian or White–Hispanic background are more easily assimilated into predominantly White culture whereas White–Black background children are generally identified with the Black community (Keerdoja, 1984). In the Enmeshment/Denial stage that follows, feelings of guilt and self-hatred may be experienced as the biracial individual struggles with her or his own rejection of a part of him- or herself. The fourth stage, Appreciation, involves exploration of previously ignored heritage(s), and the final stage, Integration, is when the biracial individual comes to value her or his multicultural identity.

Another model of bicultural personality development, by Gutierrez (1985), reconciles Erikson's (1968) stages of development with typical minority identity development stages. At each of Erikson's psychosocial developmental stages, the individual's current cultural identity plays an important role in how developmental tasks are approached (Chavez, 1986). Kerwin and Ponterotto (1995) review several other biracial identity development models.

Several scholars suggest that biracial status can be problematic: Biracial children must come to terms with a culture where standards of beauty are White and other children may ask painful questions about why they look unlike their parents (Shackford, 1984). Many biracial adolescents indicate problems with racial identity (Gibbs, 1987). On the other hand, Burnette (1995) notes that interracial children are no less well adjusted than other children of color and Brandell (1988) notes some advantages of biracial status: more tolerance of others and greater hesitancy to develop biases toward any groups of people. There is some consensus that parents may foster a healthy self-concept in interracial children by using labels such as "interracial," "mixed," or "tan" (Jacobs, 1992; Kerwin, 1993). Parents can help their children by providing them with a multiethnic label and by helping them recognize positive aspects from each ethnic background (Baruth & Manning, 2003). Hall (1980) found that two-thirds of her sample of biracial adults had resolved any earlier identity issues and identified themselves as multiracial, suggesting

TABLE 6.1. Comparison of Racial/Ethnic Identity Development Models

Racial/cultural identity development model[a]	Cross-cultural awareness development model[b]	Biracial identity development model[c]
Conformity	Unawareness	Personal Identity
Dissonance	Transition	Choice of Group Categorization
Resistance & Immersion	Conscious Awareness	Enmeshment/Denial
Introspection	Consolidated Awareness	Appreciation
Integrative Awareness	Transcendent Awareness	Integration

[a] From Atkinson, Morten, and Sue (1989).
[b] From Christensen (1989).
[c] From Poston (1990).

that they had reached the last stage of biracial identity development. We will return to biracial people in Chapter 18.

In comparing these and other models of cultural identity development, several similarities can be found. Refer to Table 6.1 for a comparison of three of these models.

Most of the models have five stages, with some outlining as many as seven. The initial stage is characterized by unawareness of culture as an important part of a person's sense of identity and the final stage is a desirable state of self-acceptance and appreciation of culture as an important dimension of the self. The stages in between involve psychological discomfort and self-examination with a middle stage of extreme feeling or overidentification with culture.

☐ Other Dimensions of Minority Identity Development

Several other dimensions of minority status, such as gender, sexual orientation, and disability status, may also be strong influences on identity formation. For example, 74% of disabled Americans recognized a common identity with other persons with a disability, according to one Harris Poll (Tainter, Compisi, & Richards, 1995).

Downing and Roush (1985) proposed a feminist identity development model that begins with a Passive Acceptance of sexism stage, followed by a Crisis stage around revelations of the influence of sexism, an Embeddedness stage marked by intense connections with other women, and ending with an Active Commitment to feminism stage in which individual personal attributes are integrated with feminist principles.

Cass (1979, 1984) pioneered discussion about gay and lesbian identity development in her Sexual Identity Formation (SIF) model consisting of Identity Confusion, Identity Comparison, Identity Tolerance, Identity Acceptance, Identity Pride, and Identity Synthesis stages. Her model became an inspiration, and baseline of comparison, for other models of gay and lesbian identity development (Zera, 1992) as well as for bisexual identity development (Zinick, 1985).

A more recent model (Troiden, 1989) includes four stages. The first stage, Sensitization, takes place before puberty, when the gay or lesbian child experiences social feelings of marginality and difference, and gender identification, not sexual behavior, is a primary concern. At this stage, being teased for cross-gender behavior may contribute to internalization of a negative self-concept. Identity Confusion, the second stage, is the most difficult and potentially dangerous. At approximately age 17 for males and 18 for females, homosexual feelings and behaviors develop and the adolescent is at risk for suicide and other self-destructive behavior as he or she tries to come to terms with societally unacceptable aspects of self. The third phase, Identity Assumption, incorporates Cass's Identity Tolerance and Identity Acceptance stages. At approximately ages 19–21 years for males and 21–23 for females, the young gay man or lesbian begins to reduce her or his isolation and increases her or his contact with other homosexual people as the sexual orientation stigma becomes more manageable. The last stage, Commitment, involves accepting homosexuality as a part of one's being and making a same-sex love commitment. Happiness and self-satisfaction increase as inner struggles diminish and homosexuality may become a less important part of the individual's total identity. This may occur roughly at ages 21–24 in gay men and ages 22–23 in lesbians.

These models of sexual orientation identity development are useful in helping counselors become aware of different issues that may be salient at different stages for clients. For example, having a counselor who is not gay may be less helpful when a client is in an Identity Confusion or Identity Pride stage (Chojnacki & Gelberg, 1995). Most importantly, these conceptual models can serve as tools for clients to better understand themselves.

The convergence of more than one minority status on identity development may have complex implications for a client's life. Morales (1992) described a five-stage process to integrate minority ethnicity and sexual orientation identity development. Some elements of the process include denial of conflict and attraction to White lovers, conflicts in allegiance to ethnic and gay communities, and the integration of various communities into a multicultural support system. Furthermore, a client who is lesbian and blind or another who is a physically disabled Latina is each dealing with a triple minority status and what this may mean in terms of self-esteem, social acceptance, and other clinical issues must be explored carefully and thoroughly by her counselor for their potential impact on the presenting problem.

☐ Counseling Implications

Sue and Sue (2003) emphasize that knowledge of cultural identity development should lead counselors to understand how oppression and racism affect the lives of minority individuals. In examining sociocultural forces that exist in society over which the minority individual has no control, these researchers recommend that therapists take a proactive stance through systems interventions. Essential to the counselor–client relationship is the need to become culturally and sociopolitically aware, in addition to recognizing as legitimate the worldview of the minority client.

Specific implications can be drawn from each of the various stage models as to relevant counseling issues and the salience of the counselor's own cultural background at a particular stage of identity development. Counselors should review appropriate models of cultural identity development that may relate to the client they are counseling. More generally, the most important result of the growing literature on cultural identity development as it applies to counseling is to reinforce the concept that how a client feels about him- or herself culturally is evolutionary and not static. This notion helps break down stereotypes that all clients from a particular cultural background would have similar feelings about themselves. An adult client could be in any stage of cultural identity development and thus very different from another client of the same cultural background who may be in a different stage. Furthermore, clients could be in one stage of cultural identity development when they first enter counseling and how they feel about their cultural identity may change during the course of counseling, whether or not culture is an explicit focus of counseling (Chavez, 1986). Thus, cultural identity should be assessed on an ongoing basis.

Comas-Diaz and Jacobsen (1987) suggest that a counselor might begin the exploration of the client's cultural identity by using reflection to acknowledge the role of ethnicity or other aspects of cultural difference in the client's life. One potential treatment goal for a client might be to transition into another stage of cultural identity development that might result in increased feelings of self-esteem and ability to act productively within her or his environment.

□ Case Vignette

Nelson Tuyuc arrived in the United States at the age of 15. He had been living in a rural village in Guatemala with his grandparents since the age of 5, when his parents had left him there in search of a better future in the United States. Nelson had missed his parents a great deal during those years. His only connection with them was through occasional phone calls. But his parents did send money and it was enough for the grandparents to raise the three children that had been left in their care. Nelson made the long trip to the United States accompanied by his older brother, who was only two years older than he. The first time they crossed the border into California they were arrested and deported to Mexico. With very little money remaining, they made a second attempt. Their second attempt into California was successful and they were able to reunite with their parents, whom they had not seen in nine years. Nelson had many dreams of going to school, learning English, and above all, of being with his parents. He had not expected to find that his father was an alcoholic and that his mother was trapped in the relationship, unable to seek help for herself and her two sons. Nelson was also confused because he had taken on so many responsibilities when he was living with his grandparents, but now living with his parents, it seemed that they treated him like a child. He had to ask them for permission for everything. Back in Guatemala, he was already considered a man. In addition to his conflicts with his parents, he did not quite understand the culture of the United States. In school, his classmates seemed to be very disrespectful of teachers. This was not how he had been raised. He wanted to succeed in his new life, but he was very unsure as to how to relate to both his parents and his teachers. He often felt that his Guatemalan upbringing had not prepared him for life with his parents or for life in the United States. He no longer knew where he fitted in.

Questions

1. As a counselor, how would you help Nelson understand his new life with his parents and the new school?

2. How might a counselor apply one of the conceptual models of identity development to help this client?

Reflection 1

Nelson had many dreams of going to school, learning English, and above all, of being with his parents; understandably he seems to be having difficulty adjusting to the new environment. If I were Nelson's counselor, I would want to explore more about his sadness and disappointment in not getting what he expected when he came to California. As a counselor, I would explore more of his identity and what it means to be a man in Guatemala, and what it feels like to be treated like a child and how this relates to his parents and teachers.

Reflection 2

A conceptual model that might be helpful in terms of understanding Nelson's process of adaptation and acculturation could be the Racial/Cultural Identity Development (R/CID) model (Atkinson et al.,1989), which could lead us to believe that Nelson, as a recent immigrant, is possibly in the first or second stage of the model, in which he questions his own culture and how it might fit in with the dominant culture. Nelson is having difficulty integrating the culture, values, role expectations, and so on of his life in Guatemala with the culture, values, and role expectations of his new life in the United States. A counselor would want to help Nelson reflect back on his Guatemalan upbringing, history, cultural values, and the like, and how it is the same or different from his U.S. life with the goal of helping him to integrate both experiences. Family counseling would be extremely beneficial due to the father's alcoholism and because the parents, too, must be experiencing many emotions in this process of reunification and bonding with their children.

☐ Recommended Cultural Resources

Print Media

Mabry, M. (1995). *White bucks and black-eyed peas: Coming of age Black in White America*. New York: Simon & Schuster. Raised by strong Black women, the author describes his road from the Black ghetto to the White mainstream.

Martinez, V. (1996). *Parrot in the oven: Mi vida*. New York: HarperCollins. Winner of the 1996 National Book Award in the Young People's Literature category, this is the story of 14-year-old Manny Hernandez's coming of age and the pressures of gangs, girls, and friends.

Morrison, T. (1970). *The bluest eye*. New York: Random House. Winner of the 1993 Nobel Prize in Literature, this is the story of an African American family struggling with issues of identity and race.

Multimedia

Lee, S. (Director). (1992). *Malcolm X* [DVD, Videorecording]. USA: Warner Home Video. Biography of Malcolm X, the famous African American leader, whose father was killed by the Ku Klux Klan, who became a gangster, and while in jail discovered the Nation of Islam writings of Elijah Muhammad.

Nava, G. (Director). (1995). *My family mi familia* [Videorecording]. Atlanta, GA: Turner Home Entertainment. Oscar-nominated drama that traces three generations of a Mexican immigrant family, their tragedies, and triumphs.

Ripoll, M. (Director). (2001). *Tortilla soup* [DVD, Videorecording]. USA: Samuel Goldwyn Films LLC, Starz! Encore Entertainment. A Mexican American master chef and father to three daughters has lost his taste for food but not for life.

Native Americans in Counseling

A sense of humor is an important characteristic of American Indian cultures. We believe there is a fine line between laughter and tears. They are both enabling means of survival.

Joseph Iron Eye Dudley (1992, p. 139)

☐ Histories and Diversity

There are over 4.4 million Native Americans in the United States (U.S. Census Bureau, 2004). States with more than 40,000 Native American inhabitants include California, Oklahoma, Arizona, New Mexico, North Carolina, Washington, and South Dakota (Axelson, 1993; Baruth & Manning, 1991; Lieberg, 1996). California had the highest number of American Indian/Alaska natives of any state in the nation, followed by Oklahoma and Arizona. About 6400 American Indians and Alaska natives were added to Arizona's population between 2003 and 2004, the largest numeric increase of any state in the nation. The proportion of Alaska's population identified as American Indian and Alaska native as of 2004 was the highest rate for this group nationally, followed by Oklahoma and New Mexico. The number of American Indians and Alaska natives in Los Angeles County, California, was 153,500 as of 2004, leading the nation's counties in the total number of people in this category. Maricopa County, Arizona, added about 3000 people of this group between 2003 and 2004, leading the nation's counties in the total number of people added in this category.

The total number of Native Americans living in the United States is very likely underreported because of difficulties in getting census information from lower-income groups and because the federal government automatically classifies American Indians whose origins are from Central or South America as "Hispanic" (Ponterotto & Casas, 1991). The federal Bureau of Indian Affairs (BIA) restricts the definition of Indian to someone enrolled or registered as a member of a federally recognized Indian tribe or someone who can legally demonstrate that he or she has at least one-fourth Indian heritage. More broadly, there are an estimated 10 to 20 million people in the United States who have some Indian blood. There is tremendous diversity among Native Americans, a term that includes American Indians, Eskimos, and Aleuts. There have been 517 federally recognized Native American entities identified (Herring, 1991) with additional groups as yet unrecognized (Heinrich, Corbine, & Thomas, 1990). The Navajo, with over 110,000 members, is the largest tribe; the smallest may have only one remaining survivor. There have been estimates ranging from 200 to 2200 distinct languages spoken by Native Americans (Baruth & Manning, 1991; LaFromboise, Berman, & Sohi, 1994). Given the vast diversity among Native American cultures, much of what is written about Native Americans is based on generalizations, primarily from specific North American Indian tribes. There is research evidence to suggest that the degree of cultural variation within a tribal group can be even greater than between Indians and non-Indians (Sage, 1991; Tefft, 1967).

When referring to the ethnicity of a Native American client, it is generally best to use the name of the person's tribe, because many Native Americans most strongly identify themselves as members of a tribe. If tribal affiliation is not known, "American Indian" is the ethnic term preferred by most Native American tribes and organizations. However, some individuals may dislike this term because "Indian" originated with European explorers who mistakenly believed they had reached India when they came to the Americas. First American, Amerindian, First Nations, or Native People are other common designations. Avoid using terms that refer to discriminatory stereotypes of Native Americans (Herring, 1991).

Roughly half the Native American population lives on federal reservations, numbering 314 (U.S. Bureau of the Census, 2004) and the others live in urban or metropolitan areas (Baruth & Manning, 1991). Many urban Indians are of mixed blood and have limited contact with reservations and may feel alienated or socially isolated (Attneave, 1982;

Sage, 1991). Meanwhile other urban Native Americans choose to return to the reservation of their people on a regular basis. On the reservation, a person's genealogy is common knowledge and the sense of community and tribal identity is strong (Sage, 1991). Thus, a return to the reservation may bring a sense of balance, increased self-esteem, and tribal identity (Sage, 1991) and at the same time help counteract feelings of isolation, rejection, or anxiety experienced when living in Anglo society outside the reservation (Sanders, 1987). Migration between the reservation and the city also brings with it greater connection to others in terms of information sharing about travel plans and some pressure to remain connected with family (Sage, 1991). Miller (cited in Attneave, 1982) found that the most successful urban Indian families were both open to the learning and technology of the majority culture around them and interested in maintaining their tribal language, values, and customs.

Although there are many variations among tribal cultures, there are several experiences shared by Native American groups in the United States that bring a sense of common history and hardship. Loss of tribal lands to the U.S. government is common to all Native Americans (Axelson, 1993). The history of Native Americans in the United States can be summarized as fraught with ambivalence, failed attempts at forced assimilation, and a general lack of respect for their humanity. Refer to the box on page 104 for a brief chronology of Native American history with the U.S. government.

Beginning in the late 1800s the U.S. government guaranteed the provision of education and health care to many Native American groups as part of treaties signed in exchange for tribal lands (Dinges, Trimble, Manson, & Pasquale, 1981). This led to the establishment of government boarding schools. By 1902, there were 25 such schools in 15 states. Native American children as young as five years of age were separated from their parents and taken to these schools, which were often far from their homes. There Native American children were punished for speaking their tribal languages as the schools were aimed at removing all traces of Indian culture and immersing the child in Western culture. In addition, the children often had to endure forced physical labor, food scarcity, overcrowding, and sickness as these institutions were underfunded (Tafoya & Del Vecchio, 1996). In addition, government practices of placing Native American children in adoptive families who were non-Native also attacked Native American cultural continuity. It has been estimated that from 25 to 55% of all Native American children have been placed in non-Native foster homes, adoptive families, boarding homes, or other institutional settings at some time in their lives (Herring, 1991). Given the known negative effects of institutionalization, the

A Brief Chronology of Native American History With the U.S. Government

1787   Policy of reserving land for exclusive use of Native Americans began the formation of reservations.

1824   Bureau of Indian Affairs organized to supervise Native Americans.

1830   Indian Removal Act moved nearly all eastern tribes west of the Mississippi and many died along the way, on the Trail of Tears.

1871   Congress ruled that tribes were no longer independent governments, thereby eliminating the need for treaties.

1887   Dawes Act gave land to individual tribe members in an effort to break up tribal groups and encourage farming.

1890   U.S. Army annihilated a band of Sioux, including women and children at Wounded Knee, South Dakota.

1924   All U.S.-born Native Americans granted citizenship.

1980   Indian Child Welfare Act gave preference to Native Americans in foster care and adoption of Native American children.

governmental treatment of Native American children in this century has been described as cultural genocide.

Social Class Considerations

Chronic unemployment and poverty are part of life for many Native Americans. The Bureau of Indian Affairs estimated a 48% unemployment rate for those living on or near reservations (Herring, 1991). Twenty-one percent of Native Americans who live on a reservation have no plumbing and 16% no electricity (U.S. Census Bureau, 1985). Native Americans also have the highest rates of diabetes, kidney disease, and accidental death nationwide. The average life expectancy of Native Americans is eight years less than for Anglo Americans (American Association of Retired Persons, 1986) and the median age for Native Americans is 20.4 years, almost 10 years younger than the national median (LaFromboise, 1988). According to the U.S. Bureau of the Census (2004), 76% of American Indians and Alaska natives age 25 and older have at least a high school diploma. High rates of unemployment, school dropouts, and teen pregnancy need to be viewed with the Native American history of 500 years of cultural trauma in mind (Sutton & Broken Nose, 1996). It is not surprising that many Native Americans share a sense of distrust and frustration with the government and these attitudes may greatly hinder the counseling relationship for any counselor working for any type of government agency.

☐ Spirituality

For traditional Native Americans, everything in nature has a spirit: all animals, inanimate objects, sky, and earth. There is respect and reverence for nature in both physical and spiritual ways. Respect may take the form of noninterference (Baruth & Manning, 1991) which can be mistaken for passivity or neglect by persons unfamiliar with Native American culture. In contrast, disrespect and overuse of natural resources is believed to lead to imbalance and disharmony in the world and dysfunction in human relationships (Axelson, 1993). Thus, harmony with nature is a very important value in many Native American cultures (Baruth & Manning, 1991). This harmony is based upon the belief in the constancy, timelessness, and predictability of nature (Herring, 1991). Harmony is desirable on a cosmic level, not only in one's nuclear and extended family, but also between the self and important others, trees, animals, land, ancestors, stars, and the Great Spirit (Herring, 1991; Matheson, 1986). Matheson (1986) gives as an example that an Indian would not waste natural resources by indiscriminately harvesting large quantities of herbs and would in addition give an "offering" back to the earth. Being ignorant of one's relationship to nature is not considered sinful, but simply the direct cause of natural destructive consequences (Axelson, 1993). Mental illness may be believed to be a justifiable outcome of human weakness or a lack of discipline in maintaining harmony (Herring, 1991).

This holistic and inclusive view of nature gives the spirit world reality, making it not unnatural to "see" or "hear" spirits in everyday life (Matheson, 1986). There may be little distinction between mind and body, spirit world and reality. Many Native American cultures believe in reincarnation (LaFromboise et al., 1994). Dreams may be considered important and visions actively sought after (Matheson, 1986). This is a definite departure from typical Western psychological dualism, in which such experiences are often deemed pathological auditory or visual hallucinations. Spirituality in Native American cultures may be described as mystical and integrated into everyday existence. Prayer may be a part of daily life (Axelson, 1993) and dance may be considered a form of religious expression (Richardson, 1981). In addition, the Medicine Wheel is a symbol connected to the sacred Four Directions of all existence and representing all knowledge of the universe (Conti, 2001). It is a symbol looked to by many, both past and present, who seek healing, wisdom, and direction. It is appropriate to look to the Medicine Wheel for answers concerning the suffering and lack of experience by many indigenous people in their educational experience today, as well as for future direction for tribes and extended families.

☐ Other Cultural Values

For many Native Americans the group, in terms of the tribe and extended family, comes before the individual (Anderson & Ellis, 1995; Baruth & Manning, 1991). Some of the ramifications of this group sense of self are that cooperation is valued, praise must come from others, and leaving the reservation may be difficult as it implies rejecting the tribe (Anderson & Ellis, 1995; Garrett & Garrett, 1994). Sharing and generosity are highly valued qualities in many Native American cultures (Attneave, 1982; Axelson, 1993; Baruth & Manning, 1991). In fact acquisition and competition may be considered abhorrent (Matheson, 1986). Instead of material wealth, family and relatives are treasured and many Native Americans may feel that to be poor is to be without family or relations (Sage, 1991). Some Native American cultures have ceremonies in which material goods are given away to recognize the help of others, achievement, or kinship at important life transitions. Sharing and gift giving toward visitors and guests is also valued. This spirit of generosity can come into conflict with modern American majority cultural emphasis on acquiring money and possessions, causing Native Americans in school and work situations to be viewed erroneously as unmotivated or unassertive if they freely share their possessions and do not try to compete for material or individual advancement. For example, sharing unemployment benefits or educational stipends with relatives whose needs are greater has been described as one of the major obstacles to career development among Native Americans (Attneave, 1982).

The "Indian Way" means families working together to solve problems (Sutton & Broken Nose, 1996). Decision making is preferably consensual (Attneave, 1982). Traditional family units often consist of a three or more generational extended family (Attneave, 1982). In many Native American cultures, the primary relationship is with grandparents (who are largely responsible for rearing children) and not parents (who are responsible for economic support) (Garrett & Garrett, 1994; Sutton & Broken Nose, 1996). Cousins may be called "brother" or "sister" and no distinction between biological relatives and in-laws is often made. It has been suggested that counselors take a family history early during the counseling process as this is not threatening and recognizes the importance of the extended family (Sutton & Broken Nose, 1996).

Because of the oral historical tradition of most Native American cultures, words are viewed as powerful and valuable (Sage, 1991). Legends are used to convey cultural knowledge in many Native American cultures (Baruth & Manning, 1991). In this manner, taboos, which have flexible mystical qualities unlike European laws, are also taught (Matheson, 1986). This suggests that counselors might consider making use of storytelling or the techniques of Milton Erickson (Rossi & Rossi, 1976) in their work with some Native American clients. Discipline often comes in the form of shaming, ridicule, or natural consequences and Attneave (1982) suggests that feelings of guilt may be less prominent among Native Americans because there are fewer assumptions regarding personal control over others or the environment.

Native American cultures often have a present orientation to time (Attneave, 1982; Baruth & Manning, 1991; Sutton & Broken Nose, 1996). Because change is not an inherent value there is more emphasis on doing things well rather than quickly. The concept of "Indian time" referring to being late might be more accurately described as doing something when the time is right (LaFromboise et al., 1994).

Noninterference in the lives of others is a value that may result in tolerance of others' behavior, even if extreme (LaFromboise et al., 1994). This can be misinterpreted as overindulgence, passivity, or a lack of concern. Direct confrontation may be limited to defining the consequences of an individual's behavior. On the other hand, a Native American client might be more open to a variety of counseling techniques because of this inclination toward tolerance (Attneave, 1982).

Some other Native American values that may have relevance for counseling include patience and control of one's emotions, honesty, bravery, strength and endurance of natural pain and suffering, self-sufficiency, and working with one's hands (Axelson, 1993; Baruth & Manning, 1991; Richardson, 1981).

☐ Indigenous Treatment Methods

Medicine people or shamans are indigenous healers who are believed to possess psychic abilities to heal and to predict weather conditions and the migration of local animals (Axelson, 1993). "Medicine" refers to a way of life or doing things (Garrett & Garrett, 1994). The Medicine Wheel or circle of life represents the Four Directions of spirit, nature, body, and mind. After sitting and talking with the medicine person and deciding what the problem is, the medicine person will typically either suggest ways of dealing with the problem or ask the person to do some specific task. The healing process also incorporates a support system and some type of ceremony or ritual. Medicine people do not solely support themselves through healing (Attneave, 1982). These indigenous healers have great influence and play a significant role in Native American communities. For example, DeAngelis (1992) writes of a Fond du Lac reservation medicine man in Wisconsin who impresses upon his people that alcohol and tobacco are both sacred substances that should not be used casually. Counselors can make their efforts with their clients more successful by consulting and working in conjunction with Native American healers whenever possible (Garrett & Garrett, 1994). Many Native Americans view both traditional and Western practices as helpful and counselors can support their clients' attendance in prayer meetings, use of herbal medicines, and participation in indigenous healing rituals (Sutton & Broken Nose, 1996). Also, any fees for counseling should be discussed explicitly and in a straightforward manner as fee-for-service may be handled differently when help is sought from a medicine person (Attneave, 1982).

Network therapy (Attneave, 1969, 1982) takes into account the Native American value of harmonious relationships from a family therapy and community psychology perspective. Counseling occurs during a network meeting in which an individual, her or his family, extended family, and any significant others in the community (e.g., neighbors, police, teacher, priest, bartender) meet to help resolve problems. Network therapy mobilizes this tribal unit or clan to help its members (Attneave, 1969). The goal of tribal network therapy is to build the client's coping skills within the context of the group (Thomason, 1995). The network therapist or counselor's role has been compared to that of a participant who sometimes intervenes, or like the conductor of an orchestra (Attneave, 1969).

Several kinds of skills are needed to conduct network therapy: family therapy and group process skills, individual assessment and crisis intervention skills, and the ability to provide links between the network and outside institutions whose services may be helpful. Although network therapy calls for much skill on the part of the counselor, it holds much promise for the successful treatment of Native Americans. Network therapy has similarities to indigenous ceremonies such as the Navajo "sing," a social and curative event in which all who play a part in the person's social life gather together. The curative properties attributed to such indigenous treatments—the reaffirmation of social bonds, social support received, hope inspired, and a general expectation of positive change (Dinges et al., 1981)—may also be activated by network therapy. There is research evidence of the effectiveness of network therapy for prevention and treatment (Schoenfeld, Halevy-Martini, Hemley-Van der Velden, & Ruhf, 1985). Even if network therapy is not attempted, community and tribal leaders can be helpful resources for counselors (Herring, 1991).

The sweat lodge and vision quest are indigenous treatment rituals common to many Native American cultures. A sweat lodge is a small hut constructed from animal hides and supported by saplings. Over a period of many hours, herbal water is sprinkled over hot stones, creating steam, for the purpose of physical and spiritual self-purification. Many aspects of the sweat lodge ceremony are symbolic. For example, the steam represents prayers ascending to the Great Spirit above (Heinrich et al., 1990).

A vision quest is a male rite of passage or renewal preceded by a sweat lodge ceremony. During the vision quest, the person has no contact with other humans and sits for days without food and water while spending the time in reflection, prayer, and search for a vision. "Whether it be in a dream state or in full consciousness, something, some one thing or series of events, will reveal to this young Native American man a strikingly real element of the future he must follow" (Heinrich et al., 1990, p. 131). A modified version of the vision quest may be incorporated in the counseling process through the use of guided imagery. The client carries out the vision quest in imagery and is instructed to seek an animal who will befriend the client and help answer the client's questions. This combination of guided imagery and inner dialogue work has parallels to the vision quest and might perhaps yield similar benefits.

Another Native American technique that has been adapted by some counselors is the "talking circle" (Heinrich et al., 1990). The talking circle is a forum for expressing one's thoughts and feelings without a time limit and in an atmosphere of acceptance. In a Native American talking circle, sacred objects (e.g., a feather or stone), a pipe, and prayer are part of the process. Thomason (1995) describes the use of talking circles in group counseling with Native American students: An object is passed around the circle of participants and only the person holding the object speaks, only for him- or herself, and for as long as he or she needs. The talking circle was also described as a highly successful activity in a treatment program for sexually abused Native American adolescents (Ashby, Gilchrist, & Miramontez, 1987).

The curative use of sand in treatment may also have possibilities. For example, the Navajo create sand paintings during special ceremonies as a means of curing afflictions (Axelson, 1993). Parallels between sand painting and the uses of the sand tray as a counseling technique have yet to be explored. Here again, consultation with Native American healers would be beneficial.

☐ Treatment Implications

Educational Concerns

Native Americans have the highest school dropout rate (35.5%) of any ethnic group in the United States (Herring, 1991; Sanders, 1987) and their representation among dropouts is over triple their proportion of all elementary and secondary students (National Center for Educational Statistics, 2002). On or near the reservation fewer Native Americans have much formal education, with as many as 16% having less than five years of schooling according to a 1987 Bureau of Indian Affairs estimate (cited in Herring, 1991). The education of Native Americans is a particularly acute concern given that Native American children function at an average-to-superior range until the third grade (Sanders, 1987), but by the 12th grade they test at three grade levels below the national average (Dillard, 1983).

Many factors have been suggested as contributing to Native American achievement difficulties in school. Baruth and Manning (1991) summarize several, including English as a second language, low self-esteem, and health problems such as fetal alcohol syndrome and ear disease. Anderson and Ellis (1995) suggest that cultural value differences may contribute to the situation. They assert that Native Americans emphasize living in the present and not long-term projects requiring delayed gratification and sacrifice such as formal education. Herring (1991) attributes the problem to chronic poverty and unemployment, which result in few positive career role models and low career aspirations.

The educational issues of Native Americans are compounded on the college level. Only 16% of Native Americans complete an undergraduate degree (Astin, 1982). Native American tribal groups have begun to develop

Some American Indian Colleges
(Members of the American Indian College Fund)

Bay Mills Community College, Brimly, MI
Blackfeet Community College, Browning, MT
Cheyenne River Community College, Eagle Butte, SD
College of the Menominee Nation, Keshena, WI
Crownpoint Institute of Technology, Crownpoint, NM
D-Q University, Davis, CA
Dull Knife Memorial College, Lame Deer, MT
Fond du Lac Tribal and Community College, Cloquet, MN
Fort Belknap Community College, Harlem, MT
Fort Berhold Community College, New Town, ND
Fort Peck Community College, Poplar, MT
Haskell Indian Nations University, Lawrence, KS
Institute for American Indian Arts, Santa Fe, NM
Lac Courte Oreilles Ojibwa Community College, Hayward, WI
Leech Lake Tribal College, Cass Lake, MN
Little Big Horn College, Crow Agency, MT
Little Hoop Community College, Fort Totten, ND
Navajo Community College, Tsaile, AZ
Nebraska Indian Community College, Winnebago, NE
Northwest Indian College, Bellingham, WA
Oglala Lakota College, Kyle, SD
Salish Kootenai College, Pablo, MT
Sinte Gleska University, Rosebud, SD
Sisseton Wahpeton Community College, Sisseton, SD
Southwest Indian Polytechnic Institute, Albuquerque, NM
Standing Rock College, Fort Yates, ND
Stone Child Community College, Box Elder, MT
Turtle Mountain Community College, Belcourt, ND
United Tribes Technical College, Bismarck, ND

their own solution to this problem. The first American Indian tribal college was founded in 1968 on a Navajo reservation (Johnson, 1994). In time, many more tribal colleges were started, most as community colleges, but three offer bachelor's and master's degrees. When counseling a Native American student preparing to attend college, it may be helpful to include in the discussion the consideration of a predominantly Native

American college. For a list of some American Indian colleges compiled by R. McNeil (personal communication, December 12, 1995), refer to the box on page 111.

Alcoholism

With an alcoholism rate estimated to be double the national average, alcohol is a significant concern for many Native Americans (Heinrich et al., 1990). Alcohol or drug abuse has been described as problematic for 52% of urban and 80% of reservation Native Americans (United States Senate Select Committee on Indian Affairs, 1985). However, alcoholism rates vary extensively among tribes (LaFromboise et al., 1994).

There is no physiological or psychological support for the myth that Native Americans have a lower tolerance for alcohol (Anderson & Ellis, 1995). Tafoya and Del Vecchio (1996) consider alcoholism, as well as other addictive behaviors such as gambling, to be consequences of the historical trauma endured by Native Americans. Addictive behavior serves as a coping skill that is used as a means of denial to avoid dealing with the impact of years of traumatic conditions. Alternatively, Anderson and Ellis (1995) suggest that alcohol is a social behavior and a social facilitator for Native Americans. Binge drinking in a group setting is done to have a good time with others and effective counseling must address the social context in which abuse was developed and maintained. Native Americans have begun to develop their own culturally relevant treatment programs for alcohol. In addition, according to Hall (cited in Heinrich et al., 1990), approximately 50% of Indian Health Service alcohol programs incorporate sweat lodge ceremonies in treatment.

☐ General Counseling Issues

Native Americans tend to underutilize mental health services and have a high dropout rate when they do seek services. Among their dissatisfactions with counseling are distance to the service location, limited operating hours, impersonal interactions, ambiguous agency procedures, long waits before they can be seen, high fees, transportation problems, and lack of child care (Baruth & Manning, 1991). It is evident that many of these barriers could be minimized by changing agency policies and procedures to be more accommodating of the needs of Native American clients. Lack of understanding of cultural differences and language are

also barriers (Martin, Frank, Minkler, & Johnson, 1988). Other contribu-
tors to low utilization may be the enduring influence of negative historical
interactions with non-Native people (Herring, 1991), who make up the vast
majority of counselors, as well as perceived conflict in acculturation goals
and power differentials within the counseling relationship (LaFromboise,
Trimble, & Mohatt, 1990). On the reservation, a Native American of mixed
blood may be reluctant to seek the services of an Indian Health Service
counselor because of concern that he or she would be perceived as not
really being an Indian if he or she sought government assistance (Sage,
1991). In urban areas, the lack of an identified central agency with whom
to communicate complicates matters (Martin et al., 1988).

Native Americans are most commonly diagnosed with alcohol abuse
and dependence, depression, anxiety, and adjustment disorders (Foster,
1995). Diagnosis of depression among Native Americans is particularly
difficult because there are several culturally appropriate behaviors that
may be misdiagnosed as signs of depression. Trimble and Fleming (1989)
describe the "cultural time out," or *wacinko* among Siouan-speaking people, which includes withdrawal. Similarly, a Native American client who
is simply waiting with hope for the natural consequences to evolve that
will resolve the problems he or she is facing may appear to others to be
hopeless or passive. The suicide rate for Native Americans is the highest
in the country and twice the national average (Baruth & Manning, 1991;
J. Pease-Pretty On Top, personal communication, July, 1977). Suicidal
behavior may be another reflection of historical trauma (Tafoya & Del
Vecchio, 1996) or even a family characteristic within some tribes and the
counselor should be aware that suicide rates vary tremendously between
tribes (Shore, 1975).

Nonverbal Behavior

Nonverbal behavior is extremely important in counseling Native Americans. Attention to how the counselor enters the room, the furnishings
in the room, and the presence of coffee or food can make the counsel-
or's office seem more comfortable (Sutton & Broken Nose, 1996). Casual
dress on the part of the counselor may be perceived negatively (Trimble & Fleming, 1989) as the degree of care the Native American client
takes in preparing her or his appearance for counseling sessions may be
an indication of her or his respect for the counselor (Anderson & Ellis,
1995). Also, the counselor needs to respect and appreciate any gifts given
(Attneave, 1982). Several authors have noted the importance of feeling
comfortable with and using silence (Foster, 1995; Garrett & Garrett, 1994;

Heinrich et al., 1990; Richardson, 1981; Sage, 1991; Sutton & Broken Nose, 1996; Thomason, 1995). Thomason (1995) suggests mirroring the client's nonverbal and verbal style. For example, some Native American children tend to speak more slowly and softly than White children (Baruth & Manning, 1991). Nonverbal signs of attention, such as head nodding or "uh-huh"s, are also uncharacteristic (Sanders, 1987). Prolonged eye contact may be considered disrespectful to Native Americans from some tribes (Garrett & Garrett, 1994; Matheson, 1986; Richardson, 1981).

The Initial Session

The first session is critical in counseling Native Americans even though the clients may disclose little information while they assess the therapist and the initial problem they present may not be the major issue (Attneave, 1982; Herring, 1991). Counselors might consider several recommendations that have been made regarding the content of the first session:

1. Disclose who you are and where you come from before asking the client to self-disclose (Sutton & Broken Nose, 1996). Anecdotes and short stories are good ways to model self-disclosure (Garrett & Garrett, 1994).

2. Ask questions. Questions that make the client the expert are a way to address client passivity (Anderson & Ellis, 1995). The first session is useful for asking open-ended questions about family history as this is nonthreatening and shows concern for the extended family (Attneave, 1982; Sutton & Broken Nose, 1996). However, avoid direct questions about religion, tribal ceremonies, politics, and traditional healing and medicine practices (Martin et al., 1988; Thomason, 1995). Broach these topics slowly, perhaps letting the client initiate the topic.

3. Acknowledge any awareness you may have of the client's tribal identity and family configuration (Herring, 1991).

4. It may be important to open the issue of Native American–White relationships if the counselor is White (Katz, 1981).

5. Be flexible in ending the session and be prepared to extend the first session (Foster, 1995).

In general, these suggestions are more applicable the more traditional the client is in terms of acculturation. The first session may be treated as time to get acquainted in an unhurried, interested fashion

(Lum, 1986) and the counselor is well advised to listen carefully and make no assumptions (Sutton & Broken Nose, 1996). The counselor demonstrates patience by not interrupting the client, and withholding advice or interpretation until invited (Garrett & Garrett, 1994).

Therapeutic Modalities

No one mode of counseling has been proven to be better than others in counseling Native Americans (Heinrich et al., 1990; Thomason, 1995). Attneave (1982) suggests that many therapeutic approaches would be acceptable to Native American clients as long as the counselor is sincere. Although there is little process research on what works in counseling Native Americans, many writers knowledgeable in the field have made a variety of recommendations. Reviews of the literature suggest that counselors use a more directive style (Trimble & Fleming, 1989), concentrate on problem solving (Richardson, 1981; Thomason, 1995), and make the counseling more informal by welcoming drop-in meetings (Heinrich et al., 1990) and conversations in social settings (Thomason, 1995). Nonverbal play and creative arts for children, spirituality, humor, storytelling, metaphors, imagery, paradoxical interventions, modeling, and role-play have been recommended (Foster, 1995; Garrett & Garrett, 1994; Lazarus, 1982; Sutton & Broken Nose, 1996). Restatement and summarizing a client's comments at the end of the session are recommended and confrontation is best avoided as it is perceived as rude and disrupts essential harmony in many Native American cultures (Baruth & Manning, 1991; Garrett & Garrett, 1994).

Family therapy has been frequently recommended for Native Americans (Baruth & Manning, 1991; Sutton & Broken Nose, 1996; Thomason, 1995). Particular attention should be paid to encouraging family stability and taking into consideration the many demands made by relatives (Thomason, 1995). At the very least, counselors need to be open to the participation of family members and tribal elders in the counseling process (Foster, 1995).

Group counseling may be helpful with Native American clients, but not if the group is heterogeneous (Baruth & Manning, 1991). Sage (1991) gives an example of a Native American women's group during which the women participated in beading and other crafts. The counseling approach was indirect, with the group focusing on problems by way of members relating stories of how similar situations had been handled. Thomason (1995) recommends small group counseling for Native American students, using values clarification and resolving cultural conflict as themes. A group program might begin with introductions that include family background and extent of identification with Native American heritage and in future sessions cover such topics as ways Native Americans differ from non-Indians and stereotypes about Indians, strengths of traditional Native American culture, conflict over societal pressure to conform to non-Indian ways, assertiveness, and sharing of Indian artwork, music, and literature.

Cultural Knowledge

It is essential that counselors become knowledgeable about Indian culture (Trimble & Fleming, 1989) and begin to read literature about specific individual tribes (Sutton & Broken Nose, 1996). Establishing credibility as a helper is a long-term, community-based process (Lowrey, 1983). It has been recommended that counselors acknowledge the depth of cultural loss that Native American clients experience, even for assimilated clients who may need to grieve for what they never had (Sutton & Broken Nose, 1996). Also, given the depth of historical trauma Native Americans have experienced in the United States, there is a need for counselors to become systemic change agents (Herring, 1991).

☐ Case Vignette

April is a Native American college student in North Carolina who is highly community-oriented and states she faces tremendous pressures to fulfill expectations and that she will return and contribute to her community. She spends time traveling between campus and home to see her family, especially on the weekends. She also states that as a counseling major role-playing with other students in class, she has a hard time looking the other student in the eye and therefore is graded lower than expected.

Questions

1. Should April be graded lower because she has a hard time keeping eye contact?

2. As a counselor would you suggest to April that she should spend more time on campus and not go home so frequently?

Reflection 1

As April's counselor, I would want to be knowledgeable about the general history and culture of Native Americans in this country, but I would also want to find out more about her specific tribe and community. I would want to help April talk about how she feels in this classroom and how her values and perspectives as a Native American may differ or be similar to those of other students in her major. By honoring April's cultural values and the importance that family and community have for her, I would hope that April would feel empowered to be true to herself. The importance that she places on community undoubtedly is a source of strength for her and by recognizing that, she will be able to set her own priorities.

Reflection 2

As a non-Native American, I want be particularly sensitive to the significant cultural differences that may exist between me and April. As such, I would work with her sensitively and carefully, being mindful of two potentially very different ways of seeing the world. I commend April for her desire to major in counseling and I appreciate the dilemma she faces in her counseling class, not looking others in the eye and hence being graded lower. One temptation I have is to encourage her to talk to her instructor about this, but I am not sure that this is the most appropriate behavior for her (e.g., she may see this as being disrespectful to her instructor). In terms of her going home or staying on campus, this is something that she would need to decide; I could certainly help her explore feelings around being on what I assume to be a dominant-culture campus, being educated in dominant-culture ways, as well as feelings regarding family and community.

☐ Recommended Cultural Resources

Print Media

Dudley, J. I. E. (1992). *Choteau Creek: A Sioux reminiscence*. Lincoln: University of Nebraska Press. A memoir of life on a South Dakota reservation.
Herring, R. (1999). *Counseling with Native American Indians and Alaska Natives: Strategies for helping professionals*. New York: Sage. A thoughtful guide for working with native peoples.

Holm, T. (1996). *Strong hearts, wounded souls*. Austin: University of Texas Press. A reflection on Native Americans who fought in Vietnam.

Miles, M. (1971). *Annie and the old one*. Boston: Little, Brown. Story of the love between a young girl and her grandparent.

Multimedia

Barnes, M. (Writer/producer). (1979). *The long walk of Fred Young* [Videotape]. Washington, DC: PBS Video. Outstanding portrayal of culture shock and ethnic differences in world outlook focusing on the obstacles confronting Fred Young, a Native American who, in spite of his success as a nuclear physicist in a technologically oriented society alien to his upbringing, still moves uneasily between two cultures.

Millar, S. (Producer). (1988). *Little big man* [Videorecording]. Livonia, MI: CBS/Fox Video. Jack Crabb is the only White survivor of a battle. Jack's story is a fantastic one: captured by Indians as a boy, reared as an Indian, shuttling back and forth between the White and Indian worlds. In the process, he befriends everyone from Wild Bill Hickock to George Armstrong Custer and is a gunslinger, a snake-oil salesman, and an Army scout.

Organizations

American Indian College Fund, 21 West 68th Street, Suite 1F, New York, New York 10023, (212) 787-6312.

National Agricultural Library links to Native American organizations, http://www.nal.usda.gov/ric/ruralres/nativeam.htm.

CHAPTER

African Americans in Counseling

If you're black, you still carry the problems that your people have been going through. You're never gonna forget that and once you know that, you wake up with that every single day. And so for me, I have to wake up every day and realize where I come from all over again, realize the struggle we went through, and understand that I am different.

Reggie Simmons, African American college student
("Voices of diversity," 1993)

☐ Histories and Diversity

As of July 1, 2004, there were an estimated 39.2 million African American residents of the United States, including those of more than one race. They made up 13.4% of the total U.S. population. This figure represents an increase of half a million residents from one year earlier (U.S. Bureau of the Census, 2004). Due to the long-standing prejudice and discrimination against African Americans throughout U.S. history, there are many descendents of African Americans who did not identify with or claim that part of their ethnic heritage. Those identifiable as African Americans are a relatively young ethnic group, with children and young people constituting close to half the population. The median age for these African

Americans is 26.9 years, compared to 32.7 years for the median European American (United States Bureau of the Census, 2004). Homicide is the leading cause of death among African American men aged 15–24 (Freiberg, 1991a) and a young Black man is six times more likely to be killed than a young White man (Pania, 1992). Nearly one in four African American males aged 20–29 are in prison, on parole, or on probation, and they outnumber those in college (Pania, 1992). Only 11.5% of African Americans have completed four years of college compared to 22.2% of Caucasians. The high school graduation rate is 66.7% for African Americans and 79.9% for Caucasians (McDavis, Parker, & Parker, 1995).

Unlike any other ethnic group who immigrated to the United States, most African Americans had ancestors who were brought to the country against their will, as slaves, beginning in the early 1600s. The effects of slavery on the majority of African Americans cannot be overstated as slavery not only created conditions of economic exploitation, it also left a legacy of disconnected family histories and, for many, a sense of hopelessness. African Americans were called "African" or "Black" during slavery and "Negro" or "Colored" during post-emancipation times, however, "Black" or "African American" became preferred terms during the civil rights era. Although slavery has been illegal for over a hundred years, the economic recovery from its effects on many African Americans has been largely unnoticed. A substantial proportion of African Americans in the United States had ancestors who were never slaves. These free people trace their roots to people who were indentured servants and worked off their financial obligations over several years. These African Americans often moved to urban areas, among them New Orleans, Charleston, Washington, DC, and Northern cities and have been prominent in the Black middle class (Axelson, 1993). Also, between 1940 and 1970 1.5 million African Americans migrated from the South to urban areas in the North and the West coast for better employment prospects (Hines & Boyd-Franklin, 1982, 2005).

The 1896 Supreme Court case, *Plessy v. Ferguson*, legalized "separate but equal" use of railroad facilities for African Americans. The ruling contributed to segregation in education and housing as well. One of the outcomes was the further development of predominantly Black colleges and universities, a trend that had first begun in 1869. Legally segregated schools ended with the 1954 *Brown v. Board of Education* Supreme Court ruling that racial segregation in public schools was unconstitutional. The Civil Rights Act of 1964 ended legalized discrimination in public restaurants and hotels, employment and union membership, and programs receiving federal assistance (Axelson, 1993; McDavis et al., 1995).

Racism and discrimination, however, continue to be strong influences in the lives of most African Americans. According to one review, people of African descent and Latinos were denied jobs which were then offered to equally qualified White people 15–20% of the time and 46% of Black people compared to 11% of White people say they have been discriminated against in the workplace during the past five years (Fendel, Hurtado, Long, & Giraldo, 1996). The overall unemployment rate remains higher for African American high school graduates than for White high school dropouts (Hoyt, 1989). Many African American parents have attempted to teach their children how to respond to discouragements such as name-calling or stereotyping (McDavis et al., 1995). They also know that they must prepare their children for dealing with police and the criminal justice system that arrest, convict, and incarcerate higher proportions of African Americans than Anglo-Americans (Jaynes & Williams, 1989). One Black mother (cited in Pania, 1992, p. 17A) instructed her son as follows.

> If you're ever stopped, … answer when spoken to. Say yes sir, no sir, and provide only what is asked. Keep your hands visible at all times and be polite. Don't question authority. And make your exit as soon as it's permitted.

Some vestiges of racism that were internalized by segments of the African American community continue to be manifested as a color "caste" system, lighter-skinned Black people being preferred over others (McDavis et al., 1995). These skin color preferences are even an issue within some families (Block, 1981).

It is important to note that the term "African Americans," as used in the United States, is very broad, including Spanish-speaking Blacks, American Indian Blacks (Ponterotto & Casas, 1991), West Indian Blacks, Haitian Americans, as well as recent immigrants from Africa. Counselors are cautioned against making assumptions about people from some of these subgroups inasmuch as the vast majority of research on African Americans in the United States is based on people whose ancestors experienced the American version of slavery and racism and their effects for generations. For example, whereas many West Indian Blacks also have a history that includes slavery, in the West Indies slaves were emancipated earlier and were able to become landowners and enter the middle or upper classes. Many skilled, educated, middle-class West Indian Blacks immigrated to the United States between 1940 and 1978. These African Americans often identify ethnically more as immigrants with island, regional, or even colonial (e.g., British) roots (Brice, 1982). Haitian Americans, some of whom speak Creole, a blending of French and African languages, are another distinct subgroup who have immigrated to the United States in large numbers since 1970 (Axelson, 1993).

Social Class Considerations

In 1987, 36% of Black families had middle class incomes of $25,000 or above on an annual basis. From 1970 to 1989, the percentage of African American and Black people with annual incomes greater than $50,000 grew by 182% (Edwards & Polite, 1992). These statistics suggest that there is a large African American middle class that has developed despite societal racial barriers and that the number of affluent African Americans is growing substantially. On the other side of the economic spectrum, 29% of Black households had no net worth in 1987 (Edwards & Polite, 1992) and the chances of a Black person finding employment are half that of someone who is White (Pania, 1992). There is a great diversity of economic conditions among African Americans, but images of unemployment and poverty continue to predominate in both print and televised media.

☐ Cultural Values

Spirituality

For many African Americans, religion has been an integral part of their ancestral cosmology and an important resource during hard times (Boyd-Franklin, 2003; Hines & Boyd-Franklin, 1982; Hooks, 2003). A national survey of Black Americans conducted in 1979–1980 (cited in Billingsley, 1992) indicated that 84% of African Americans consider themselves religious and 77% said that the church was very important in their lives. In addition to providing a sense of hope, communal religious practices also provide a network in which to socialize, exchange support, develop leadership, and take social action. Consequently, African Americans with a strong sense of spirituality may initially seek help from spiritual resources before approaching a counselor (Martin & Martin, 2002).

The "African American church" is a generic term for religious institutions within African American communities, which include a multitude of Christian denominations, such as African Methodist Episcopal Zion; African Methodist Episcopal; Apostolic; National Baptist Convention of America; National Baptist Convention, USA; National Primitive Baptist Convention; Progressive National Baptist Convention; Church of God in Christ; Church of God; Congregational; Episcopal; Lutheran; Roman Catholic; Seventh Day Adventist; and others (Axelson,

1993; B. L. Richardson, 1991). The Nation of Islam practices an American version of Islam (Axelson, 1993). In general, 80% of African Americans are Protestant (Billingsley, 1992). B. L. Richardson (1991, p. 65) wrote that

> Slavery and then segregation denied African Americans access to the rights and privileges accorded other Americans. The church was the only institution that African Americans had to meet their emotional, spiritual, and material needs.... Today, the church remains at the center of community life, attending to the social, spiritual, and psychological needs of scores of African Americans. No other institution claims the loyalty and attention of African Americans as does the church.

The church continues to serve many functions in addition to spiritual guidance: (a) It is a source of support and enhancement of self-esteem gained through service to the church, (b) it is a source of role models, and (c) it is a community base around which to organize collective efforts to confront oppressive systems and practices. For example, some African American parents who live in White neighborhoods and whose children attend predominantly White schools may seek African American churches as a means of balancing their children's identity development (B. L. Richardson, 1991). This may counteract the possibility of feeling alienated from both Blacks and Whites and experiencing interpersonal rejection as personal rather than cultural, which may occur when growing up in a White community.

In 1984 a Gallup survey found that 74% of Black adults belonged to a church, compared to 68% of White adults (cited in Hill, 1993). More recently, however, Jackson (cited in Foster, 1995b) suggested that although the African American church was a primary focus and had a calming effect on the family, its influence has diminished because many African American men no longer attend as regularly. He recommended that counselors encourage their African American male clients, in particular, to become more involved in church, among other treatment options.

Family

The myth regarding the deterioration of the Black family as a major cause of African American problems suggests a lack of understanding of the Black family. Strong kinship and tribal ties common among African cultures were damaged by slavery, which often physically separated family members (Hines & Boyd-Franklin, 1982). However, the resilience of African American family values may be currently evidenced in a variety of ways, including acceptance of children born out of wedlock, frequent extended family contact, and multigenerational households. A child raised by persons other than her or his parents is not rejected in the community, as alternative living arrangements are a practical solution to economic and other problems (Hines & Boyd-Franklin, 1982). The mother is often considered the family's strength and emotional center, acting as a stabilizing influence if the father does not have the level of education or employment needed to protect or provide for the family (Pinderhughes, 1982). However, the father may be considered the head of the household even when he is physically absent from the family. Long separations may be more tolerable than the idea of divorce when marital conflicts occur, and marital issues may be addressed indirectly.

At the same time, there may be pressure on family members to remain close to home and to assist family members in need (Hines & Boyd-Franklin, 1982). In some families, economic necessity results in a de-emphasis on sex role-related division of labor within the household and encouragement of educational accomplishment for women. Grandparents may take on the responsibility of raising their grandchildren (McDavis et al., 1995) and, indeed, 85% of African American teenage mothers live in three-generational households with their grandparents at the head (Billingsley, 1992). Black families also have been characterized as having a strong work and achievement ethic and a strong religious orientation (Baruth & Manning, 1991; D. W. Sue & Sue, 1990). The family is often used as a solution to individual problems. According to Hines and Boyd-Franklin (1982), a high tolerance for problems in the family may be related to religious convictions or to having dealt with a long history of oppression. African Americans may be disinclined to view the family as a source of problems, and the counselor would do well to draw on the family as a strength and consider including or consulting extended family members. For example, a "parent effectiveness group" may not appeal to African American families with extended or nonnuclear structures, whereas a more inclusive description, such as a group on "raising children," may be better received (Thomas & Dansby, 1985).

The Afrocentric Worldview

In an Afrocentric view of the world, the individual is validated in terms of others (Asante, 1987; Cheatham, 1990). This is a definitive concept, and this basic value is complemented by emphases on family and collective survival. The family is a reference point for interconnecting the person to all other family members—past, present, and future—and includes relationships based on blood, marriage, and both formal and informal adoption (Rogers-Dulan & Blacher, 1995). The traditional vocational choices of African Americans, teaching and the social sciences, tend to actualize Afrocentric values. Other elements of an Afrocentric worldview include a holistic rather than dualistic mind-versus-body focus, self-knowledge revealed through symbolic image and rhythm, interpersonal relationships that are cooperative and interdependent, harmonious blending with others and the universe, emphasis on the present more than the future, animated emotional expression, obedience to authority, and respect for the elderly because they have accumulated life's wisdom (Pinderhughes, 1982; Robinson & Howard-Hamilton, 1994; White & Parham, 1990).

Oral tradition is another important aspect of African American cultures (White & Parham, 1990). Parables, folk verses, folk tales, biblical verses, songs, and proverbs contribute to this oral tradition. A sample of Black proverbs collected by White (1984) is listed in the box below.

Much Black humor has evolved from the strong oral traditions of many African cultures. African American vernacular, or *Ebonics*, is a variation of American English that evolved in the United States over several hundred years. In fact, many African Americans are bilingual, speaking

---

Some African American Proverbs

The truth will out.

Don't sign no checks with your mouth that your ass can't cash.

Hard head make a soft behind.

You better be yourself or you gonna be by yourself.

One monkey don't stop no show.

Only a fool plays the golden rule in a crowd that don't play fair.

If you lay down with dogs you gonna come up with fleas.

What goes around, comes around.

You better learn how to work before work works you.

You don't git to be old being no fool.

Ebonics as well as the more widely accepted American English. Recently, controversy has arisen over programs that use Ebonics as a means of teaching African American schoolchildren American English (Darling, 1997). An African American client's decision to speak the mainstream American version of English could be indicative of responsiveness to the social context in which he or she is speaking.

Wilson and Stith (1991) noted that poor Blacks may have difficulty communicating their feelings, behaviors, and thoughts in American English. They recommend that counselors become familiar with Ebonics and accept its use by their clients. Counselors unfamiliar with Ebonics might do well to consider getting training in or increased exposure to Ebonics as a means of more fully understanding their clients. African American clients do not expect their counselors to imitate either Ebonics or Black humor in an attempt to create rapport, however, because African American clients frequently are more adept at switching back and forth between Ebonics and American English than most counselors. The African body language is a modality for maintaining rhythm in expression as well as dramatizing that which the language fails to communicate (Akbar, 2004).

☐ Indigenous Treatment Methods

The African American church may be a source of great assistance to some African American clients. B. L. Richardson (1991) noted that some African Americans may associate the counseling process with institutional or individualized racism they have experienced, and such perceptions promote defensiveness and hinder the counseling process. This tendency is exacerbated when counselors have limited knowledge of and sensitivity to racism. African American clergy are a form of traditional healer, and the counselor may benefit from consulting them (Hines & Boyd-Franklin, 1982; B. L. Richardson, 1991). Richardson (1991) offered some guidelines for consulting with traditional healers. When a client's spiritual beliefs are counterproductive to positive mental health, consultation is recommended. The church can also provide resources and support for families in crisis or who have experienced loss and assist isolated families in forming a new social network. Counselors might also consider the benefits of "pastoral initiative," the expectation that clergy will go to people and intervene on their own initiative and without specific invitation. Counselors can establish contact with African American clergy, for example, by giving a workshop at a ministerial alliance, a weekly meeting where clergy discuss clerical and community concerns, and later, presenting a workshop to the congregation (B. L. Richardson, 1991).

There has been interest in studying indigenous healing as currently practiced in Africa (Anwar, 1995; Levers & Maki, 1995). This process may have potential benefits with respect to understanding African American concepts of healing. Medicine and religion are connected in several African cultures and the healing process is characterized by spiritual transformation (Levers & Maki, 1995). Generally, healers had been ill for some years themselves and perceived their abilities as inherited or received as a gift from God or ancestral spirits. Healing is spiritual in that it involves a sense of community, of being reunited with ancestors (Levers & Maki, 1995, p. 139):

> Transformation occurs from the state of being afflicted to being healed; transcendence occurs in the act of being healed and in the process of becoming healer. Becoming healer and the process of healing allow for reconnection—the reconnection of the healer as well as of those the healer heals—to self, to community, to ancestors, and to universe.

Identification with a mythical figure and adopting the role of the spirit is another way traditional healing occurs (Anwar, 1995).

Kwanzaa is "a movement that seeks to establish, express, and celebrate aspects of African-American cultural identity" (Axelson, 1993, p. 103). Dr. Maulana Karenga developed it in 1966 on the basis of the African harvest celebration. The seven-day festival celebrates the life principles of unity, self-determination, collective work and responsibility, collective sharing, purpose, creativity, and faith (Axelson, 1993). Kwanzaa can be viewed as an indigenous healing ritual for some African Americans.

Robinson and Howard-Hamilton (1994) proposed that the African value system called *nguzo saba* can be integrated into the counseling process in a more Afrocentric approach. The seven major principles of *nguzo saba* are *umoja* (unity), *kujichagalia* (self-determination), *ujima* (collaborative work and responsibility), *ujaama* (cooperative economics), *nia* (purpose), *kuumba* (creativity), and *imani* (faith).

Yet another form of indigenous treatment was described in an article by Charles (cited in Lefley, 1989), who used cultural values and strengths in treating African Americans from the Caribbean. For example, the Haitian value placed on not lying or stealing was used to generate motivation to attend vocational training. Similarly, achievement orientation and group commitment values were used as incentives to treat depression.

☐ Treatment Implications

Black Rage and Trust

One of the most important issues for the counselor to initially consider when counseling an African American client is that of trust. Because of the legacy of slavery and realities of present-day racism and discrimination, trust in counselors and the counseling process may be difficult to develop. The history of slavery in the United States continuously makes African Americans angry and, whether consciously or unconsciously, every African American deals with it internally, according to Clemmont Vontress (Foster, 1995b). In some segments of the African American community, a client might ask her- or himself, "Is counseling something Black people do? Will counseling help me?" This is especially salient when the counselor is White. It may be easier for some African American clients to develop a counseling relationship with a counselor of color, but a degree of wariness might still exist. Block (1981) compared a Black getting help from a non-Black therapist as "like asking a Jew to be treated by a German, an Irish Catholic by an Irish Protestant, an Arab by a Jew, a white South African by a black" (p. 191). The real reason for counseling may be disguised, and a pseudoneed may be presented instead to first test the safety of the counselor and the counseling process (Block, 1981).

Because counseling or therapy may be perceived as something for "crazy" people, other sources of help, such as ministers, doctors, aunts, or grandmothers, may have been tried first (Hines & Boyd-Franklin, 1982). By the time many African American clients encounter a professional counselor they may feel desperate and at the end of their rope. According to Morris Jackson (Foster, 1995b), the counselor must ask him- or herself, "Can I deal with the rage that African Americans may be having?" knowing that that rage may be directed at people very similar to the counselor and, "Do I have enough confidence and competence as a counselor to work through that, or am I too timid?"

The counselor is cautioned not to interpret African American anger as simple transference; the client's feelings are a realistic response to the counselor as a part of a social system that has historically proven inhospitable and deserving of mistrust. Client issues concerning trust may constructively be viewed as healthy suspiciousness (Hines & Boyd-Franklin, 1982). Sometimes clients' expression of affect or other responses may be subdued because the clients expect a negative response from the counselor. The counselor may help the client feel more comfortable expressing emotions by responding to a client's description of a situation with "Some people might feel ... (discouraged, outraged, etc.) with that experience."

The client being "cool," acting unconcerned and worldly, has been mistakenly interpreted at times as limiting the personal risk of counseling and promoting a sense of power and control, especially for African American men (Freiberg, 1991a). On the other hand, counselors need to keep in mind that verbal directness does not necessarily imply hostility (Baruth & Manning, 1991). A somewhat different, but also stigmatizing issue is that of internalized oppression (see Chapter 3). Some African American clients may have internalized societal messages about racial inferiority with the results being self-hatred and self-limiting of potential, with concomitant hostility and mistrust (Akbar, 2004; McDavis et al., 1995). This self-hatred hypothesis has been destructive to understanding Black adjustment and may result in a counselor erroneously blaming the client, when the client may actually have been victimized.

Historically Black Colleges and Universities

According to the U.S. Census Bureau (2004), among blacks age 25 and older, 81% of the population had at least a high school diploma. This proportion rose by 8% from 1994 to 2004. In addition, among blacks age 25 and older, 18% had at least a bachelor's degree in 2004—up 5% from 1994. Among blacks age 25 and older, 1.1 million had an advanced degree in 2004 (e.g., master's, PhD, MD, or JD). Ten years earlier—in 1994—only 624,000 blacks had this level of education. Finally, there were 2.3 million Black college students in fall 2004, roughly double the number 15 years earlier.

Low expectations, lack of role models, disregard for cultural diversity, and grouping or tracking practices have been identified as barriers to African American educational success in schools (Locke, 1995). Counselors with African American clients who are considering college can be of great assistance by helping them consider the potential benefits of attending a historically Black college, which may minimize many of these barriers. Some traditionally Black educational institutions are Clark Atlanta, Howard, Florida A&M, Fisk, Hampton Institute, Morehouse, Morgan State, North Carolina Central, John C. Smith, Southern, Tennessee State, Tuskegee Institute, and Virginia State (Backover, 1992; DeAngelis, 1992; Pruitt & Isaac, 1985; "Voices of diversity," 1993). Many historically Black colleges and universities (HBCUs) are private institutions. HBCUs provide a distinctive, positive educational experience for their students.

According to Locke (1995), getting good grades in high school can lead to an African American student being accused of "acting White" and can result in her or his questioning the value of academic achievement because it puts him or her at odds with peers. This dilemma loses significance at HBCUs. African American students at Black colleges and universities are often more diverse with respect to socioeconomic and educational background. Historically, Black colleges and universities have produced a large majority of African American PhDs, Army officers, physicians, and federal judges (Kemp, 1990). Graduation rates for African American students are higher at HBCUs compared to graduation rates at predominantly White institutions. According to a 1992 report, 44% of all bachelor's degrees earned by African Americans were awarded by HBCUs, even though only 17% of all enrolled African American college students attend them (Backover, 1992).

Some of the advantages of attending a Black institution of higher education are a higher level of psychosocial adjustment and a better self-image gained from being part of a majority experience (Kemp, 1990). Communication and identification with faculty also happen more spontaneously (Backover, 1992). The disadvantages include fewer campus resources and more limited choice of majors and advanced-study programs (Kemp, 1990). Faculty may be less nationally recognized than at predominantly White institutions, but they frequently place more of their emphasis on teaching.

In 1990, 73% of African American students attended predominantly White universities (Kemp, 1990). Counselors may have little knowledge about Black institutions as an educational alternative. The choice of colleges for African Americans is complex and also interacts with issues of ethnic identity. Tatum (1993) found that many African American students did not consider attending a historically Black college for the reason that they were afraid to be labeled "too White" by their college peers. Interestingly, Edwards and Polite (1992), in their book, *Children of the Dream,* found that a common trait among successful African Americans was a positive sense of ethnic identity. Other similarities included a strong sense of family, self-confidence, a willingness to get along with Whites, and an ability to keep anger or resentment from detracting from their goals (Siegel, 1992).

Diagnostic Issues

Psychological disorders may express themselves differently depending on the client's ethnic and economic background. The rate of depression among Black people is actually no different from among White people when socioeconomic status is taken into account (Boyd-Franklin, 2003). African Americans with depressive disorders may also display more agitation and aggression, weight gain, difficulty crying, and self-destructive symptoms such as not going to work or victim-precipitated homicides (Block, 1981). As with depressive disorders, no differences have been found between Black people and White people in rates of sociopathy or antisocial personality (Cloninger, Reich, & Guze, 1975; Robins et al., 1984).

Historically, African Americans have had more access to health services than to mental health services, and somatic complaints sometimes have helped bring about positive change in terms of relief from situational stresses. However, African Americans continue to have differentially higher rates of infant mortality, hypertension, heart disease, obesity, anemia, AIDS, and other physical conditions than European Americans (Axelson, 1993; Baruth & Manning, 1991; DeAngelis, 1992; Mayo, 1974; Pinderhughes, 1982). On average, Blacks die seven years earlier than Whites (DeAngelis, 1992).

Counselors must be sensitive to issues of bias in diagnosing African Americans. Jordan (1993) reviewed studies that indicated that African Americans tend to be rated by clinicians and therapists as less verbal, more impaired, and having poorer family relations, moreso when the therapist is White.

Other Counseling Issues

There are several ways in which the counselor may want to modify her or his behavior when working with African American clients. For some African Americans, eye contact may not be a sign of attentiveness (Baruth & Manning, 1991), and the counselor needs to look more closely at other nonverbal behavior instead. Although many African Americans may value openness and action, being out of control is not valued (Block, 1981). Self-disclosure may be low, and the counselor may want to share more personal information and opinions of her or his own (Block, 1981; McDavis et al., 1995) and provide an orientation to the counseling process to first-time clients (Boyd-Franklin, 2003; Hines & Boyd-Franklin, 1982; McDavis et al., 1995). The orientation might include:

1. Discussing the importance of being present at the time of the appointment.

2. Emphasizing the need to notify the counselor about cancellations.

3. Telling the client that he or she needs to bring up important issues.

4. Explaining to the client that trust will develop over time.

5. Explaining to the client that counseling occurs outside the session as well, in terms of how he or she thinks and acts between sessions (Block, 1981; Boyd-Franklin, 2003; Hines & Boyd-Franklin, 1982).

Giving specific, explicit answers to client questions also has been recommended (Locke, 1995). In addition, it may be helpful to specifically address cultural differences (Wilson & Stith, 1991). This may be appropriate during the initial session. The counselor may want to give the client a summary of what the counselor understood from the session, particularly at the end of the first session.

African American clients may prefer a more active, problem-focused, time-limited therapeutic style (Hines & Boyd-Franklin, 1982) from an authoritative counselor who will be vigorous and committed in her or his interactions (Pinderhughes, 1982). A cognitive behavioral approach has been recommended for African American women and people of color in general because of its active, present orientation (McNair, 1992; Ponterotto & Casas, 1991). However, role playing with some adult clients may be resisted as childish (McRoy & Oglesby, 1984). More passive approaches, such as psychodynamic or client-centered approaches, may increase clients' anxiety about counseling and may be more appropriate with African American clients who have more education. Others have recommended an eclectic approach with an existential philosophical base (McDavis et al., 1995). An additional recommendation has been that counselors be ready to assume the role of client advocate in working with African American clients (Locke, 1995; Paster, 1985).

Specific questions a counselor might ask to get a more accurate picture of the family of an African American client are, "Who is in the family?" or "Whom can you depend on for help when needed?" instead of "Who lives in the home?" (Hines & Boyd-Franklin, 1982). Pinderhughes (1982) recommended that, because powerlessness is a major issue in the lives of many African Americans, the counselor should focus on client strengths rather than weaknesses. It may be helpful to connect discussions of actions with other people in the community: "What would your parents, other kinfolk, church members, etc. think about this behavior?" (Locke, 1995). Among the goals a counselor might consider with an African American client could be helping the client understand more about her or his cultural history and learning to express anger effectively, and to convert negative feelings into creative productivity (Foster, 1995).

Group counseling may be beneficial, because it is consistent with the communal focus of many African American cultures (Locke, 1995). Counseling in an all-Black group would provide opportunities for clients to deal with issues of cultural identity, feelings of racial hostility, identification of new goals, and getting feedback on their presentation to others.

Family therapy with African Americans, as commonly practiced, is somewhat controversial. Gwyn and Kilpatrick (1981) reported an 81% dropout rate for family therapy with low-income Blacks. Counselors may make many errors that may contribute to premature termination. For example, a counselor who uses first names before asking permission may be perceived as treating African American clients disrespectfully (Hines & Boyd-Franklin, 1982). Bowen family systems therapy, on the other hand, has been specifically recommended for West Indian Black families because it is compatible with the education and upward mobility values of this African American subgroup (Brice, 1982). In general, Pinderhughes (1982) recommended focusing on African American family strengths to counteract societal experiences of powerlessness.

In conclusion, words of advice by Jones (1985, p. 175) may best describe how to work with African American individuals:

> Knowing that a client is Black fails to inform adequately about his views of psychotherapy, about his personality and psychological conflict, and about his inspirations and goals in therapy, let alone about educational level, social background, or environmental context. There is enormous within-group variability. The question is not how to treat the Black client, but how to treat this Black client.

Remember that all African Americans/Blacks are not alike. Using these words to live by while working with African American clients should decrease dropout rates for African Americans in therapy.

☐ Case Vignette

Sophia is a 20-year-old African American female student at a predominately White Institution (PWI). She comes from a two-parent family and is the eldest of three children and the first to go to college in her family. Her immediate family lives in another state. She lives in campus housing and her roommate is White. Sophia's grades have been very good (mostly As and Bs) with a 3.5 grade point average. Despite her grade point average, Sophia often reports she is very sad. She expresses her disappointment in herself for not getting better grades. She does not have any outside activities other than attending church every Sunday.

Questions

1. What do you think is Sophia's diagnosis or does she need a diagnosis?

2. Why do you think Sophia has a hard time adjusting to college?

3. As her counselor, what would you recommend for Sophia?

Reflection 1

As the first in her family to attend college, Sophia understandably seems to be having difficulty adjusting to the college environment, sharing a room with someone who may be very different from herself, and living away from home for the first time. If I were Sophia's counselor, I would begin by trying to develop trust with Sophia. I would want to explore more about her sadness and disappointment in not getting better grades. In reality, a grade point average of 3.5 is quite respectable, but it seems that she has higher expectations for herself. Helping Sophia see her strengths would, it is hoped, build her self-esteem. I would also want to help her discover extracurricular activities and organizations, both on and off campus, to strengthen her sense of community by bringing her into contact with people with whom she could identify and feel comfortable. I am glad to see that she is attending church every Sunday as her church will be an excellent source of support and a resource in helping her build community connections.

Reflection 2

Sophia might be diagnosed with an adjustment disorder. As a first-time freshman and the first in her family to go to college, she is having to get used to a very different environment and be away from family and familiar surroundings. Although her grades have been very good, we do not know if they have dropped markedly since high school. Sophia is in a socially isolating situation in a PWI and even though she has a roommate, she may not feel comfortable sharing her thoughts and feelings with someone who is so different from herself. A counselor might give her a safe place to express both her satisfactions and concerns about starting college and encourage her to become involved with extracurricular activities that might allow her to meet other African American students on campus.

☐ Recommended Cultural Resources

Print Media

Campbell, B.M. (2005). *72 hour hold*. New York: Knopf. A powerful story of a mother trying to cope with her daughter's bipolar disorder. Keri, the owner of an upscale L.A. resale clothing shop, is hopeful as daughter Trina celebrates her 18th birthday and begins a successful-seeming new treatment.

Haley, A. (Ed.). (1992). *The autobiography of Malcolm X*. New York: Ballantine. This book recounts his transformation from a bitter, self-destructive petty criminal into an articulate political activist, the continued relevance of his militant analysis of White racism, and his emphasis on self-respect and self-help for African Americans.

Journal of Black Psychology

Journal of Black Studies

Lincoln, C. E., & Mamiya, L. H. (1990). *The Black church in the African American experience*. Durham, NC: Duke University Press. In addition to their status as houses of worship, Black churches function as centers of social life, ethnic identity, and cultural expression in the African American community. Although African American music is derived from a variety of sources, religion has historically served as one of its major inspirations.

Mabry, M. (1995). *White bucks and black-eyed peas*. New York: Simon & Schuster. A 25-year-old Paris correspondent for *Newsweek* writes a memoir of being a Black urban professional and the uneasy price of that success. His grandmother and mother were the driving forces that sent him from poverty to prep school and beyond, in contrast to his "deadbeat dad," a wealthy judge who didn't acknowledge Mabry for years.

McCall, N. (1994). *Makes me wanna holler, a young Black man in America*. New York: Vintage Books. McCall's autobiography tracks his trajectory from the streets of Portsmouth, VA, to prison, rehabilitation, and a job at the *Washington Post*.

Morrison, T. (1970). *The bluest eye*. New York: Random House. Winner of the 1993 Nobel Prize in Literature, this is the story of an African American family struggling with issues of identity and race.

Murray, P. (1956). *Proud shoes*. New York: Harper. The story of a family over 100 years, especially the experiences of Murray's maternal grandparents.

Walker, M. (1966). *Jubilee*. Boston: Houghton Mifflin. The story of a Black woman from slavery through the Civil War, including her daily life, thoroughly researched and caringly written.

Ward, E. (2005). Keeping it real: A grounded theory study in African-American clients engaging in counseling at a community mental health agency. *Journal of Counseling Psychology, 52*(4), 471–481.

Multimedia

Margulies, S. (Producer). (1992). *Roots* [Videorecording]. Burbank, CA: Warner Home Video. This saga begins with a birth in an African Village in 1750 and ends seven generations later in Arkansas.

Riggs, M. (Producer). (1995). *Black is, Black ain't* [Videorecording]. San Francisco: California Newsreel. Racial identity is a difficult subject, fraught with controversy. For some, *Black Is, Black Ain't* challenges deeply held beliefs.

Shange, N. (1976). *For colored girls who have considered suicide when the rainbow is enuf* [Sound recording]. New York: Buddah Records. A celebration of Black womanhood in poetry and prose.

Spielberg, S. (Director). (1995). *The color purple* [DVD]. New York: Warner Brothers. Alice Walker's Pulitzer Prize-winning story about an abused and uneducated black woman's struggle for empowerment.

Latinos and Latinas in Counseling

Es algo que jamás esperé ver (grandes manifestaciones de Latinos): que bendito sea Dios estamos demostrando nuestra cultura, nuestra educación. Y también quiero darle las gracias a todos los de las demás razas, a los de la raza afroamericana, a los de otros países, por su apoyo. Y que esto nos sirva de pie para evitar más confrontamientos con otras razas, porque a fin de cuentas todos estamos en la misma situación en este país. Es muy bonito sobre todo ver a los jóvenes de todas las escuelas, que se están comportando a la altura. A mi me llena de alegría, me gana de emoción.

I never thought I would see this (huge marches of Latinos): thank God that we are showing our culture, our education. I also want to thank everyone from other races, those from the Afro-American race, those from other countries, for their support. And I hope that this also serves as an example for us to avoid further confrontations with other races, because we are, after all, all in the same situation in this country. More than anything it's beautiful to see the young people from all the schools who are behaving at their best. I'm overcome with joy, overwhelmed with emotion.

Felipe, Fresno, CA, speaking on May 1, 2006,
"A Day Without Immigrants" on the national Spanish-language talk
show, *Línea Abierta*, produced by Radio Bilingüe, Latino public radio.

On May 1, 2006, more than a million people, mostly Latinos, took to the nation's streets to demand that U.S. immigration laws be reformed. Both legal and illegal immigrants and their supporters demonstrated by the thousands in major cities such as Los Angeles, San Francisco, Chicago, and Denver. Calls for justice, dignity, and legal residence for illegal immigrants in the United States became the rallying cries. Not since the war in Vietnam had the country witnessed such a large coordinated demonstration. "A Day Without Immigrants" included boycotts, store closures, and student walkouts intended to show the economic role of immigrants and to protest legislation passed by the House of Representatives that would declare illegal immigrants and those who help them to be felons (Cabanatuan, Hendricks, & Johnson, 2006). A month later, respondents of a phone survey of Latinos conducted by the Pew Hispanic Center reported that they felt empowered to create change after the pro-immigration marches that took place as a result of the debate over immigration legislation. Survey results indicated that 58% of those polled, including both native and foreign-born respondents, believe that Latinos are working toward similar political goals, despite their varying national, ethnic, cultural, and political backgrounds (Fears, 2006).

☐ Histories and Diversity

Latinos and Latinas are people of diverse ethnic, racial, and cultural backgrounds living in the United States and constituting the largest minority group in the country, numbering 31 million in 1999 (U.S. Bureau of the Census, 2001). The population is significantly larger when the estimated 11 million undocumented workers are included (Pew Hispanic Center, 2005). Latinos and Latinas are the fastest-growing ethnic minority group in the country (Santiago-Rivera, 1995). By 2004, the total Latino population was estimated to be 40.4 million (Pew Hispanic Center, 2005). Latinos and Latinas can be found in every state in the United States, with the majority living in California, Texas, New York, Florida, Illinois, Arizona, and New Jersey (Gloria & Segura-Herrera, 2004). In California, one out of every three persons is Latino and, by the year 2040, Latinos are expected to comprise half of that state's population (Hayes-Bautista, 2004).

Most Latinos live in urban areas (Arredondo, 1991; Sue & Sue, 2003; Zapata, 1995) and work in blue-collar jobs as laborers or machine operators if they are male and as service personnel if they are female (Arredondo, 1991; Zapata, 1995). Latinos and Latinas are undereducated (Zapata, 1995), even in comparison to African Americans, with an average educational level of the sixth grade and a high school dropout rate of more than one in three (Sue & Sue, 2003). Latino youth take a less rigorous curriculum in high school, and tend to score lower on national assessments and college entrance exams (Pew Hispanic Center, 2005). In the population aged 25 and older, only 56% of Latino and Latina adults have a high school diploma or better (compared to 74% of White non-Hispanics) and 11% have at least a bachelor's degree (compared to

60% of White non-Hispanics). In 1999, the percentage of Latinos with a bachelor's degree or higher was not significantly different from 10 years earlier (U.S. Bureau of the Census, 2001). Latinos and Latinas are a young population compared to other ethnic groups; their birthrate is twice as high as that of non-Latinos (Pew Hispanic Center, 2005). Approximately one in four Latinos and Latinas live in poverty (Zapata, 1995), with more Latino families (26%) living in poverty than White non-Hispanic families (8%) (U.S. Bureau of the Census, 2001). Although Latinos and Latinas make up approximately 14% of the population, they accounted for 19% of new AIDS cases reported in 2000, according to findings from a national survey conducted by the Henry J. Kaiser Family Foundation (2001). That same survey found that adult Latinas contract AIDS at a rate of 13.8 per 100,000, which is more than six times the rate for White women (2.2 per 100,000).

In this book we have decided to use the term "Latino" over the term "Hispanic," although they are often used interchangeably. The term "Hispanic" is a federal government designation that was instituted by President Richard Nixon in 1973 when he mandated that all federal records include the identifier to describe people from Mexico, Puerto Rico, Cuba, and other countries of Spanish culture or origin including El Salvador, Guatemala, Honduras, Dominican Republic, Spain, and so on (Hayes-Bautista, 2004). The use of the term Hispanic is controversial because it lumps together millions of individuals who are different in terms of race, class, language, national origin, and the like (Gloria & Segura-Herrera, 2004) and it emphasizes a Spanish heritage thus ignoring the vast contributions of indigenous Americans and Africans to Latino life and traditions (Sue & Sue, 2003).

"Chicano" is a term that originated in an era of mass social and political student mobilization for social and racial equality. American students of Mexican descent involved in the Chicano Power Movement of the 1960s coined the term as a way of recognizing and reclaiming their Mexican indigenous culture and history, which up to that point had been silenced. It tends to be used as a positive symbol of ethnic identification more often by young, educated, urban, bilingual English- and Spanish-speaking Mexicans born in the United States. Cesar Chavez is viewed as the leading founder of the Chicano Movement for his leadership in mobilizing the United Farm Workers to demand better working conditions and fair wages.

"Mexican" may be a term favored by older, often working-class, rural, monolingual, Spanish-speaking Latinos and Latinas of Mexican heritage. People who call themselves "Mexican Americans" are likely to be somewhere in between Chicanos and Mexicans politically and in terms of educational status. "La Raza" (the race), Mexicano, and

Spanish-American are other terms for Latinos and Latinas (Sue & Sue, 2003). Puertorriqueño, Newyorican, and Tejano are additional terms Latinos may use to describe themselves which refer to their birthplace (Puerto Rican, New Yorker of Puerto Rican heritage, and Texan of Mexican heritage, respectively).

Clearly, the specific words a client may use to describe her or his ethnic background may provide important clues to her or his cultural identity and further exploration with the client may be worthwhile. The counselor's cultural sensitivity to the client's choice of terms is also important when talking about immigration status. The term "undocumented workers" rather than "illegal aliens" should be used because it does not convey a negative judgment or stereotype, but rather takes into account the working status of people in these circumstances, acknowledging a lack of official papers.

There is a long history of discrimination against Latinos and Latinas in the United States beginning after the United States–Mexico War. In 1848, the Treaty of Guadalupe Hidalgo was signed, which ended the war and ceded almost half of Mexico's territory, including Texas and most of the Southwest, to the United States. Under the treaty, Mexican landowners retained their citizenship and land rights. According to Article IX of the treaty, Mexicans were guaranteed "the enjoyment of all the rights of citizens of the United States according to the principles of the Constitution; and in the meantime shall be maintained and protected in the free enjoyment of their liberty and property, and secured in the free exercise of their religion without restriction." Article X guaranteed protection of "all prior and pending titles to property of every description" (Acuña, 2000, p. 54). Despite this legal contract, however, Mexican lands were eventually taken away and Mexicans treated as second-class citizens. As Rodolfo Acuña states: "In practice, the treaty was ignored and during the nineteenth century most Mexicans in the United States were considered as a class apart from the dominant race" (2000, p. 55).

The realization that racism and discrimination are part of life in the United States may take Latino and Latina immigrants by surprise. In many of their countries of origin, a wide variation in skin color among people is the norm (Smart & Smart, 1995). Also, 98% of "Hispanics" identified their racial background as White according to U.S. Bureau of the Census data (A. Leal-Idrogo, personal communication, March 28, 1995). In 1940 the Census Bureau mandated that Latinos were White, giving Latinos official status as a race, while at the same time limiting their access to schools, public facilities, and real estate (Hayes-Bautista, 2004). At that time, for example, restrictive covenants forbade that property be sold to Mexicans.

Linguistic discrimination is one of the major modes in which Latinos and Latinas are discriminated against today. In 1974 the Supreme Court ruled (in *Lau v. Nichols*) that public schools must provide programs that do not prevent non-English speaking students from receiving meaningful education. Bilingual education programs were developed as a result of this ruling but remain controversial even now, more than 20 years later. Part of the controversy is due to a belief held by many English-speaking majority people that the English language is preferable to Spanish because it is the language of the majority and in part due to suggestions that bilingual education provides Spanish speakers with a segregated, lesser quality educational experience.

Social Class Considerations

Latinos and Latinas are a very diverse group socioeconomically and demographically (Rogler, Cortes, & Malgady, 1991) with differences in subgroup membership, immigration status, skin color, and bilingual ability (Arredondo, 1991). One major dimension of diversity is along the lines of country of origin. Whereas some Latinos trace their family histories in the United States going back several centuries, others are more recent arrivals with roots originating in many countries with varied cultures. With respect to place of origin, 63% trace their families to Mexico, 10% to Puerto Rico, 5% to South America, 4% to Cuba, 3% to El Salvador, 3% to Dominican Republic, 4% as Other Central American, and 8% as Other Latino (Pew Hispanic Center, 2005). Leal and Menjivar (1992) noted that Latinas whose ethnic roots are in different countries are not necessarily supportive of one another.

Latinos of Mexican origin form the largest Latino ethnic subgroup in the United States. Mexican Americans are frequently of "Mestizo" ancestry, the ethnic mixing that resulted from Indian, African, European, and Asian heritages (Hayes-Bautista, 2004). Because the United States and Mexico share a border, the proximity of the two countries makes it easier to maintain cultural ties with family on both sides of the border.

Puerto Ricans, the second largest Latino ethnic group, represent about 10% of all Latinos (Pew Hispanic Center, 2005). They are the least educated, having the highest dropout rate (Sue & Sue, 2003; Zapata, 1995). They are also most likely to be unemployed and poor (Zapata, 1995), with 40% living below the poverty level (Sue & Sue, 2003). Given their level of environmental stress as a result of those conditions of poverty, it is not surprising that Puerto Ricans have the highest rate of depression among Latino ethnic groups (Moscicki, Rae, Regier, & Locke, 1987).

Cubans have the most economic power of any Latino ethnic group (Zapata, 1995). This might be related to several factors: Many Cubans in the United States appear to be of White European descent (Smart & Smart, 1995), the average Cuban is older than other Latinos and has had longer potential time in the workforce, and more Cuban immigrants may have initially come from middle and upper classes. Compared to other Latino and Caribbean populations, Cubans in 1990 had the highest educational level; in fact, their educational levels are comparable to those of mainstream Americans and they have the highest number of workers in upper white-collar jobs and the highest percentage of people who own their homes (Trueba, 1999, citing Rumbaut, 1995). Interestingly, Cubans had the second highest use of public assistance in 1990 (Trueba, 1999, citing Rumbaut, 1995).

☐ Cultural Values

Simply stated, Latinos are a very diverse group. The cultural values associated with Latinos vary with each individual, depending on ethnic identity, acculturation level, social class, generational affiliation, and so on. One must not assume that the values listed below are all inclusive; rather, they are intended solely as a brief introduction. The ability to speak English in order to be a part of American society is considered to be very important by a majority of Latinos, according to public opinion surveys conducted in 2003 and 2004 (Pew Hispanic Center, 2006). Although Latinos as a whole are the least-educated ethnic group, with only 62% of Latinos finishing high school compared to almost 90% of all young adults finishing high school in this country, 84% of native-born Latino young adults have finished high school (Pew Hispanic Center, 2005).

Family

Loyalty to the family is highly valued among many Latinos and Latinas. *Compadrazgo* describes a formalized system of kinship relationships that tends to be both hierarchical and patriarchal (Arredondo, 1991). A large extended family may be part of the client's interpersonal world. Strong kinship bonds may exist between friends as well as family (Lee &

Richardson, 1991). Godparents, often the parents' closest friends, can play an integral role in the client's life and may be an integral part of the family system. F. Sabogal, G. Marin, R. Otero-Sabogal, B. V. Marin, and E. J. Perez-Stable (1987) describe *familism,* or the importance of the family, among Latinos and Latinas as having three components: (1) family obligations, (2) perceived support, and (3) family as referents or role models. In their research, Latinos and Latinas were found to be familistic, even when acculturated. Indeed, family support is a cultural resource for many Latinos and Latinas. Family support has been shown to be associated with success in college for Chicanas (Gándara, 1995; Vasquez, 1982). It would be helpful for many Latino and Latina clients that the counselor explore ways in which they can draw on their family as a source of strength.

Children in the family are taught to value respect, *respeto,* and obedience to parents, and adults in general (Gonzales, 1979). An individual who shows proper respect for an elder is considered to be *una persona bien educada,* which literally means a well-educated person, whereas the individual who is *mal educado,* or poorly educated, has not learned how to treat others properly (Gloria & Segura-Herrera, 2004). *Respeto* may come into play in the counseling setting as deference to the counselor and an unwillingness to disagree, ask questions, or speak up in order not to show a lack of respect (Ho, 1987).

Trueba (1999) refers to loyalty to one's ethnic group as a highly important value for Latinos. Discussed frequently by families and alluded to often in popular songs, loyalty signifies that one not only acknowledges the presence of other Latinos but also that one treats them as equals. One of the worst offenses is for someone to act superior or arrogant or to speak only English. The derogatory term *pocho* is used to describe persons who either refuse or are unable to speak Spanish.

Machismo

Within Latino cultures, "machismo" has a meaning that is far different from the male chauvinistic stereotype typically associated with the word in the United States. In Spanish, the term originally referred to honor, loyalty, and the following of a gallant code of ethics, comparable to that often associated with knighthood and chivalry in European history. Misinterpretation of the term in mainstream American culture has led to misconceptions and erroneous negative stereotypes. The situation is complex. For example, research has shown that marriages between Latinos and Latinas are no more traditional in terms of sex roles than other marriages, yet anecdotal clinical evidence suggests that sex role expectations may be problematic for many Latinas (Zuniga, 1988).

The rate of separation and divorce is higher for Latinas (14.1%) than for other women (9.8%) according to a 1981 study (cited in Arredondo, 1991). Duty, self-sacrifice, chastity, and *aguantar*, or enduring, a quality involving passivity and deference to male authority, are valued in women from many Latino cultures and have come to be known as *marianismo*, a model of perfection based on the Virgin Mary (Gil & Vazquez, 1996) that implies a female spiritual superiority (Lee & Richardson, 1991). Providing care for others, especially for the men in her life, is central to the woman's role, which is circumscribed to the home. Meanwhile, the man's role is to be in the world. Although these roles may have functioned in the country of origin, conflict arises as women assume new roles in the United States. For example, Hispanic men and women participate in the labor force at a rate of 67.4%, which is higher than for all Whites (66.2%) and for all African Americans (63.8%). This workforce participation forces Latinas to choose between the *marianista* mandate of being homemakers and housewives or achieving the status and respect of the workplace to which their own mothers could never aspire (Gil & Vazquez, 1996). Trueba's (1999) study of Mexican women in Migrant Town documented women who were as capable and resilient as men, assertive, and powerful in many critical areas of the family, a far cry from the stereotypical image of Latinas as passive victims.

The value placed on machismo among Latinos might play a role in the higher incidence of AIDS among Latinos and Latinas compared to the U.S. population in general (Freiberg, 1991b). In a study conducted by Amaro (cited in Freiberg, 1991b), two-thirds of Latinos who were diagnosed with AIDS or were HIV-positive reported having had unprotected sex with a woman in the preceding year. Machismo may contribute to a cultural homophobia that masks sexual contact between Latinos who are not gay-identified. It is important to note, however, that other factors, such as a lack of educational information about AIDS prevention in Spanish, may have an even greater role in the higher impact of AIDS upon Latinos and Latinas.

Spirituality

Religion and spirituality have a great influence in the lives of many Latinos and Latinas. Most are Christian, usually specifically Roman Catholic (Arredondo, 1991). Religion and family life may be intertwined and the church may be regarded as a social gathering place and community center as well as a place of worship. The strong influence of Catholicism on Latinos and Latinas may have several implications for counseling. The teachings of the church may suggest that health and illness are influenced by God and as a result some Latinos and Latinas may be less likely to seek preventive medical exams or procedures. Mental illness may be viewed similarly as an act of God. The influence of Catholicism on the client may sometimes be perceived by the counselor as an attitude of fatalism. In counseling, the client might appear to be unmotivated to change. The client may appear to behave unassertively if he or she acts consistently with beliefs in sacrifice leading to salvation, charity to others, and the value of enduring wrongs (Sue & Sue, 1990). A tendency toward larger families and an avoidance of divorce may also be related to religious teachings regarding contraception and divorce. Continuing with an unhappy marriage or maintaining a permanent separation may be preferable to divorce for some traditional Latinas who believe they will be treated as outcasts or prostitutes within their own community if they ever begin a new relationship.

In addition to the influences of Catholicism, some Latino cultures have elements of spirituality that may include witchcraft, sorcery, and belief in anthropomorphic or animistic supernatural beings, sacred objects, rites, and ceremonies that are complementary or coexistent with Catholicism (Fabrega & Nutini, 1994; Sandoval, 1979). For example, in a rural Mexican community, grief reactions over several cases of SIDS were tempered by indigenous spiritual beliefs that catastrophes and unhappy events happen for a reason (Fabrega & Nutini, 1994). Paniagua (2005) notes that Latinos tend not to use witch doctors or *brujos/brujas* in the same way as *curanderos/curanderas*, associating witch doctors with the power of the devil, whereas the spiritual power of *curanderos* comes from God.

Personalismo

Personalismo refers to a preference for personal contact and individual interactions over more formal or bureaucratic dealings (Ruiz & Padilla, 1977). *Personalismo* emphasizes the importance of people over tasks. For the client, this could mean a preference for more personal small talk and for the counselor, this might suggest engaging in more self-disclosure and communicating with warmth and genuineness. In a first session, however, Paniagua (2005) recommends that counselors avoid *personalismo* and instead use formality because proper respect needs to be paid to the client and her or his concerns. Less formal and more personable conversations can take place in subsequent sessions or at the end of the first session.

In summary, some of the cultural values important to understand when counseling Latino and Latina clients are:

- The importance of family

- *Respeto*

- *Machismo* and *marianismo* and their effect on sex roles

- The influence of the Roman Catholic Church and other forms of spirituality

- *Personalismo*

☐ Indigenous Treatment Methods

Curanderos are folk healers who use herbs and spirituality to treat the mystical or supernatural roots of psychological disturbance and physical ailments in indigenous people, *campesinos*, or laborers, and large sectors of urban populations (González Chévez, 2005). In modern Mexico, traditional healing is a cultural mix rooted in the Meso-American worldview, peninsular folk healing brought by the Spanish missionaries, as well as elements from the biomedical model. A *curandero* might make use of candles, a rosary, an altar, incense, praying in Spanish, massage, or ointments made from natural sources in their treatment (Davidson, 1993). True *curanderos* are believed to be "chosen" and receive further training through an apprenticeship process. *Boticas* and *farmacias* dispense non-prescription remedies for psychological and physical ailments.

Another approach to indigenous counseling with Latino clients has been to make use of cultural folk tales and proverbs in the counseling process. *Cuento therapy* (Costantino, Malgady, & Rogler, 1986; Malgady, Rogler, & Costantino, 1990) was developed as a treatment for young children that makes use of Puerto Rican folk tales, or *cuentos*. The *cuentos* have themes, for example, delay of gratification or controlling aggression, and are read, discussed, enacted, and videotaped, and summarized for full effect. *Cuentos* adapted to U.S. settings were found to be more effective,

Some Mexican *Dichos*, Translated Into English
(From R. Gonzales & Ruiz, 1995)

Getting up at dawn will not make the morning come sooner.

Experience is the Mama of science.

Pig out while you have the chance.

If you don't ride, you can't fall.

A good listener needs few words.

If you hang out with wolves you will learn how to howl.

A good rooster can crow anywhere.

After the rain comes the sun.

If you get wet early, you'll have time to dry off.

Small, but very hot.

When you use force, not even your shoes fit.

One bee doesn't make a hive.

Many littles make a lot.

You only visit the cactus when it is bearing fruit.

Sing every day and chase the mean blues away.

If you know how to swim you won't drown.

A lesson well learned is never forgotten.

Each head is a world of its own.

A painting is a poem without words.

compared to either their original Puerto Rican versions or art therapy. Similarly, Zuniga (1991) describes the use of *dichos,* or Spanish-language proverbs, for use with Latino clients. Some examples of *dichos* collected by Gonzales and Ruiz (1995) are included in the box above.

☐ Counseling Issues

Language and Acculturation

Language is a very important consideration when counseling Latinos and Latinas. English language use is an important component of acculturation and accounts for much of the variance attributed to acculturation (Rogler et al., 1991). One study found that Mexican Americans who were either bilingual or primarily English speaking perceived mental health issues no differently than Anglo Americans whereas those who were primarily Spanish speakers tended to believe mental illness was inherited and used more somatic attributes to describe mental problems (Edgerton & Karno, 1971). Mexican Americans who prefer to speak Spanish are more likely to be monolingual, born in Mexico, and have lower levels of education and stronger ties to religion than other Mexican Americans. The language(s) spoken is a key indicator of cultural traditionalism in Latinos, with Spanish-speaking-only clients tending to be more traditional. However, whatever languages they speak, it is important to note, Latino parents strongly encourage their children to speak both Spanish and English (Edgerton & Karno, 1971; Fernandez, 1989). Many second-generation Latinos and Latinas, although having spoken Spanish at home and being considered bilingual, may prefer to function in English, which they learned in school and via television (Sue & Sue, 1990).

Lijtmaer (1993) suggests that it is important to explore when and where a client learned English. If at all possible, give the client the choice of which language he or she wishes to use in counseling. In addition, the counselor may be able to make use of the client's bilingualism in therapeutic ways. For example, using a nonnative language may allow the client to temporarily separate from intense emotions. The counselor may use "language switching" to moderate the client's level of emotional involvement rather than freely allowing the client to choose the language used during sessions (Santiago-Rivera, 1995).

In addition to languages spoken, other important areas to assess are: socioeconomic status, religious training and current spiritual identification, politics, birthplace and immigration status, generational level of immigration, geographic location of ancestors (including any effects of continuing immigration, proximity of the mother country, etc.), level of acculturation, and experiences with prejudice or discrimination.

Adolescents

Baruth and Manning (2003) list several potential counseling issues that may come up for Latino adolescents: identity issues, effects of negative stereotypes, cultural value conflicts, struggle between individual advancement versus family commitments, failure to comply with traditional family roles, academic problems, language problems, developmental differences in height and weight, and the effects of racism and discrimination. Gang involvement among Latino youth may serve to give members a sense of identity (Curry & Spergel, 1992); however, Latinos and Latinas, in general, have a lower delinquency rate compared to that of the majority group in the United States (Lyon, Henggeler, & Hall, 1992).

Career Concerns

Given the lack of educational and economic success for many Latinos and Latinas, career counseling needs are great. Information about the world of work would be helpful in combating the tendency toward low educational goals, unrealistically high career goals, and less specific educational and career goals. When expectations are high, disappointment can be great, and many Latinos and Latinas leave the corporate world to start their own businesses, which further limits the potential role models available to new workers. Discrimination in the work world is also an important factor. One review suggests that when Blacks and Latinos are denied jobs, 15–20% of the time these same jobs were later offered to equally qualified Whites instead (Fendel, Hurtado, Long, & Giraldo, 1996).

Some suggestions for increasing the workforce participation of Latinos and Latinas include recruiting at minority job fairs, offering employer-paid training programs, sponsoring career events that feature popular musicians or athletes in order to draw a larger audience, and distributing information to a wider audience through ethnic clubs and ethnic studies departments on college campuses. Figueroa (1996) also added advertising jobs where they will be seen by a wider range of applicants, expanding internship and outreach programs, developing mentoring partnerships with inner-city schools, and providing educational scholarships as ways to increase the pool of qualified minority applicants.

There may be some conflict between workforce values and the personal values of the Latino or Latina. For example, traditional Latino values of community, cooperation, modesty, and hierarchical relationships do not mesh well with modern values of individualism, competition, achievement, and egalitarianism in many work environments. Also, effective communication in individual interpersonal relationships may differ from what is effective in management. Finally, prejudice and discrimination may make advancement and promotion in the workplace even more difficult.

Undocumented Workers

The Pew Hispanic Center (2005) estimates that there are between 11.5 and 12 million undocumented people in the United States: 56% from Mexico and 22% from the rest of Latin America, especially Central America. Undocumented persons have limited access to the job market as well as education and economic benefits. They live in fear of deportation and their lives are filled with caution and mistrust because anyone could report them. They are vulnerable to exploitation, blackmail, and pressure to work for substandard wages. Although the Immigration Reform and Control Act of 1986 declared an amnesty and allowed access to citizenship for many of these people, fear and distrust may have kept many from seeking amnesty. One suggestion for counseling this population is to provide training in problem-solving and social skills to combat stress and to increase social support. In addition, counselors need an understanding of immigration law to be maximally helpful with this population. Undocumented immigrants are ineligible for food stamps; however, they are eligible for emergency medical care and some programs for children. American-born children of undocumented persons are eligible for full educational and public assistance (Smart & Smart, 1995).

Other Counseling Issues

In terms of nonverbal communication, when counseling Latinos and Latinas, the counselor may want to decrease interpersonal distance by placing chairs a little closer together. Lapses in eye contact may signify respect rather than pathology and should be evaluated with the client's level of traditionalism in mind.

There are many barriers, both economic and psychological, to Latino and Latina clients getting counseling. Arranging childcare, forfeiting hourly wages, and lack of public transportation contribute to low utilization rates. Latinas, in particular, may approach counseling with mixed feelings of relief and embarrassment or apprehension inasmuch as self-disclosure by women outside the home may be discouraged in some Latino cultures (Arredondo, 1991). Similarly, Mexican Americans with a traditional cultural orientation may have some difficulty with being open and self-disclosing in the role of the client (Paniagua, 2005), *personalismo* notwithstanding. For clients with limited English proficiency, the use of translators brings a third person into the psychotherapeutic process, which may be disagreeable to the client (Paniagua, 2005).

Although clients rarely enter counseling stating that culture is a concern, cultural differences may have an impact on many presenting problems. It may be helpful for the counselor to help the client distinguish between individual difficulties in functioning and the effect of broader social problems on the client. A. Ruiz (1981) recommends examining external causes first, among them exposure to environmental toxins, fears of deportation or creditors, poverty, poor housing, lack of English facility, and difficulties in dealing with governmental agencies. Some suggestions that have been made regarding counseling Latinas, that would apply to Latinos as well, include identifying sources of personal and environmental stress, exploring the positive aspects of the client, locating community resources, and identifying specific cultural assets (Rodriguez-Nelson, 1993).

The counselor is advised to take a present-time orientation during counseling and to focus on getting the client current relief. The counselor's role might include listener, problem solver, advocate, and interpreter. Waiting a little longer in using confrontation with the client and in general proceeding slowly to allow trust to develop have been recommended when counseling Latinos and Latinas. In their review of the literature, D. W. Sue and D. Sue (1990) noted recommendations for active, concrete, problem-solving, behavioral, or cognitive behavioral approaches lasting four to five sessions.

The client may prefer an active orientation and direct advice; however, there is no evidence that Latinos and Latinas are not good candidates for gaining insight. Wampold, Casas, and Atkinson (1981) found a majority of practicing psychotherapists to have subtle stereotypic attitudes in which Latinos were perceived as lazy, unintelligent, unclean, and overemotional. Negative stereotypes may influence the counseling process and counselors should be especially wary of such counter-transference.

Family therapy has also been recommended, particularly structural family therapy, which complements the often hierarchical pattern of many Latino families (Sue & Sue, 1990). Although the mother may be the spokesperson for family, it is usually the father who holds the power. The family counselor is encouraged to be active, polite, willing to offer advice (Padilla, 1981), and nonconfrontational (Ho, 1987). However, family therapy may not work if the parents do not bring out issues for fear of being embarrassed in front of their children. In such cases it might be better to meet with parents and children separately.

Paniagua (2005) recommends that the counselor assess the family's level of acculturation in the first session. A traditional Latino family, for example, will value *machismo* and *marianismo*, but as members of the family become more acculturated, that value may change. The wife may desire to have a more egalitarian relationship with her husband or the young daughters may aspire to have professional careers outside the home. It would be a serious mistake for a therapist to strongly put out the idea that women should have the same kinds of opportunities as men in the first session. However, if a similar issue came up in a more acculturated family, the mother or the daughters might not feel supported if the counselor did not recognize and acknowledge their growing need for independence.

In summary, when counseling Latinos and Latinas, the counselor needs to be cognizant of the potential impact of cultural differences and external stresses on the client. Either an active individual approach or family therapy may be especially useful.

☐ Case Vignette

On May 1st, 2006, 17-year-old Silvia Cisneros walked off campus at her high school with a group of about 30 other students in support of the "Day Without Immigrants." All week students at her high school had been talking about how important it was to protest the Sensenbrenner Bill being discussed in Congress, which many Latinos believed would split up families. Silvia and her father were born in this country, and her mother is an immigrant. Silvia is very close to her grandparents and she knows that her grandparents entered the United States as undocumented workers many years ago. Silvia wanted to discuss the protest and the Sensenbrenner Bill with teachers at her school, but she wasn't close enough to any of them and none of the adults offered any discussion on the topic. The homeroom teachers had read a memo stating that any student who walked out of school would be considered truant and would be suspended from school.

Although Silvia had never stood out academically in school, she consistently scored at the top percentiles on standardized tests. Personal problems related to her parents' divorce kept her highly distracted and without focus. But when she heard talk about possible marches to protest the Sensenbrenner Bill, she felt personally connected to the issues. On the morning of May 1st, as soon as she walked onto campus, Silvia noticed the buzz among students whispering and nudging one another about what to do. Silvia found herself anxiously waiting for one of her peers to speak up, but no one felt comfortable saying much because of the presence of several school staff. In the cafeteria, Silvia nervously approached a group of students and asked them if they had thought about doing something to support the marches. An administrator overheard and quickly walked over to the group.

The informal gathering turned into a full meeting. Silvia switched to Spanish and asked the students whether anyone was going to do what they had been talking about all week, walk out and march in protest. She reminded the students as to the reasons why they had talked about doing this; it was for their families. When the group of about 20 students followed her lead, Silvia was surprised but happy. Other students quickly fell into place behind the initial group and a total of about 30 students left campus, followed by counselors and administrators. A student used her cell phone to call the local media and the group had walked only a few blocks when TV cameras and the local newspaper reporters showed up. Student protests and rallies were unheard of in the history of this farming town. Once the interviews with the media were over, the students returned to classes.

All day students kept coming up to Silvia to congratulate her for getting them to walk out. Silvia herself was in awe as she remembered how things had evolved. She had not planned on speaking out in favor of the march in front of her peers. And now her peers were congratulating her for having done so. Her peers were also impressed with how well Silvia spoke Spanish. Silvia felt flattered by the compliments, but she was more worried about how her father would react when he found out. He would disapprove of her having left school. Several days later she was suspended for having walked out of school.

Questions

1. What steps might counselors take to provide students with healthy outlets for self-expression, particularly with respect to social justice issues?

2. How can counselors work with youth such as Silvia who appear to be unmotivated academically, but who are obviously very bright?

3. What is the role of the counselor in this specific situation where schools knew that there was the very real possibility that students were going to walk out en masse?

Reflection 1

In this very interesting case, I can't help but be struck by the environmental dimension. It appears that school personnel had an understanding that a student walkout was likely. Instead of developing a punitive response, I would like to have seen the administrators be more proactive and adaptive in finding other, creative ways of responding. On a more personal level, it is understandable that Silvia (and many other students) acted as she did, and we likely could have predicted her behavior, given the strong influence of *familismo* in Latina (Latino) culture.

Refection 2

It's curious to see the strong interest generated by the pro-immigrant marches on students like Silvia who are not doing well academically. This event held much meaning for Silvia because she has family and friends who could potentially be affected by anti-immigrant legislation. Counselors might have foreseen the importance of this issue for students and helped to facilitate discussion of the topic by involving the students, teachers, and administrators. It seems that Silvia and other students wanted their voices heard. By providing classroom forums, allowing students to write in their journals, revisiting historical moments that would shed light on this issue, developing art projects where students can express how they feel, and other such activities, students can be helped to gain critical thinking skills, insight, and perspective not only for the issue at hand, but for their learning in general. The pro-immigrant marches represented a teachable moment, particularly for students who are turned off by school. At a personal level, Silvia received recognition from her peers in terms of her public speaking skills and her fluency in Spanish. These skills could be reinforced by school personnel, both in the classroom and in personal counseling, to help her build on these strengths. Whether we agree with a person's right to demonstrate for what he or she believes in, as counselors we can actively listen to our clients and try to understand their values and worldview.

☐ Recommended Cultural Resources

Print Media

Canales, V. (2005). *The tequila worm.* New York: Random House. A heartwarming story of a young Latina's coming of age and her stories growing up in the barrios.

Cull, N., & Carrasco, D. (Eds.). (2004). *Alambrista and the U.S.-Mexico border: Film, music and stories of undocumented immigrants.* Albuquerque, NM: University of New Mexico Press. Stories of undocumented immigrants.

Esquivel, L. (1992). *Like water for chocolate.* New York: Doubleday. Using a magical realism approach, the author incorporates an imaginative mix of recipes, home remedies, and the love story of Tita de la Garza, a young Mexican woman whose mother forbids her to marry the man she loves.

Gonzales, R., & Ruiz, A. (1995). *My first book of proverbs (Mi primer libro de dichos).* San Francisco: Children's Book Press. A humorous collection of popular Mexican-American sayings. Bilingual English/Spanish. Beautifully illustrated.

Hispanic Journal of Behavioral Sciences

Journal of Latinos and Education

Martinez, E. (1991). *500 Años del pueblo Latino: 500 Years of Chicano History in pictures.* Albuquerque, NM: Southwest Organizing Project.

Martinez, V. (1996). *Parrot in the oven: Mi vida.* New York: Harper Collins. Winner of the 1996 National Book Award in the Young People's Literature category, this is the story of 14-year-old Manny Hernandez's coming of age and the pressures of gangs, girls, and friends.

Rodriguez, L. T. (1993). *Always running: La vida loca.* New York: Simon & Schuster. Winner of the 15th Annual Carl Sandburg Literary Arts Award for Nonfiction, this book is the autobiography of poet Luis Rodriguez's coming of age amid the gangs of East L.A.

Shorris, E. (1992). *Latinos.* New York: W.W. Norton.

Urdaneta, M.L., Livingston, J., Aguilar, M., Enciso, V., & Kaye, C. (2002). *Understanding Mexican American cultural beliefs and traditional healing practices: A guide for genetic service providers on the U.S./Mexico border.* University of Texas Health Science Center at San Antonio/Department of Pediatrics.

Multimedia

Arau, A. (Director/Producer). (1992). *Like water for chocolate* [Videorecording/movie]. Based on the book of the same title by Laura Esquivel. The love story of Tita and Pedro and how Tita was not allowed to marry because she had to take care of her mother.

Arau, S. (Director), & Artenstein, I. (Producer). (2004). *A day without a Mexican* [DVD/Movie]. Inexplicably, one day California wakes up and not one Latino can be found.

Bieberman, Herbert J. (Director). (2004). *Salt of the earth* [Videorecording]. Narberth, PA: Alpha Video Distributors. A semidocumentary of the year-long 1950 struggle by Mexican American zinc miners in New Mexico. Produced at the height of the McCarthy era by a group of blacklisted filmmakers.

Blank, L. (Director), & Strachwitz, C. (Producer). (1994, 2003). *Chulas fronteras* [Videorecording/Movie]. El Cerrito, CA: Brazos Films. Features music and culture of Mexican Americans living in southern Texas.

Cardozo, P. (Director). (2003). *Real women have curves* [Videorecording/Movie]. U.S.A.: HBO Films. The story of a first-generation Mexican American teenager on the verge of becoming a woman.

De los Santos, N., Dominguez, A., & Racho, S. (Directors). (2002). *The bronze screen: 100 years of the Latino image in American cinema* [Videorecording/ Movie]. Chicago: Questar, Inc. Documentary on Latinos in Hollywood.

Galan, H. (Producer). (1996). *Chicano: History of Mexican American civil rights movement* (Series of 4 videorecordings). Los Angeles: National Latino Communications Center in association with KCET Los Angeles. Chronicles the struggles for equal rights by Mexican Americans. Part 1: Quest for a homeland; Part 2: The struggle in the field; Part 3: Taking back the schools; Part 4: Fighting for political power.

KPBS-TV (Producer), Espinosa, P. (Writer), & Christopher, F. (Director). (1985). *The Lemon Grove incident* [Videorecording/Movie]. New York: Cinema Guild. Documents one of the earliest cases of school desegregation involving Mexican Americans using dramatizations, archival footage, and recollections of witnesses. In English and Spanish with English subtitles.

Menéndez, R. (Writer/Director), & Musca, T. (Writer/Producer). (1988). *Stand and deliver* [Videorecording/Movie]. Burbank, CA: Warner Home Video. An inner-city minority teacher motivates marginal students to learn calculus and they do so well that the students are accused of cheating.

Perez, S. (Director). (1997). *And the earth did not swallow him* [Videorecording/ Movie]. New York: Kino International. Story of a young boy and his farmworker family, based on an adaption of Tomas Rivera's short novel ... *Y no se lo tragó la tierra (And the earth did not devour him)*, depicts Hispanic social/ religious values and the challenges of Latino migrant workers.

Redford, R., & Esparza, M. (Producers). (1993). *Milagro beanfield war* [Videorecording]. Universal City, CA: MCA Home Video. Nothing has changed in Milagro, New Mexico in the last 300 years, but now there are plans to build a major new resort at the expense of local Hispanic farmers. Won an Oscar.

Riker, David (Writer/Director). (2005). *La ciudad the city* [Videorecording/Movie]. New York: Zeitgist Films. The stories of four Hispanic immigrants living in New York.

Rodriguez, R. (Writer/Director). (2003). *El mariachi* [Videorecording/Movie]. Culver City, CA: DVD Video, Columbia Tristar Home Entertainment. A traveling mariachi looking for work in a new town is mistakenly thought to be a criminal.

Southwest Organizing Project and Collision Course Video Productions (Producers). (1995). *Viva la causa: 500 years of Chicano history* (2-part series of videorecordings). San Francisco: Collision Course Video Productions; Albuquerque, N.M.: Southwest Organizing Project (Distributor). Based on the book by Elizabeth Martinez.

Valdez, L. (Writer/director). (1998). *La bamba* [Videorecording/Movie]. Culver City, CA: Columbia Tristar Home Entertainment. Biographical story of the life of singer Ritchie Valens.

Valdez, L. (Writer/director). (2003). *Zoot suit* [Videorecording/Movie]. Universal City, CA: Universal Pictures. Part fact and part fiction, *Zoot Suit* is the film version of Luis Valdez's critically acclaimed play, based on the Sleepy Lagoon murder case and the zoot suit riots of the 1940s in Los Angeles.

Ya Basta! (Director/Producer). (2001). *Hijos del silencio (Sons of silence)* [Videorecording/Movie]. San Francisco: Q Action. Based on the book by Jose Antonio Martinez Coronel. Interviews with young gay Latino men regarding their families, coming out, and sex. Examines the cultural silences that affect safe sex practices.

10

CHAPTER

Asian and Pacific Islander Americans in Counseling

Asians are silent people
Never speaking of distress
Bearing much in their heart
The burden of the silent one.

Standing up to their rights
Trying to prove loyal by working hard.
America, a place of hopes …
For White people only!

Leah Appel, elementary school student
(Sue, 1973, p. 398)

☐ Histories and Diversity

Asian Americans are people of Asian ethnicity who are making their home in the United States. They are a very diverse group. Chinese, Japanese, Koreans, Filipinos, Malays, Vietnamese, Cambodians, Laotians, Hmong, and Mien living in the United States are among the many ethnic groups categorized as Asian American. Depending on the classification system used, Hawaiians, Samoans, Guamanians/Chamorro, Tongans, and Fijians (all Pacific Islanders), and South Asian Indians are also included. The history of Pacific Islanders in the United States and their cultural traditions are in many ways more similar to those of Native Americans than to those of Asian Americans, and classifying these peoples with Asian Americans is often a matter of convention rather than utility. Among Asian American women, more Hawaiian women, 16.7%, live in poverty than do women of any other Asian American ethnic group (Caiazza, Shaw, & Werschkul, 2004). Although there are a few references to Pacific Islander Americans in this chapter, the reader is also referred to Chapter 7, "Native Americans in Counseling," for further material that may be relevant when counseling Pacific Islander Americans.

In 2001, 12.5 million Asian Americans lived in the United States, making up 4.4% of the population (U.S. Census Bureau, 2003). Asian Americans are the second fastest-growing ethnic group in the United Status, with only the Latino population growing more quickly (Texeira, 2005). From 1990 to 2000, the Asian American population increased at least 48%, compared to an overall U.S. population increase of 13% (Barnes & Bennett, 2002). Estimates range from 30 to 50 different cultural subgroups of Asian Americans (in part depending upon whether Pacific Islanders are included). The most populous subgroups are the Chinese, Filipinos, and Asian Indians, who, combined, make up 57% of all Asian Americans (Barnes & Bennett, 2002). The Chinese, Japanese, and Filipinos were the earliest Asian ethnic groups to begin immigrating to the United States in the 19th century. Many other groups followed, with a large number of Southeast Asians arriving after 1975. Because of recent immigration, the majority of any Asian American subgroup is foreign born, except for Japanese Americans (Sue & Sue, 1995).

To make any generalizations about Asian Americans is extremely difficult, given the variety of ethnic groups included under the designation and the changes in migration patterns that the population continues to undergo. The diversity within Asian American subgroups is dramatic. For example, Asian American women earn both the highest and lowest hourly wages among all U.S. women (Cohen, 2002). Among Asian American women, Japanese, Asian Indian, and Chinese women have the highest earnings and Hawaiian/Pacific Islander and Vietnamese have the lowest. Japanese American women earned $39,300 per annum, even more than White women who earned $30,900 per annum, but Vietnamese American women earned only $26,500 (Caiazza et al., 2004).

The history of each ethnic group, including dates and circumstances of immigration/refugee resettlement and ensuing treatment within the United States, is entirely different. For example, the forced

internment of 110,000 Japanese Americans for up to five years without due process of law during World War II is an integral part of the
history of Japanese Americans as a group (Tomine, 1991). This traumatic experience still affects not only the elderly adult survivors of the
camps, but also the families they have raised. Another example is the
devastating level of war atrocities and refugee camp experiences of many
Southeast Asian Americans, particularly, according to Rumbaut (1985),
the Hmong and Cambodians, for whom post-traumatic stress symptoms
may go unnoticed by individuals themselves because they are so common within a community.

In addition, any two Asian Americans may differ in degree of
acculturation, English fluency, socioeconomic status, and education.
Unfortunately, more of the available literature in counseling and psychology related to Asian and Pacific Islander Americans has been written
about Chinese and Japanese Americans than any of the other groups.
However, all Asian Americans in the United States may be subjected to
racism (see box on page 162). Asian American youth are sometimes subjected to ethnic slurs, intimidation, or beating in schools and such racism
may be worsening. Some young Asian Americans join gangs or carry
weapons for protection (Texeira, 2005). One study found that 11.5% of
Vietnamese Americans reported being discriminated against by teachers,
more than for any other immigrant or refugee group studied, including
all other Asian American subgroups (Hobbs, 2000) and in other studies, Southeast Asian students experienced more past discrimination and
expected more future discrimination than other immigrant and refugee
groups (Rumbaut, 1999).

Social Class Considerations

More Asian and Pacific Islander families have annual incomes above
$75,000 than do non-Hispanic White familes yet more Asian and Pacific
Islander familes also have annual incomes below $25,000 (Reeves &
Bennett, 2003). Ten percent of Asian and Pacific Islander Americans live
in poverty, compared to 8% of non-Hispanic White Americans (Reeves
& Bennett, 2003). Similarly, statistics indicate that earnings are higher
while at the same time poverty rates are higher for Asian American
women compared to White women (Caiazza et al., 2004). Among ethnic groups in the United States, Asian Indians have the highest level
of education and median Socioeconomic Index (SEI) score, a measure
of occupational prestige among workers, whereas Cambodians, Hmong,
and Laotians have the least education and the lowest median SEI score

Chronology of Asian American Immigration
and Ethnic Discrimination

1848 Gold discovered in California. Chinese begin to arrive in numbers.

1854 *People v. Hall* rules that Chinese may not testify in court.

1858 California passes a law to bar entry of Chinese and "Mongolians."

1865 Central Pacific Railroad Co. recruits Chinese workers for the transcontinental railroad.

1869 Several dozen Japanese taken to California to establish the Wakamatsu Tea and Silk Colony.

1872 California's Civil Procedure Code drops law barring Chinese court testimony.

1878 *In re Ah Yup* rules Chinese not eligible for naturalized citizenship.

1880 Section 69 of California's Civil Code prohibits issuing of licenses for marriages between whites and "Mongolians, Negroes, mulattoes and persons of mixed blood."

1882 Chinese Exclusion Law suspends immigration of laborers for 10 years. Renewed in 1892, 1902, and made indefinite and applicable to U.S. possessions as well in 1904.

1894 U.S. circuit court in Massachusetts declares in *In re Saito* that Japanese are ineligible for naturalization.

1898 *Wong Kim Ark v. U.S.* decides that Chinese born in the United States cannot be stripped of their citizenship. United States annexes Hawaii and the Philippines.

1903 First group of Korean workers arrives in Hawaii.

1907 First group of Filipino laborers arrives in Hawaii.

1913 California passes alien land law prohibiting "aliens ineligible to citizenship" from buying land or leasing it for longer than three years. Over the next 10 years, Arizona, Washington, Louisiana, New Mexico, Idaho, Montana, and Oregon follow.

1922 Cable Act declares that any American female citizen who marries "an alien ineligible to citizenship" would lose her citizenship.

continued on next page

Chronology of Asian American Immigration and Ethnic Discrimination
continued from previous page

1923 *U.S. v. Bhagat Singh Thind* declares Asian Indians not eligible for naturalized citizenship. *Frick v. Webb* forbids aliens "ineligible to citizenship" from owning stocks in corporations formed for farming.

1924 Immigration Act denies entry to virtually all Asians.

1941 After declaring war on Japan, 2000 Japanese community leaders along Pacific Coast states and Hawaii are rounded up and interned in Department of Justice camps.

1942 President Franklin D. Roosevelt signs Executive Order 9066 authorizing the secretary of war to delegate a military commander to designate military areas "from which any and all persons may be excluded," primarily enforced against Japanese. Congress passes Public Law 503 to impose penal sanctions on anyone disobeying orders to carry out Executive Order 9066.

1944 Draft reinstated for Nisei. 442nd Regimental Combat Team gains fame. Exclusion orders revoked.

1956 California repeals its alien land laws.

1965 Immigration Law abolishes "national origins" as basis for allocating immigration quotas to various countries; Asian countries now on equal footing.

1975 More than 130,000 refugees enter the United States from Vietnam, Kampuchea, and Laos as Communist governments are established there.

1976 President Gerald Ford rescinds Executive Order 9066.

1978 Massive exodus of "boat people" from Vietnam.

1981 Commission on Wartime Relocation and Internment of Civilians (set up by Congress) concludes the internment was a "grave injustice" and that Executive Order 9066 resulted from "race prejudice, war hysteria and a failure of political leadership."

1986 Immigration Reform and Control Act imposes civil and criminal penalties on employers who knowingly hire undocumented aliens.

1989 President George Bush signs into law an entitlement program to pay each surviving Japanese American internee $20,000.

Note: Adapted from Chan (1991).

(C. N. Le, 2006b). These data underscore the vast diversity among Asian Americans with respect to their economic circumstances related to educational attainment and immigration status.

☐ Cultural Values

Many Asian cultures are influenced by the philosophies of Confucianism, Buddhism, and Taoism. Among the values that appear common to many Asian cultures are those of harmony; humility; and respect for family, authority, and tradition. Within the United States, however, there are also many Asian Americans who are Catholic (mostly Filipinos and Vietnamese) or Protestant (Koreans) (C. N. Le, 2006a).

Harmony is a widely held value in many Asian cultures. To promote interpersonal harmony, emotional restraint and indirect communication as opposed to confrontation are often preferred (Homma-True, 1990; Huang, 1994; Mattson, 1993). The Buddhist concept of moderation is valued by some Asian Americans, and humility is valued over competitive pride. For example, at times it might be preferable to take second place in a contest rather than first, because this facilitates interpersonal harmony, does not provoke as much envy from others, and does not embarrass others that their performance was inferior. Similarly, moderation of affect may be valued as a means of expressing intrapersonal harmony, and in a counseling setting this can result in a client's problems being understated or ignored.

The Confucian notion of filial piety teaches respect and obedience to authority figures beginning with the males in the family (Cerhan, 1990). The family in general, including extended family, is often highly valued in Asian cultures (Homma-True, 1990; Kitano, 1989). Hierarchical relationships within and without the family are prevalent (Kitano, 1989). The significance of roles in interpersonal relationships is very important, and birth order and sex roles are strongly emphasized (Huang, 1994). The group often takes precedence over the needs of the individual. For example, when emphasis is placed on education, as in many Asian cultures, its purpose may be more to directly increase the status and wealth of the family as a whole, not to advance one's individual career, as is more common in northern European American families. The societal group focus also tends to emphasize dependency and respect for authority as compared to independence and egalitarian relationships. As part of a respect for authority, some Asian Americans may expect advice or specific direction from their counselor. Internal means of control, such as guilt, shame, obligation, and duty, rather than individual freedom of choice and expression, also are more valued in many Asian cultures. In a related fashion, the concept of dating and choosing one's spouse does not exist in some Asian cultures where arranged marriages are traditional; so when a first- or second-generation Asian American dates, the relationship may be taken very seriously by the individual or her or his family.

The extended family as well as the nuclear family are important. In many Asian cultures a sense of the time continuum includes past and future generations, not just present family. Sometimes comparisons are made by parents, aunts, uncles, or grandparents between a client and someone else in her or his extended family as an indirect form of motivation. The family counselor should consider including extended family members, especially if they are living in the same household.

A more passive (listening, observing) versus active (doing, experimenting) approach to learning is typical in some Asian cultures, and this has implications for counseling. Counseling techniques that demand more activity from the client during the session—for example, role playing or hitting a pillow—may be less comfortable for some Asian Americans.

An especially important point to note is that each Asian culture is different in its values, and greater familiarity with a particular culture is important to understanding the values a client may bring to the counseling setting. In Japanese culture, for example, the concept of "self" may have multiple facets: an interactional self, an inner self, and a boundless self (Yamaguchi, 1995). Behavior may change on the basis of the social context without threatening an individual's coherent sense of self. Thus, a client's behavior may appear as more inconsistent, unpredictable, or inscrutable to a counselor who is unaware of Japanese cultural viewpoints.

One Japanese value has been termed *enryo,* or not dominating others in a social situation. Hesitancy to speak up in class or to contradict someone in authority and devaluing or disparaging oneself, one's children, or one's possessions to others so others will not feel inadequate are examples of *enryo* (Uba, 1994). *Enryo* can easily be mistaken by a counselor who is unaware of Japanese culture as passivity or low self-esteem. Another Japanese value is that of *gaman,* meaning the endurance of hardships (Kristof, 1996). This value has been offered as a possible explanation of the low rate of divorce in Japan. The somewhat fatalistic orientation of some Japanese to problems, called *shikata ga-nai*—literally, "it cannot be helped" (Kitano, 1981)—may originate in a Buddhist attitude toward living life without struggle. In the worst case, *shikata ga-nai*, when combined with *gaman,* may render a victim of spousal abuse dangerously resistant to leaving a violent relationship.

One sample of Asian American practitioners identified the cultural values they felt were most important to understand when counseling Asian American clients. These were, in descending order of importance (as summarized by Uba, 1994):

- Importance of family

- Shame and guilt

- Respect for others based on their role and status

- Interpersonal styles of behavior

- Stigma of mental illness

- Restraint of self-expression

- Group orientation

- Achievement

- Sense of duty and obligation

- Role expectations

☐ Indigenous Treatment Methods

Traditionally, many Asian Americans may believe that hard work, effort, and character development are the best cure for mental disorders (Kitano, 1989). Handling problems through internalization has been described as common for Japanese Americans (Kitano, 1981), and it may be frequent for other Asian Americans as well. Keeping active also is often viewed as helpful (Homma-True, 1990), and behavioral counseling techniques are culturally consistent with this view.

One view of mental illness in many Asian cultures is that it is related to organic factors, and physical remedies may be expected (Kitano, 1989). Because many Asian cultures do not promote a mind–body dichotomy, a concept that is more common from a Western view, somatic symptoms are often reported and may be indicative of concurrent psychological disorders (Homma-True, 1990; Mattson, 1993).

Family support is a form of treatment. Asian Indian psychiatrists may combine drugs, spiritual advice, and family counseling in treating schizophrenia and there is some evidence that living with families and working in low-stress jobs has proven more effective for this diagnosis in India than in more Western cultures such as the United States. Family support can help in getting work as well as monitoring dosages and ensuring medication compliance (Vedantam, 2005).

Many first-generation and more traditional Asian Americans may turn to indigenous cultural healers and remedies when distressed. Much diversity exists within Asian cultures as to whom they will go to seek assistance outside the family. Some Hmong may seek out herbalists or shamans, who may use herbal remedies, animal sacrifices, or other religious rituals (Cerhan, 1990; Kitano, 1989). Some Lao (Bliatout and colleagues, cited in Kitano, 1989) and Vietnamese (State of California Department of Mental Health, 1981b) may consult Buddhist monks, whereas other Vietnamese may opt to consult Catholic priests (State of California Department of Mental Health, 1981b) or Taoist scholars (Bliatout et al., cited in Kitano, 1989). Acupuncture, massage, fortune telling, and physiognomy (reading palms and facial features) also are among the folk remedies used by Southeast Asian Americans (Chung & Okazaki, 1991). See Das (1987) for a review of the folk, mystical, and medical traditions of Buddhist, Hindu, and Islamic societies. Thai traditional healers have been discussed by Hiegel (1983). In general, C. C. Lee and Armstrong (1995) recommended working in conjunction with traditional healers in a concerted effort to assist clients.

There has been limited discussion of Asian cultural concepts in Western psychological literature. Okonogi (1978) described the *Ajase complex*, which is based on Buddhist writings and focuses on the consequences of a strong mother–child relationship and forgiveness after conflict. In an interestingly related manner, Doi (cited in Homma-True, 1990) described the Japanese concept of *amae* as the intense dependence of a child on her or his mother.

Morita therapy also incorporates the mother–child relationship through the acknowledgment of client indebtedness to significant people in her or his life. This therapy is based on the work of Shoma Morita of Japan and emphasizes the recognition and acceptance of feelings. Clients are assumed not to be able to control their feelings and are not responsible for them (Willms, 1990). Morita therapy has been adapted for use in the United States and is called *constructive living*. It has been compared to rational-emotive therapy and other cognitive therapies (Ishiyama, 1990; Le Vine, 1993) and, although the focus is on altering thoughts, the emphasis is more on constructive actions rather than regulating feelings as the goal. Morita therapy, like client-centered counseling (Rogers, 1951), promotes the acceptance of subjective experiences and, like existential therapy (Frankl, 1978), the concept of facing anxiety and taking responsibility for life choices is central. Morita therapy incorporates some Zen Buddhist philosophy in guarding against too much effort as being possibly immobilizing rather than successful. One example given (Ishiyama, 1990) is that of a donkey tied to a post. The donkey can get tangled in its own attempts to walk around the post in order to get free, or it could graze freely around the post without becoming trapped. Morita therapy interventions are confrontational with the goal of "anxious action taking" as preferable to inaction.

There are many other indigenous treatment approaches. *Naikan therapy* has been described as group centered, ritualistic, behavioristic, and focused on the here and now (Kitano, 1989). A group-oriented indigenous approach is the Samoan *fa'a aiga* family unity process (State of California Department of Mental Health, 1981a). In this process, a leader entreats all family and community members affected by the client's problems to meet. At the meeting, prayers are said; the problem is identified; each person discusses the problem; and errors by the client are admitted, repented, and forgiven. Restitution may be made as well. Chung and Okazaki (1991) suggested using folk tales with Eastern concepts and philosophies (see box on facing page for examples) as a culturally consistent technique in counseling Southeast Asian Americans. These folk tales could be integral within the counseling process a lá Milton Erickson (Haley, 1973).

☐ Counseling Issues

Spirituality

Buddhist, Confucian, Taoist, Shinto, and Catholic spiritual views underlie many of the beliefs of Asian Americans toward mental health, as mentioned previously, and this should be considered in forming treatment plans. For example, Taoist spirituality emphasizes the harmony between yin and yang, the female and male, dark and light, passive and active aspects of life. Avoiding direct confrontation and respecting the natural course of events also are part of the philosophy. This suggests that client-centered counseling (Rogers, 1951) might be a complementary approach for counseling someone with Taoist beliefs, because the process of self-actualization may assist in releasing the natural tao in the client.

Two Chinese Folk Tales

The Story of the Bamboo

During a fierce storm, the bamboo bends every which way the wind blows, while the other trees (e.g., oak) stand straight and resist the wind. But after the storm the bamboo tree stands proudly, looking into the heavens and reaching for life, dreams, and hopes. The other trees lie on the ground lifeless and without hope because they resisted the wind; they were not flexible and did not move with the wind.

The Frog

A frog sitting at the bottom of a well looks up toward the opening of the well and asks, "Oh! That's the size of the sky?" In reality the frog will not know how big the sky is until it steps out of the well. The frog in a well is limited in its knowledge by a narrow vision.

Note: Adapted by Chung and Okazaki (1991).

This approach also tends to minimize confrontation and, through unconditional positive regard, accepts the natural course of the client's life.

Many Cambodians put great importance on the attainment of personal spiritual enlightenment in accord with Thervada Buddhism, whereas many Laotians believe in animism, in which gods and spirits pervade much of daily life (Chung & Okazaki, 1991). Relaxation or visualization techniques may be helpful in counseling some of these clients. Engaging in spiritual activities is often the self-help remedy chosen by Cambodians in America (D'Avanzo, Frye, & Froman, 1994). Given the diversity within the Asian American population, spending some time early in the counseling process to explore the spiritual beliefs of the individual client is paramount in order to avoid stereotyping that could negatively affect treatment planning.

Myth of the Model Minority

The academic and economic success of Asian Americans as a group has led to Asian Americans sometimes being described as the "model minority." According to the 2000 U.S. Census, 25.2% of Asian Americans aged 25 and over held bachelor's degrees or higher, compared with 15.5% of Americans overall (Yang, 2004). However, a high level of education is not uniform for all Asian American subgroups. For example, the proportion of people with bachelor's degrees ranged from only 5.9% to 14.8% among Southeast Asian American subgroups, proportions that are more similar to those of African Americans, Latinos, and Native Americans, than those of Asian Americans in general (Yang, 2004).

The positive stereotype of Asian Americans being successful can have damaging repercussions. On a societal level, this stereotype suggests an erroneous notion that any minority can (and should) succeed if the members work hard enough. Also, the model minority myth separates Asian Americans from other ethnic minority groups by pointing them out as an example to others (Sue & Sue, 1990). Indeed, there have been suggestions of "white flight," white families moving their children out of schools with substantial proportions of Asian American students because of stereotyped perceptions that Asian American students are excessively competitive and too academically driven, focusing on math and science and ignoring other subjects such as liberal arts, extracurricular activities, or sports (Hwang, 2005). Finally, in many instances Asian Americans are not categorized as a minority group and are not eligible for affirmative action programs (Sue & Sue, 1995), even though specific subgroups of Asian Americans may be underrepresented in terms of graduation, employment, or promotion rates.

On an individual level, teachers may not only have higher expectations of Asian Americans, but they also may judge them more negatively when they do misbehave or fail to achieve, and other students may be hostile toward them because of their reputation as good students (Baruth & Manning, 1991). Individuals with problems or concerns counter to the positive stereotype may be ignored (Fendel et al., 1996). Counselors may neglect to assess Asian Americans for substance abuse, teen pregnancy, domestic violence, and so on.

In order to allow their children to receive what they feel are superior educational experiences, affluent parents from some Asian countries, Taiwan in particular (P. Le, 1996), may split up their family in order to send their children to school in the United States. Children may be living with a grandparent, with only their mother while their father remains in Asia, or even with a paid guardian, all situations that could potentially be emotionally stressful in themselves for students and put additional pressure on them to do well in school. In addition, schoolwork may be a source of stress for some Asian American students who face family expectations to support their parents and other family members as soon as they graduate. This may not only put excessive pressure on them for academic success, but it may also affect their choice of field of study and subsequent career satisfaction (Scott-Blair, 1986).

Mordkowitz and Ginsburg (1986) attributed the academic success of Asian Americans to what they termed *academic socialization*, meaning a combination of authoritative families, high expectations, emphasis on effort, supervision of children's time, allocation of resources for educational purposes, and reinforcement of beliefs and behaviors conducive to learning. In this interview study of Asian American college students at a prestigious university, families placed studying as the students' principal obligation and limited other chores expected of them. The other side of academic success, however, could be social discomfort, as these same families seemed to engage in little family conversation, discourage inviting guests into the home, and compare their children's performance to exemplary others. Another explanation of the higher average grades of Asian Americans may be attributed to increased time spent studying at the expense of leisure time or social relationships.

Career Concerns

Effort and family pride may be more important to many Asian American families than individual interests. One review of the literature on the career development of Asian Americans concluded that as a group they are more field dependent and segregated in their occupational choices, less tolerant of ambiguity, and more socially anxious than European Americans. Being *field dependent* means that external factors such as security, money, and status play a large role in vocational choice (Leong, 1991). Asian Americans tend to cluster in computer science, engineering, pre-med, and business majors. Underrepresentation of Asian Americans in certain majors and subsequent occupations may be due to several influences: demonstrative self-expression is not encouraged in many Asian cultures, counselors may unintentionally steer students toward sciences because of stereotypical notions of their aptitudes, and some Asian Americans may choose technical career fields in which more objective evaluation occurs and discrimination may be more easily avoided (Sue & Sue, 1995).

A frequent issue in career counseling with Asian Americans may be a mismatch between a vocation chosen for external factors and contradictory individual interests or aptitudes. A counselor assisting an Asian American client with such an issue is cautioned not to mistake what may be a collectivist decision-making style that takes family concerns into account as being an overly dependent style (Leong, 1991). One-third of students of Asian descent taking the SAT intend to seek vocational counseling, more than any other ethnic group (Leong, 1991). This may indicate a perception of vocational counseling as relevant to educational goals and an acknowledgment of the increased complexity of career decision making for Asian Americans. There is great potential for a counselor to make a significant difference in the lives of Asian American clients through skillful handling of career issues.

For Asian Americans already participating in the workforce, still other counseling issues may arise, such as discrimination in hiring or advancement or role strain for Asian American women. Each year of college education yields an additional $522 per year in earnings for White Americans, whereas Japanese Americans earn only an additional $438 yearly and Chinese Americans only $320 (R. Jiobu, cited in Chan, 1991). Similarly, Asian-Pacific Islanders with college degrees have average earnings 26% less than the average earnings of Whites with similar degrees (Fendel et al., 1996).

Although a larger percentage of Asian American women work compared to other ethnic groups in the United States, the stereotype of Asian American women as "hardworking, uncomplaining handmaidens" (Homma-True, 1990) may result in being exploited at work or denied promotions. Asian American women are disproportionately represented in some low-wage occupations such as garment industry sweatshops and high-tech microchip manufacturing, and domestic work (Caiazza et al., 2004). Some employers may hire Asian American workers under the stereotypic notion that they may be less likely to protest poor working conditions and are adaptable to tedious and repetitive work (Foo, 2003). Asian American women who believe strongly in their duty to be homemakers may more keenly experience the discomfort of role strain between their career and family obligations that is common among working women (Homma-True, 1990).

Other Counseling Implications

When Asian Americans seek counseling they may present with more severe symptoms and are more likely to utilize outpatient or day treatment programs than inpatient services (Chen, Sullivan, Lu, & Shibusawa, 2003). They continue to be underrepresented in mental health treatment. The stigma attached to psychological problems may contribute to these tendencies. However, once treatment has begun, Asian Americans may have lower dropout rates and stay in treatment longer, especially if the services are ethnic specific (Lau & Zane, 2000).

During the initial assessment phase of counseling some Asian Americans may appear to be doing more "complaining" than seeking help, which could be indicative of a more fatalistic, accepting approach to life. For some Asian Americans personal problems may come up only indirectly whereas physical, school, or vocational difficulties are readily discussed. W. M. Lee and Mixson (1995) noted the need for counselors to address presenting academic or career problems and simultaneously reduce client reluctance to deal with personal concerns. Because so many Asian Americans are born outside the United States and are experiencing cultural transition, intergenerational conflicts are especially common, including difficulties in communication, struggles over moving out of the family home, and interracial relationships.

Berg and Miller (1992) recommended emphasizing the client's goal during the first meeting, because many Asian Americans, like members of many other ethnic minority groups, are focused on problem solving and are not likely to stay in extended treatment otherwise. Relationship questions are suggested as a way to elicit information about the client's worldview and her or his view of others' perceptions of them. An example of a relationship question would be, "What do you think (fill in name) would say he or she likes about you?"

Because interpersonal relationships are often defined by roles, clients may be more comfortable once roles have been clearly established. The counselor, for example, is in a role of authority and expertise. Silence and avoidance of eye contact could be signs of respect from an Asian American client. A client may express agreement in order to be polite when he or she really does not agree with or does not understand the counselor and instead may not return for another session. Once counseling has begun, client transference regarding age or sex may be more likely because of the importance of such distinctions and roles in many Asian cultures.

Several authors have written about culturally consistent counseling approaches for Asian Americans. Homma-True (1990) summarized the recommendations to include the following.

1. Use bilingual–bicultural counselors whenever possible.

2. Respect the client's reluctance to express him- or herself verbally or emotionally.

3. Be attuned to somatic complaints as potential indicators of psychological distress.

4. Focus on issues within the context of the family.

5. Consider taking a more active role in the sessions.

6. Take an educational or informational approach.

Other counseling recommendations have included use of behavioral counseling, structured family therapy, assertiveness training, communication skills training, cognitive therapy (especially Morita therapy), supportive therapy, client-centered therapy, and role exploration (e.g., life script). When counseling families, M. K. Ho (1987) recommended addressing the parents first, which heightens the role differentiation in the family and is consistent with the hierarchical family structure of many Asian cultures. Berg and Miller (1992) recommended discussing exceptions to the problem when counseling Asian Americans as this helps the client "save face" and provides information about the client's strengths for further development.

Some caveats also have been raised regarding what not to do in counseling with most Asian Americans:

1. Avoid putting the client at odds with her or his family.

2. Traditional group therapy is not recommended (Kitano, 1989; Nakao & Lum, 1977); however, when appropriate, use a support group (Mattson, 1993).

3. Be generally cautious with psychodynamic, Gestalt, and confrontational approaches (Nakao & Lum, 1977) or approaches that seem to demand expression of feelings.

☐ Case Vignette

Charlie is a 21-year-old, heterosexual, second-generation Chinese American student at a respected state university. He was referred to the university counseling center because he was on probation with a C– average in his chemistry major. At his first session Charlie related that he was pre-med because his parents wanted him to become a doctor. He felt depressed and hopeless because he might not be able to graduate in the next semester. He did his best and studied hard, but found the course work challenging and had struggled to get the mediocre grades he had earned. Charlie was interested in science and thought it would be great to be a crime scene investigator, as in the *Crime Scene Investigation (CSI)* television show he liked to watch.

The counselor worked with Charlie on study skills and time management and after many months Charlie got himself off probation and was eligible to graduate. At the graduation ceremony, he introduced the counselor to his parents. They spoke proudly about Charlie's older sister who was in graduate school earning her MBA and barely mentioned Charlie in the conversation at all.

Questions

1. What cultural influences (e.g., model minority myth) may be relevant to Charlie's situation?

2. Would you as the counselor treat Charlie any differently if he were seen in a community mental health clinic setting? Would you include Charlie's family in the counseling and, if so, how?

3. What diagnosis would you give Charlie?

Reflection 1

This case presents an interesting confluence of academic, career, and personal/social dimensions. It seems that Charlie chose the pre-med field based on what his parents wanted him to do, which is understandable given the high value that family has in his culture. I might begin working with this client by exploring career issues as a way to build trust. How important is it for Charlie to have a high-status career such as being a medical doctor? At the same time, does the the pressure to excel come from the model minority myth that is so prevalent in society? With time, I would hope that the client could explore personal/social dimensions such as being a second-generation Chinese American and how his values may or may not be different from those of his parents. It may be important for Charlie to explore what he thinks about his parents barely mentioning his accomplishments on such an important event as graduation, while speaking proudly about his older sister working on her MBA. I would also want to check with Charlie to see if he might feel more comfortable receiving services from a counselor of similar ethnic background or at a mental health clinic in his community, which could be a very appropriate setting for family counseling to take place, if Charlie and his parents were open to that idea.

Reflection 2

Charlie has been negatively affected by the model minority myth as his lack of success with science courses may seem surprising to teachers and parents who may expect him to have an easy time with such subjects because academic success is common among Asian Americans. If Charlie were in a community clinic and not a college counseling center, family therapy might be appropriate to help his family set realistic expectations for his academic life and find a valuable place for Charlie within the family. In individual counseling, Charlie can explore his reactions to his parents' expectations and disappointment, especially compared to his sister, and develop his own realistic career goals. No psychiatric diagnosis is relevant for Charlie as he is experiencing a normal range of emotions and successes.

☐ Recommended Cultural Resources

Print Media

Buck, P. S. (1958). *The good earth*. New York: Pocket Books. Epic classic about a poor Chinese farmer and his wife who have a family and become rich, written by a Pulitzer Prize-winning author to increase cultural understanding.

Carlson, L. M. (Ed.). (1994). *American eyes: New Asian-American short stories for young adults*. New York: Holt. Ten short stories for young people about the conflicts faced in balancing ethnic heritage and modern culture.

Han, A., & Hsu, J. (Eds.). (2004). *Asian American X : An intersection of 21st century Asian American voices*. Ann Arbor: University of Michigan Press. A collection of stories by Asian Americans.

Kingston, M. H. (1989). *The woman warrior: Memoirs of a girlhood among ghosts*. New York: Vintage Books. Passionately written memoir of a Chinese American woman who grew up in Stockton, CA, with her mother's stories of warriors and ghosts and her own experiences being Chinese in America.

Okada, J. (1979). *No-no boy*. Seattle: University of Washington Press. Powerful description of the effects of internment on Japanese American families through the experience of one.

Proudfoot, R. (1990). *Even the birds don't sound the same here: The Laotian refugees' search for heart in American culture*. New York: Peter Lang. Poignant description of the facts and experiences that have shaped Laotian refugee communities and the impact of these people on the author.

Yep, L. (Ed.). (1993). *American dragons: Twenty-five Asian American voices*. New York: HarperCollins. A children's book of short stories, poems, and play excerpts from plays about growing up Asian American.

Multimedia

Hegyes, S., & Waddell, R. L. (Producers). (1995). *Double happiness* [Videorecording]. Los Angeles: New Line Home Video. Generations and cultures collide in this comedy about a young Chinese woman struggling to satisfy both her traditionalist father and her modern dreams.

Hope, T., Schamus, J., & Lee, A. (Producers). (1994). *The wedding banquet* [Videorecording]. Beverly Hills, CA: Fox Video. Comedy about a gay Taiwanese man who tells his parents he is engaged to end their match-making efforts only to find that they fly to New York to meet the bride and plan the wedding.

Ina, S. (Producer). (1999). *Children of the camps* [Videorecording]. San Francisco: Center for Asian American Media (CAAM). Vivid documentary telling the stories of six adults who were children during the WWII internment of Japanese Americans in concentration camps and the impact of the experience in their lives.

Onodera, L., & Mark, D. M. L. (Producers). (1995). *Picture bride* [Videorecording]. Burbank, CA: Miramax Home Entertainment. Story of a young, beautiful Japanese woman who marries a man in Hawaii (known to her only from his picture) and her life in America.

Nozik, M., & Fair, M. (Producers), & Fair, M. (Director). (1992). *Mississippi masala* [Videorecording]. Burbank, CA: Columbia TriStar Home Video. Interracial love story about an African American small business owner and an Asian Indian immigrant who meet resistance from both their families.

Ridzon, C. (Producer). (2001). *Silent sacrifices: Voices of the Filipino American family/ Patricia Heras, PhD* [Videorecording]. San Diego, CA: Concepts in Motion. First- and second-generation Filipino American experiences are explored and discussed including growing up in an immigrant family, childrearing, and ethnic identity.

Sternberg, T., Wang, W., & Yung, D. (Producers), & Wang, W. (Director). (1987). *Dim sum: A little bit of heart* [Videorecording]. Beverly Hills, CA: Pacific Arts Video. Entertaining comedy about a Chinese American family in San Francisco and the clashes between their cultural heritage and a changing world.

Stone, O., & Yang, J. (Producers), & Wang, W. (Director). (1994). *The joy luck club* [Videorecording]. Hollywood: Hollywood Pictures Home Video. Four Chinese women, lifelong friends, play mah jong together in San Francisco, and their poignant stories affect their relationships with one another and their daughters, who are living their own stories in America.

Tajima-Peña, R., & Thai, Q. (Producers). (1996). *My America, or, honk if you love Buddha* [Videorecording]. Los Angeles: National Asian American Telecomunications Association and Independent Television Service. Documentary about Asian Americans from New York to California, from recent past to present, from the arts to high society.

Thomas, J. (Producer), & Bertolucci, B. (Director). (1999). *The last emperor* [Videorecording]. Santa Monica, CA: Artisan Entertainment. An epic about Pu Yi, who, at age three, became China's last emperor.

Yamamoto, K., & Kelly, N. (Producers). (1992). *Thousand pieces of gold* [Videorecording]. Los Angeles: Hemdale Home Video. Fascinating fictional rendition based on the true story of a young Chinese woman brought to frontier America and her personal experiences with racism and sexism.

Organizations

Asian American Legal Defense and Education Fund, 99 Hudson Street, 12th Floor, New York, NY 10013, (212) 966-5932, http://www.aaldef.org.

11

CHAPTER

European Americans in Counseling

It's a complex fate, being an American, and one of the responsibilities it entails is fighting against a superstitious valuation of Europe.

Henry James (Bartlett, 1992, p. 548)

Although the term "European American" is meant here to include Americans whose ancestors immigrated to the United States from a country in Europe, many European Americans would not immediately identify themselves with this label for their cultural background. Many European American clients are likely to use the expressions "American," "Caucasian," or possibly "Anglo American," "Southerner," or "White." Some European Americans are either unaware of or do not identify with the European aspects of their culture. However, because Americans from Europe are the dominant cultural force in the United States today, it is hoped that examining the cultural background of European Americans will not only promote greater understanding of the counseling issues particular to this group of people but that it also will illuminate the extent to which counseling itself, as it has developed to date, is a Euro-centric process (Das, 1995).

According to the 2000 census, German (42.9 million), Irish (30.5 million), and English (24.5 million) ethnic groups from northern Europe and Italians (15.7 million) from southern Europe are the most popu-lous European ethnic groups in the United States (U.S. Census Bureau,

2006). Another 20.6 million Americans list their ancestry as "American" or the "United States."

Some scholars have noted the lack of emphasis on encouraging White people to explore what it means to be White or have called for White people to explore their own cultural identities (Carter, 1990; J. H. Katz, 1989; Pope-Davis & Ottavi, 1994). The relative dearth of information about counseling European Americans published in the last decade is remarkable; during the same period, the number of articles about counseling people of non-European ethnic backgrounds has grown tremendously. This discrepancy may be an indication of a lack of cultural awareness among majority White or European American researchers about the importance and uniqueness of their own ethnic backgrounds even though research results have found White racial identity attitudes to be related to racism toward others (Pope-Davis & Ottavi, 1994; see also Neville, Worthington, & Spanierman, 2001). The best resource about counseling European Americans continues to be *Ethnicity and Family Therapy* (3rd ed.), by Monica McGoldrick, Joe Giordano, and Nydia Garcia-Preto (2005), which includes specific chapters devoted to family therapy with many distinct European cultural groups in America.

☐ Within-Group Characteristics and Variability

Northern European Americans

Northern European Americans may include people whose families immigrated from England, Scotland, Wales, Ireland, France, Germany, Sweden, Norway, Denmark, Finland, Belgium, and so on. Although there are many differences between, among, and within ethnic groups that emigrated from northern Europe, some important similarities are worth noting, especially as they have in turn shaped current American culture. Four of these characteristics seem frequent among northern European immigrants: the importance of work in self-identity, an emphasis on individuality, suppression of feelings, and distancing as a mode of coping with interpersonal conflict.

Work as a predominant value may have roots in British culture. Sixty-five percent of the top executives of the largest American corporations in 1950, and 78% of Supreme Court justices through 1957, were of British heritage (Axelson, 1993). It is worth considering that these accomplishments may be indicative of political as well as economic power. A strong work value is also consistent with German, French, and other northern

European cultures (Langelier & Langelier, 2005; McGill & Pearce, 2005; Winawer & Wetzel, 2005). In general, the work ethic has evolved in the United States to an emphasis on individual achievement, such that there is a dominant cultural expectation of individual success (McGill & Pearce, 2005). This core value, which may have originated in Calvinist philosophy, is evidenced in negative attitudes toward anyone who is not obviously successful: for example, some people of color, disabled persons, and people on welfare. In counseling, this value may be reflected in high self-expectations and corresponding feelings of failure as well as in positive motivation to "work" on relationships and other problems.

The northern European American, especially British, emphasis on individuality may bring with it feelings of alienation, emotional isolation, and withdrawal (McGill & Pearce, 2005). Das (1995) noted that many successful middle-class Americans feel alienated and lack a sense of community after putting their emphasis on individual achievement and the self.

Another commonality in northern European countries that appears to have become characteristic of mainstream American culture is a reluctance to directly express feelings, which has been noted in British, French, German, and Irish cultures (Langelier & Langelier, 2005; McGill & Pearce, 2005; McGoldrick, 2005; Winawer & Wetzel, 2005). Perhaps as a consequence, the expression of feelings often becomes a goal of counseling with European Americans, and several counseling techniques seem to have developed to address this need. Some examples are psychodrama, Rogerian reflection of feeling, and Gestalt "empty chair" techniques.

Northern European Americans may cope with interpersonal conflicts by distancing or cutting off the relationship, as is common in British, German, and Irish cultures (McGill & Pearce, 2005; McGoldrick, 2005; Winawer & Wetzel, 2005). Current European American concerns with divorce and teenage runaways may be indicators of this problem-solving style. Counseling techniques that focus on communication training and family therapy may have developed as remedies for such problematic interpersonal coping strategies.

Some other stereotypically American characteristics appear to have their roots in northern European culture, for example, the British tendency to use the legal system, and especially money and property, to regulate human relationships, as currently evidenced in American divorce and custody battles. Similarly, the German propensity for structuring time and relationships may have contributed to the sense of hurriedness and need for time management so common to current American life. The political and social pressure on German Americans not to claim their German heritage, which grew out of World War II, has no doubt further blurred the influence of German culture on American life.

Southern and Eastern European Americans

After 1900, and prior to the 1965 Immigration Act, most immigrants to the United States came from southern and eastern European countries, such as Italy, Greece, Poland, and Russia (Stave, Sutherland, & Salerno, 1994). In 1882, 87% of immigrants were from northern and western European countries, but by 1907 the focus of immigration had shifted, and 81% were from southern and eastern European countries instead. Immigrants from southern and eastern European countries are sometimes called "White ethnic Americans" (Axelson, 1993). This term, however, seems to ignore the ethnic roots of northern and western European Americans. As cultural groups, southern and eastern European immigrants have some general cultural differences from northern Europeans that bear discussion: the importance of the family over the individual, expression of feelings, and prescribed roles as a mode of coping with interpersonal conflict.

As is commonly the case in Latino American cultures, family is of great importance to many southern European Americans (Giordano, McGoldrick, & Guarino Klages, 2005; C. L. Johnson, 1985b; Killian & Agathangelou, 2005), so much so that the needs of the individual may be considered secondary. This can make individuation from the family a difficult issue, especially in contrast to popular emphases on American independence. In fact, it may be contrary to southern European American cultural norms to label particular family issues as individuation-enmeshment issues. Moving out of the house, going away to college, or marrying outside the culture could each be viewed by the family as an act of betrayal and might become a presenting problem in counseling (C. L. Johnson, 1985; Killian & Agathangelou, 2005; Sleek, 1995). It is essential that counselors inquire about and identify cultural values related to these issues.

Variability exists within European cultures with respect to individual achievement, ranging from idealistic family demands in Jewish culture that seem to render individual accomplishments as more like failures (Herz & Rosen, 1982); to Italian American culture, which may seem to support achievement only when compatible to family solidarity (Giordano et al., 2005); to Polish Americans, who may have ambivalence about upward mobility (Folwarski & Smolinsk, 2005). In the case of Italian Americans, for example, an Ivy League college might be judged too distant or expensive if the student cannot continue to live at home (C. L. Johnson, 1985).

Emotional expression is another common theme among southern European cultures (Giordano et al., 2005; Rosen & Weltman, 2005).

For example, among many families with Jewish cultural backgrounds, expression of feelings may not only be accepted but may also be a highly valued part of family interaction (Rosen & Weltman, 2005). In other southern and eastern European cultures—Polish and Greek American, for example—some emotions related to joy or sexuality may be easily expressed, whereas other emotions that might indicate anxiety or weakness may be censored (Killian & Agathangelou, 2005; Mondykowski, 1982).

Proscribed roles for men and women may contribute to a more formalized behavioral conformity in carrying out relationships, with men often viewed as the authority and provider and women viewed as the nurturer within the family sphere (Giordano et al., 2005; C. L. Johnson, 1985; Killian & Agathangelou, 2005; Rosen & Weltman, 2005). The implication for counseling is that models for interpersonal negotiation and gender role flexibility may be lacking in some southern European American homes (Giordano et al., 2005; Rosen & Weltman, 2005).

☐ Indigenous Treatment Methods

Many indigenous treatments for European Americans are already part of traditional counseling practice. Because most counseling techniques taught today were developed by European Americans (Ivey, Ivey, & Simek-Morgan, 1993), it seems logical that they would be effective when applied to European Americans. The rational explanations of psychodynamic approaches to counseling may be especially suited to British Americans (McGill & Pearce, 2005) and Jewish Americans (Rosen & Weltman, 2005). Sigmund Freud, originator of psychoanalysis, was northern European and Jewish. Carl Rogers and Virginia Satir, both European Americans living in the Midwest, developed counseling approaches that may be especially compatible to midwestern British Americans, whereas structural and strategic family therapy approaches may be less helpful with these European Americans (McGill & Pearce, 1982). In contrast, structured paradoxical techniques or positive refraining have been noted as possibly being more helpful to Irish Americans than nonverbal or body techniques (McGoldrick, 1982, 2005). Behavioral or action-oriented approaches have been described as culturally consistent for French Americans (Langelier & Langelier, 2005) and Polish Americans (Mondykowski, 1982). In addition, Milan-style family counseling was developed by northern Italians and may be suited for issues of family enmeshment when it becomes problematic (Rotunno & McGoldrick, 1982) as may Bowenian family counseling (Giordano et al., 2005).

☐ Counseling Issues

Social Class Considerations

European Americans as a group have enjoyed social, political, and economic privileges not afforded others. For example, as of 2004, European Americans had higher household incomes ($49,101) than Latinos ($34,299), American Indians/Alaska Natives ($33,132), or Blacks ($30,355) and were less likely to live in poverty than were Blacks, American Indians/Alaska Natives, Latinos, or Asians. European Americans, too, were more likely to have health insurance (89%) than were Asians (82%), Blacks (80.2%), American Indians/Alaska Natives (71%), or Latinos (67.4%) (DeNavas-Walt, Proctor, & Hill Lee, 2005). This economic power may be the result, in part, of race-based privilege in that White Americans may receive economic benefits and advantages just on the basis of being White.

These statistics overlook, however, large numbers of European Americans (oftentimes in Appalachia or in the Southwest) who live in poverty or are marginalized (see, e.g., McGill & Pearce, 2005). Some European Americans see their successes solely to be the result of hard work and may ignore or deny the social benefits of White racial identity. Sometimes issues that arise in counseling a European American client may be related to a lack of understanding of the impact of privilege on the client and ignorance related to race.

Spirituality

The Association for Spiritual, Ethical, and Religious Value Issues in Counseling has defined *spirituality* as "the animating force in life, represented by such images as breath, wind, vigor and courage. Spirituality is the infusion and drawing out of spirit in one's life" ("Summit Results," 1995, p. 30). Spirituality is further described as both an active and passive process, innate and unique to all people, which moves the individual toward knowledge, love, meaning, hope, transcendence, connectedness, and compassion, encompassing the religious, spiritual, and transpersonal.

Spiritual differences, only one facet of culture, are often confused with ethnic differences. For example, one study of Italian Americans frequently compared them to Protestants rather than to another specific ethnic group (C. L. Johnson, 1985). As such, differences between groups might be more related to differences between Catholics and Protestants than between Italians and other ethnic groups. When counseling European Americans, the spiritual differences within these ethnic groups are particularly diverse and relevant to counseling. A client from one ethnic group, German American for example, might be Catholic, Protestant, Jewish, or have other spiritual beliefs.

It is important for the counselor to assess the client's individual views of spirituality and to not assume that membership in a particular ethnic group implies religious convictions common to that group. The counselor should explore the dynamics and religious practices of the client's family of origin and ask about the importance of these customs for the individual. The history and practices of each partner's religion in a couple can be helpful in avoiding misunderstandings and resolving differences (Sleek, 1995).

There are other counseling considerations related to religion. One suggestion has been for the counselor to make use of *clerical transference*, a tendency to see a counselor as a powerful clergyperson who can help with advice and problem solving (Langelier & Langelier, 2005). However, McGoldrick (1982) warned that it may be counterproductive for a Catholic client to view counseling as if it were confession, a place to tell one's sins and seek forgiveness. Srole, Langner, Michael, Opler, and Rennies (1962) found that Jews were more likely to seek outpatient treatment than were Protestants or Catholics. Talking, insight, and complex explanations are culturally consistent with Jewish culture, making psychodynamic approaches to counseling a treatment of choice (Rosen & Weltman, 2005). Church activities can be utilized in counseling as a source of social support for Greek Orthodox clients, Protestant clients, and clients from other organized religions.

☐ Case Vignette

Jenny, a 23-year-old marketing researcher, is a third-generation Anglo American of English, Scottish, and Welsh heritage. She is engaged to Carlo, a 24-year-old immigrant from a small village in southern Italy. Jenny explained that they met in college, where they had a whirlwind romance and where Carlo, in her words, "swept me off my feet." She complains that Carlo talks more and more about her being a stay-at-home wife and mother after they marry, roles she is interested in, "… but not right now." She says that every time she tries to talk to Carlo about this, he tells her not to worry because once they're married he'll take care of everything. Also, Jenny would like one or two children, while Carlo,

"… wants a big family like he grew up in." She has come in for counseling because she is having second thoughts about their upcoming marriage.

Questions

1. What is your personal opinion about what Jenny should do? What is your professional opinion? If these differ, how do you resolve the difference between your personal and professional values?

2. Are Jenny and Carlo good candidates for couples therapy? Why or why not?

3. If you chose to see them in couples therapy, what theoretical orientation would you use?

Reflection 1

What we may be seeing here is culture clash, with different values between the two members of this couple. Carlo appears to desire a very traditional, southern European marriage arrangement in which the husband is provider for his family and the wife is homemaker and mother. Jenny, on the other hand, appears to want more flexibility in her role, with the option of continuing in her career for some period of time as well as considering the possibility of the roles of homemaker and mother sometime in the future. She is a member of the dominant culture, given her northern European background as well as the fact that her family has been in the United States for several generations. Carlo, as a recent southern European immigrant, may continue to identify more with his culture of origin than with North American culture. I cannot say that they should go ahead and marry; nor can I say that they should not. I do think they might very well benefit from culturally sensitive couples therapy.

Reflection 2

My personal opinion is that Jenny and Carlo have many differences to face in continuing their relationship and Carlo's traditional view of a woman's role as a full-time homemaker and mother of many children, consistent with his southern European cultural background, is particularly problematic for Jenny. My professional opinion is that couples counseling would be a good place for their differences to be shared and compromises explored. Through the counseling process, Jenny may decide that marrying Carlo would or would not result in the life she would want for herself. I would be inclined toward behavioral communications training in couples therapy.

☐ Recommended Cultural Resources

Print Media

Guest, J. (1977). *Ordinary people*. New York: Ballantine. A European American family has severe difficulties directly confronting a family tragedy.

Lazarre, J. (1996). *Beyond the whiteness of whiteness*. Durham, NC: Duke University Press. A European American mother of Black sons deals with the reality of racism in America.

Wise, T. (2005). *White like me: Reflections on race from a privileged son*. Brooklyn, NY: Soft Skull Press. A European American's quasi-memoir arguing that racial privilege hurts all people.

Multimedia

Feldman, E. S. (Producer). (1985). *Witness* [Film]. Hollywood: Paramount Pictures. A moving thriller that takes place in the world of the Amish.

Hammond, R. (Executive Producer). (n.d.). *The German Americans* [Video]. New York: WLIW. Cultural history of Germans in the United States.

Hammond, R. (Executive Producer). (1998). *The Greek Americans* [DVD]. New York: WLIW and Veras Communications Inc. Cultural history of Greeks in the United States.

Hammond, R. (Executive Producer). (n.d.). *The Italian Americans* [Video]. New York: WLIW Entertainment. Cultural history of Italians in the United States.

Hammond, R. (Executive Producer). (n.d.). *May the road rise to meet you* [Video]. New York: WLIW. Cultural history of Irish in the United States.

Hammond, R. (Executive Producer). (1998). *The Polish Americans* [Video]. New York: WLIW. Cultural history of Polish Americans.

Ivory, J. (Director). (1990). *Mr. & Mrs. Bridge* [Videorecording]. Burbank, CA: Miramax. A lush film about a European American couple in 1930s and 40s America.

Kramer, S. (Director). (1967). *Guess who's coming to dinner* [Videorecording]. Hollywood: Columbia Pictures. Academy Award-winning film about a European American family's response to race relations.

Schwary, R. L. (Producer). (1981). *Ordinary people* [Videorecording]. Hollywood: Paramount Home Video. A brilliant film about a European American family torn apart by a tragedy.

CHAPTER

Middle Eastern Americans in Counseling

☐ Histories and Diversity

Middle Eastern Americans originate from a geographical region stretching from Syria in the north, to Yemen in the south, and from Morocco on the Atlantic Ocean in the west to the Persian Gulf countries in the east. It should be noted that Middle Easterners have been given many social and political designations, such as Palestinians, Jordanians, Egyptians, Lebanese, Iraqis, Syrians, and Yemenis, terms which refer to their country of origin. Such designations as Maronites, Copts, Melkites, Chaldeans, Greek Orthodox, Antiochian Orthodox, Protestants, Sunni Muslims, and Shiite Muslims refer to religious affiliations (Khoury, 2002). Arab Americans are descendants of the Semites who originated in a vast region of enormous historical and cultural complexity. Today the region is called the Middle East. It is rich in natural resources as well as in religions. It is estimated that approximately three million Middle Eastern Americans are currently living in the United States (Al-Deen, 1991). Middle Eastern Americans came to the United States in two waves, which occurred before and after World War II.

The first wave of immigration began during the last quarter of the 19th century. Most of the newcomers were "from the lower social classes and with little education" (Khoury, 2002). They were mainly Christian (90%), single males, and 75% of them were between 15 and 45 years of age (Khoury, 2002). Other religious groups such as Muslims and Druze constituted minorities. About 50% of the first wave settled in the South and the other 50% split into two groups, each emigrating to the East Coast and Midwest, respectively (Al-Deen, 1991). The second wave of immigration began after World War II and continues to the present time. This immigration appears to have been primarily caused by the need to escape the political turmoil in the Middle East. This wave has tended to be composed of highly educated professionals such as doctors, lawyers, and engineers. They are predominantly Muslim (60%), married, and 50% range in age from 20 to 49 years old. Females constitute about 45% of the total (Al-Deen, 1991). In 2000, there were over one million people in the United States who reported at least some Arab ancestry (Brittingham & de la Cruz, 2005). Of this group, 29% identified themselves as Lebanese, another 20% as "Arab," 15% as Egyptian, and other groups each accounted for less than 10% of the Arab population.

Race and Social Class Considerations

On the average, both Arab men and women earn more per year than men and women in the general U.S. population (Brittingham & de la Cruz, 2005). Although the median family income for Arabs was higher than the national median, not all Arab Americans are financially better off. Census statistics indicate that 17% of Arab Americans live in poverty, compared to 12% of the general population, and fewer have been able to own their own homes.

Stereotypes

Middle Eastern Americans are one of the most misunderstood ethnic groups in the United States. Frequently misrepresented and even vilified in the press (e.g., depicted as terrorists, "fanatics," or "oil-sheiks"), Middle Eastern Americans are routinely negatively portrayed in the media and entertainment and are often the victims of stereotypes (Abraham, 1995; Erickson & Al-Timimi, 2001). Stereotyping has led to hostile attitudes toward the Middle Eastern American community. For instance, during the 1990–1991 Persian Gulf conflict, Arab Americans were called "A-rabs," "Camel Jockeys," "Ragheads," "Sand Niggers," "Sandsuckers," "Towel heads," and other denigrating terms (Al-Deen, 1991). Hate crimes increased, including harassment, threats, offensive language, physical aggression, religious aggression, discrimination, vandalism, and other hostile acts against this community (Al-Deen, 1991).

In addition, the advent of "9/11" has increased such negative attitudes. In one Associated Press report, 44% of Americans were inclined toward "at least some restrictions on the civil liberties of Muslim Americans" and more than a quarter of those polled thought Muslim Americans should be placed on government rosters, monitoring where they live (McGaraghan, 2006). This negative attitude toward Muslims is carried over to Middle Eastern Amcricans even though most Middle Eastern Americans are Christian (Kulwicki, 2000) and has led some Middle Eastern Americans to deny their heritage out of fear of discrimination and for fear of their lives. These stereotypes not only present serious challenges to Middle Eastern Americans' development of positive ethnic identity (Erickson & Al-Timimi, 2001; Jackson, 1997), but also lead to biases and mistaken assumptions among the mental health professionals who serve them. These biases and assumptions can significantly compromise the effectiveness of mental health services for Middle Eastern Americans and yet have received little or no attention in the counseling or mental health literature.

☐ Cultural Values

Religious Factors

Religion often dictates the way of life in the Middle East. Religion continues to play an integral role in the lives of many Middle Eastern Americans and may be a central component of their identity (Abudabbeh, 1996; Erickson & Al-Timimi, 2001). Middle Eastern immigrants tend to reside in the United States near people from their respective homeland or who share the same religion. The reason for such proximity is based upon the preservation of cultural values, customs, and traditions. The religious affiliations of Middle Eastern Americans are as diverse as their national origins. In general, the community is divided into two distinct religious groups: Christian and Muslim. The majority of Middle Eastern

Americans are Christians, although Islam is the predominant religion practiced throughout the Middle Eastern world. Within the Christian faith, Middle Eastern Americans may belong to one of the following sects: Maronite, Melkite Catholic, Greek Orthodox, Antiochian Orthodox, Protestant, or Roman Catholic. Within the Islamic faith, Middle Eastern Americans belong to one of the two major sects, Sunni or Shiite Muslims (Al-Deen, 1991; Baker, 1999; Erickson & Al-Timimi, 2001; Khoury, 2002).

Communication

Communication can be illustrated by both the spoken and written forms of language. Arabic (Semitic language) was the mother tongue of the ancestors of Middle Eastern Americans. Also, most Middle Eastern Americans are conversant in some additional languages such as English, French, Italian, or Spanish, to name a few. Nonverbal communication can be explained as "all those stimuli within a communication setting, both humanly and environmentally generated, with the exception of verbal stimuli, that have potential message value of the sender or receiver" (Samovar, Porter, & Jain, 1981, p. 156). Middle Eastern nonverbal communication may be illustrated by examples of physical touch, such as greeting the opposite sex, as well as examples of appearance. During greeting, the Americanized group may touch by kissing, hugging, or shaking hands with a person of the opposite sex, depending on their relationship. These acculturated people may or may not touch the opposite sex depending on the participants in a communication situation. The traditionalists, meanwhile, cannot touch due to either religious values or restrictive customs and traditions; their greetings tend to remain strictly verbal (Al-Deen, 1991).

Family and Affiliation Factors

The family is the central structure of Middle Eastern culture and plays a critical role in Middle Eastern society and in collective identity. This means that the development of an individual identity separate from that of the family or the community is typically not valued or encouraged (Al-Deen, 1991; Erickson & Al-Timimi, 2001). Middle Eastern cultures consider the enhancement of family honor and status an important goal for each family member and conformity and placing family interests over individual ones are expected (Erickson & Al-Timimi, 2001). The concepts of honor, *sharaf*, and shame, *ayb*, control individual behavior as they reflect on the reputation of the family (Aswad, cited in Kulwicki, 2000). Extended families are very important in Middle Eastern culture and relatives often live near or with one another. Within some Middle Eastern cultures, parents or families sometimes arrange a couple's marriage or aid in the selection of a partner (Al-Deen, 1991; Baker, 1999; Erickson & Al-Timimi, 2001).

Arab societies are patriarchal, with traditional Arab women often viewing themselves as self-sacrificing with their place being in the home (Kulwicki, 2000). Mothers are responsible for raising their children, particularly their daughters, properly. Divorced Arab women may suffer both socially and emotionally and sometimes will endure years of marital discord in order to avoid becoming divorced (Al-Krenawi & Graham, 2005). When counseling a more traditional client, gender matching between client and counselor might be considered (Mass & Al-Krenawi, cited in Al-Krenawi & Graham, 2005). More acculturated Middle Eastern Americans are less strict about gender differences (Kulwicki, 2000).

☐ Counseling Issues

Relocating to a foreign culture can be complicated, challenging, and stressful. Among the factors that may affect Middle Eastern Americans' acculturation experiences are country of origin, length of time in the United States, reasons for emigration, whether they have family still living abroad, their ability to return to or visit their home country, and their long-term plans to stay in the United States (Ahmed & Lemkau, 2001). Additionally, language factors such as the ability to speak English or the presence of a discernible accent may affect individuals' acculturation experiences or be a source of stress in their lives. Another factor to consider in understanding Middle Eastern Americans' cultural adjustment is their family's educational and economic status in their home country and the degree to which these have changed since coming to the United States, because such differences can be dramatic and represent a significant source of stress for families. Another source of stress may stem from being constantly "profiled" since 9/11 when Middle Eastern Americans attempt to board planes or other means of transportation, go through security checkpoints, or are more frequently questioned about their "whereabouts" by others.

☐ Indigenous Treatment Methods

Psychosociocultural Factors

There are several psychosociocultural aspects of Middle Eastern culture that are important for mental health professionals to understand because Middle Eastern culture, religion, and history are all believed to be related to Middle Eastern Americans' attitudes toward seeking psychological services (Abudabbeh, 1996; Erickson & Al-Timimi, 2001; Nadler, 2001). Middle Eastern Americans may have a general skepticism of the authority of mental health professionals in part because of their negative connotations regarding mental illness. Clients may have strong fears about being branded *majnun* (pronounced "muhj-noon"), or crazy, a term that can carry considerable stigma (Baker, 1999; Erickson & Al-Timimi, 2001; Okasha, 1999). Another factor contributing to reluctance to seek mental health services is the lack of experience with or exposure to Western counseling approaches. Family members are sought out for guidance and most of the time men seek guidance from an older man and women from an older woman (Abudabbeh, 1996; Erickson & Al-Timimi, 2001; Okasha, 1999). In addition, individuals have a tendency to display emotional pain in physical terms or through physical complaints. For example, anxiety or depression may be described as an aching body or gastrointestinal concerns (Erickson & Al-Timimi, 2001; Okasha, 1999). Another characteristic that may affect counseling is a tendency to be less "psychologically minded" than Westerners (Erickson & Al-Timimi, 2001).

☐ Recommendations for Providing Mental Health Services

The following recommendations are intended to assist mental health professionals in these processes (Al-Deen, 1991; Baker, 1999; Erickson & Al-Timimi, 2001; Okasha, 1999).

• Middle Eastern Americans are inclined to maintain their family ties.

• Middle Eastern Americans may be reluctant to engage in self-disclosure and therefore any services rendered will involve a longer period of time in order to develop the trust necessary for effective treatment.

- The concept of shame is widely held and expressed in the daily life of Middle Eastern Americans.

- The concept of "mental disturbance" may be very difficult to accept as a diagnosis by Middle Eastern Americans.

- A large number of Middle Eastern Americans, particularly those from rural areas, are not educated about good mental health and will not seek help even for temporary mental disturbances precipitated by social situations.

- Middle Eastern Americans may generally believe in demons as the causative factor for mental illness or "madness."

- Many people coming from the Middle Eastern world have negative feelings regarding government and public institutions.

- Disciplinary practices differ considerably due to cultural differences.

- There are also nonverbal responses or implicit communications that may be difficult for mental health professionals other than Middle Eastern Americans to understand.

To provide effective services to Middle Eastern clients, mental health professionals need to have an awareness of history, culture, and experiences beyond what they are exposed to in the popular press.

☐ Case Vignette

Rashid, a 34-year-old electrical engineer, and his wife, Samia, a 25-year-old housewife, came to family therapy because they were in constant conflict. Rashid had changed from being a supportive spouse to being abusive. Rashid expected Samia to behave as a Western woman in some contexts, such as in their sexual relationships, and meeting his close friends, and so on. Samia complained of loneliness, despite the fact that she lived in the same neighborhood as her extended family and in the same building as her husband's family. During therapy, she suffered from postpartum depression and threatened to kill herself. (Adapted from Baker, 1999.)

Questions

1. How would you counsel Samia given the dual standards (Western vs. Middle Eastern) that her husband applies to her?

2. What issues should the couple work on as individuals and as a couple?

Reflection 1

Rashid and his family may have contributed to Samia's feelings of isolation and rejection, which resulted in Samia's depression. Supportive therapy to help Samia discover and feel good about her own unique identity would be beneficial. In terms of her feelings of loneliness, it is recommended that Samia find other support groups in the community in order that she might feel more connected.

Reflection 2

Samia and Rashid have many differences to face in continuing their relationship. Rashid's traditional view of a woman's role is infused as a Westerner and Middle Easterner, which continues to aggravate this situation. The counselor should suggest that couples counseling would be a good place for their differences to be shared and compromises explored.

☐ Recommended Cultural Resources

Print Media

Abu-Jaber, D. (1993). *Arabian jazz*. New York: Harcourt Brace. Accessible and enjoyable for a general audience, this is a delightful book about a Jordanian American family's life in a lower-middle-class town in upstate New York. Past tragedies haunt the grown daughters and their widowed father, as well as their Aunt Fatima.

Baker, K. (2003). Marital problems among Arab families: Between cultural and family therapy interventions. *Arab Studies Quarterly* (September 22), 471–477.

Erickson, C., & Al-Timimi, N. (2001). Providing mental health services to Arab Americans: Recommendations and considerations. *Cultural Diversity and Ethnic Minority Psychology, 7*(4), 308–327.

Kanafani, F. A. (1998). *Nadia, captive of hope: Memoir of an Arab woman*. New York: M.E. Sharpe. An Arab Muslim woman born in Beirut in 1918 weaves together reflections on her personal struggle for independence with an account of her extended family's dislocation in the violent political upheavals of the Middle East.

Khoury, R. (2002). Refugee mental health manual: Culturally competent practice with Arab-Americans. Retrieved July 26, 2006, from http://www.arabacc.org/Refugee_Manual/body_refugee_manual.html

Middle Eastern American Resources Web site: http://www.scu.edu/diversity/mideast.html. General information, electronic journals, reference materials, and so on.

Nafisi, N. (2004). *Reading Lolita in Tehran: A memoir in books*. New York: Random House Trade. We all have dreams, things we fantasize about doing and generally never get around to. This is the story of Azar Nafisi's dream and of the nightmare that made it come true.

Multimedia

Middle Eastern videos at Berkeley Web site: http://www.lib.berkeley.edu/MRC/MidEastVid.html

Perelman, V. (Director). (2003). *House of sand and fog* [Videorecording/Movie]. Universal City, CA: Dreamworks Home Entertainment, Distributed by Universal Studios Home Video. Fictional account of Iranian immigrant homeownership.

13

Counseling Women

Wives, submit yourselves unto your own husbands, as is fit in the Lord.

Colossians 3:18 (Starr, 1991, p. 122)

It is the law of nature that woman should be held under the dominance of man.

Confucius (Starr, 1991, p. 118)

☐ Histories and Diversity

Women in the United States do not have status that is comparable to that of men. Women comprise 10.9% of the board of directors' seats at Fortune 1000 companies and only 2.5% of the top executives in U.S. companies are female (Babcock & Laschever, 2003). Women make up only 1.4% of the Fortune 500 CEOs, 14% of the Senate, 15.4% of the House of Representatives, and 23% of full professors (American Association of University Professors, 2004; Catalyst, 2005; Center for American Women and Politics, n.d.). Although women own approximately 40% of all U.S. businesses, companies owned by men receive 97.7% of the equity capital available for business growth (Babcock & Laschever, 2003). Women are reportedly also more frequently sexually harassed, interrupted in conversations, and addressed with inappropriate forms of familiarity than are men (Enns, 1992).

Attempts have been made to combat discrimination against women (Wolfe, 1995). Congress passed the Equal Pay Act of 1963, and some government commissions were appointed to examine changes in the roles of women. The Women's Educational Equity Act of 1974 allocated funding for counseling women. The 1975 passage of Title IX of the Educational Amendments Act was aimed at eliminating sexual discrimination in college admissions, financial aid, physical facilities, curricula, sports, counseling, and employment in educational institutions receiving federal funds. However, relatively minimal real gains have been made because of lax enforcement and subsequent court decisions that restricted the impact of legislation. In the late 1970s, the Comprehensive Education Training Act began programs to retrain displaced homemakers, but these limited programs were ended by the Reagan administration in the early 1980s. During the same time, failure to ratify the Equal Rights Amendment contributed to further stagnation and erosion of women's rights.

Women of Color

Women of color have specific issues that in part reflect their dual minority status as both ethnic minorities and women. Women of color are more likely to be poor and this may be related to higher levels of unemployment, lower levels of marriage, lower wages, and lower spousal income (Caiazza, Shaw, & Werschkul, 2004). In addition, Black and Hispanic women represent 83% of women diagnosed with AIDS, yet they constitute only 25% of all women in the United States (Centers for Disease Control & Prevention, 2004). Ethnic minority women have been described as having little trust in the health care system, believing that they will encounter racism (Burnette, 1996), and this reluctance may apply to seeking counseling as well.

Among all women, Native American women aged 25–44 have the highest suicide rate (National Women's Health Information Center, 2003). Seventy-six percent of Native American women using the Indian Health Service are diagnosed with some form of depression. This has been attributed to a variety of causes, including historical trauma, feelings of discrimination, acculturation stress, or greater personal losses (LaFromboise, Berman, & Sohi, 1994). Native American women have a higher rate of alcoholism than American women in general. According to the Indian Health Service, the death rate for alcohol/substance abusers among Native American women aged 15–24 is 40% higher than their male counterparts (LaFromboise et al., 1994). However, it is worth noting that alcoholism rates vary from tribe to tribe. For example, among the Navajo and Plains tribes, fewer women drink any alcohol at all compared to national surveys of women in general.

African American women have been more likely than White women to endorse the goals of the women's movement (1979 Harris poll cited in Reid, 1993). Because of slavery, African American women have historically been in the position of working outside the home and raising children (Davenport & Yurich, 1991). Many never-married Black female college graduates are single heads of households raising children. Counselors need to be prepared to work with their nonnuclear families. Depression has been diagnosed more frequently among Black women than among White women and alcoholism and suicide are on the increase among African American women (McGrath, Keita, Strickland, & Russo, 1990). Many Black women feel that they are ugly when they compare themselves to European American majority standards of beauty, and if they are intelligent, strong, persistent, or express anger they may be told they are "too masculine" (Brown, 1993). According to Brown (1993), some Black women isolate themselves from other women to protect themselves from rejection and hurt for being considered "not Black enough," and counselors need to encourage these women to develop a friendship with a Black "sister" for support.

Among Latinas of Mexican heritage, many have been taught not to express affection openly, with marriage containing the only acceptable role (wife) for a woman. Many Latinas have not been encouraged to strive for higher education or a career. S. A. Gonzales (1979) cited a source which suggested that some men of Mexican heritage may be even more reluctant than White men to hire a Chicana for an administrative position. Instead, unselfish self-sacrifice is often extolled for Latinas: *abnegada y sufrida*. In Spanish, *la vida de la mujer es dura y asi ha sido siempre*, meaning that a woman's life is hard and that is the way it has always been. Access to 24-hour childcare and contraceptives are particularly salient issues for Chicanas. Because of factors such as discrimination or lack of education, many Chicanas have limited employment prospects. Jobs with odd work hours are out of the question unless evening and late-night child care are possible. The strong influence of the Catholic Church makes any decision about how many children to have a particularly difficult one. Latinas in general are at greater risk for contracting AIDS than other women ("Waking up," 1988). A majority of Hispanic males who are either diagnosed with AIDS or intravenous drug users at risk for contracting HIV report unprotected sex with a woman in the past year (Freiberg, 1991b). AIDS education, especially for Spanish-speaking Latinas, is needed.

A larger percentage of Asian American women work outside the home compared to other groups of American women (Homma-True, 1990). Asian American women may often be exploited at work and denied promotions in accord with stereotypes of their hardworking and uncomplaining nature. Counseling regarding specific skills needed for advancement and successful role models may be particularly useful. Meanwhile, many Asian American women value the role of homemaker and subsequently experience much role strain between career and family obligations. Emphasis on traditional sex roles may make language learning and cultural adjustment in general more difficult for Asian American female immigrants. Somatization and social isolation have been frequently reported among Southeast Asian refugee women (Mattson, 1993). Additionally, many of these women have experienced sexual abuse, putting them at risk for depression or post-traumatic stress disorder (McGrath et al., 1990).

Middle Eastern American women face a "double life" if they are Muslim, with experiences of equality in the workplace yet limited access to mosques and religious leadership. Some of them are beginning to call for more representation and the Islamic Society of North America, the largest organization of mosques in the United States, has begun to train imams to give more prayer space and leadership roles to women (Watanabe, 2005).

Social Class Considerations

The economic status of women is not equal to that of men. From 1973 to 1989 the number of women working two or more jobs increased by 3.5 times (Amott, 1993). In 2000, women were still reported to earn less than men in all comparable job classifications (National Committee on Pay Equity, 2001b). Although the disparity between what women earn and what men earn has been gradually getting smaller (decreasing by 0.4% per year over the last 40 years), U.S. Census Bureau statistics indicated that in 2003 women still earned only 75.5% of the amount men earned (National Committee on Pay Equity, 2004). At this rate of change, it will take at least 61 more years for women's pay to be equal to that of men. Pay inequity is magnified for women of color. For example, black women earn 64.1% and Hispanic women earn only 54.4% of what white men earn (National Committee on Pay Equity, 2001a). Women make up only 45% of the world's workforce, but constitute 70% of those living in poverty (American Federation of Labor—Congress of Industrial Organizations, 2006). The poverty rate for households headed by women increased to 28% in 2003 and 12.4% of adult women live in poverty (U. S. Census Bureau, 2004).

☐ Cultural Values

It has been said that women tend to define themselves in relation to others (Miller, 1976). Chodorow (1978) and Gilligan (1982) similarly assert that female development emphasizes attachment and connection, whereas male development emphasizes separation and independence. A woman's sense of ethics may be based on caring, whereas male ethics seem based on logical principles of justice. However, both female and male "voices" can be equally valid. A more relational focus can lead women to place the needs of others before their own or have difficulty being aware of their own needs (Murphy, 1992).

Society gives women the message that they should not be too smart in order to protect men's feelings. Knowledge and power are often devalued for women (Saakvitne & Pearlman, 1993). In adolescence, when traditional societal views of women as less competent become salient, girls are much more at risk for loss of self-esteem than boys are (American Association of University Women, 1991). This is a crucial time for girls, as self-confidence drops and they begin to restrict their views of their future potential and place in society. *Fear of success* is a term used to describe women's anxiety or avoidance of success that is due to a belief that career success would jeopardize their relationships with men (Horner, 1972).

Women value intimacy. This is reflected in their communication patterns (Tannen, 1990). It seems that women talk as a means of becoming more intimate, whereas men talk more to share information. Men also tend to talk more in public or with lesser-known people as a way to negotiate their status, and they may talk less at home because their status is not in question there. The resulting mismatch in communication styles can leave women feeling unheard and invalidated and men feeling helpless to assist their partners in solving problems.

☐ Indigenous Treatment Methods

Feminist Therapy

Feminist therapy is a theoretical orientation toward counseling that was developed by and for women. A comprehensive review of feminist therapy by Enns (1993) concluded that feminist therapy is difficult to define. A wide variety of theories and techniques has been used by counselors who practice feminist therapy. Also, feminist therapy evolved out of political, sociological, and philosophical perspectives of feminism as opposed to traditional psychological theories (Enns, 1993). Feminist theories have been characterized as more relational, more egalitarian, and emanating from women's experiences compared to the major theories of counseling, which tend to stress individualism, autonomous decision making, and a linear cause-and-effect worldview (Nwachuku & Ivey, 1991). Two other differences are that feminism calls for a commitment to activism and value-laden activity, in contrast to mainstream therapies, which encourage the counselor to be value free, and that feminist counselors intentionally blur boundaries between clients and counselors (Enns, 1993). Ballou and Gabalac (1984) described six characteristics of feminist therapy:

1. The counselor promotes an egalitarian counselor–client relationship.

2. Use of community resources is emphasized.

3. The counselor takes an active participatory role.

4. Giving information is appropriate.

5. Personal validation of the client is encouraged.

6. Traditional theories are used with an awareness of their cultural implications.

Feminist therapy developed out of women's consciousness-raising groups. Early premises were that the "personal is political," which symbolized women's solidarity, and that counselor–client relationships should be egalitarian and collective rather than hierarchical. Social conditioning was attributed to be the cause of women's distress. Personal change and support were the primary beneficial outcomes of consciousness-raising groups. Over time feminist therapy groups became more focused on specific issues. By the early 1980s individual feminist therapy had become the most frequent form of feminist practice. Social and gender role analysis, working on expressing anger, and self-disclosure are among the techniques that are most often associated with feminist therapy (Enns, 1992, 1993).

Gender role analysis may involve examining gender role constrictions, how behavior is currently maintained, costs and benefits of change, and commitment to take action (Enns, 1992). Clients can be helped to rename and reconceptualize their issues in a feminist framework, place problems within a social context, confront myths that contribute to self-blame, and identify ways that symptoms serve as survival mechanisms within American culture. Gender role analysis can be facilitated by a variety of techniques, including guided inquiry, transactional analysis of cultural scripts, Gestalt two-chair exercises, and guided imagery (Enns, 1992). For example, the counselor might ask the client questions such as, "What did it mean to be female or male in your environment? What direct and indirect lessons did you learn about gender? What happened when you deviated from gender role norms?" (Enns, 1992, p. 10). Another example is to have the client first visualize herself in an imaginary box that represents gender role definitions, then explore the interior of the box that constrains her and, finally, imagine breaking out of the box.

Women have been socialized to inhibit expressions of anger (Murphy, 1992). Assertiveness training has often been incorporated into feminist therapy as a means of developing new skills for women. Assertiveness training is consistent with a feminist perspective in that it can involve becoming aware of interpersonal rights, altering negative beliefs, transcending stereotypical gender roles, and influencing the environment. Women who completed assertiveness training programs did tend to increase their range of behaviors and self-esteem; however, they also had to face negative perceptions by others that they had become aggressive or pushy. Enns (1992) summarized earlier criticisms of assertiveness training techniques as defining assertive responses too narrowly, assuming that assertiveness leads to positive social consequences, reinforcing traditional emphases on power, and defining human "rights" without consideration of gender role complexities.

Other techniques used by feminist therapists have included use of fantasy and imagery, role playing, behavior modification, coping and decision-making training, cognitive restructuring, self-confirmation and nurturing, body therapy, poetry and storytelling, creating new support systems, and client advocacy. The overall goals of feminist therapy have been described as personal effectiveness, independence, autonomy, and a feminist social perspective (Enns, 1993).

Goddess Spirituality

Another indigenous approach to counseling women is through spirituality and one manifestation of this is goddess psychology. Goddess psychology applies the Jungian concept of female archetypes to counseling women. By exploring the myths of female archetypes, women are able to gain an awareness of the coping behaviors they use to deal with their lower status in contemporary society and release self-blame. Goddess psychology tends to draw heavily on Greek mythology. Major goddess archetypes often include Athena (intellectual life, wisdom, achievement), Aphrodite (love and intimacy), Persephone (spiritual and mystical experiences), Artemis (adventure and the physical world), Demeter (nurturing and motherhood), and Hera (leadership and power). This kind of archetypal psychology encourages clients to look for the heroine within and place less emphasis on material and external satisfactions. It is consistent with feminist values in that Jung, like feminists, de-emphasized pathology and the authority of the analyst (Enns, 1994).

When counseling from a goddess psychology approach, clients may be invited to identify favorite fairy tale or mythical characters or role models from their real lives, visual media, or biographies. The counselor may use questions to guide the client in identifying strengths and limitations in these characters, what attracted them to these people, and how the characters deal with adversity. In this manner, the client can be helped to reflect on how stereotypes can be transcended in establishing individuality. Similarly, clients can create their own myths by drawing or describing themselves as they would like to be, noting important qualities of their images, and identifying characters from books, television, and fairy tales with similar qualities. In this manner, clients come to create their own stories in counseling. One caution in using archetypal approaches is that some archetypes may magnify gender differences or limit behavioral or emotional responses of clients, making it important to identify archetypal models who defy stereotypes (Enns, 1994).

☐ Counseling Issues

Gender and Diagnosis

Men and women are equally likely to be diagnosed with a mental health disorder; however, women are more likely to be diagnosed with an affective, anxiety, or somatization disorder (Morrissey, 1995b). More specifically, major depressive episodes, agoraphobia, simple phobia, dysthymia, obsessive-compulsive disorder, schizophrenia, somatization disorder, and panic disorder are all more prevalent in women than in men (Robins et al., 1984). Women are also disproportionately diagnosed as having dependent personality disorder compared to men (Landrine, 1989).

Women are especially at risk of experiencing clinical depression. Roughly twice as many women as men are diagnosed with depression

(Bhatia & Bhatia, 1999). Worldwide, women tend to be more likely to be depressed than men, and this relationship holds true for White, Black, and Hispanic women (Ritter, 1993), and is likely for other women as well. Poverty, marital dissatisfaction, being the mother of several young children, and having experienced physical or sexual abuse are all related to the presence of depression in women (McGrath et al., 1990). Roughly 70% of antidepressant medications prescribed are given to women, with sometimes questionable diagnosis and monitoring.

Premenstrual syndrome (PMS) has been a recent mental health issue for women. Between 20% and 90% of American women experience one or more premenstrual symptoms, among them irritability, tension, anxiety, depression, fatigue, mood swings, fluid retention, headaches or backaches, breast tenderness, acne, and food cravings (Adler, 1990; Hamilton, 1984; Snyder, 1990). Treatments for these symptoms include progesterone therapy, dietary changes, vitamin supplements, stress reduction techniques, and exercise (Hamilton, 1984; Snyder, 1990). Counseling, diuretics, and oral contraceptives also have been selectively recommended ("PMS," 1989). Before seeking a medical intervention, a trial of nondrug self-care lasting at least three months is recommended (Hamilton, 1984). Reducing caffeine, alcohol, sugar, and salt, along with relaxation and regular exercise, may have a substantial impact on symptoms. Increasing a woman's awareness of her body and its cyclical changes may also help in giving validity to her feelings and experiences, thereby reducing the effects of PMS. Self-statements such as "I'll feel better in a few days," "My feelings are more intense than usual right now," and "I need to take good care of myself now," may be useful.

PMS is controversial for many reasons. Little is known about the exact biological mechanisms involved. Research in this area is extremely complicated because it is difficult to validate self-reports of PMS with objective measures; PMS differs for women who have borne children or are taking contraceptives; and a majority of women seeking treatment for PMS have another ongoing condition, often depression, that tends to worsen prior to menstruation (Payer, 1989). In fact, 84% of women with PMS were diagnosed as having a major affective disorder, according to one psychiatrist (Adler, 1990). Sociopolitically, PMS conforms to Western cultural apprehensions about the female reproductive cycle. Only 2–5% of women actually require treatment for their PMS, suggesting that the lives of many women are not significantly affected (Payer, 1989). However, PMS as a bona fide psychiatric diagnosis would carry with it a social stigma, fueling the myth that women have "raging hormones" and poor emotional stability, which might provide an easy excuse for not hiring, promoting, or electing a woman. PMS could then be used as a legal defense, as it has been in Great Britain. In *DSM–III–R*

(American Psychiatric Association, 1987), PMS was given the term *late luteal phase dysphoric disorder* and, after political controversy, was relegated to the appendix. Subsequently, *premenstrual dysphoric disorder (PMDD)* was included in *DSM-IV* (American Psychiatric Association, 1994) and an estimated 2–10% of women of childbearing age receive the diagnosis PMDD (American Academy of Family Physicians, 2004).

Self-defeating personality disorder (SDPD), presented in *DSM–III–R* (American Psychiatric Association, 1987), is another controversial diagnostic classification because it seems to negatively label co-dependency or affiliation. It could also potentially be misused to blame victims of abuse. Landrine (1989) found that respondents assumed that a description of someone with SDPD was female. There was little evidence to support it as a separate disorder and it was removed from *DSM–IV* (Skodol, Oldham, Gallear, & Bezirganian, 1994).

Violence Against Women

Many women are victims of violence at some time in their lives. An estimated 25% of all girls in the United States are victims of sexual abuse (Whealin, 2006). At some time in their lives, nearly one-fourth of adult women experience at least one physical assault from a partner and 17% of women experience attempted or completed rape (National Center for Injury Prevention and Control, 2006b). Approximately 1.5 million women in the United States are raped or physically assaulted by an intimate partner each year (National Center for Injury Prevention and Control, 2006a). Women are most at risk for violence from people they know. Nearly half of child sexual assaults and more than two-thirds of sexual assaults on adult women are perpetrated by acquaintances, including family members (Russo, 1990). Poverty increases women's risk for sexual violence because poor women may participate in high-risk survival activities involving sex (National Center for Injury Prevention and Control, 2006b).

Walker (1984) delineated three phases of a cycle of violence affecting battered women. In the first, the tension-building phase, stress and frustration build in the relationship, along with communication difficulties. During this phase the woman may try to pacify the batterer's anger. When the tension can no longer be controlled, the second phase, violence, occurs. The third phase is the aftermath, a honeymoon period during which the batterer apologizes and tries to convince the woman that it will never happen again. Tension eventually mounts again, and the cycle repeats itself.

The first goal in counseling an abused woman is getting her to a safe physical environment. Then, examining the client's experience as part of a larger political, social, familial, and spiritual context can help transform the trauma into something meaningful beyond the self (Saakvitne & Pearlman, 1993).

The costs of violence against women are unknown. Many women with eating disorders have a history of sexual abuse, incest, or both. Counseling goals with a client who has an eating disorder might include increasing self-esteem, eliminating maladaptive behaviors, and focusing on factors other than external appearance for one's identity (Mintz & Wright, 1993). Effective treatment for eating disorders may combine behavioral, cognitive, and insight-oriented affective strategies as well as nutritional information.

Pay Discrimination and the Glass Ceiling

Equal education or occupational pay does not make a difference in remedying the disparity between women's earnings and that of men. U.S. Representative Carolyn Maloney noted that, "After accounting for so many external factors, it seems that still, at the root of it all, men get an inherent annual bonus just for being men" (Longley, 2006).

Women with five or more years of college earned 62% of what men earned with equivalent education (Weiss, 1991). In law, for example, a less traditional field for women, women who were lawyers earned 27% less than male lawyers (National Committee on Pay Equity, 2001b). Women scientists earn less than their male counterparts and women in academia earn only 80% of what male faculty earn (American Association of University Professors, Committee on Women, 2005). In highly paid occupations such as physicians and securities and financial services sales, women earned only 58% and 57%, respectively, of what men earned (National Committee on Pay Equity, 2001b). Women in upper management are subject to similar inequities. In other fields pay was relatively equitable, but access was still problematic ("Women narrow the paycheck gap," 1996). Among working women, 39.5% were employed in technical, sales, and administrative support fields, areas long traditional for women (Caiazza et al., 2004).

These statistics suggest that there remains a substantial inequity in both pay and employment opportunities for women. The shortage of women in upper management and leadership positions is often attributed to a "glass ceiling," an invisible barrier that keeps women from further career advancement (Wolfe, 1995). Morrison and Von Glinow

(1990) suggested that discrimination and systemic barriers are responsible for the lack of representation of women in management positions. Women themselves often perceive sex discrimination and childrearing as career barriers (Swanson & Tokar, 1991). Lack of information and self-esteem issues may also play a role because most women don't know how to engage in salary bargaining and tend to underestimate their worth in pay negotiations (McGowan, 1993; Babcock & Laschever, 2003).

Research suggests that female clients are especially drawn to feminist therapy approaches when career and employment issues are the presenting concerns (Enns, 1993). Wolfe (1995) recommended that counselors help women examine alternatives so that they can surmount workplace barriers. She also recommended training in communication skills such as self-promotion and projecting confidence and in deciding on a long-term career plan. Bartholomew and Schnorr (1994) described several practical exercises for broadening career options for school-age girls; they also recommended exposure to female role models by way of biographies, videotapes, and guest speakers in math- and science-related fields.

Sexual Harassment

Sexual harassment on the job is a reality for many women. Current estimates are that between 40–70% of women are sexually harassed on the job (About, n.d.). Of the 13,136 sexual harassment charges logged in 2004 alone by the U.S. government, 85% were filed by women (United States Equal Employment Opportunity Commission, 2005). Sexual harassment can include sexual innuendo, suggestive stories or jokes, remarks about personal appearance, sexual advances, sexual assault, or sexual coercion. The effects of harassment can include depression, insomnia, and feelings of frustration and anxiety. Fouad and Carter (1992) suggested that the counselor first help the client become aware of what sexual harassment is and help the client realize that she has a right not to be subjected to it. Next, the counselor should help the client to not blame herself for the actions of others and, finally, to develop ways to confront and effectively respond to the undesirable behavior. As mentioned previously in the discussion of how to counsel someone who has experienced discrimination, other recommendations are that the counselor validate the victim's feelings, provide information, encourage the safe expression of anger, assess maladaptive coping patterns by the victim or any impact on her family, provide a place to mourn losses, and offer hope (Koss, 1990).

Multiple Role Strain

Most women with families work because of economic necessity, but many of them would continue to work if given a choice, perhaps because of job satisfaction and commitment, adult companionship and support, and contact with the larger world (Scarr, Phillips, & McCartney, 1989). However, women are especially susceptible to role strain between their family and work roles. More than half of two-parent families have two wage earners. Yet even when a woman is employed full time outside the home, the majority of household and childrearing tasks is still accomplished by her (Levant, 1990). When employed, the average adult woman spends more time on housework, childrearing, and caregiving to sick or elderly family members than the average adult man, yielding a 74-hour total week for women, compared to 56 hours for men, according to studies conducted by Nolen-Hoeksema (as cited in Azar, 1996a). The effects of employment on a woman's mental health are moderated by her husband's approval and support and by her own level of satisfaction with childcare (Elman & Gilbert, 1984; Van Meter & Agronow, 1982). Employed mothers with unsupportive partners and childcare problems tend to be the most depressed (Russo, 1990). Dual-career concerns, childcare, and maternal employment issues may all compound routine work stress. The sum total of role demands can result in fatigue, guilt, and irritability, as well as depressed mood. Betz and Fitzgerald (1987) enumerated nine coping mechanisms for adapting to role conflict that were suggested by Epstein:

1. Eliminate unsupportive social relationships.

2. Reduce the number of contacts with others.

3. Reduce the number of obligations.

4. Redefine the occupational role as adjunctive to the family.

5. Plan schedules to emphasize the most salient role at the time.

6. Carefully separate work and family.

7. Delegate tasks to family or outside help.

8. Increase the salience of demands so that others will be aware of time demands.

9. Rely on rules, deadlines, or other devices to legitimize nonparticipation in family or social events.

Lessening expectations for oneself within roles is yet another way of reducing role strain (Stoltz-Loike, 1992). On a family level, discussion of time management, role overload, childbearing plans, role conflict, identity issues, and career orientation may be useful (Wolfe, 1995). Improved childcare, flextime, and maternity leave benefits on the part of employers also are needed.

Other Counseling Implications

Women are more likely to seek help for mental health problems from their general medical practitioner than from a counselor. Women also are more likely than men to be seen in outpatient treatment (Russo, 1990). Ironically, more money is spent on mental health treatment for men even though women are more likely than men to seek mental health services. Women are more likely to receive a prescription for psychotropic medication than are men (Morrissey, 1995).

Counselors need to become knowledgeable about resources and information relevant to women, including childcare and eldercare services (Wolfe, 1995), laws regarding sexual harassment and spousal abuse, and information about nontraditional careers.

☐ Case Vignette

Rajani is a 24-year-old international graduate student from India who came to the Counseling Center because she had a problem with her parents. For many years she had been betrothed to a young man chosen by her parents. When she first came to the United States to pursue her graduate studies the transition was hard for her. The foods, customs, and other American ways were quite foreign to her. She did well in her studies and over the past three years had really come to like living in the United States. She liked the music and had made friends. She related that she had begun dating and that she had come to realize that she no longer wanted to return to India after completing her doctoral studies and, most distressing to her, did not want to go through with the arranged marriage. In the second session, Rajani mentioned that one of the men who had asked her out was one of her professors, a young assistant professor of European American ethnicity. They had had several lunches together to discuss her research and her professor suggested they next go to dinner and a club to listen to music later.

Questions

1. What cultural issues may be present?

2. As the counselor, how would you address Rajani's relationship to the professor?

3. How might feminist therapy be applicable when counseling Rajani?

Reflection 1

In many aspects, Rajani is adapting well to her new life in the United States. Her transition into this new way of life, however, is creating some cultural conflict, as evidenced by her desire not to go through with her arranged marriage. Her wish not to return to India may be a way to avoid conflict with her parents. A counselor could validate the difficulty for Rajani in the conflicting values and customs of the two countries and help her reach some clarity as to how she sees herself integrating these seemingly disparate values. At the same time, Rajani is now in contact with the inappropriate behavior of her professor, who holds a position of power over his student, when he suggests that they go out for dinner and then to a club for music. Rajani would benefit from information about sexual harassment and her rights to a relationship free of sexual expectations (harassment) from individuals in positions of power. Helping Rajani explore the pros and cons of arranged marriages in her country of origin might also shed light on the nature of the dating relationships in the United States, including that of her professor. Feminist therapy could be used effectively with this client as a way of examining the changes in gender roles that she is experiencing as she becomes more exposed to life in the United States. Because it promotes an egalitarian counselor–client relationship, this therapy could also in practice demonstrate a new way of being in a relationship.

Reflection 2

Rajani has gone through culture shock and become happy with her new life in the United States. Culturally, disobeying and disappointing her parents by not going through with her arranged marriage is an important issue. As a woman, being asked out by her male professor is sexual harassment, even though she likes him and his attention. The power differential and potential negative consequences for her studies should the relationship go awry are cause for concern. In some higher education institutions, this behavior should at least be discussed with, if not reported to, the sexual harassment officer of the college. Feminist therapy aspects such as gender role analysis, decision-making training, and client advocacy might apply. Gender role analysis might be useful in comparing the role of women in India and the United States. Decision-making training might be helpful in weighing the alternatives and consequences of her engagement and dating. Finally, client advocacy may be helpful if the sexual harassment issue becomes known within the institution.

☐ Recommended Cultural Resources

Print Media

Alvarez, J. (1991). *How the García girls lost their accents*. Chapel Hill, NC: Algonquin Books. Fifteen tales about a wealthy Dominican family who become refugees in the Bronx and the four sisters' adjustment to their new life.

Chester, P. (1997). *Women and madness*. New York: Four Walls Eight Windows. Classic exposé first published in 1972 about women and mental illness.

Comas-Diaz, L., & Greene, B. (1994). *Women of color: Integrating ethnic and gender identities in psychotherapy*. New York: Guilford. An excellent resource combining scholarship and clinical insights about multicultural women.

Gaines, E. J. (1971). *The autobiography of Miss Jane Pitman*. New York: Dial. Multifaceted novel about a Black woman who lived over a century, from slavery and through the Black Power movement of the 1960s.

Gilligan, C. (1993). *In a different voice: Psychological theory and women's development*. Cambridge, MA: Harvard University Press. Very influential book that challenged traditional views of moral development for the sexes.

Heim, P. (2005). *Hardball for women*. New York: Plume. A guide for professional women using sports as a metaphor for how men approach business and success.

Hochschild, A. (2003). *The second shift*. New York: Penguin. A sociological exploration of dual-career households and who really does the work.

Kim, E. (1983). *With silk wings: Asian American women at work*. San Francisco: San Francisco Study Center. Real-life Asian American women in varied and nontraditional occupations.

Lamb, W. (1997). *She's come undone*. New York: Pocket Books. A heroic novel about a woman whose life is full of mishaps and tragedy.

Miller, J. B. (1986). *Toward a new psychology of women*. Boston: Beacon. Famous text about sexual stereotypes and psychological development.

Morrison, T. (1994). *The bluest eye*. New York: Plume. The story of an African American girl who begins to want to become beautiful by White, Hollywood standards.

Naylor, G. (1982). *Women of Brewster Place*. New York: Viking. Novel about the group strengths of seven Black women living in a poor urban neighborhood.

Robbins, T. (1990). *Even cowgirls get the blues*. New York: Bantam. A girl with large thumbs learns about her body as she hitchhikes across the country and becomes a model.

Wasserstein, W. (1998). *The Heidi chronicles*. New York: Dramatists Play Service Inc. Pulitzer Prize and Tony Award-winning play about a woman's evolution from the 1960s through the 1990s.

Wiseman, R. (2002). *Queen bees and wannabes*. New York: Crown. A description of adolescent girls' culture and socialization.

Multimedia

Butler, S. (Producer & Director). (1998). *The way home* [Videorecording]. Oakland, CA: World Trust. Eight ethnic councils of women meet over many months to discuss topics such as love, beauty, assimilation, power, identity, oppression, and resistance.

Jhally, S. (Producer & Director). (2002). *Killing us softly 3* [Videorecording]. Northampton, MA: Media Education Foundation. Jean Kilbourne's documentary about media treatment of women's bodies through advertising. Also see the original *Killing us softly* and *Still killing us softly*.

Marshall, R. (Director). (2005). *Memoirs of a geisha* [DVD]. Culver City, CA: Sony Pictures. Drama about a geisha's life from childhood through training in many arts and her working and love life as an adult.

Spielberg, S. (Director). (1995). *The color purple* [DVD]. Burbank, CA: Warner Brothers. An uneducated woman who has suffered much from her father and husband is transformed by her relationship to two women.

Wagner, J. C., & DiFeliciantonio, T. (1997). *Girls like us* [Videorecording]. New York: Women Make Movies. Documentary about four working-class teenage girls over four years and the impact of classism, sexism, and violence.

Whitaker, F. (Director). (1996). *Waiting to exhale* [Videorecording]. Beverly Hills, CA: Fox Video. An ensemble of four Black women friends who support each other through various relationships with men.

Young, V. L. (Producer & Director). (1980). *The pinks and the blues* [Videorecording]. Paramus, NJ: Time Life Video. NOVA program depicting sex role stereotyping from birth.

Organizations

9to5 Working Women Education Fund, National Job Survival Hotline (800) 522-0925, 238 W. Wisconsin Ave., #700, Milwaukee, WI 53202.

Catalyst. 120 Wall Street, 5th Floor, New York, NY 10005. (212) 514-7600, info@catalyst.org.

National Organization for Women. http://www.now.org/index.html.

CHAPTER

14

Counseling Men

At a time when women want men to love, raise babies and remember our birthdays, it is also required that they be the ones who rescue people in burning buildings.

Gloria Emerson (1985, p. 14)

☐ Histories and Diversity

Men in the United States are the recipients of many privileges. All of the U.S. presidents have been men, along with the vast majority of corporate executives, members of the Senate and House of Representatives, and university professors. The wealth and power in this country are primarily available to White men.

Current societal sex roles have negatively affected men as well as women. Men also experience *gender role conflict.* Gender role conflict can be defined as internal conflict or violation of others' rights that result from socialization messages that are either unrealistic or contradictory. It has been conceptualized as having six patterns: socialized control, power, and competition issues; restrictive sexual and affective behavior; obsession with achievement and success; homophobia; restricted emotionality; and health care problems (O'Neil & Good, 1997). Gender role conflict has been reported to be linked to depression, lower psychological well-being, physical illness, poor self-care in men (Enns, 1993), substance abuse (Blazina & Watkins, 1996, cited in Mahalik, Locke, Theodore, Cournoyer, & Lloyd, 2001), and psychosocial rigidity (Mahalik, 2000, cited in Mahalik et al., 2001). Relatedly, male college students rated concern about sex-role conflicts as a potential barrier in their careers, whereas women were more concerned about sex discrimination and childrearing issues as barriers (Swanson & Tokar, 1991).

The normative sex role for men in this country can be hazardous to their health. Men have been reported to have higher rates of several physical illnesses compared to women: heart disease, lung cancer, cirrhosis of the liver, and AIDS. Men also are more likely to experience homicide, suicide, and accidents than women. Men, in general, have a lower life expectancy than women by several years and the gap has widened during this century (Leafgren, 1990a; May, 1990). On average males born in 2003, for example, can expect to live 74.8 years, about 5 years less than females (80.1 years; Hoyert, Heron, Murphy, & Kung, 2006).

Social Class Considerations

In Liu's (2002) analysis of how social class affects men's lives, he notes that it has an impact on men's psychological and physical health and well-being. For example, in men, lower social class is associated with higher incidences of heart disease, obesity, alcohol use, premature death, work-related stress, and high-risk sexual activity. Lower social class also is associated with higher incidences of depression, anxiety, aggression, and other psychiatric disorders. Furthermore, higher social class might be associated with its own particular health issues. In order to help the therapeutic relationship and the client, Liu (2002) posits that when working with a male client, counselors must attend to his context, worldview, and classism.

Men of Color

In 2000, White males constituted only 35% of the U.S. population (United States Census Bureau, 2006). White males are overrepresented, however, in positions of power and influence, and even as late as the mid-1990s making up 80% of the U.S. House of Representatives, 85% of tenured professors, and 90% of U.S. Senators (Fendel, Hurtado, Long, &

Giraldo, 1996). In contrast, men as well as women of color experience much less political, social, and economic success in the United States.

Many of the traditionally respected gender roles for *First Nations* (i.e., Native American) men, for example, hunter or warrior, are no longer viable. First Nations women have associated the anger and physical abuse First Nations men direct toward them as related to the loss of these roles (LaFromboise, Berman, & Sohi, 1994).

African American men are at risk for increased death by violence, inadequate health care, and lower life expectancy rates, imprisonment, decreased educational opportunities, unemployment, and underemployment (Parham & McDavis, 1987). Most avenues of power in American society are relatively inaccessible to African American men (Davenport & Yurich, 1991). The suicide rate for African American men is increasing and by some accounts, "Black men are rapidly becoming an endangered species" (Parham & McDavis, 1987, p. 24). Counselors may continue to represent a social system that has rendered African American men powerless and the counseling process may be perceived as unmanly, so Lee (1990) has recommended an active outreach approach for African American men that utilizes Black churches, fraternal organizations, and other African American community organizations. He proposes an intensive, developmental group consciousness-raising experience that incorporates African American music, literature, and theater into the group process.

Asian American men in general seem to acculturate to life in the United States more slowly than Asian American women. They experience great pressure upon them for academic success and greater career restriction than Asian American women. Although Asian American men are heavily represented in the physical sciences, the reasons this occurs may be related to greater perceived financial returns, lower perceived potential for discrimination, or even counselors' stereotypical beliefs about their abilities in these fields (Sue, 1990).

☐ Cultural Values

It is particularly hard to delineate male cultural values because they are so intertwined with the dominant mainstream values of U.S. society. It is difficult to differentiate men, in particular, from Americans in general. Because men lead, own, or manage most of the major institutions in this country, it might be assumed that most of what is currently the status quo is what is valued by men. Wealth, power, sexuality, and competitiveness have been emphasized in mainstream American culture and those who are successful in these areas seem to have a higher status and may feel more worthy (Moore, Parker, Thompson, & Dougherty, 1990). Achievement, power, and strength have been particularly associated with masculinity in our society (Forrester, 1986). It is important to note that there is much overlap between the cultural values placed on individual achievement and strength in many Northern European cultures and the values associated with being male in the United States.

Achievement

Men in the United States have been socialized to validate their sense of maleness through achievement-oriented behaviors such as winning in sports, physical fights, intellectual debates, financial success, and attaining power over others. They are trained to be goal-oriented and productive and consequently, to base their sense of self on external standards, particularly their achievements (Leafgren, 1990b). Some men, who for whatever reason are not able to be successful according to these external societal definitions, may instead involve themselves in compensatory masculine role behaviors such as risk-taking, aggression, and violence (Leafgren, 1990a).

Perhaps consequentially, many men are not comfortable with the intimate sharing and one-down position of being a client if they have adopted power-oriented values and they may expect or prefer more self-disclosure from counselors (Wilcox & Forrest, 1992).

Power and Strength

Cultural expectations encourage men to remain strong and do not encourage expressions of intimacy, gentleness, caring, weakness, or needing help. Weakness is associated with a loss of masculinity and an ensuing loss of self-worth. Feelings other than aggression or anger are kept hidden. "Boys were told that 'big boys don't cry,' or, in sports, that they should learn to 'play with pain,' exhortations that served to train them to be out of touch with their own feelings, particularly those feelings on the vulnerable end of the spectrum" (Levant, 1990, p. 84). Research suggests that although men and women self-disclose equally (Wilcox & Forrest, 1992), men tend to mention their strengths and conceal their weaknesses. This may contribute to the difficulty many men have in communicating personal concerns and the fact that men participate less frequently in counseling than do women (Leafgren, 1990b).

In contrast, O'Neil and Egan (1993) contend that men are more comfortable with overt social, political, and economic power, relative to women, because they have more practice and support using it. Boys are often trained to resolve conflict through the exercise of power, in terms of physical strength, verbal facility, or superior strategy (Levant, 1990). In contrast, girls are socialized to use power indirectly through emotionally expressive and nurturant roles.

Independence and Connection to Other Men

According to Gilligan (1982), separation and independence are thought to be central to male development, which also includes identification with roles and positions, individual achievements, rational cognitions, and a sense of ethics based on principles of justice. "Coming to terms with one's loneliness, with one's isolation, with one's independence is part of becoming a man" (Moore et al., 1990, p. 281). However, an important part of male development also involves connection to a group of other men.

Western cultures have few formal initiation rites for a boy entering manhood. The Boy Scouts, military schools, Little League baseball, and other team sports are informal substitutes for initiation rites (Moore et al., 1990); oftentimes these substitutes are not friendly—and are actively hostile—toward gay male youth. Dougherty (1990) contends that until the mid-1950s, the U.S. Armed Forces was perhaps the most influential group for most men, with its initiation ritual of boot camp and emphases on commitment, competition, and cooperation. (In an increasingly militarized American culture, the same argument may be made regarding today's young men.) Associations with other men in either formal or semiformal groups provide men with rules for behaving in relationships. Intimacy in such groups is usually indirect, often around working on another task (Moore et al., 1990).

☐ Indigenous Treatment Methods

Men's Groups

The Chicago Men's Gathering group, begun in the 1970s, was aimed at facilitating growth through awareness and consciousness raising (Leafgren,

1990b). Men's studies have developed more slowly than that of women, however. Although many individual courses about men exist, there were no departments of men's studies for several decades (Femiano, 1990). In 1991, the American Men's Studies Association was founded and there are now a few men's centers and departments of men's studies on college campuses (American Men's Studies Association, n.d.).

In the context of group counseling, men can learn about what is unique and special about being male (Dougherty, 1990). Men need this because they grow up in a world dominated by women because women continue to be the primary caregivers and nurturers of children. The group may explore masculine ways of feeling and communicating and how these styles may be different from those of women. What it means to be a lover, husband, or father, the powerful and dangerous aspects of manhood, need for control, fear of appearing feminine in the presence of other men, and physical contact among men may also be examined in a men's group (Dougherty, 1990; Wilcox & Forrest, 1992). These issues may perhaps be revealed in storytelling, which is men's primary mode of telling about themselves. Poetry, drawing, role playing, and other techniques can also be utilized in men's groups (Dougherty, 1990).

These groups stand in sharp contrast to and must be distinguished from other men's movements, such as the Promise Keepers (a Christian group that holds an attraction to a subset of men who are interested in reclaiming their roles as heads of household), which promotes an image of a hypermasculine Jesus as the role model for men. Although verbally eschewing violence, this movement promotes a "gender-based family hierarchy" with the man at the head, a structure that has been associated with the social ill of violence within the family (Rosen, 2005).

Spirituality: The Mythopoetic Men's Movement

The mythopoetic men's movement, which draws somewhat less public interest than it did a decade ago, is inspired by Jungian psychology. Like goddess psychology, archetypal images are a focus. The primary archetypes are the warrior, representing self-discipline and self-defense; the king, representing confidence, effective decision making, and executive organization; the lover, representing passion and creativity; and the magician, representing spirituality. According to mythopoetic thought, life is fully integrated when all four influences are expressed appropriately (Enns, 1994).

The philosophy behind this movement is similar to men's groups in that men have been taught to compete, win, achieve success, and equate economic success with their worth as human beings. However, the mythopoetic movement suggests that through isolation from their fathers, the loss of male initiation rites, and overidentification with the world of women, men learn to be passive followers, absorbing attacks from others. Men's sense of patriarchy is built on immature masculinity, abuse of power, and enactment of fantasies, and their behavior wavers from passivity and weakness to abuse and intimidation (Enns, 1994; May, 1990). Men are victimized by performance expectations associated with work, sex, and war (Enns, 1994). Some men may develop fixed ego boundaries and deny feelings of vulnerability and dependence to protect themselves from the pain of separation from maternal influence (May, 1990).

The mythopoetic men's movement calls for a rediscovery of masculinity from among men, not in contrast to femininity. There is emphasis on initiation rites that mark the passage from immature masculinity and the world of women to the world of men. Some of these are actually new rites that have been adapted from Native American tribal traditions. These rites are aimed at assisting men in opening up to their own feelings, including emptiness and loneliness, replacing false optimism with honesty, and replacing compulsive activities for self-exploration (Enns, 1994).

Perhaps the most important contribution of the mythopoetic men's movement is that it permits men to explore their inner experiences, promotes emotional closeness with other men, and de-emphasizes material and external satisfactions. However, several criticisms of the mythopoetic men's movement have also been raised. The primary archetypes tend to reinforce traditional societal views of masculinity, overlooking qualities such as compassion, caring, and empathy. Another criticism is that men's pain is blamed on women, particularly their mothers. Also, Native American tribal rituals are being co-opted. Finally, the movement proposes only individual solutions for societal problems. Enns (1994, p. 130) writes,

> It is unlikely that images of warriors and wild men and experiences of fierceness will help men feel more positively about sharing power with women in the work world, become more comfortable with emotions related to vulnerability and responsiveness, or assume greater responsibility for providing emotional nourishment to the next generation.

The mythopoetic men's movement might be helpful to some male clients, but, as with goddess psychology, the counselor is again cautioned about utilizing archetypes that magnify gender differences or restrict the client's behavior and emotions (Enns, 1994).

☐ Counseling Issues

Men's Issues

Men are more likely than women to be diagnosed with substance abuse or antisocial personality disorder (May, 1990; Morrissey, 1995). The traditional masculine role encourages hiding weakness, solving problems independently, keeping feelings to oneself, and taking action; furthermore, these values are in direct contrast to those of traditional counseling: revealing weakness, collaborative problem solving, disclosing feelings, and verbal dialogue (Wilcox & Forrest, 1992). Robertson and Fitzgerald (1992) found that men with more traditional opinions about masculinity were less willing to seek counseling. Along a similar line, Warren (1983) proposed that depressive symptoms are incompatible with the traditional male sex role, rendering men reluctant to admit having problems or to seeking help from others. Interestingly, when men do receive mental health services, more money is spent, on average, than women (Morrissey, 1995). This difference could be an artifact of the kinds of treatment received, for example, more expensive inpatient substance abuse treatment compared to outpatient counseling.

Work

Taffel (1991, p. 53) describes the "work-identified man" who seems to define himself solely in terms of his work. The counselor working with such a client might inquire about work and emphasize the kind of relatedness to others required by the client's work environment. Who the client respects, what he takes pride in, and who he feels closest to on the job may prove helpful in understanding other problems in the client's life. Taffel maintains that exploring work often leads to family of origin issues because a man's choice and manner of occupational relationship has its roots in his family of origin.

Violence and Partner Relational Abuse

Boys who witness domestic violence are three times as likely to grow up into abusers as those who do not witness domestic violence during their youth (Protective Order Project, 2006). This history contributes to some men viewing their behavior as normative rather than abusive. Whereas females continue to be socialized to be passive and yielding in family relationships, males are socialized to be aggressive and in control at all costs (see, e.g., Kindschi Gosselin, 2003). Male role socialization, a contributing factor, has the effect of restricting the expression of feelings other than anger and discourages interpersonal conflict resolution modes that are not based on power (Grusznski & Bankovics, 1990).

Treatment for male batterers instructs the man to physically leave the situation when aggression is escalating. He is taught to identify physical cues, situational cues, self-statements, and feelings that occur prior to incidents of violence. Once his level of tension has decreased and he regains self-control, he learns to return to the situation and calmly discuss the issue. Grusznski and Bankovics (1990) assert that assisting men in changing their violent behavior involves teaching them to be assertive, release stress, decrease isolation, identify and express feelings including remorse and shame, accept responsibility, recognize self-statements, and to examine male roles, sex role stereotypes, attitudes toward women, and behavior learned in their family of origin. Through the learning of these new skills, thoughts, and feelings, it is hoped that at least some perpetrators of violence will acquire more adaptive relationships with women (see Kemp, 1998).

Fathering

According to Levant's (1990) review of the literature, a man's family role is more significant to him than his paid work role. This means that multiple role strain is an issue for men as well as women involved in parenting. Lack of time, difficulty finding affordable, high-quality childcare, inflexible workplace policies, and role-cycling, having to shift from one mode of functioning at work to another at home, all contribute to multiple role strain for working parents. Men may also face internal conflict over not fulfilling their provider role adequately (Levant, 1990). Some men respond by virtually abandoning the parental role to their wives, whereas others "assume the most superficial ('quality time') dimensions of the role" (Rosen, 2005, p. 135).

There are few male models of childrearing available for men who wish to be involved parents. Training in listening and negotiation skills might be helpful and a Fatherhood Course is one method of teaching these skills to men (Levant, 1990). The course is structured as an educational program for skill development, not "counseling," and focuses on communication skills, awareness and expression of feelings, child development, and child management. Role play, videotaped feedback, and homework exercises in addition to lectures are utilized.

Other Counseling Implications

Several authors have written about culturally consistent counseling approaches for counseling men. Shepard (2005) notes that boys learn to become disconnected from self and from their emotions. Silverberg (1986) suggests that the major goal in counseling men is the integration of traditional masculine and feminine components of the male role, that is, combining analytical instrumental elements with emotional expressiveness, warmth, sensitivity, and tenderness. May (1990) reasons that client trust in the counselor is critical in helping men explore their lives because many of the issues men face are unconscious and pre-verbal. He also warns that internalized homophobia is a primary obstacle in exploring emotions for many men. Taking into account male preferences for more personal space, counselors may want to position their chairs a little farther away from male clients than female clients.

Ipsaro (1986) suggests that the counselor use more direct, analytical, educational techniques rather than ambiguous, emotionally laden interventions when counseling men. For example, Robertson and Fitzgerald (1992) recommend using terms such as "classes," "workshops," or "seminars" rather than "personal counseling" as a way to help encourage more traditional men to obtain counseling services. J. M. Sullivan (personal communication, June 14, 1998) sometimes "coaches" male clients. He notes the importance of respecting a male client and maintaining his dignity. Time management, career development, and stress reduction through physical fitness may initially appeal to more men. A review of the literature by Wilcox and Forrest (1992) suggests the use of cognitive, problem-solving, and action-oriented strategies. They mention the potential use of argument and debate as productive in counseling as a parallel to engaging competition. This suggests that rational emotive therapy may also be a helpful theoretical approach with men.

In contrast, Heesacker and Prichard (1992) point out the importance of storytelling as a mode of communication by men as part of the counseling process. They also emphasize the recognition of silence as a crucial aspect of men's affective processes and the observing of actions, either from memory or in session, as a manner of accessing and integrating feelings. May (1990) recommends that an awareness of feelings can be developed through utilizing devices such as popular songs, artwork, old photographs, sentence completion and other structured exercises, and massage. May (1990) maintains that including an element of social consciousness-raising in counseling to help men confront the societal attitudes that devalue women may be needed in order for men to permit themselves to develop their more feminine aspects.

An awareness of outcomes is particularly important when counseling men. Many men may be especially interested in counseling sessions being productive, perhaps applying a value of competitive achievement to their time in counseling (Scher, 1979).

☐ Case Vignette

Fred is a 58-year-old, married, White male with two grown children, who recently was diagnosed with colon cancer. He presents in session as very formal, wearing a dark business suit, white shirt, and maroon tie. His hair is impeccably cut, his black shoes shine brightly, and his nails appear manicured. In a somewhat flat affect, he complains of feeling depressed and anxious. He explains that his prognosis is actually good and he is expected to recover from his cancer treatment. He states,

> I feel like I have wasted my life. All I've done is work ... as if anyone cares. Sure, I didn't spend much time with the kids when they were growing up, but then how could I have.... I worked hard to make sure they had a good life ... and it got me the good life, too ... a beautiful wife, a nice home, new cars, practically everything I wanted. I feel like I'm being given a new chance in life, but I don't really know what to make of it. Should I continue working? Should I retire early? What would I do if I retired? Play golf all day? I have some buddies, but my wife is my only friend and she doesn't want to retire yet.

Questions

1. What are your feelings about Fred? Do you like him? Why or why not?

2. What do you believe to be the core issue that Fred is facing?

3. What steps would you take therapeutically to help Fred work through this issue?

Reflection 1

Fred appears to be facing an existential "crisis" of sorts. He has made a successful life for himself, at least materially, but his recent diagnosis has pressed him to ask if there is more. To a degree, he may be emotionally distanced from his spouse and his children. I'd certainly like more information about his relationship with them. Given his formal presentation, I have concerns about how he handles issues related to control or lack thereof. I would more formally want to assess him for depression before deciding on the next steps therapeutically.

Reflection 2

Fred is a good, likable man who, like many middle-aged men, finds himself re-evaluating his priorities. Although the presenting problem is related to his adjustment to a diagnosis of colon cancer, questions about feelings and relationships are emerging related to his life stage and male role. Some structured exercises around career-life planning, exploration of current and desired relationships, and life review may be helpful.

☐ Recommended Cultural Resources

Print Media

Bly, R. (1990). *Iron John: A book about men*. New York: Addison-Wesley. The classic men's movement book.

Goldman, F. (1998). *The ordinary seaman*. New York: Grove/Atlantic. Central American men transcend abysmal conditions after being coaxed into working aboard a freighter abandoned in New York.

Hemingway, E. (1995 reissue). *The old man and the sea*. New York: Scribner. Classic story of a man who struggles against something bigger than himself.

Kingston, H.M. (1989). *China men*. New York: Vintage Books. Stories of three generations of Chinese immigrant men as they make their way in America.

Multimedia

Hopper, D. (Director). (1969). *Easy rider* [Videorecording]. Hollywood: Columbia Pictures. Two male bikers travel across the United States in search of experiences and adventures; a classic.

LaBute, N. (Director). (1997). *In the company of men* [Videorecording]. Toronto, ON: Alliance Atlantis. A tragicomedy exploring the relationship between two men—one a misogynist—and a woman.

Lee, S. (Director). (1998). *He got game* [Videorecording]. Los Angeles: Disney. Spike Lee's story of the relationship between a basketball player and his father.

Scorsese, M. (Director). (1976). *Taxi driver* [Videorecording]. Los Angeles: Sony. A war veteran is compelled to act out.

Spiking, B., Deeley, M., Cimino, M., & Peverall, J. (Producers). (1982). *The deer hunter* [Videorecording]. Universal City, CA: MCA Videodisc. Young working-class men from a small town are sent to Vietnam and captured by the Viet Cong.

Stone, O. (Director). (1989). *Born on the fourth of July* [Videorecording]. Hollywood: Universal Studios. True story of Ron Kovic, a Vietnam vet who becomes an anti-war activist.

Organizations

American Men's Studies Association, http://www.mensstudies.org/. An organization promoting the study of men via conferences and publications.
Check online for other men's groups and organizations in your area.

15

CHAPTER

Counseling Lesbian, Gay, Bisexual, and Transgender (LGBT) People

To be honest, gay persons are not just plain folk; we are quite extraordinary.... We are not—heaven forbid—"the same as" heterosexuals, but are uniquely different with our own positive and lasting contributions to humanity.

Rictor Norton, writer (Judell, 1997, p. 23)

You understand that in homosexuality, just as in heterosexuality, there are all shades and degrees, from radiant health to sullen sickness, from simple expansiveness to all the refinements of vice.

Andre Gide, writer (Judell, 1997, p. 25)

What do you think caused your heterosexuality? ... Is it possible that your heterosexuality stems from a neurotic fear of others of the same sex? ... Why do you insist on flaunting your heterosexuality? Can't you just be who you are and keep it quiet?

Martin Rochlin, therapist (Rochlin, 1982)

☐ Histories and Diversity

Persons who are sexual or gender minorities may identify in one of many different ways, including, but not limited to, lesbian, gay, bisexual, transgender, transsexual, or queer. The best way to understand how sexual or gender minority clients want to be referred to is to ask.

Due to pervasive institutionalized social, religious, and governmental discrimination against sexual and gender minorities, it is very difficult to estimate with accuracy the percentages of these populations. For example, the percentage of the population that has been estimated to manifest same-sex behaviors ranges from a high of about 37% (males) and 13% (females) (people who have had at least some overt same-sex behavior to orgasm; Kinsey, Pomeroy, & Martin, 1948; Kinsey, Pomeroy, Martin, & Gebhard, 1953) to less than 1% (those identified as exclusively homosexual; Smith, 1991). Gonsiorek, Sell, and Weinrich (1995) place the estimate of homosexuality at 4–17%. Three million male and female adolescents in the United States may have a homosexual orientation (O'Connor, 1992), although many of them may not have yet actually participated in sexual behavior consistent with their orientation.

Definitions of LGBT

Estimation difficulties are also due—in part—to differences in definitions (e.g., Are "gay males" those who identify as gay, those who have same-sex fantasies, or those who engage in same-sex behavior?) as well as in survey techniques (e.g., Are questions asked face to face? Are responses confidential or anonymous?). These differences may reflect the great difficulty our society has had with the cultural acceptance of people with a nonheterosexual orientation.

LGBT might be defined on the basis of self-identification, sexual behavior, sexual desire, or a combination of these ("Sex Survey," 1994). For example, sexual orientation has been described as a person's choice of sexual partners and could be heterosexual, homosexual, or bisexual (Patterson, 1995). However, researchers in the field have pointed out the need for workable definitions of gay, lesbian, and bisexual (DeAngelis, 1994b); the same may be said for transgender and transsexual.

For the purposes of this chapter, we define LGBT and other sexual minority people as the following:

- *Lesbians.* Individuals who self-identify as female gender and express either *self-identities* as lesbians, sexual or romantic *fantasies* involving other women, or sexual or romantic *behavior* with other women.

- *Gay Men.* Individuals who self-identify as male gender and express either *self-identities* as gay, sexual or romantic *fantasies* involving other men, or sexual or romantic *behavior* with other men.

- *Bisexual.* Individuals who self-identify as one gender (male or female) and express either *self-identities* as bisexual, sexual or romantic *fantasies* involving same- and other-gender persons, or sexual or romantic *behavior* with same- and other-gender persons.

- *Transgender.* A person who identifies as a transsexual or a person who identifies with neither male nor female gender and who experiences the self as neither male nor female gender or experiences the self as a third gender.

- *Transsexual.* A person born with the culturally sanctioned characteristics of one gender (male or female) and whose psychological experience is that of the other gender. Transsexuals, like nontranssexuals, may identify as gay, lesbian, bisexual, straight, queer, or none of the above.

- *Queer.* A person who self-identifies as not belonging to the dominant cultural view of sex or gender.

- *Intersex.* A person who is born with some of the sex characteristics of males and of females.

The issues of sexual orientation and gender identity are complex and socially charged, and in reading the literature, one will find both variety and disagreement in the definitions of the above terms.

Basis of Sexual Orientation

Most organized institutions that seek to marginalize and discriminate against lesbian and gay people claim that sexual orientation is a choice, and in the case of gay or lesbian people, an immoral choice at that. Medical research increasingly, however, is identifying biological factors that may influence development of sexual orientation. These lines of research suggest that the development of sexual orientation may be the result of or influenced by prenatal hormonal or genetic factors (LeVay & Valente, 2006). Differences between homosexual and heterosexual brain structures, for example, have been documented. Twin studies have indicated that the more genetically similar two brothers are, the more likely it is that the second brother will have the same sexual orientation as the first. If this is the case, sexual orientation (whether heterosexual or homosexual) rightly should be seen as biological in origin and not social or psychological. Furthermore, if homosexuality—like heterosexuality—is biological, then it is not a choice, hence it is not immoral. Homosexuality and heterosexuality both should be recognized as normal variations of sexuality.

Basis of Transgenderism and Transsexualism

In recent North American history, transgender/transsexual persons have been seen by the current medical establishment as suffering from a psychiatric disorder (see, e.g., American Psychiatric Association, 2000). Psychiatric disorders are defined by the psychiatric community, and definitions change, as was the case with homosexuality more than 30 years ago. In fact, transgenderism/transsexualism has existed in many different cultures and has been embraced as sacred in many cultures, such as the *two-spirit* persons of First Nations (Native American) cultures or the *hijra* of India (Istar Lev, 2004; LeVay & Valente, 2006).

Homoprejudice, Transprejudice, and Pathological Bias

Gay, lesbian, and bisexual people have long been subject to anti-gay bias or homophobia (Weinberg, 1972), and transpeople to transphobia (Istar Lev, 2004) or, more accurately, *homoprejudice* (Logan, 1996) and *transprejudice*. A number of people in the United States—typically affiliated with right-wing religiopolitical groups—perceive homosexuality and transgenderism as sick, immoral, or criminal (see, e.g., B. C. Murphy, 1992), although this view is changing.

The Stonewall riots of 1969 signaled the birth of the modern gay liberation movement. Four years later the American Psychiatric Association declassified homosexuality as a mental disorder (Bayer, 1987).

Shortly thereafter, the American Psychological Association followed the American Psychiatric Association's leadership in this matter. Homoprejudice continues to persist even though, aside from sexual orientation itself, there are no significant differences between gay men and lesbians and heterosexual men and women (DeAngelis, 1994b); for example, domestic violence is no less a concern for lesbian couples; and perpetration of child sexual abuse is no less prevalent among straight men (Patterson, 1995).

Some psychiatrists suggest that people who are homophobic (and we may add transphobic) suffer from *pathological bias*. We define pathological bias as prejudice (e.g., racism, sexism, heterosexism) that interferes with that individual's ability to function as a member of society. These psychiatrists argue that pathological bias can be and indeed should be identified as a psychiatric disorder; and there is at least one report that treatment with antipsychotic medications can result in a reduction in the severity of racist and heterosexist symptoms (Vedantam, 2005).

Hate Crimes

Hate crimes against LGB individuals are verbal and physical assaults motivated by the perception that the victim is gay, lesbian, or bisexual (Herek, 1989). The assaults may include verbal insults, taunts, threats, spitting, kicking, punching, throwing objects, vandalism, arson, attacks with weapons, rape, and murder. As many as 92% of gay men and lesbians have experienced anti-gay verbal abuse, and as many as 24% have experienced physical violence. Hate crimes against people based on sexual orientation lagged behind only those hate crimes founded on race or religion and represented over 15% of all reported hate crimes (see Human Rights Campaign, 2006). Transpeople are often targets of hate crimes as well. Only seven states provide legislation protecting citizens independent of gender identity or expression (National Center for Transgender Equality, 2006).

According to Bohn (cited in Bridgewater, 1992), attacks on gay men are most frequently carried out by an armed group, typically numbering four persons, who outnumber the victim or victims. Common victim reactions to anti-gay violence include resignation, shame, self-recrimination, guilt, numbness, despondency, depression, and anger.

Gay men, lesbians, and bisexuals may themselves succumb to the anti-gay prejudices of our society, and this *internalized homophobia* has been associated with depression, low self-esteem, defensiveness, and impaired intimacy (Sleek, 1996). Frederick (cited in Sleek, 1996) suggested that it may be helpful for the counselor to treat internalized homophobia by discussing the client's early experiences and ways that homosexual feelings were adapted to or repressed. Malyon (1982) recommended using cognitive restructuring and, if the counselor is gay, carefully considering the pros and cons of revealing this to the client.

Transpeople may suffer from *internalized transphobia*. Istar Lev (2004) noted some of the benefits of the Internet for connecting transpeople who feel apart from one another. This connection may be a first step in reducing internalized transphobia.

Diversity Among Sexual and Gender Minorities

There is much diversity within the gay, lesbian, bisexual, and transsexual/ transgender population in terms of the development and impact of sexual orientation or gender identity or expression on each individual's life. Any generalities about these groups may not necessarily represent the experience of a specific client.

Gay Men

The psychological experiences of gay men are in many ways similar to those of other men in this country. For example, the coming-out process for gay men sometimes includes anonymous sex (Hersch, 1991), which is consistent with the object-oriented sexuality of many men in the United States (Hawkins, 1992). (The coming-out process is an important issue in counseling and is discussed later in this chapter.) DeAngelis (1994b) suggested that intimacy difficulties may arise because it may be easier for a gay man to have a sexual relationship with another man than to allow himself to love another man because of our culture's taboo against men expressing affection to each other.

However, in other ways the experiences of gay men are different because of the effects of cultural discrimination. In fact, psychological problems may be the result of an oppressive society that discriminates against sexual minorities. Hawkins (1992), for example, noted that when gay men are under stress, needs for validation, splitting behavior, or acting out may be defenses for dealing with hostile, unsupportive environments and are not necessarily signs of personality disorders. Among undisclosed older gay men, career achievement has been one way to cope with the stigma of homosexuality (Adelman, 1990).

Lesbians

Lesbians endure the double effects of social oppression based on both gender and sexual orientation. They are at risk for depression, suicide, and substance abuse (Ritter, 1993; Rothblum, 1990) and are more closeted in the workplace compared to gay men (Ness, 1993). Between 30% and 35% of lesbians report excessive alcohol use, compared to 5% of heterosexual women (Rothblum, 1990). Depression is the most common reason lesbians seek counseling. Many lesbians are open to the counseling process. One survey (Bradford & Ryan, 1987, as cited in Brown, 1989) revealed that 78% of the lesbian respondents either were or had been in therapy, and lesbians frequently request lesbian-identified or lesbian-sensitive counselors (B. C. Murphy, 1992). As lesbians age, important counseling issues include the need to develop strong friendship ties, in essence, to create their own families; societal homophobia and internalized negative stereotypes about being old and a lesbian; and more general women's issues related to taking risks and pleasing others (Sang, 1992).

Bisexuals

Unlike the majority of gay men and lesbians, most bisexual people eroticize heterosexually when they enter adulthood and later discover their homosexual interests (Wolf, 1992). Bisexuality may be more problematic for men than women because of society's more restrictive male sexuality expectations. It is not unusual for a bisexual client to have never known someone with similar feelings, never talked to anyone about bisexuality, or never read about bisexuality. Counseling may be helpful in terms of giving permission and information regarding bisexuality, helping build a support network, providing specific suggestions as to how and when to disclose bisexuality, and discussing how to deal with bisexuality within a relationship.

Transgendered and Transsexual People

There is considerable discourse today about the nature of gender and gender identity (see, e.g., Rudacile, 2006). Yet for many transgender or transsexual people, the hallmark of the trans experience is an incongruity between their socially sanctioned gender and their gender sense of self. To a degree, this feeling of incongruity is the result of the dominant culture's unreflective and unquestioning assumption of the duality of gender (Istar Lev, 2004), an assumption not shared by all cultures. Counselors might assist transgender persons in the process of coming out, what might be called transgender emergence, in helping a client deconstruct gender and sex, in depathologizing transgender identity, and in working through family and community challenges (see Istar Lev, 2004). Perhaps transgender activist Kate Bornstein (1994) is right in believing that humans might be better off if we were not so preoccupied with gender.

☐ Sexual or Gender Minority People of Color

It has been noted that ethnic gay people face a "double indemnity" of race as well as sexual orientation and are more closeted in the workplace (Ness, 1993). Many gay men and lesbians of color must find a way to exist in three communities simultaneously: interacting with other gay people, with others of their ethnic group, and with the predominantly White heterosexual majority (Morales, 1992).

First Nations

Several Native American tribes have historically accepted homosexual behavior without requiring a rigid classification of sexual orientation (Midnight Sun, 1988); the same may be said for transgender behavior. For example, the Mohave and Navajo cultures had specific acceptable social roles for people who engaged in predominantly cross-gender behavior, including cross-dressing and same-sex sexual behavior. As tribal traditions have become diluted by majority culture, acceptance for gay Native Americans in some tribes ironically is more difficult today than in the past.

African Americans

Many African Americans still perceive *gay* or *lesbian* to be White terms tied to a White identity ("Sex Survey," 1994). This is not surprising given that racial discrimination in advertising, employment, and admission to bars is reported to be just as prevalent in the gay community as in the rest of

U.S. society (Gutierrez & Dworkin, 1992). Similarly, African Americans have supported anti-gay legislation in at least one state (J. M. Sullivan, personal communication, June 14, 1998). Many gay African Americans see themselves as African American first and gay or lesbian second, and therefore support from other African Americans is especially important (Riggs, 1989). Validation is an important adjustment theme for African American gay men and lesbians: validation within the African American community, validation within the gay and lesbian community, and the integration of these two identities (Loiacano, 1989). Gutierrez and Dworkin (1992) recommend that counselors do as much as they can to validate their gay African American clients and be aware of resources in both the African American and gay and lesbian communities.

Latinas/Latinos

Gay Latinos and Latinas may have difficulty being accepted in either ethnic or gay communities. Morales (1992) noted that, in general, Latino communities may be homophobic, and attitudes toward gay men and lesbians are negative; furthermore, many gay and lesbian communities may have racist attitudes toward Latinos and Latinas. Many Latinos do not consider themselves to be gay if they take the active role in same-sex sexual encounters. The incidence of AIDS is almost twice as high among Latinos and Latinas compared to the total U.S. population, and one of the contributing factors may be sex between men who do not identify with being gay because of cultural homophobia (Freiberg, 1991b).

Asian Americans

Some gay Asian Americans may remain closeted within their ethnic community while being open about their sexual orientation in all other parts of their lives (Chan, 1992). Although they may need the support of other Asian Americans, the fear of rejection and stigmatization is too great. In a study by Chan (1989), 77% of gay Asian Americans reported that it was difficult to disclose their sexual orientation to other Asian Americans, and only 26% had come out to their parents. The most difficult task for gay Asian Americans in the coming-out process, according to C. S. Chan (1992), is disclosing their sexual orientation to their parents, because they may expect a lack of understanding and fear rejection from their families. Additionally, issues of independence from sex role socialization also are relevant for Asian American lesbians. Some Asian American lesbians disclose their sexual orientation to their parents to dispel expectations for marriage and to assert that they are capable of being responsible for themselves.

☐ Social Class Considerations

There is no evidence that LGBT people differ demographically from the general population. In fact, LGBT people come from all walks of life, all social classes, and all educational backgrounds. There is a common myth that gay men have higher disposable incomes than their straight counterparts. This myth arose from some limited marketing research in the late 1980s and early 1990s on the readership of some gay and lesbian newspapers and magazines; the purpose of this research, however, was to identify gay consumers (and not gay people in general) as a market segment (see Bronski, 1998).

☐ Cultural Values

Perhaps because of the invisible nature of sexual minority populations, cultural values for these groups are difficult to state. Sexual role equality is valued among many gay men and lesbians. Among lesbian couples, role flexibility is frequent, and a butch–femme pattern is rare (B. C. Murphy, 1992). Many lesbians place emphasis on power equality, intimacy, and communication. Role inflexibility is rare, too, in gay couples.

Language

As a general rule in counseling, do not assume that your client is hetero-sexual. Counselors need to be careful not to use language that is indica-tive of heterosexual bias. Examples of heterosexual bias include asking a lesbian couple which partner is in the "male" role or referring to sex-ual intimacy as "having sex," which describes heterosexual intercourse (B. C. Murphy, 1992). Nonheterosexist terms such as "partner" for gay male and lesbian relationships or "husband" or "boyfriend" for gay male and "girlfriend" or "wife" for lesbian relationships are preferred. Care in constructing informational forms is needed because many questionnaires unwittingly presume that all respondents are heterosexual. For example, a question as to whether a client is sexually active is frequently followed with a question on the type of birth control used (Logan, 1997). This can be awkward for some gay clients, forcing disclosure, deceit, or discomfort.

☐ Indigenous Treatment Methods

Community Interventions

Although there have been few reports of indigenous treatments developed by and for gay, lesbian, or bisexual people, those that exist seem to build on the strength of the community. Many gay men and lesbians develop families of choice and interlocking friendship networks that can be mobilized for treatment intervention. This "village" concept was first used during the AIDS crisis in the early 1980s (Logan, 1997). Gay men and lesbians from all walks of life came together to identify resources and allocate funds to provide support services such as food delivery, transportation, and "buddy" programs. Another positive outcome of these activities was that they provided an opportunity for many people to come out and live out, finding a sense of purpose and community with other people who were gay. A variation of the village concept comes from HIV-prevention research. Training gay community leaders to disseminate risk-reduction information, for example, resulted in a substantial reduction in unprotected anal intercourse among men who frequented gay bars (Azar, 1996c).

In 1996, a Houston, Texas, group of lesbians developed the AssistHers program to serve lesbians with breast cancer, lupus, AIDS, other chronic illnesses, and mental health disorders (AssistHers, n.d.; Logan, 1997). AssistHers provides services such as companionship, transportation, food delivery, and assessment and correction of environmental barriers. Volunteers organize into treatment teams and meet monthly with a mental health professional for supervision and to process their feelings and issues about their clients. Through participation in the program, volunteers gain increased insight into their own issues, self-esteem, and knowledge about the parameters of caregiving.

Among the complications of the village concept are issues of dual relationships, because in these groups individuals may have multiple roles. For example, friends may become clients, and romantic partners or former partners may become fellow helpers. Logan (1997) suggested that these complications urge counselors to move toward a redefinition of boundaries to permit the kind of complex relationships associated with traditional village life.

☐ Counseling Issues

Adolescence

Adolescence is an especially difficult period for many LGBT people. Between the ages of 12 and 14, many gay adolescents begin to realize that their attraction to members of their own sex could mean that they are part of a stigmatized minority group (D. Anderson, 1987); many transgender adolescents in their increasing understanding of their gender identity may come to the same conclusion. Peterkin and Rison (2003) suggest LGB youth suffer more than non-LGB youth from issues related to family, violence, substance use, suicide, and sexually transmitted infections (including HIV).

If lesbian and gay adolescents disclose their sexual thoughts to their parents, the feelings often are denied as just being part of a phase the teen is going through (Zera, 1992). Other initial parent responses may be shock or anger. D. Anderson (1987) described parental reactions to their gay children as similar to a grief process that may include denial, anger, bargaining, and acknowledgment. If gay adolescents do not disclose their feelings to their family, awkward and inauthentic communication may result, leading to mutual isolation (B. C. Murphy, 1992). Indeed, in reviewing the literature, O'Connor (1992) noted that 20–30% of gay adolescents attempt suicide, a rate two to three times higher than for other adolescents. Gay youths are also at risk for drug use, truancy, academic problems, dropping out of school, and running away from home. In addition, A. D. Martin and Hetrick (1988) found that 40% of gay adolescents had experienced violence perpetrated by family members or others. Rates may be even higher for transgender and transsexual youth. However, the adolescents themselves rated isolation and family rejection as their most important problems. Along the same lines, Hunter and Schaecher (1987) reported that one out of five of the lesbian adolescents and half of the gay male adolescents in their sample had experienced either verbal harassment or physical assault at school because of their sexual orientation. A recent survey by the Gay, Lesbian & Straight Education Network (GLSEN, 2005) found that 22% of LGBT students did not feel safe at school (7% of non-LGBT students do not feel safe at school);

furthermore, in the previous 12 months, 90% of LGBT students reported being harassed or assaulted at school.

Gay males under age 25 have one of the fastest-growing HIV infection rates and have a higher than average incidence of mental health problems (Azar, 1996c). Many male adolescent prostitutes are gay male adolescents who have been expelled from their homes (Hetrick & Martin, 1987). Among lesbian adolescents, pregnancy may be a way of either denying or testing their sexual orientation (Zera, 1992).

All in all, 40% of gay adolescents do seek psychiatric help, but when they do so they do not necessarily disclose their sexual orientation (Remafedi, 1987). This suggests that there is much opportunity for counselors to be of help to gay adolescents. Counselors need to support and positively affirm the gay feelings an adolescent may be experiencing. Bringing up the topic when the client has not, and disclosure to and involvement of parents, is potentially complicated. J. M. Sullivan (personal communication, June 14, 1998) asks about who the client notices and inquires about the content of sexual fantasies during masturbation as possible clues to sexual orientation. Zera (1992) noted that gay adolescents need positive, visible role models and socialization with gay peers. D. Anderson (1987) suggested forming support groups for gay adolescents. Such groups exist in New York, San Francisco, and other urban areas. The more than 3000 Gay–Straight Alliances found in public schools throughout the United States (GLSEN, 2006) may serve as sources of social support for GLBT adolescents.

Coming Out

Unlike most ethnic minority, elderly, female, or physically disabled people, people who are gay, lesbian, or bisexual are part of a hidden or invisible minority, because their sexual orientation is not automatically visible to others. The experience of being a minority of one is common (O'Connor, 1992) and can contribute to a strong feeling of isolation. *Coming out* has been described as a developmental process in which gay people recognize their sexual orientation and make choices to integrate this knowledge into their lives (Zera, 1992). A gay person may choose to come out to certain people and in certain situations before others. Counselors need to assess more than whether the client is out. Many additional questions arise, including, "To whom?" "What was their reaction?" "How is your current relationship with them?" "Whom have you not yet told?" and so on.

Coming out is difficult for many reasons. Because of the homophobic nature of our society, coming out means risking the loss of interpersonal relationships, economic hardship, and physical danger due to prejudice and discrimination. Bridgewater (1992) noted that periodic regression to previous stages of identity development is a natural part of the coming out process when homophobia is confronted. Coming out may be psychologically painful, because sometimes the gay person's old sense of self must be grieved before a new sense of self can emerge (Ritter, 1993). Coming out is complicated also because gay men and lesbians by and large must be bicultural, living concurrently in both heterosexual and homosexual cultures (L. S. Brown, 1989). Coming out issues may also re-emerge when a gay couple takes steps toward additional intimacy, such as moving in together or deciding to parent (Ariel & Stearns, 1992; B. C. Murphy, 1992).

Coming out is positively correlated with mental health and with relationship satisfaction (Berger, 1990; DeAngelis, 1994b). However, the coming out process is easier for some than for others. For example, level of education is strongly related to self-identification as a gay person, especially among women ("Sex Survey," 1994). For a counselor working with a client who is dealing with coming out, the use of role play has been recommended to practice disclosure (B. C. Murphy, 1992). Bibliotherapy also can be useful, as well as participation in a support group with other gay people.

Career Concerns

Sexual orientation may affect the work life of many gay people in several potential areas, among them career choice, workplace benefits and stresses, and career advancement. For example, when compared to other female college students, lesbian students tended to decide on their career paths later, choose less traditional careers, and planned to have fewer children (Azar, 1996b). Also, lesbians who took their sexual orientation into account in making career decisions have more often chosen to work in the helping professions. They tended to be more open about their sexual orientation and accepted their gayness earlier than other lesbians. These findings suggest that sexual orientation and level of sexual identity formation both have an impact on career decisions. Orzek (1992) recommended that when engaging in career planning with a gay client the counselor identify the client's level of sexual identity formation and accept the client's sexual orientation as viewed from within the client's own frame of reference.

Gay adults frequently are aware of being different, according to Zera (1992), and this difference is made salient in the workplace. Gay workers are often not able to integrate their personal lives into the workplace as freely as their heterosexual colleagues do, in simple actions such as displaying a photo of their partner or talking about a new home (Ness, 1993). Corporate nondiscrimination policies, including those concerning sexual orientation, are becoming normative in many parts of the country, and there are many large corporations (e.g., Apple, Levi Strauss, and Microsoft) who now grant full domestic partner benefits to gay employees. The "lavender ceiling" is the biggest reason professional people who are gay, lesbian, or bisexual may choose not to disclose their sexual orientation at work (Ness, 1993). Gay people in middle management see almost no examples of disclosure among those at the highest executive levels. Counselors can help their gay clients handle the additional stress they may experience regarding their sexual orientation in the workplace.

Relationship Issues

Gay couples have some unique relationship issues, because in our homophobic society they are denied most of the legal, religious, economic, and social benefits typically bestowed on heterosexual couples (B. C. Murphy, 1992). For example, with the exception of one state (Massachusetts), lesbian and gay people may not legally marry in the United States, although they may in Canada and several other countries. Denial of marriage rights may actually contribute negatively to the mental health of gay and lesbian people (see Herdt & Kerzner, 2006). For example, a gay couple may feel sadness over not having a wedding shower, ceremony, or presents. Alternative legal signs of commitment for gay men and lesbians might include buying a house, making a will, or filing a power of attorney with the county clerk. Counselors can help gay couples anticipate and perhaps plan rituals or celebrations around changes in their relationships.

When two men build a relationship together, the double influence of male sex role socialization in terms of low interpersonal skills, aggression, independence, achievement, competition, and object-oriented sexuality may become problematic (Hawkins, 1992). In addition, when relationship difficulties arise, gay men may be more prone to seek isolation, a coping mechanism from childhood used to deal with gay feelings, which makes intimacy even more difficult. One instance where this may occur is when one member of a gay male couple is HIV seropositive. The partners, especially the seronegative member, may tend to avoid facing their relationship problems, conflicts may escalate, and relationship satisfaction and support may decline (Murray, 1996). For HIV-mixed couples, group interventions designed to teach communication and problem-solving skills have been recommended as a means of affirming the validity of the relationship, increasing hope, reducing isolation, and improving communication.

Most lesbians have a previous history of relating to men; 95% have dated men, and between one-fourth and one-third of them have been married to a man (B. C. Murphy, 1992). However, when the relationship involves two women, couple issues more frequently concern difficulties with differentiation and maintaining a sense of self (Dupuy, 1993; B. C. Murphy, 1992). Indeed, feelings of merger and identity fusion may be a primary presenting problem (Dupuy, 1993). Roth (1989, as cited in Dupuy, 1993) suggests several ways to promote individual autonomy in lesbian couples: (a) encourage statements of individuality; (b) teach the couple about boundaries, triangulation, and fusion; and (c) reframe undifferentiated caretaking as disrespectful.

Parenting Issues

Anywhere from 6 to 14 million children in the United States have a parent who is gay or lesbian (Sullivan, 1995, cited in National Adoption Information Clearinghouse, 2000); furthermore, somewhere between 8 and 10 million children are being raised in households identified as lesbian or gay (Editors of the *Harvard Law Review*, 1990, cited in National Adoption Information Clearinghouse, 2000). Estimates suggest that there are 2 million to 20 million lesbian mothers and gay fathers in the United States (Ariel & Stearns, 1992; Laster, 1993). Lesbians and gay men can become parents in a multitude of ways, including adoption, alternative insemination by donor, heterosexual intercourse during marriage, heterosexual intercourse for the purpose of procreation, and foster parenting (Ariel & Stearns, 1992; Falk, 1989). For example, one family might consist of a lesbian couple with a child whose father is a gay man who is also part of a couple. Both couples may actively participate in childrearing, whether they choose to share a residence or live in close proximity (Laster, 1993).

Several legal issues are potential concerns for gay parents. Given the homophobic nature of our society and, hence, the legal system, gay parents may have realistic concerns about losing physical custody of their children, visitation restrictions, and prohibitions against adoption (Abbitt & Bennett, 1984; Patterson, 1995). "Second-parent adoption," or legal adoption by a nonbiological parent without the original parent losing any rights, is legal in seven states (Laster, 1993). Without legal status defining family relationships, unwanted complications may arise in the event of medical emergency, separation, or death (Ariel & Stearns, 1992).

Much more is known about lesbian mothers than about gay fathers. Research indicates that there are no major differences between lesbians and heterosexual women in terms of either their mental health or their approaches to childrearing (Patterson, 1995). One of the family issues that might affect lesbian mothers is overparenting or competition for the primary parent role if both women identify with a maternal role (Ariel & Stearns, 1992). Another potential concern for gay and lesbian parents is whether to come out to children in consideration of (a) psychological or physical harm to the child by peers; (b) the child's rejection of the parent; or (c) the child telling other people, which might lead to employment, social, or custody problems (Abbitt & Bennett, 1984).

There is considerable research evidence that children of gay parents are no different from children of heterosexual parents in terms of gender identity development; sexual orientation; preferences in toys, activities, interests, or occupations; personal adjustment; or social relationships (Ariel & Stearns, 1992; Hersch, 1991; Laster, 1993; Patterson, 1995). The most difficult period for children of gay parents is early adolescence, when homophobia in general is high, and children who are told of parental gay, lesbian, or bisexual identity either in childhood or late adolescence may find the information easier to handle (Laster, 1993; Patterson, 1995). Feelings of isolation also are a potential concern, as only 29% of young adult children of gay parents report ever having known anyone else with a gay, lesbian, or bisexual parent (Patterson, 1995).

Spirituality

There is wide diversity among religious organizations regarding LGBT people. Liberal religious organizations, independent of their religious identity (e.g., Christian, Muslim, Jewish, or Buddhist), tend to integrate logic, reason, and empiricism into their *weltanschauung*, or worldview, and tend to consider LGB orientations or trans-identities as natural variations of human sexuality. Conservative religious organizations tend to base beliefs on self-defined "tradition" (oftentimes without considering the historical evolution or fluidity of traditions) or on self-perceived "divine" revelations. Their beliefs about LGBT people tend to be more rigid, exclusive, and condemnatory (see Ontario Consultants on Religious Tolerance,

2006). LGBT people who are raised in liberal traditions may mature with a healthy sense of self and of spirituality in life; LGBT people raised in conservative traditions may grow up holding thoughts and feelings of self-loathing and confusion about spirituality. The Metropolitan Community Church developed, in part, as a refuge for those LGBT people who are excluded from their religious communities of origin.

General Treatment Implications

Ariel and Stearns (1992), in their discussion of gay and lesbian families, stated that "The legacy of secrecy and fear of losing close, familial relationships ... is an integral part of the fabric of the gay and lesbian experience." These themes are important and relevant to counseling many gay clients, whether in individual, relationship, or group counseling. Slater (1988) emphasized the effects of homophobic socialization on both client and counselor and the importance of bringing these into conscious awareness. Bibliotherapy is recommended to counter myths and stereotypes. To counteract homophobia, counselors need to be gay affirmative, which means actively affirming the validity of gay relationships (B. C. Murphy, 1992).

Clinical supervision is sometimes recommended to guard against sexism, homophobia, and heterosexism in counseling, and for gay male and lesbian counselors to prevent overidentification. Mosher (1991) further noted that heterosexual counselors must be committed to justice in order to be effective with gay, lesbian, or bisexual clients, who live in an unjust world. Crisis counselor and advocate roles may be appropriate at times (Bridgewater, 1992). Counselors need to be knowledgeable about safe sex practices and HIV/AIDS education and should assess clients for the possibility of grief issues or post-traumatic stress disorder. Finally, counselors who work with gay clients need to familiarize themselves with common sexual practices and sex therapy for gay men and lesbians (see, e.g., Nichols, 2000), legal and financial resources, activist organizations, gay newspapers and magazines, couple support groups, and gay professional organizations (B. C. Murphy, 1992).

☐ Case Vignette

Joanne is a 28-year-old biracial (Asian and European American) female who has been with her wife, Marie (also 28, and European American) for eight years. Joanne and Marie recently wed in Canada and are considering becoming parents. They reside in the United States. Their discussions, sometimes heated, revolve around whether to adopt or have a biological child. Joanne wants to carry a biological child and use their longtime friend Fred, an African American gay man, as the donor. Joanne very informally has approached Fred about being the donor. Marie wants to adopt, but grudgingly has stated that she will consider a biological child only if they use an anonymous donor. Marie fully wants to be the child's mother as much as Joanne does. Marie states that she is concerned that if they use Fred, then he might be more involved in their child's life than she desires. Joanne came in for counseling because she feels that she is at a standstill with Marie.

Questions

1. What is your first objective in providing counseling treatment?

2. Would you bring in Marie for counseling also? Would you bring in Fred?

3. How do you feel about Joanne and Marie becoming parents? Are they ready for the responsibilities of having a child?

4. What are your thoughts and feelings about the interracial dimensions of this case? What are your thoughts and feelings when you overlay the interracial dimension with the sexual orientation dimension and the fact that the child will have two lesbian mothers and a gay father?

Reflection 1

This potentially is a complex case. The first thing we would want to consider is couples counseling for Joanne and Marie. We might continue to see Joanne for individual counseling, but with the exhortation that she and Marie be in couples counseling. (We have a good couples counselor with whom we often work.) At this point, there is no good reason to pull in Fred. One of the major meta-issues to be addressed is how Joanne and Marie resolve disagreements and negotiate compromise. We would be interested in their history of resolution of conflicts and would assume that they have some experience and wisdom in this area given their number of years together. As to whether they are ready to have a child is for them, not us, to decide.

Reflection 2

The focus of treatment with Joanne is a couples issue about becoming parents and therefore it would be best to have Marie and Joanne come to counseling together as a couple. Fred could be involved in the process later if the couple decides to ask him to be the donor. The eight-year length of their relationship and recent marriage suggests that Joanne and Marie are definitely ready for the responsibilities of parenthood. The issue of who to choose for the donor may in part be related to the couple having recently reached a new level of commitment and definition in their relationship; how they make decisions as a couple, in the past versus now that they are married, may be worth exploration. Marie may have some unacknowledged racial prejudice against Fred being the donor and this should also be potentially acknowledged in the counseling process. The possible family constellation of White and biracial lesbian mothers and an African American gay male father is more complicated, but certainly provides the possibility of a loving family environment for a child.

☐ Recommended Cultural Resources

Print Media

Berzon, B. (2004). *Permanent partners* (revised ed.). New York: Plume Books. Revised edition of this very popular book on gay and lesbian relationships.

Bornstein, K. (1994). *Gender outlaw: On men, women, and the rest of us*. New York: Vintage Books. A fun and important read on one person's experience of transgender identity.

Brown, R. M. (1983). *Rubyfruit jungle*. New York: Bantam. A classic lesbian coming-of-age novel.

Clark, D. H. (2005). *Loving someone gay* (4th ed.). Berkeley, CA: Celestial Arts. Newly updated edition of this popular book for friends and families of gay people.

Eugenides, J. (2003). *Middlesex: A novel*. New York: Picador. A sweeping, best-selling novel about history, family, and one person's gender identity.

Green, J. (2004). *Becoming a visible man*. Nashville, TN: Vanderbilt University Press. True story of a female-to-male transgender person.

Johnson, F. (1997). *Geography of the heart*. New York: Scribner. A poignant account of a gay couple's life together in the face of AIDS.

Proulx, A. (1997). *Brokeback mountain*. New York: Scribner. Moving story of two men who fall in love in 1960s Wyoming.

Multimedia

Epstein, R. (Director). (1984). *The times of Harvey Milk* [Videorecording]. San Francisco: Black Sand Productions. A moving documentary of San Francisco's first openly gay elected official; a must see.

Ganatra, N. (Director). (1998). *Chutney popcorn* [Videorecording]. San Jose, CA: Wolfe Video. An engaging look at being South Asian and lesbian.

Lee, A. (Director). (2005). *Brokeback mountain* [Videorecording]. Hollywood: Universal Studios Home Entertainment. Annie Proulx's award-winning short story of the love between two cowboys lovingly brought to the big screen.

Nichols, M. (Director). (2004). *Angels in America*. New York: Home Box Office Home Video. Tony Kushner's Pulitzer Prize-winning play about the early days of the AIDS epidemic in the United States brilliantly brought to life on the small screen.

Showtime Networks Inc. (Producer). (2001–2005). *Queer as folk* [Videorecording]. New York: Author. This five-season melodrama follows a group of gay and lesbian friends, partners, and families as they navigate their way in a sometimes hostile world.

Showtime Networks Inc. (Producer). (2004–2005). *The L word* [Videorecording]. New York: Author. This engaging melodrama follows the lives of a close group of lesbians.

Tucker, D. (Director). (2005). *Transamerica* [Film]. New York: Belladonna Productions. Explores the relationship between a pre-op male-to-female transsexual and her son on a trek across America.

Organizations

AssistHers, P.O. Box 541095, Houston, TX 77254. URL: www.assisthers.org/mainwebsite_html/about.htm.

Bisexual Resource Center, P.O. Box 1026, Boston, MA 02117-1026. URL: www.biresource.org.

Gay and Lesbian Alliance Against Defamation (GLAAD), 5455 Wilshire Blvd, #1500, Los Angeles, CA 90036. URL: www.glaad.org.

Gay, Lesbian & Straight Education Network (GLSEN), 90 Broad Street, 2nd Floor, New York, NY 10004. URL: www.glsen.org.

Human Rights Campaign (HRC), 1640 Rhode Island Ave. NW, Washington, DC 20036. URL: www.hrc.org.

Marriage Equality USA, 4043 Piedmont Ave #334, Oakland, CA 94611. URL: www.marriageequality.org.

National Center for Lesbian Rights, 870 Market St., Suite 370, San Francisco, CA, 94102. URL: www.nclrights.org.

National Center for Transgender Equality, 1325 Massachusetts Ave., Suite 700, Washington, DC 20005. URL: www.nctequality.org.

National Gay and Lesbian Task Force, 1325 Massachusetts Ave NW, Suite 600, Washington, DC 20005. URL: www.thetaskforce.org.

Parents, Families and Friends of Lesbians and Gays (PFLAG), 1726 M Street, NW, Suite 400, Washington, DC 20036. URL: www.pflag.org.

16
CHAPTER

Counseling Old Adults

> Grow old along with me!
> The best is yet to be,
> The last of life, for which the first was made ...

> Robert Browning (1864)

> How good we all are, in theory, to the old; and how in fact we wish them to wander
> off like old dogs, die without bothering us, and bury themselves.

> Edgar Watson Howe (Ehrlick & DeBruhl, 1996, p. 475)

☐ Histories and Diversity

It is said that there is one minority status every one of us will experience—
if we're lucky enough—old age. In fact, people in the United States live
one-fourth or more of their lives over age 60 (Myers & Schwiebert, 1996).

Currently, almost 13% of the U.S. population is over age 65 and
by 2030 old adults will comprise 20% of the population (Administration on Aging, 2004). Although the U.S. general population is expected
to increase by nearly 50% from 2000 to 2050, the number of persons

aged 65+ is expected to increase by 114%, and the number aged 85+ is expected to increase by a whopping 389% (U.S. Census Bureau, 2005a)! Currently, about 17% of old people are racial-ethnic minorities and about 58% of old people are female (Federal Interagency Forum on Aging-Related Statistics, 2005).

Most old people live in metropolitan areas and typically in the same geographical location where they lived in midlife (Administration on Aging, 2004). By age 65, 40% of adults residing in the community require assistance with activities of daily living (ADLs) or instrumental activities of daily living (IADLs); by age 85, nearly one in five old adults is living in a nursing home (Administration on Aging, 2004). Clearly, there is a revolution under way in terms of the numbers and percentages of old adults, a population with a number of special needs.

Ageism

Ageism is a term first used by Butler (1969) to describe discrimination against old people and a tendency to view all old people similarly and negatively. Old age oftentimes is viewed as an undesirable time full of physical and emotional decline and loss. Some stereotypes of old people are that they are physically or cognitively impaired, cannot learn new things, are senile, are depressed and anxious and typically have psychological problems, and are isolated, lonely, and not socially connected (Belsky, 1999). Many health care professionals hold *ageist* views that interfere with the provision of adequate health care (Alliance for Aging Research, 2003). Many old people do not receive help for treatable depression, for example, because depression erroneously is viewed as a normal part of aging.

Statistics dispute the stereotypes we hold. Although many old people do experience physical conditions that limit their daily activities in some way, most are able to continue living independently. Only about 5% of old people live in a long-term care setting at any one time. Nearly half of old adults see or talk to their children daily, and old parents— when they move—tend to move closer to their children (Lefrancois, 1993). Furthermore, old adults tend to have lower diagnostic rates for mental disorders—except for cognitive impairment—than other age groups (Belsky, 1999).

A number of pieces of legislation have been put in place in order to protect the rights of old Americans. The Older Americans Act of 1965, for example, was one of the first steps taken on a national level to combat ageism. Its general purpose was to help old people live independently for as long as possible. The Age Discrimination in Employment Act of 1978, as another example, protects people aged 40–70 from ageism in the workplace (Myers & Schwiebert, 1996).

Gender and Social Class

Old age is a different experience for men than for women. For example, there are four times more widows than widowers (U.S. Census Bureau, 2005b). Old men are more likely to live with their spouses, whereas old women are more likely to live alone (Federal Interagency Forum on Aging-Related Statistics, 2005). Given that those who live alone are more likely to live in poverty than those who live with others, old women are more likely than old men to live in poverty (Federal Interagency on Aging-Related Statistics, 2005). Among old women who live alone, 26% of European Americans, 48% of Latinas, and 60% of African Americans have incomes below the established national poverty level (Eichler & Parron, 1987). These conditions are particularly notable because, on average, a woman in the United States can expect to be a widow for 25 years (Special Committee on Aging, 1983). Old age affects women in a second major way as well: About 75% of informal caregivers to old adults are female and they spend 50% more time engaged in caregiving activities than do males who are caregivers (U.S. Department of Health and Human Services, 1998).

Marginalized Old Adults

Although there are exceptions, old people of color tend to be poorer, less well educated, and experience earlier death (Administration on Aging, 2001), have fewer and lower quality housing choices, more illness, and a generally lower quality of life (Baruth & Manning, 1991). The number of old European Americans is expected to increase by 81% by 2030; however, as noted below, the numbers of old people of color are increasing at a far faster rate (Administration on Aging, 2001).

By 2030, the population of old First Nations people (i.e., Native American, American Indian, Alaska Native elders) is expected to increase by 147% (Administration on Aging, 2001). Today, more First Nations people live in urban areas than in rural or tribal lands. Hendrix (2001) notes that many First Nations old adults may have common cohort experiences including living on reservations, acquiring U.S. citizenship, serving in WW II or the Vietnam War, and more recently becoming educated as a professional. They may have been forced to attend boarding schools, lost their land, had their tribes terminated, seen their offspring return to traditional practices, and more recently seen the rebirth of tribal self-determination. Their traditional culture at one point may have been seen as bad, they may have suffered from laws banning traditional spiritual practices, may have been forced to assimilate, moved to urban areas for schooling and employment, and become involved in collaborative First Nations projects; most recently they may have seen the rise of gaming on tribal lands. Any of these cohort experiences may be significant when counseling First Nations old adults.

Furthermore, communication patterns of First Nations old adults may differ significantly from those of the dominant culture. Some hallmarks of First Nations communication that may be noted include, but are not limited to, showing respect by avoiding direct eye contact, being economical in speech, listening more than speaking, placing high value on nonverbal communication, and not criticizing directly (Hendrix, 2001). When counseling First Nations old adults, it is important to be sensitive to the possibility that clients may hold as normative some or many of the above values and behavioral patterns.

The number of old African Americans is anticipated to increase by 131% in the coming years (Administration on Aging, 2001) and old African Americans represent the fastest-growing segment of African Americans (American Association of Retired Persons, 1995). Old African American men are more likely to be separated, divorced, or not living with their spouses than are European American men (American Association of Retired Persons, 1995). Old African Americans are also more likely to live in an urban area with an adult child (Baruth & Manning, 1991; Myers & Schwiebert, 1996). Relative to European Americans, old African Americans tend to rely on extended family, church, and other informal support networks. Hospital stays for older African Americans are longer and more frequent, perhaps because they have a high rate of multiple chronic diseases. Among African Americans aged 65–74, for example, one in four has diabetes (Pouliot, 1996); other common medical issues include heart disease and stroke (American Association of Retired Persons, 1995). With respect to counseling, Vontress (1976) noted that some older African Americans may loudly verbalize the opposite of their real feelings or "play it cool" to avoid revealing their true emotions; among African American men, this may be a manifestation of the "ethic of toughness" as a coping mechanism (Rooks & Whitfield, 2004).

The number of old people who identify as having Latino, Hispanic, or Spanish descent is anticipated to increase by 328% by 2030 (Administration on Aging, 2001). These old adults have the least education of any group of old people, with only 27% having completed high school (American Association of Retired Persons, 1995). They frequently were employed as unskilled laborers or farmworkers, jobs that did not offer retirement benefits, and tend to remain in the workforce many years after most other old people have retired. Unemployment among Latina/o elders is higher than among African American or European American elders (American Association of Retired Persons, 1995); hence, more old Latinos and Latinas seek work. Sources suggest that Latinos and Latinas treat old age as beginning earlier, at age 60, compared to Blacks at age 65, and Whites at age 70 (Baruth & Manning, 1991).

These conditions may contribute to the lower levels of life satisfaction expressed by old Latinas/os when compared to African American and European American old people (Johnson et al., 1988). Many old Latinos and Latinas have poor health, in terms of chronic illness, activity limitations, and days spent in bed (American Association of Retired Persons, 1995). Twice as many older Latinas and Latinos than European Americans are hospitalized in state mental institutions (Baruth & Manning, 1991). Many Latino and Latina elders are cared for at home, and 85% of those living outside nursing homes have at least one chronic illness and problems in day-to-day activities (see American Association of Retired Persons, 1995; Baruth & Manning, 1991). Common medical problems include hypertension, diabetes, arthritis, cancer, and high cholesterol (American Association of Retired Persons, 1995).

Asian Americans are a diverse group linguistically and culturally and comprise people with ancestry from Asia (e.g., China, Tibet, Japan, Korea), Southeast Asia (e.g., Cambodia, Vietnam, Thailand), South Asia (e.g., India, Sri Lanka, Bangladesh), and the Pacific Islands (e.g., the Philippines, Samoa, Tahiti, Fiji, Hawaii). By 2030, the number of old Asian Americans and Pacific Islanders will increase by 285% (Administration on Aging, 2001). They also are more likely to continue working than other old ethnic minorities or European Americans, with 16% remaining in the workforce after age 65 (American Association of Retired Persons, 1995). Many Asian American elders never learned English and about 30% are linguistically isolated; 13% or more live in poverty, a rate higher than old European Americans (see American Association of Retired Persons, 1995; Yeo & Hikoyeda, 2000; Young & Gu, 1995). Although cancers linked to smoking, as well as diabetes, hypertension, and other health matters are a concern (see Yee, 2004), intergenerational family issues are the most frequent reason older Asian Americans come to counseling (Baruth & Manning, 1991).

Many old Asian Americans believe and expect that younger family members will take care of them (a culture-of-origin norm) and if this does not happen it becomes a source of stress (Baruth & Manning, 1991). Counselors may consider assessment of old Asian American clients for suicide potential, as the suicide rate for Asian American old people is three times the national average. Especially vulnerable are old Chinese women as well as old Asian American men without families (see Shi, 2005).

There are between one and three million old lesbians, gay men, bisexuals, and transgender/transsexual people in the United States (Cahill, South, & Spade, 2000), yet this population is little understood. Concerns that are prevalent among old LGBT people include lack of access to health care, housing, and other social services, due in large part to institutionalized discrimination against LGBT people by federal, state, and local governments and communities (Cahill et al., 2000). Problems are further compounded by the presence of social isolation and ageism even in LGBT communities.

☐ Cultural Values

Little information is available to guide counselors in regard to the specific values of old people. Even the information that is available may change, as the values of one old cohort, who grew up with the impact of certain historical events (e.g., the Great Depression or the world wars), may differ substantially from those of the next generation of old people. Pipher (1999) suggests that the current cohort of old adults grew up in a more communal culture, are marked by lack of irony (i.e., they are less cynical and more direct in their communication), focus more on time than on money, and value resiliency in the face of adversity. Myers and Schwiebert (1996) suggest that old Americans value their ability to function independently. This makes an event such as the loss of the capacity to drive particularly difficult, symbolizing the beginning of loss of independence. Similarly, many old people may prefer to live on their own and not be dependent on or a burden to their adult children.

Keeping things to oneself or "not airing one's dirty laundry in public" is another commonly held value among old people (Myers & Schwiebert, 1996). This may contribute to their reluctance to seek counseling (see Pipher, 1999; Waxman, Carner, & Klein, 1984) and difficulty with self-disclosure during the counseling process (Myers & Schwiebert, 1996). Old people may lack a comfortable vocabulary for discussing their feelings, which may lead them to somaticize (i.e., report emotional concerns in terms of physical difficulties). Old people, however, value conversational skills and narratives (Pipher, 1999), qualities that may be predictive of successful counseling outcomes.

Even though over two million old adults are victims of crime each year, in fact, old adults are less likely to be victims than are teens or young adults (National Institute on Aging, 2003). Counselors, therefore, can help old clients determine which of their fears regarding crime victimization are realistic and which are exaggerated.

☐ Relevant Theories

There are many psychosocial theories of later life development and aging that are relevant to counseling old people, including those of Erikson (1963, 1985), Tornstam (2003), Whitbourne (2005), Marsiske, Lange, Baltes, and Baltes (1995, cited in Belsky, 1999), and Kuypers and Bengtson (1973).

Erikson's (1963, 1985) theory of *psychosocial crises resolution* probably is the most widely known theory addressing development in late life. According to Erikson, over the course of life, people grow as they successfully resolve eight psychosocial crises, the last of which—integrity versus despair—is most closely identified with old age. The person who resolves this final stage will possess the quality of wisdom.

Identity process theory (Whitbourne, 2005) applies concepts from Piaget's cognitive-developmental theory to Erikson's life-span developmental approach and suggests that as we age people engage in identity assimilation (interpreting experiences in life in terms that are congruent with conceptions of self) and identity accommodation (changing one's conception of self, based on experiences that cannot be assimilated into one's current sense of self).

Marsiske et al. (1995, cited in Belsky, 1999) propose a theory of *selective optimization with compensation.* They believe that success in aging necessitates selection (choosing the most important area to focus on from among the universe of possible areas), optimization (investing one's internal energies in that area to ensure success), and compensation (i.e., depending more on external resources for an area in order to make up for one's lack of proficiency in that area).

Social breakdown theory, described by Kuypers and Bengtson (1973), is particularly relevant from a cultural perspective. This theory suggests that being old in U.S. society creates a predisposition toward vulnerability.

Negative external social messages about incapacity and age become internalized and bring about decreased self-esteem and increased feelings of vulnerability, which may interact in a continuing downward spiral, eventually contributing to the untimely death of the older person.

Spirituality

Tornstam (2003) posits that as people age—and especially in late life—they move from a materialistic view of life to a more transcendent, spiritual view. According to Tornstam, persons move toward *gerotranscendence*, a fundamental change in relationship to life marked by three factors: cosmic transcendence (a feeling of connection with the universe and all it contains), coherence (i.e., meaning in life), and solitude (satisfaction with being alone and philosophizing).

☐ Indigenous Treatment Methods

Reminiscence, Life Review, and Guided Autobiography

Although there are no published accounts of specific treatments that have been developed by and for old people, reminiscence, life review, and guided autobiography groups have proven to be culturally compatible approaches that have gained widespread use in counseling older people.

Reminiscence comprises remembering (having a memory), recalling (sharing that memory with others), reviewing (evaluating the significance of the remembered experience), and reconstruction (understanding the memory in some new or different way; Gibson & Burnside, 2005).

Life review may be considered a structured intervention that involves guiding the client to look back over her or his life events and experiences, and tell stories of her or his life—from youth through old age—with the objective of gaining greater appreciation for and assimilation of the stories of one's life into a more unified narrative (Gibson & Burnside, 2005). The counselor may ask the client to reflect on a certain period or specific life events to evoke memories for discussion and review.

Guided autobiography is perhaps the most structured approach. Comprising individual and group interventions, individuals are led to identify the most significant life events they have experienced and reflect upon those experiences. In a guided autobiography group, individuals write life stories expounding upon predetermined themes; they then read their stories and share their reflections upon the stories within the context of a supportive group of like-minded persons (Birren and Deutchman, 2005). Written or taped autobiographies, reunions, genealogies, scrapbooks, diaries, photographs, and other material can be used as stimuli for a reminiscence, life review, or guided autobiography process (see, e.g., Malde, 1988). Furthermore, reminiscence, life review, and guided autobiography may be particularly useful in resolving Erikson's (1963, 1985) adult development stage of ego integrity versus despair. The counselor can help clients identify events that are remembered negatively and reframe them in a more meaningful, positive fashion.

☐ Counseling Issues

Aging and Diagnosis

Depression, cognitive impairments, and dementias are the most frequent psychiatric diagnoses given to old people. Roughly 15 to 20% of old adults may exhibit depressive symptoms; up to 45% of oldest old adults (age 85+) may exhibit cognitive impairments or dementias (Gallo & Lebowitz, 1999). Diagnosis of, for example, dementia versus depression (especially if it manifests as pseudodementia) must be accurate; each of these disorders may have expressed symptoms that look very similar, yet treatment and prognosis for these disorders are very different. Diagnosis is complicated; however, many old adults have serious medical illnesses, and old adults and their health care providers oftentimes perceive comorbid depression as a normal response to medical illness. This normalizing of depression may result in undertreatment of this oftentimes debilitating comorbid condition (National Institute of Mental Health, 2003).

Some of the common physical conditions that complicate fully understanding and appropriately counseling old people are arthritis, diabetes, hypertension, and heart disease. Medications are a further complication. Many old people take several medications, and these are often prescribed by different physicians, filled at different pharmacies, or both. Symptoms could be due to either side effects or drug interactions, each of which is a common phenomenon in old adults. One of the best strategies for minimizing side effects or drug interactions is to follow the adage, "Start low, go slow." Old adults take more drugs, whether they are prescription drugs or nonprescription drugs (i.e., over-the-counter) than does any other age demographic. In fact, 30% of all prescription drugs sold and 40% of all nonprescription drugs sold are purchased by old adults (i.e., people age 65+). Old adults average four prescription plus two nonprescription drugs per day. Forty to seventy-five percent of old adults do not take their medication properly (not in the correct amount or not at the correct time of day; Food and Drug Administration, 2003).

Mood Disorders

Mood disorders are one of the most common mental health problems in old adults. Furthermore, they occur concurrently with other health problems in late life, including stroke, cancer, Parkinson's disease, diabetes, and heart disease (Depression Guideline Panel, 1993, cited in National Institute of Mental Health, 2003). About two million old people (approximately 6% of the population of old adults) have a mood disorder—either major depressive disorder, dysthymic disorder, or bipolar disorder—and another five million (about 14%) may have depressive symptoms; in other words, about 20% of old adults have a full-blown mood disorder or have a range of depressive symptoms (Narrow, n.d., Alexapoulos, 2000, cited in National Institute of Mental Health, 2003). It is important to keep in mind, however, that the prevalence of depression in old adults is lower than among adults aged 25–44 (Robins et al., 1984). Unfortunately, most people seek treatment for their depression from a primary care physician rather than a mental health professional, and in roughly half the instances their depression is undiagnosed (Human Capital Initiative, 1993; Sturm & Wells, 1995). Depression in old people manifests itself somewhat differently than in other adults (Myers & Schwiebert, 1996); old people report more physical symptoms of depression, which may include lack of appetite, constipation, fatigue, headaches, and difficulty breathing.

The suicide rates for old men and old women are higher than that of the general population (National Institute of Mental Health, 1999). European American males age 85+ are six times more likely than the general population to commit suicide (National Institute of Mental Health, 1999); old Chinese American females, too, are at a much higher risk than the general population to commit suicide (Shi, 2005). Although old adults comprise only 13% of the population, they account for 18% of all suicides (National Institute of Mental Health, 2003). Tragically, up to 75% of old adults who commit suicide have contact with a medical professional in the four weeks prior to their suicide (Conwell, 2001, cited in National Institute of Mental Health, 2003). Suicide rates may actually be underestimated, because the statistics do not include less obvious means, such as not eating or taking medication, delaying treatment, or taking unnecessary physical risks (Butler & Lewis, 1995). Old people who attempt suicide also tend to do so more successfully (Osgood, 1985). They may give fewer warning signals prior to their attempts. The most dangerous time for suicide in severely depressed older people may be two to four weeks after medical treatment for depression begins, when energy levels increase to the point where they are able to attempt suicide (Myers & Schwiebert, 1996).

Suicide in older people is perhaps best prevented by diagnosis and treating depression early. Either pharmacological treatments (e.g., the use of selective serotonin reuptake inhibitors [SSRIs] or other medications) or psychotherapeutic treatments (particularly cognitive-behavioral or interpersonal approaches) may be effective in reducing depression in old adults (Lebowitz et al., 1997, cited in National Institute of Mental Health, 2003). Most effective may be a combination of pharmacological and psychotherapeutic approaches (Reynolds et al., 1999, cited in National Institute of Mental Health, 2003). Primary prevention of depression might include reducing isolation through participation in community center activities, involvement in church, wearing prescribed hearing aids, continuing physical exercise, increasing social and communication skills, and doing volunteer work (Human Capital Initiative, 1993; Myers & Schwiebert, 1996).

Grief and Loss

Among the major sources of stress for old people are loneliness and isolation due to loss of life partner/spouse, family members, friends, or pets; loss of purpose due to retirement, no longer feeling needed, or feeling like one has lower status in one's community; loss of independence due to inability to drive, lack of readily available public transit, or feeling far from loved ones; lessened financial independence due to increases in the cost of health maintenance; loss of health, oftentimes resulting in an increased dependence upon family members; loss of physical or cognitive abilities, oftentimes resulting in the need to move in with a caregiver or move to an assisted living or nursing environment (see Bosch, 2003; Cox, 1988). Loss has been described as the predominant theme in the lives of older people (McDougall, 1993).

Grief is a natural and normal response to loss: In fact, it is *the* natural and normal response to loss. Old adults who are grieving may complain of feelings of emptiness, physical problems, trouble sleeping, loss of appetite, anger at others, feelings of guilt, or nightmares. There is no normal length of time for grieving to last, and there is wide variability in this regard, ranging from days to months or even years. A typical grieving process may require the griever to accept the loss(es), work through the grief, adjust to living without the lost person or objects, and move on (National Mental Health Information Center, 2005).

Kubler-Ross (1969) described several stages of grief (e.g., shock, numbness, denial, and acceptance) that people may experience to varying degrees after a loss. Grief over the loss of a spouse, for example, may take two or more years to be resolved; pathological grief, however, might be indicated by severe interference with daily functioning over long periods of time (Butler & Lewis, 1995). People who lose a spouse must often also learn to cope with a change in income, spending time alone, or acquiring household skills (TIAA-CREF, 1996). A counselor may assist an old client by helping her or him prepare for her or his own or a loved one's death by helping resolve conflicts with family and significant others, discussing the client's feelings about death and the perception of death as the final stage of life, helping the client make final legal, social, and other arrangements, and helping him or her review her or his life (Myers & Schwiebert, 1996).

Chronic Illness and Alzheimer's Disease

Illnesses in old people tend to be chronic, progressive, and multiple (Myers & Schwiebert, 1996). Chronic illness may lead to grief over changes in body image, physical limitations, and increasing dependence on others. Counselors can help old clients who are dealing with chronic illness plan their day-to-day activities, manage their medications, and modify their homes for safety purposes. Counselors also can help family members learn to differentiate between normal changes accompanying age and changes that are caused by ongoing physical illness.

One chronic illness that affects many old people is Alzheimer's disease (AD), a progressive, degenerative organic brain syndrome marked by memory loss, inability to recognize family members, loss of physical functioning, and ultimately death. AD is the most common dementia in old adults (those age 65+) and currently affects about four million people in the United States (National Institute of Mental Health, 2001). Approximately 10% of people 65+ and nearly 50% of people 85+ have AD (Alzheimer's Association, 2005). With a growing population of old adults, we may expect an increase in the coming years in the number of people who suffer from Alzheimer's. AD is progressive, with most people living 8–10 years with the disease after its onset (National Institute of Mental Health, 2001).

Myers and Schwiebert (1996) suggest that counselors educate clients with AD about the nature and course of the disease, help them express their feelings, and aid them in getting their personal affairs in order while their cognitive functioning is less impaired. It also is imperative for counselors to intervene with family members of the impaired old adult to aid them in dealing with practical day-to-day management issues regarding the person with AD as well as with issues related to loss.

Work and Leisure

Retirement is an important transition for old people. Financial assets are a major predictor of voluntary early retirement, and health is a major predictor of involuntary retirement (Human Capital Initiative, 1993). In addition to a decrease in income, a retired person may lose her or his sense of identity and personal worth as well as experience a shrinking of her or his social network (Myers & Schwiebert, 1996). Old people who continue to work have to deal with stereotypes that they are more expensive to hire, use more sick days, and are "... intractable, untrainable, and behind the times," even though research studies have shown that old people are reliable and they tend to report higher job satisfaction (see Clark, Oswald, & Warr, 1996, cited in Belsky, 1999).

Counselors can assist clients who are considering retirement in planning for future finances, housing, lifestyle, family interactions, socialization, medical care, nutrition, exercise, relationships, recreation, education, and re-employment once they retire (Myers & Schwiebert, 1996). Regular exercise before and after retirement, continued contact with young people, beginning retirement planning before age 40, and sufficient funds contributed to a satisfactory retirement, according to a 1995 survey of 1851 older people receiving annuities (TIAA-CREF, 1996). Two-thirds of those surveyed also either moved or considered moving, and those who moved did so to be closer to family or friends or for a better climate. Counselors who work with old people should remain current regarding specific laws and regulations relevant to this population (e.g., limits to the amount a retired person may earn before her or his Social Security benefits are reduced or lower tuition fees for old people who attend public colleges or universities or other recreation, transportation, and housing benefits).

Caregiving

Caregiving for an impaired old adult occurs in about 25% of all households in the United States (National Alliance for Caregiving and American Association of Retired Persons, 1997). The typical primary caregiver is an adult daughter or other female relative (Spector, Fleishman, Pezzin, & Spillman, 2000; U.S. Department of Health and Human Services, 1998). Caregiving in families differs by ethnicity, with Asian, African, and Latina and Latino Americans more likely to provide care than White Americans (National Alliance for Caregiving and American Association of Retired Persons, 1997); furthermore, immigrants are twice as likely to be caregivers as are nonimmigrants (American Association of Retired Persons, 2001). On average, caregivers spend nearly 18 hours per week providing care (U.S. Department of Health and Human Services, 1998) and continue to do so on average for four and a half years (National Alliance for Caregiving and American Association of Retired Persons, 1997).

Although caregiving on some levels may be very satisfying, it may also result in feelings of depression or anxiety, especially for women (Family Circle and Kaiser Family Foundation, 2000). The stress of giving care to a parent can bring about uncomfortable feelings as caretaking roles are reversed or earlier unresolved conflicts resurface. This suggests that in working with clients in families with old adults, it is incumbent upon the counselor to inquire about caregiving tasks and responsibilities and the emotional impact upon caregivers. Knight (2004) has proposed considering a stress and coping model and family systems model when working with caregivers, and suggests using cognitive-behavioral interventions, group counseling, and family or individual counseling to help caregivers cope.

Elder Abuse

Between 2–10% of old adults are victims of elder abuse (Lachs & Pillemer, 2004), and 90% of the time, their abuser is a family member, most often an adult child or a spouse (Administration on Aging, 2005). Stress, lack of respite care, inadequate emotional support for caregivers, and lack of resources may contribute to elder abuse. Mistreatment may include physical abuse, emotional abuse, sexual abuse, exploitation, neglect, or abandonment (National Center on Elder Abuse, 2005). Emotional abuse in terms of verbal assault, isolation, lack of affection, and so on, occurs most frequently, followed by financial abuse, neglect, and physical abuse

(Reis, Nahmiash, & Shrier, 1993). Elder abuse is reported less frequently than child abuse. The actual rate of elder abuse is probably higher than statistics indicate, because many old people are reluctant to report abuse received while living with an adult child or spouse for fear that the alternative—institutionalization—would be even worse. Neither victims nor perpetrators are likely to voluntarily seek treatment.

Successful interventions for elder abuse have emphasized education and counseling for the caregiver and concrete assistance, such as nursing, homemaking, or bath care, for the care receiver (Reis & Nahmiash, 1995). Empowerment groups in which abused old people can vent their feelings, support one another, and raise self-esteem are another, less frequently used treatment option. Counselors should become familiar with symptoms of elder abuse—for example by using the Brief Abuse Screen for the Elderly (Reis et al., 1993)—and their individual state's laws regarding mandatory reporting of suspected elder abuse.

Sexuality

One way that dominant culture marginalizes groups is through manipulation of the targeted group's sexuality. For some groups, this results in perceptions of hypersexuality or being oversexed; for others—including old adults—the images are of asexuality or disinterest in sex. For old adults, however, the reality is quite different. Most old adults can and do have satisfying sex lives. A recent American Association of Retired Persons study found that for many old adults sexual relationships were an important factor in maintaining a high quality of life and—for those in good health and who have a sexual partner—there is not an inevitable loss of sex (Fisher, 2005). In old adults, untreated health problems oftentimes have a pronounced negative effect on sex (Fisher, 2005). This suggests that in counseling old adults around issues of sex, it is profoundly important for the client to rule out, have treated, or learn to manage health problems.

☐ General Treatment Implications

In 1983, Myers reported that only 36% of counselor education programs offered a course on working with old people and that only 1–4% of old people received outpatient mental health services. Low use of mental health services has been attributed to negative attitudes on the part of both clients and counselors and to a lack of specialized training for mental health practitioners (Myers & Schwiebert, 1996). Other factors that affect use of mental health services may include real or perceived costs of treatment, and a lack of attention to indigenous values and development of counseling techniques consistent with those values.

Today gerontological counseling is evolving into its own specialization within the field of counseling. There are several counselor education programs that now offer a training specialization in gerontological counseling. Counselors who work with older clients rated their most important roles as those of pre-retirement counselor and educator, bereavement counselor, family counselor, and in-service counselor educator (Johnson & Riker, 1982). The American Counseling Association has developed 10 minimum essential gerontological competencies for all counselors (see box below) and 16 minimum essential competencies for gerontological counseling specialists (Myers & Sweeney, 1990). The minimum competencies for all counselors primarily focus on counselor attitudes and knowledge, and the competencies for gerontological counseling specialists emphasize skills.

Minimum Essential Gerontological Competencies

1. Exhibits positive, wellness-enhancing attitudes toward older people, including respect for the intellectual, emotional, social, vocational, physical, and spiritual needs of older individuals and the older population as a whole.

2. Exhibits sensitivity to sensory and physical limitations of older people through appropriate environmental modifications to facilitate helping relationships.

3. Demonstrates knowledge of the unique considerations in establishing and maintaining helping relationships with older people.

---

continued on next page

Minimum Essential Gerontological Competencies
continued from previous page

4. Demonstrates knowledge of human development for older people, including major psychological theories of aging, physiological aspects of "normal" aging, and dysfunctional behaviors of older people.

5. Demonstrates knowledge of social and cultural foundations for older people, including common positive and negative societal attitudes, major causes of stress, needs of family caregivers, and the implications of major demographic characteristics of the older population (e.g., numbers of women, widows, increasing numbers of older minorities).

6. Demonstrates knowledge of special considerations and techniques for group work with older people.

7. Demonstrates knowledge of lifestyle and career development concerns of older people, including the effects of age-related physical, psychological, and social changes on vocational development, factors affecting the retirement transition, and alternative careers and lifestyles for later life.

8. Demonstrates knowledge of the unique aspects of appraisal with older people, including psychological, social, and physical factors that may affect assessment, and ethical implications of using assessment techniques.

9. Demonstrates knowledge of sources of literature reporting research about older people and ethical issues in research with older subjects.

10. Demonstrates knowledge of formal and informal referral networks for helping older people and ethical behavior in working with other professionals to assist older people.

Note: Myers, J. E., & Sweeney, T. J. (1990). *Gerontological competencies for counselors and human development professionals.* Alexandria, VA: American Association for Counseling and Development.

Group Counseling

Group work with older clients is a popular form of counseling, particularly in inpatient settings. Haight and Burnside (2005) suggest several specific principles for group work with old adults:

1. In order to maximize effectiveness, group leaders may need to be more active, directive, and self-disclosing when working with old adults than when working with other age groups.

2. Problem solving, rather than insight or personality change, should be stressed; especially if the group is addressing issues related to loss or death.

3. Group leaders must attend to the physical constraints and special needs of group members, given old adults' greater likelihood of impairments in vision, audition, mobility, and generally decreased energy.

4. Group leaders should offer psychological support to group members; this will increase confidence in group members and will also enhance group cohesiveness.

5. Member-leaders who emerge from within the group should be encouraged and supported, especially as a way to raise self-esteem.

6. It is important to carefully screen group members, attending to the group's purpose and objectives.

Some specific modes of group counseling for severely impaired older people in an inpatient setting that have been particularly effective are reality orientation, remotivation, and resocialization (Myers & Schwiebert, 1996). *Reality orientation* techniques—which may be particularly helpful in work with forgetful adults (see Haight & Burnside, 2005)—include coordinated staff efforts to help residents maintain orientation to time, place, and person. *Remotivation therapy* involves structured inpatient groups that promote discussion of topics related to the "real" world and building relationships with other group members with the aim of lessening confusion and disorientation. *Resocialization* is akin to psychodynamic group therapy in that it focuses on interpersonal relationships and feelings. Touch can be an important affirmation of dignity and worth, especially for clients who live alone or in institutional settings, and when touch seems appropriate, Myers and Schwiebert (1996) suggested asking the client if a hug would be all right.

Bibliotherapy

Bibliotherapy is another approach worth considering with older clients. The counselor needs to assess the client's level of literacy and select reading material with the size of type appropriate for the client's eyesight. Following are some questions a counselor might ask to help process the meaning of a book or other material for a client (Myers & Schwiebert, 1996, p. 183): "With which character did you most identify? How did the book make you feel? Whom did you like best or least in the book? What themes did you see in the book?"

Early Recollections

Another approach is to make use of early recollections. This is a technique adapted from Adlerian theory in which older clients are asked to remember and recount their earliest memories (Sweeney & Myers, 1991). The themes and patterns the client generates reflect her or his guiding principles for living, given that people selectively recollect early life experiences to create their personal mythology (Corsini & Wedding, 2004). Increasing awareness of a life script then allows the client the freedom to validate or change underlying themes.

Other Approaches

Many other specific approaches and techniques have been suggested for counseling old people, among them biofeedback and other behavioral techniques for pain management (Human Capital Initiative, 1993), family therapy, peer counseling, art therapies, making therapeutic use of pets or horticulture, guided imagery, and self-hypnosis (Myers & Schwiebert, 1996). However, more research and development of counseling techniques that are culturally consistent or indigenous to old clients are needed, and the recent advances toward developing gerontological counseling specializations and essential competencies offer hope that this will occur.

In addition to becoming familiar with counseling methods and issues relevant to old people, counselors also need to educate themselves about community resources, such as Meals on Wheels, home health care, personal care, respite services, and hospice programs (Myers & Schwiebert,

1996). Information about local senior centers; assisted living; retirement; nursing facilities; and laws related to wills, trusts, and conservatorships also is useful.

☐ Case Vignette

Marlon is a 68-year-old heterosexual White male in good physical health who sought counseling after the death of his wife of 40 years from a protracted and particularly debilitating illness. He was articulate although a bit disheveled. He presented with feelings of sadness, restlessness, lack of interest in eating, and trouble sleeping. He told the story of how, the night his wife died in the hospital, on his way home he stopped at a bar and had a drink while chatting with a woman; he did not tell the woman that his wife had died just hours earlier. Marlon expressed feeling extreme guilt over this incident. He has no children and is estranged from his siblings. Although he had retired three years ago, he now works 20 hours a week volunteering at a local middle school. The counselor focused her work with Marlon on expression of feelings about his deceased wife, encouraging him to talk about both the good times and the not-so-good times, talking about his feelings of guilt over going out for a drink the night his wife died, and normalizing the sadness and emptiness he expressed. She also referred Marlon to a psychiatrist for a medication evaluation and to a support group for bereft spouses. At his support group, Marlon met a woman with whom he could have a coffee or attend a movie from time to time. During the first year after the loss of his wife, Marlon's condition waxed and waned: He still tended to have what he called "bad days," but these seemed to be occurring with less frequency.

Questions

1. Does Marlon suffer from bereavement, depression, both, or neither?

2. Why might the counselor have encouraged Marlon to talk about both the good times and the not-so-good times he had had with his wife?

3. As a counselor, how would you have responded (personally and professionally) to the fact that Marlon went out for a drink the night his wife died?

Reflection 1

One big issue in this case revolves around gender. Although females are more likely to be bereft of their spouses or partners than males, still a significant number of males suffer the death of a spouse or partner. Furthermore, males generally utilize counseling less than do females, and this might be especially true in late life, given cohort considerations. We might want to consider Marlon as existing in at least two cultures—that of men and that of old adults—and provide counseling sensitive to these two considerations. Of the former, it is important to keep in mind that men may have weaker social supports (e.g., in terms of friendships) than do women.

Reflection 2

Marlon seems to be developing a stronger social support system through his counselor's referral to a support group for bereft spouses, as well as through his volunteer work at a local middle school. This is particularly important as it appears that he is estranged from his own siblings and has no children of his own. The support group will offer adult peers to whom he can relate and the volunteer work with children will give him an opportunity to share his wisdom and experience. By talking about the good and the bad times he had with his wife, Marlon will be able to discover important themes and lessons learned, which will undoubtedly help him gain perspective on his life that will contribute to his self-fulfillment.

☐ Recommended Cultural Resources

Print Media

Kidder, T. (1993). *Old friends*. Boston: Houghton Mifflin. Pulitzer Prize-winner's true account of life in a nursing home and the unlikely friendship that develops between two residents.

Martz, S. H. (Ed.). (1987). *When I am an old woman, I shall wear purple*. Watsonville, CA: Papier Mache Press. Award-winning anthology of poems and prose about late life and aging.

Moore, P., & Conn, C. P. (1985). *Disguised: A true story.* Nashville, TN: W. True story of a young woman who disguises herself as an old woman and goes out into the world.

Pipher, M. (1999). *Another country: Navigating the emotional terrain of our elders.* New York: Riverhead. Nationally noted counselor and author writes about the culture of old age and the current cohort of old adults.

Thomas, W. H. (2004). *What are old people for?: How elders will save the world.* Acton, MA: Vanderwyk & Burnham. A persuasive indictment of ageism in North America.

Multimedia

Gilbert, B. (Producer). (1982). *On golden pond* [Videorecording]. Farmington Hills, MI: Twentieth Century-Fox Video. A daughter reconnects with her increasingly cognitively impaired father and her aging mother.

Hoffmann, D. (Producer). (1995). *Complaints of a dutiful daughter* [Videorecording]. New York: Women Make Movies. A true, poignant account of a daughter's relationship with her mother who suffers with Alzheimer's disease.

Zanuck, R., & Zanuck, L. F. (Producers). (1989). *Driving Miss Daisy* [Film]. Burbank, CA: Warner. Sentimental portrayal of the relationship between an old woman and her chauffeur in the deep South.

Organizations

American Association of Retired Persons (AARP), 601 E St. NW, Washington, DC 20049. Phone: (202) 434-2277. URL: www.aarp.org. Premier political action organization for older adults.

American Society on Aging (ASA), 833 Market Street, Suite 511, San Francisco, CA 94103. Phone: (800) 537-9728. URL: www.asaging.org. A major professional organization for those individuals who work with old adults or have an interest in aging issues.

Family Caregiver Alliance (FCA), 180 Montgomery Street, Suite 1100, San Francisco, CA 94104. Phone: (800) 445-8106. URL: www.caregiver.org. Exceptional organization that provides education, services, research, and advocacy for family caregivers.

Older Women's League (OWL), 1750 New York Ave. NW Suite 350, Washington, DC 20006. Phone: (800) 825-3695. URL: owlinfo@owl-national.org. Provides research, education, and advocacy for mid- and late-life women.

CHAPTER

Counseling Persons
With a Disability

Disability only becomes a tragedy for me when society fails to provide the things we need to live our lives; job opportunities or barrier free buildings for examples. It is not a tragedy for me that I'm living in a wheelchair.

Judy Heumann, disability activist and
assistant secretary for the Office of Special
Education and Rehabilitative Services
(Tainter, Compisi, & Richards, 1995, p. 31)

For me, "physically challenged" or "differently abled" do not capture the serious-ness and depth of our pain and struggle. A friend of mine who is visibly disabled described her daily struggle as being "center stage but invisible"—stared at but avoided. I want to be appreciated, and appreciate myself, for what I really deal with. From that I derive pride and self-esteem.

Ricki Boden, MFCC (Boden, 1988, p. 157)

☐ Histories and Diversity

People with disabilities are the nation's largest minority group, numbering more than 50 million persons (U.S. Census Bureau, 2006a). Nearly one in five people in the United States has a disability (U.S. Census Bureau, 2006a), and nearly one in six people in the United States has limited abilities to perform some major life activity (Murphy & Murphy, 1997). Among children aged 6–14, about 11% have a disability (U.S. Census Bureau, 2006a). Approximately two million persons with a disability are inpatients in some type of institutional setting (Tomes, 1992). This is the only minority group that a person may become a member of at any time (Foster, 1996a).

Persons with disabilities constitute a very diverse group. The Americans with Disabilities Act (1990) defines persons with disabilities as anyone possessing a physical or mental impairment that substantially limits one or more major life activities, or a person on record or regarded by others as having such an impairment. Caring for oneself, performing manual tasks, walking, seeing, hearing, speaking, breathing, learning, and working are all among the major life activities whose performance may be impaired. Some of the many disabling conditions included are orthopedic, visual, speech, and hearing impairments, cerebral palsy, epilepsy, muscular dystrophy, multiple sclerosis, cancer, heart disease, diabetes, mental retardation, emotional illness, specific learning disabilities, HIV disease, tuberculosis, drug addiction, and alcoholism. In addition to variations in the specific nature of their disability, persons with disabilities also vary in terms of the age of onset of their disability, the severity of their condition, the extent to which they identify with their disability status, and the degree to which their specific condition is accepted by others (Vernon & Andrews, 1989), in addition to diversity in age, sex, ethnicity, sexual orientation, and socioeconomic status. Given the amazing diversity among people grouped together because they have disabilities, it is imperative that counselors fully assess their clients and refrain from presumptive stereotyping based solely on one aspect of their client, for example, the nature of the disability. In order to present an overview of some of the conditions included, some general information regarding specific disabilities follows, but the possibility of overgeneralization must again be noted.

Types of Disabilities

Approximately 35 million people (13% of the U.S. population) report some degree of hearing loss; specifically, about 600,000 are deaf, 6 million report having a lot of trouble hearing, and over 28 million report having a little trouble hearing (Gaulladet Research Institute, 2006). From 46 to 60% of the deaf population deal with unemployment, substance abuse, criminal behavior, and poor mental health (Vernon, 1995). In one study, 53% of the deaf mothers whose children had been referred to Child Protective Service had problems with substance abuse (Moser & Rendon, 1992). Although an estimated 40,000 deaf people in this country may have substantial psychopathology, only 1 in 50 receives the mental health services he or she needs (Pollard, 1996). There is only one inpatient substance abuse program, in St. Paul, Minnesota, specifically designed to meet the needs of deaf patients and fewer than half of the states have any inpatient mental health units for deaf persons at all (Vernon, 1995).

There are approximately 1.3 million persons in the United States who are legally blind (National Federation of the Blind, 2006); however, not all legally blind persons are totally without sight, and few persons who report some impairment in their sight are legally blind (consider all the persons who wear glasses). Among persons with a visual impairment (i.e., those who have some degree of a problem with sight) there is great variability within the population based on degree of impairment alone inasmuch as 70–80% of all legally blind persons in the United States have some sight (Murphy & Murphy, 1997). For someone with a visual impairment, getting to the counselor's office can be daunting. During the initial phone contact it would help to give very thorough and explicit directions to the office, including the size and shape of the building, the number of buildings, driveways, or pathways from the nearest cross street, the location of the door, the layout of the floorplan and furniture, a description of the waiting area, and other information that may be relevant (Harsh, 1993).

A large subpopulation of people with mobility impairments are persons with a spinal cord injury. Among people with a spinal cord injury, 82% are male and the men tend to have more serious injuries than women (Page et al., 1987). Age of onset is most frequent in the 15–24-year age group. No other disability affects sexual functioning as profoundly as spinal cord injury (Parker, 1983). The effects include difficulties with mobility, sexual performance, and forming and maintaining relationships with the opposite sex (Page et al., 1987). These difficulties may contribute to the erroneous myth that persons with spinal cord injuries are asexual. Counselors can educate themselves about alternate sources of sexual arousal and gratification. Some recommendations for teaching students with mobility impairments that may apply to counseling as well are to make sure that the room is accessible, plan for unavoidable tardiness due to transportation delays, and understand and accommodate any absences caused by required medical treatment (Murphy & Murphy, 1997). If a client prefers later appointments, this may be due to anticipation of personal assistants being often tardy or unreliable, as opposed to resistance to counseling.

The U.S. Census Bureau estimates that nearly 14 million Americans (about 5% of the population) suffer from a mental disability (2006c); this, however, may be an underestimate. Given that 15% of all adults report signs or symptoms of mental illness in the preceding month (Tomes, 1992), the number of people affected by emotional disabilities is enormous. The major impact of mental health problems in terms of lost disability-adjusted life years is from depressive disorders, self-inflicted injuries, Alzheimer's or dementia, and alcohol dependence ("Disability from Mental Health Problems," 1995). However, the full impact of emotional and cognitive disabilities may not be known because people with learning disabilities or other hidden disabilities may not be included in reported statistics. Many adults now diagnosed with learning disabilities may not have known they had a disability for years as diagnostic testing was less available when they were in their youth. Also, children and adolescents with learning disabilities often develop low self-esteem or passive learning styles that later affect their productivity or ability to ask for help as adults (Murphy & Murphy, 1997; Palombo, 1979).

Like many other minority groups, persons with disabilities have been subject to stereotypes and discrimination and these negative perceptions and actions have been described as *ablism* (Tainter, Compisi, & Richards, 1995). According to Riger (1992), people with disabilities have a personal and collective history of devaluation, marginalization, and exclusion. A 1985 Harris poll revealed that 74% of Americans with disabilities recognize a common identity with other disabled people and 45% believe they are a "minority group in the same sense as African Americans and Hispanics" (Tainter et al., 1995). Stereotypes of persons with disabilities portray them as abnormal, helpless, heroic and inspirational, invisible, childlike, in need of pity or charity, and as the smiling poster child, appreciative of even second-class status (Harsh, 1993; Murphy & Murphy, 1997; Tainter et al., 1995).

The *spread phenomenon* refers to the mistaken belief that if one disability is present there must be others, such that a person with a physical disability is impaired mentally or emotionally as well (Murphy & Murphy, 1997). There is also a medical model belief that having a disability means being less than whole and therefore a person with a disability must want and need to be "cured." Examples are a person preferring to try to walk painstakingly rather than make use of the greater mobility afforded by a wheelchair or struggling to lip-read or speak when using an

A Brief Chronology of Events Relevant to Persons With Disabilities

1965   *Dictionary of American Sign Language* (Stokoe, Casterline, & Croneberg, 1965) is published, showing that ASL is a sophisticated, complex language distinct from English.

1988   Deaf Freedom Day (March 13) redefined the focus and qualifications for Gallaudet University's president and board of trustees after students protested the election of a non-deaf president.

1990   Americans with Disabilities Act (ADA) protects persons with disabilities from discrimination in employment, public accommodations, transportation, and telecommunications.

1994   *Tugg v. Towey* ruling in U.S. district court decrees that mental health services provided through sign language interpreters are not equivalent to services hearing people receive, thereby violating the Americans with Disabilities Act.

interpreter or pad and pencil would actually yield better communication (Tainter et al., 1995; Vernon & Andrews, 1989).

A brief chronology of events relevant to people with disabilities (adapted from Pollard, 1996) is listed in the box above. Although many of the events are specific to persons with hearing impairments, they have implications for people with other disabilities and may be suggestive of political changes and legal rulings to come.

Race and Social Class Considerations

Disability may have a profound impact on social class, and vice versa. In some circumstances, the presence of a disability may result in overt or subtle discrimination in educational or employment opportunities, thereby limiting the income (and social class status) of the person with a disability. In other circumstances, poverty or limited resources may result in the inability to acquire accommodations for the person with a disability. The median annual income for people with a nonsevere disability is $22,000 and for those with a severe disability it is $12,800 (compared to $25,000 for those with no disability), and the poverty rate for adults with a nonsevere disability is 11% and for those with a severe disability it is 26% (compared to 8% for those with no disability) (U.S. Census Bureau, 2006b). Clearly there is a relationship between ability and social class. For example, one study found that older farmers and blue-collar workers reported higher levels of functional disabilities than did white-collar workers (Rahkonen & Takala, 1998). Brantlinger (2001) takes a broad view of how poverty and social class influence the perceptions and definitions of disability (especially within the context of the school system) and argues for an egalitarian, nonexclusive, social justice approach to ability and disability.

☐ Indigenous Treatment and Cultural Views of Disability

Native Americans have the highest proportion of persons with disabilities among ethnic minority groups in the United States (Tomes, 1992). One urban study of Native Americans with disabilities found diabetes, followed by arthritis in women, and substance abuse in men, to be the most frequent disabling conditions (Marshall, 1996). Specific tribal beliefs may be attached to certain disabilities, which can complicate the counseling process. For example, the Dine'h have a legend that attributes seizures to incest between siblings, a belief that contributes to greater feelings of stigmatization and shame among Dine'h who are epileptic (Levy, 1987).

Common barriers to rehabilitation services for Native Americans include lack of transportation, long distances to treatment centers, and lack of vocational training and employment opportunities (Marshall, 1996; Martin, Frank, Minkler, & Johnson, 1988). Cultural barriers also hinder treatment, as evidenced by a survey of 332 vocational rehabilitation counselors who work with American Indians (Martin et al., 1988). The counselors tended to rate clients who were more acculturated to the dominant society as having more success with rehabilitation and rated vocational rehabilitation as more willing to support Native American healing practices for clients who lived on a reservation.

African American mothers of children with disabilities consistently reported less stress, feeling less overwhelmed, and feeling less personally burdened than other mothers in general, according to research reviewed by Rogers-Dulan and Blacher (1995), who suggested that flexible family roles, informal adoption, and help from extended family and the Black church all contribute to family support in making it easier to raise a child with a disability. African American family values that (a) all children are important, (b) the family is collectively responsible for raising children, (c) "fictive" kin and foster children are part of the family, and (d) family ties should be strong, all help provide a buffer when a family member has a disability. For African Americans, religion may have an influence on family adjustment to disability, but its effects are not clearly known. Religious beliefs may facilitate accepting and finding meaning in the disability; however, religious implications of guilt, wrongdoing, or failure on the part of the parent could contribute to overprotectiveness and feelings of inadequacy. Counselors and other service providers should coordinate their efforts to augment rather than replace the assistance exchange already present in many African American communities.

Cultural values may have an effect on how Latinos and Latinas deal with disabilities. Clients who subscribe to a sense of fatalism about their lives may be more difficult to motivate toward rehabilitation. An injured Latino or Latina who values family over work may be reluctant to relocate away from her or his extended family for better employment prospects elsewhere. For those men who place great importance on the integrity of their bodies, having to stay home "like a woman" due to a disability may contribute to depression or alcoholism. In contrast, other disabilities may receive little emphasis. Mild disabilities that do not impinge on a child's ability to form and maintain social relationships may not be considered disabilities at all (DeLaGarza, 1996).

Asian Americans have the lowest proportion of persons with disabilities among the ethnic minority groups in the United States (Tomes, 1992). However, cultural beliefs may contribute to possibly inaccurate reporting rates. Some Asian cultures promote the belief that disabilities are the result of the actions of previous ancestors, making public knowledge of a disability a cause for family shame. An attitude of acceptance of trauma or suffering as part of life may aid in adjustment to disability, but hinder rehabilitation efforts. For example, the Chinese are less positive toward people with disabilities than Whites are, and they are even less positive toward people with mental disabilities than they are toward people with physical disabilities. An attitude of acceptance of trauma or suffering as part of life may aid in psychological adjustment to disability but hinder rehabilitation efforts (F. Chan, Lam, Wong, Leung, & Fang, 1988).

Most caregivers are female and this overlaps with women's issues around multiple role strain and making time for oneself. Disability may have additional effects on the lives of gay men and lesbians, because health insurance policies, legal wills, and other survivor preparations may be either unavailable or more complicated if someone in the family is homosexual (Roland, 1994).

☐ Cultural Values

Language

Language is an important concern when counseling some persons with a disability. This is especially important with deaf clients. Roughly only 30% of spoken English is understandable through lip reading ("Deaf Culture," 1995), making American Sign Language the primary language for full communication for most deaf persons. American Sign Language is a much different language from English, having its own vocabulary, syntax, grammar, homonyms, and pattern of discourse (Pollard, 1996). In addition, facial expressions, body movements, and space around the body may have specific semantic or grammatical functions, unlike in English. Even if a counselor is fluent in ASL it is important that he or she keeps in mind that all hearing-impaired persons do not necessarily like to use sign, nor do they all lip-read. Murphy and Murphy (1997) make several recommendations for teachers that can also be applied to counselors: Get the client's attention before talking, face the client and not an interpreter, speak slowly and clearly, use short sentences, make use of facial expressions and gestures, and ask the client to repeat or write down anything that was not understood by the counselor.

Disability Culture

Prior to the early 1980s there was little written about disability that wasn't clinical in nature, and even less was written by people with disabilities (Braunstein, 1997). Since then a "disability culture" of art, music, and literature has evolved. "Disability culture is disabled people talking about ourselves," according to writer and performance artist Cheryl Wade (Braunstein, 1997, p. 30). Disability culture implies a cultural identity based on a shared history of oppression. Steven Brown, cofounder of the Institute on Disability Culture (Braunstein, 1997), states that "Most importantly, we are proud of ourselves as people with disabilities. We claim our disabilities with pride as part of our identity."

Cultural transmission is difficult because most disabled children are not born to disabled parents. There is a disability press, including publications such as *The Disability Rag,* and a weekly nationwide live radio show, *On a Roll.*

Deaf Culture

More has been written about the cultural aspects of deafness than of any other disability. Indeed, most deaf persons view themselves as part of a linguistic and cultural minority and not as disabled ("Deaf Culture," 1995). Those who identify with deafness as a minority group experience tend to capitalize the "D" in Deaf as an indication of cultural identification, whereas deaf with a small "d" refers to the physical condition of hearing impairment and is used more frequently among people who lost their hearing as adults. The solidarity and strength of Deaf culture is notable given that 90% of deaf persons have hearing parents (Sudbury, 1993; "Deaf Culture," 1995) and their language acquisition and introduction to the culture is primarily through peers.

Schools for the deaf, often boarding schools that provide a sense of "home," and Deaf Clubs, social organizations owned and operated by Deaf people, are vital institutions that help to pass on Deaf cultural traditions (Bienvenue & Colonomous, 1988). For example, Deaf culture tends to value direct communication more than does hearing culture (Sudbury, 1993). This has many implications for counseling with respect to how humor, assertiveness, and family communications are perceived between Deaf and hearing persons.

Deaf culture values deaf children. Deaf adults may make special efforts to spend time with them in order to help the children develop positive attitudes and self-acceptance (Bienvenue & Colonomous, 1988). Mainstreaming deaf children may make it more difficult for them to make connections with the Deaf community. The likelihood that a deaf child will be improperly evaluated or treated by a professional who has had no training in deafness is also greatly increased (Vernon, 1995).

Cochlear implantation, a medical procedure that may enable a deaf person to hear, is a controversial issue. Deaf people who view deafness as a cultural minority status oppose the more medical view of deafness as an undesirable disability that must be remedied (Pollard, 1996). The cultural view has been adopted by the American Deafness and Rehabilitation Association, a multidisciplinary network of professionals who work with the Deaf, which uses the acronym ADARA in order to de-emphasize the negative connotation of "rehabilitation" in its name. Pollard (1996) notes that cross-cultural legitimacy and sign fluency are only achievable through consistent interaction with deaf persons above and beyond the service provider's professional training.

☐ Counseling Issues

Although two out of three people with a disability want to work, only half of them are employed due to hiring discrimination or a lack of transportation (Tainter et al., 1995). According the U.S. Census (2006a), 56% of people with a disability were employed in the past year (versus 88% of nondisabled people who were employed in the past year). Underemployment is also a significant problem. For example, many deaf clients feel stuck in their jobs yet don't assert themselves because they feel lucky to even have a job (Marino, 1996).

Employment discrimination is difficult to eliminate. The ADA does not allow employers to collect health or mental health histories, ask whether an applicant has a disability, test for disabilities, or require a pre-employment medical exam (ADA, 1990; Romei, 1991; Youngstrom, 1992). The ADA does allow employers to ask about abilities needed to perform a job. But although the ADA prohibits overt discrimination, Foster (1996a) asserted that more subtle bias still remains. This occurs even though accommodations for disabled workers are relatively inexpensive. A U.S. Department of Labor (1982) survey of federal contractors who made efforts to hire workers with disabilities reported that 81% of the respondents spent $500 or less on accommodations. Turnover is low among employees with disabilities, so companies can easily justify any accommodation costs (Romei, 1991). When appropriate, highly skilled workers are more often provided environmental adaptations or special equipment, whereas less-skilled workers more often receive job redesign, retraining, or selective placement as accommodations (U.S. Department of Labor, 1982).

The career counseling considerations for a client with disabilities depend greatly on the specific nature of their disabilities. For example, for persons with autism, the social aspects of work may be the most problematic and certain occupations may decrease the likelihood of social problems occurring (Grandin, 1996). Some freelance businesses such as piano tuner, automobile repair, computer programming, or graphic arts use skills that many autistic persons possess, such as perfect pitch, mechanical ability, or artistic talent.

Using nontraditional job-seeking strategies, such as networking, and avoiding personnel departments, has been recommended for people with autism, who may not interview well (Grandin, 1996). This may also be helpful advice for clients with emotional or communicative disabilities. Harsh (1993) suggested that a counselor of a visually impaired client become knowledgeable of the types of skills he or she can acquire though rehabilitation training, and this kind of knowledge would be useful with respect to many other disabilities as well.

Family

The effects of disability on family functioning may in part depend upon which phase the family is in relative to dealing with disability. Roland (1994) describes three phases: crisis, chronic, and terminal.

The *crisis phase* includes the symptoms the family must deal with prior to obtaining a diagnosis, the diagnosis, and the period of initial adjustment after diagnosis. The primary issue during this phase is managing change, determining what must change and what can stay the same in the family's and the individual's sense of identity. The family's and the individual's history of dealing with change is relevant here (Roland, 1994). Feelings of shock, denial, anger, and depression typical of the grief process may permeate the initial adjustment to disability.

The *chronic phase* involves day-to-day coping and stamina in dealing with a condition that may be permanent or last for many years. The family's history of dealing with constant stressors can give an indication of their strengths and help anticipate problems that may arise (Roland, 1994). The magnitude of daily stress the client experiences needs to be understood from the client's own perspective. For example, Riger (1992) notes that the continual frustration architectural barriers present to some people with disabilities can instill feelings of shame, alienation, victimization, hurt, and outrage that can be as strong as the emotions resulting from physical or sexual assault.

The *terminal phase* includes pre-terminal preparation, death, and grief. Emotions are especially significant in this phase, along with attitudes toward hospice and death and culturally normative rituals around death (Roland, 1994).

Wright (1983) describes overprotectiveness as a primary issue for families of children with disabilities. The counselor can work directly with the parents to help dissipate their feelings of guilt or urge them to participate in a parent discussion group, which can be useful in setting realistic expectations. Cultural reactions to disability may provide secondary gains for the client or family that may help or hinder the adjustment process. Responsibilities and expectations of the client or family may be temporarily suspended in some cultures. The counselor may also want to explore the role of a patient in the client's culture (Roland, 1994).

Spirituality

Schulz (2005) defined spirituality as connection to self, others, the world, or a greater power (see also Soissons-Segal, 2004). In Schulz's (2005) research, she noted that some persons with disability felt disconnection rather than connection to self, others, the world, or a greater power, and that they expressed their spirituality through actions to change the feeling of disconnection. Coulter (2001) advises those who work with persons with disability to identify the spiritual in them, even in the face of severe intellectual or physical disabilities. Interestingly, at least one disability rights organization, the National Organization on Disability (NOD), has instituted a program to assist congregations, faith groups, and seminaries in becoming more welcoming to persons with disability. This welcoming includes removal of physical and psychological barriers that hinder a person with disability's full participation in the life of the congregation, faith group, or seminary (National Organization on Disability, 2006). It behooves counselors to become sensitive to issues of spirituality and connection in the lives of clients with disabilities and to actively advocate for full integration of persons with disabilities into spiritual communities.

Abuse

A counselor should be particularly watchful for signs of physical or sexual abuse when working with a client with a disability. Research has indicated that disabled children are more likely to have been physically or sexually abused than their peers (Courtois, 1988), even 1.7 times to 3.4 times more likely (Arizona's Child Abuse InfoCenter, 2006). Women with disabilities who are abused may not report the abuse because they may have no accessible shelter to go to and no alternatives for long-term help if the abuse is perpetrated by a care provider.

☐ General Treatment Implications

When working with a client with a disability a helpful general approach may be to offer rather than automatically provide assistance (Murphy & Murphy, 1997). For example, Harsh (1993) suggests that the easiest way to determine the level of assistance required by a person with a visual impairment is to ask, "Would you like to take my arm?" This kind of helpful but flexible stance addresses the great diversity among persons with a disability in terms of level of impairment and their degree of identification with having a disability. In a similar vein, counselors should be prepared to expand their role to include coordination among community agencies and advocacy on behalf of their clients with disabilities when appropriate (Vacc & Clifford, 1995).

Counselors must be on their guard for counter-transference issues that may inhibit empathy for their clients with disabilities. Michael Berube, an able-bodied man, wrote that "Understanding disability as an integral part of the human condition ... means imagining ourselves in their places—and that may be too much of a psychological burden for us to bear" (Berube, 1997, p. B5).

Some frequent counseling themes when working with persons who are dealing with a disability are feelings of abandonment, inclusion and exclusion, anger, and specialness (Boden, 1992). Rehabilitation counseling is a specialization in its own right within the field of counseling and it is beyond the scope of this text to try to cover all counseling issues relevant to people with disabilities. The reader is encouraged to take additional coursework related to rehabilitation counseling for more specific information about the psychological and physical adjustments that occur when a client is living with a disability.

☐ Case Vignette

Arthur is a 19-year-old, Japanese American male in the first semester of his sophomore year in college. He was referred by one of his professors who noticed that Arthur had some difficulties in comprehending class lectures as well as assignments. Arthur stated that he was a modest student in high school, making above-average grades. He stated that he always felt he wasn't as smart as other kids, but that he always gave school his best try. When asked about alcohol and substance use, Arthur looked down and shook his head, "No." He found his freshman year in college difficult, making mostly Cs and a couple of Bs. He expressed considerable anxiety about the increasing difficulty of his studies and his fear that he would fail and disappoint his parents.

Questions

1. As a counselor, would you refer Arthur for testing for learning disabilities? Why or why not?

2. How would you deal with the emotional aspect of this case (i.e., Arthur's anxiety over possible failure and feelings of disappointing his parents)?

3. What might you recommend to professors facing students who appear like Arthur?

Reflection 1

In this interesting case, we have a young man who is presenting with comprehension difficulties. He also states a history of problems in school. The specific nature and etiology of these difficulties is unknown. Arthur may have a learning disability, he may be suffering the effects of substance abuse or anxiety, or there may be some other totally different explanation. As his counselor, I would want to explore further his comprehension difficulties, the possibility of substance use, and the possibility of language difficulties (especially if English were not his first language). Also important would be to give Arthur some techniques to reduce his anxiety, which may contribute to his academic performance problems. There are many, many more potential aspects to this case (e.g., family dynamics, friendship networks, cultural considerations, possible hearing impairment) that at present are a mystery. These too in time would need to be explored in order to come to some initial conclusions.

Reflection 2

Arthur's difficulty with comprehension may be caused by many factors. He may have a learning disability, difficulty comprehending English as a second language, hearing loss, substance abuse, or a combination of two or more of these factors. Referral for testing for a learning disability may not be successful if Arthur feels a strong stigma attached to having a disability. It would be helpful to send students like Arthur to a college counselor who might help Arthur figure out whether his difficulties with school are influenced by cultural or physical factors and give him support in finding ways to both understand and ameliorate his comprehension difficulties and his feelings and the reactions of his parents.

☐ Recommended Cultural Resources

Print Media

Berube, M. (1998). *Life as we know it*. New York: Random House. Moving story of a family who reflects on life with a child born with Down syndrome.

Davis, L. J. (1995). *Enforcing normalcy*. New York: Verso. A hearing child of deaf parents, the author deconstructs disability.

Dolnick, E. (1993, September). Deafness as culture. *The Atlantic Monthly*, 272, 37–53. A readable analysis of the culture of deafness.

Mairs, N. (1996). *Waist-high in the world: A life among the nondisabled*. Boston: Beacon Press. A woman with multiple sclerosis writes about her experiences in a wheelchair.

Shapiro, J. (1994). *No pity*. New York: Random House. A history of the disability rights movement.

Trent, J. W., Jr. (1995). *Inventing the feeble mind*. Berkeley, CA: University of California Press. A history of developmental disability.

Multimedia

Bienvenue, M., & Colonomous, B. (1988). *An introduction to American deaf culture* [Videotape]. Silver Spring, MD: Sign Media Inc. This series covers social interactions, language, group norms, values, and identity in American deaf culture.

Cornfield, S. (Producer). (1981). *The elephant man* [Videorecording]. Hollywood: Paramount Home Video. Poignant, true account of the life of a man with severe physical disconfigurement.

Sugarman, B., & Palmer, P. (Producers). (1987). *Children of a lesser god* [Videorecording]. Hollywood: Paramount Pictures Corporation. A new teacher at a school for the deaf begins to fall in love with a deaf janitor.

Organizations

American Deafness and Rehabilitation Association (ADARA), PO Box 27, Roland, AR 72135, (501) 868-8850, www.adara.org. ADARA has as its mission to improve service delivery to person's who are deaf or hard of hearing.

American Foundation for the Blind (AFB), 11 Penn Plaza, Suite 300, New York, NY 10001, (212) 502-7600, www.afb.org. AFB advocates for greater technology access and the promotion of independent and healthy living for persons with vision loss.

The ARC of the United States, 1010 Wayne Avenue, Suite 650, Silver Spring, MD 20910, (301) 565-3842, www.thearc.org. The ARC promotes support and services for persons with developmental disabilities and their families.

National Association of the Deaf (NAD), 814 Thayer Avenue, Silver Spring, MD 20910, (310) 587-1788 & (310) 587-1789, www.nad.org. An advocacy organization for deaf persons.

Counseling Bicultural/ Biracial People

I am a person of color.
I am not half-"white."
I am not half-"Asian."
I am a whole "other."

A Chinese, Japanese, German, Hungarian,
English woman (Fulbeck, n.d.)

☐ Histories and Diversity

The number of mixed-race people in the United States is growing quickly. In 1970, 460,000 children lived in mixed-race families. By 1980 this number had doubled to 996,070 and by 1990 almost 2 million children lived in mixed-race households (U.S. Census Bureau, 2001). Thus, the number of mixed race children in the United States had increased by 400% in only 20 years. In 2000, the first year that respondents were allowed to claim more than one race, more than 7 million people acknowledged being of more than one race in the United States, or about 3% of the population (U.S. Census Bureau, 2005). There are many successful actors, singers, artists, and athletes who are biracial. Some examples are Joan Baez, Jennifer Beals, Halle Berry, Benjamin Bratt, Yul Brynner, Mariah Carey, Cher, Jimi Hendrix, Frida Kahlo, Ben Kingsley, Bob Marley, Anthony Quinn, Keanu Reeves, Jimmy Smits, and Tiger Woods. However, the multiracial heritage of these famous people is often not highlighted. When visible in the media, they may be pressed to identify only with their ethnic minority backgrounds (Streeter, 1996).

Intercultural Marriage

The burgeoning increase in mixed race people is related to the increase in intercultural marriage. As the population of the United States has become increasingly ethnically diverse, intercultural marriages have become more frequent. Less than 40 years ago, 17 states still had laws prohibiting interracial marriages and the last miscegenation laws were repealed by the *Loving v. Virginia* Supreme Court decision of 1967 (Bachman, 1996; Burnette, 1995; Marino, 1995; Tucker & Mitchell-Kernan, 1990). Intercultural marriages may occur between members of many ethnic groups. Indeed, concerns of intercultural couples may occur between persons from different ethnic groups within the same broad "racial" group, for example, a Chinese American and Japanese American couple. In addition, intercultural couples could differ in terms of religion rather than race.

Currently three million interracial married couples are estimated to reside in the United States (U.S. Census Bureau, 2000). These marriages most frequently occur between middle-class individuals who have been married before and live and work in integrated areas (Marino, 1995). Americans, in general, have been somewhat ambivalent about interracial marriage, verbally expressing their approval as long as the marriage does not occur within their own family.

As in other marriages, partners in intercultural marriages need to come to a common definition of marriage, family, fidelity, and privacy. Agreements about sex roles, the role of extended family, and the language to be spoken in the family are necessary. Beyond the usual difficulties in maintaining a marriage, interracial marriages may face societal discrimination and other complications due to cultural differences in gender roles, childrearing, language and communication style, food preferences, and spirituality (Burnette, 1995).

The degree of prejudice and discrimination the couple may experience may depend on many factors, including their place of residence, level of education, and socioeconomic status (Marino, 1995). A European American partner in an interracial marriage may be shocked by the experience of racism from other European Americans (Burnette, 1995; Marino, 1995). If the couple lives in an area that is not integrated and is foreign to one of the partners, there needs to be a recognition that the person who is living in a "foreign" culture will always have some needs that will go unfulfilled (Bishop, 1989).

Perhaps as a consequence of additional stresses, the divorce rate for interracial marriages is higher than for other marriages (Marino, 1995). Along similar lines, one author suggests that children raised in interfaith households may possibly be more at risk for depression and unruly behavior, particularly if they are not raised in one of their parents' faiths (Sleek, 1995).

Labeling

There are many terms that have been used to describe people of biracial descent, among them "mixed," "brown," "tan," "biracial," "interracial," "multiracial," "multiethnic," "Eurasians," "LatiNegras," "Hapas," "mestizos," "mulatos," "Oreo," "banana," "apple," "Heinz 57 Variety," and "half and half," (Comas-Diaz, 1996; Gibbs & Moskowitz-Sweet, 1991; Jacobs, 1992; Kerwin, Ponterotto, Jackson, & Harris, 1993; Wardle, 1992). Some have negative connotations and some more positive. For example, the term "Hapa" was originally a derogatory slang word for a person of mixed racial descent and derived from the word for "half" in Hawaiian. Now it is a term of pride and self-definition embraced by many Eurasian, Amerasian, and other people of part Asian or Pacific Islander ethnic heritage.

Social Class Considerations

As noted previously, interracial marriages are most frequent among the middle class and the degree of prejudice a biracial person experiences may be moderated by social class. In addition, a lighter skin tone implies positive connotations about social class (Neal & Wilson, 1989). It is important to assess a biracial client's social class background as a context for the degree of acceptance a client may have experienced.

☐ Cultural Values

According to Wei Ming Dariotis, "The difficulty is that we don't have a common culture. We don't share things with each other that we share with our different ethnic groups, like language, food, mannerisms and accents. These daily things make it difficult to have a hapa culture" (Nishioka, 1999). However, popular literature suggests a couple of common values for mixed race people. One is a desire to embrace the duality or multiplicity of all a person's heritages, to be inclusive rather than exclusive. Mixed race organizations may be open to members who are interested in multiracial issues, rather than only those who are themselves biracial.

A second value is that of self-definition. It is important that the label used to describe one's ethnicity is self-selected by the mixed race person. For example, Tiger Woods once described his ethnicity as "Cablinasian," a term which includes his Caucasian, Black, Indian, and Asian heritages ("Hapas in the Spotlight," 1999).

Spirituality

It has been suggested that the counselor explore the dynamics and religious practices of each client's family of origin, asking about the importance of these customs for the individual. In interfaith couple counseling, partners can be encouraged to learn about the history and practices of each other's religion so they can avoid misunderstandings and create new options for overcoming differences (Sleek, 1995).

For example, Catholics have been described as tradition-oriented, guilt-ridden, and concerned about outward appearances whereas Protestants have been contrasted as stressing individual responsibility and emotional isolation (McGill & Pearce, 1982). The work ethic in America has at times been attributed to the Protestant faith. In Protestantism, work and productive activity are considered an expression of the spiritual being and eventually as indicative of one's self-worth. The external controls and behavioral conformity attributed to Catholicism in American culture have been contrasted with a Protestant emphasis on self-direction (Johnson, 1985). The implications for counseling are many: possibly more difficulties with guilt for Catholics and with dependency or workaholic tendencies for Protestants.

Most of the six million Jews in the United States, as of 1982, emigrated from eastern European countries, Russia, and Poland in response to religious persecution. The retention of the Jewish faith is important, especially for first-generation immigrants. One cultural issue for Jews in counseling may be interfaith marriage. Jewish–Christian interfaith marriages have a higher rate of divorce than same-faith unions and this has become an issue of cultural survival because the frequency of marrying outside the faith has risen to 52% in recent years (Sleek, 1995).

☐ Indigenous Treatment Methods

Biracial people have begun to express themselves in writing, photography, and on the Internet as a way to self-define their experiences and network with other biracial people (Fulbeck, n.d.). Cornell, Stanford, U.C. Berkeley, and some other college campuses have biracial student organizations. These groups can have political as well as social agendas. There is a Bill of Rights for Racially Mixed People (see box below, Root, 2001), which includes basic assertions of self-definition, self-expression, and multiculturalism.

Bill of Rights for Racially Mixed People
Maria P. P. Root

I HAVE THE RIGHT ...
Not to justify my existence in this world.
Not to keep the races separate within me.
Not to be responsible for people's discomfort with my physical ambiguity.
Not to justify my ethnic legitimacy.

I HAVE THE RIGHT ...
To identify myself differently than strangers expect me to identify.
To identify myself differently from how my parents identify me.
To identify myself differently from my brothers and sisters.
To identify myself differently in different situations.

I HAVE THE RIGHT ...
To create a vocabulary to communicate about being multiracial.
To change my identity over my lifetime—and more than once.
To have loyalties and identification with more than one group of people.
To freely choose whom I befriend and love.

☐ Counseling Issues

Identity Issues

Claiming a positive racial identity has been noted as the primary issue for biracial people as they develop (Herring, 1992; Wehrly, 1996). Zack (1996) described firsthand the shame she felt not being all White and the inherent conflict of being both Black and Jewish. Most biracial children would prefer to classify themselves as biracial and not identify solely with one ethnic group, if given a choice (Newsome, 2001). However, in early adolescence many biracial children feel pressured to choose one of their ethnic backgrounds over others. Winn and Priest (1993) interviewed 34 biracial children, ages 8–20, and reported that 82% felt compelled to choose a monocultural racial label and felt uncomfortable choosing one parent's ethnic identification over that of the other parent. "Mixed," "brown," and "tan" are among their preferred ethnic labels (Jacobs, 1992).

Over the years several biracial identity development models have been suggested and they acknowledge the pressure of having to choose only one ethnic group identification and the eventual desirable acceptance of multiple cultural identities (Jacobs, 1992; Kerwin & Ponterotto, 1995; Poston, 1990). Adolescence may be the most difficult developmental period for biracial children. For example, Gillem, Cohn, and Thorne (2001) tell of a 17-year-old biracial Black/White girl who was unaware of her family's difference from others or her parents being of different races until the sixth grade. She became depressed upon entering junior high when her former White friends became less friendly and the significance of her ethnic difference became evident.

Gibbs and Moskowitz-Sweet (1991) studied 20 biracial/bicultural females and males 14–18 years old who had been diagnosed with identity disorders. Some of these teens felt rejected from both groups when they entered high school. However, many studies with nonclinical samples suggest that the concept of marginality for most biracial adolescents may be exaggerated or nonexistent (Foeman & Nance, 1999; Harrison, 1997; J. E. Jones, 2000; Kerwin, 1991; Shih & Sanchez, 2005). For example, J. E. Jones (2000) studied 251 adolescents and found no differences in either psychological adjustment or self-esteem between multiethnic adolescents and others. Moreover, there may be benefits to being biracial. Brandell (1988) suggests that biracial children may be more tolerant and less willing to develop biases toward others. Gibbs and Hines (1992) found biracial teens liking their appearance, being unique or different, and flexibility to fit in with more groups as positive aspects of being biracial. Biracial people can feel that they have the best of both worlds (Hall, 1992).

Hall (1992) described the critical period for ethnic identity development as beginning at age 13–15 and lasting for three to four years. Experiencing racism, attending a new school with a different racial mix than the previous school, or other such critical incidents may trigger a time of ethnic identity confusion as the biracial adolescent is forced to deal with issues of ethnic allegiance (Kerwin & Ponterotto, 1995). Counselor exploration of ethnic identity issues is particularly important with mixed race adolescents.

Bicultural adolescents who have one ethnicity and a minority sexual orientation may have identity issues similar to those of biracial adolescents with more than one ethnic background. Gay or lesbian youth of color may feel a lack of acceptance of their sexuality among their friends of color and a lack of acceptance of their ethnic background when associating with gay or lesbian youth.

Social and Sexual Issues

Adolescence is also a challenging time socially and sexually for multiracial youth. Other people may have varying social reactions to the ambiguous features of many biracial individuals, contributing to feelings of ambivalence about their physical specialness (Root, 1994).

In many places in the United States, standards of beauty are White (Shackford, 1984). One biracial autobiographer noted that as a teen, "looking beautiful meant looking white" (Scales-Trent, 1995, p. 52). Another wrote about being mocked for the shape of her eyes as early as age four and growing up feeling different and resentful (Fukuyama, 1999).

On the other hand, there is a media stereotype regarding biracial beauty suggesting that biracial women are more exotic, sexual, passionate, immoral, and promiscuous (Nakashima, 1992; Root, 1994). Thus, biracial teenage girls and women may experience more freedom to be flexible with their appearance than biracial men. In careers where physical appearance plays an important role, such as fashion, acting, or newscasting, a biracial woman can use this stereotype to advantage. Conversely, a biracial teen who doesn't question the authenticity of the stereotype could put herself at risk for promiscuity and sexually transmitted disease.

☐ General Treatment Implications

Counselors need to be fully aware of their own attitudes toward inter-racial marriage and biracial people, especially as their attitudes may vary depending upon the particular ethnic mix of the client. Root (1994) found differences in attitudes toward Asian–White, Black–White, and Black–Asian Americans. The counselor's own level of racial identity development may contribute to counter-transference toward a biracial client with respect to perceptions of client attractiveness, severity of experienced racism, and social isolation.

Additionally, the counselor's own ethnic background may bring up transference issues for a biracial client related to the client's experiences with people of a similar ethnic background. A Black–White American client might have a different reaction to a Black counselor compared to a White counselor, depending on the client's stage of biracial identity development and prior experiences with Blacks and Whites.

Mixed race heritage is not typically the primary presenting problem in counseling (Herring, 1992; Root, 1994), although many client concerns may be related to biracial identity issues (Brandell, 1988). For example, Root (1994) suggests that some biracial women develop a communication style that others may perceive as compulsive or paranoid in their attempt to provide more context for others in order to be better understood. In contrast, a biracial woman who has become comfortable with her unique experiences and perceptions could appear narcissistic or "entitled" to others. Even if not a presenting problem, in formulating counseling goals for biracial clients, the counselor might consider affirming positive multi-racial identity development and supporting the client's sense of individuality and cultural assets. Strengths-based therapeutic approaches such as solution-focused therapy and narrative therapy have been recommended for counseling biracial clients (Edwards & Pedrotti, 2004).

The environment surrounding a biracial/bicultural client should be assessed for influences that may help or hinder the counseling process. Gibbs and Moskowitz-Sweet (1991) raise several questions relevant to biracial children that might also apply to biracial adults: What are the ethnic backgrounds in the client's immediate and extended families? How supportive have parents been in discussing racial feelings? How frequent and positive is family communication? What is the ethnic composition of the client's school or workplace and what have been the client's ethnic experiences there? Is the neighborhood White, one ethnic minority group, or mixed? A White–Asian American woman described how her family embraced multiculturalism, but the surrounding community did not (Fukuyama, 1999). A Black and Jewish woman noted that there was no Black-Jewish community to which she could belong (Zack, 1996). A supportive environment may be especially important in early childhood when a biracial child first experiences being different and the counselor, parents, and teachers can be part of this support system (Wardle, 1987, 1992).

Biracial Children

Lee (2004) summarizes treatment recommendations for counselors of biracial girls that have implications for biracial boys and bicultural children in general. The recommendations have four foci: introducing a sociopolitical perspective, developing/affirming multicultural identity, forming community, and educating parents (Lee, 2004).

A biracial child's presenting style for interacting with the world may evolve from her or his sociopolitical experiences (Root, 1994). It may be helpful to acknowledge the stereotypes and social barriers that biracial people face in the United States. Feelings of being frequently judged or evaluated by others may have some basis in reality. Being stared at is a common experience that can contribute to self-consciousness. The counselor can help the biracial child discuss her or his desired response to queries such as, "What are you?" "Why don't you look like your mother/father?" or "How come your name doesn't match how you look?" (Fukuyama, 1999; Root, 1994; Wehrly, 1996). Role play and *stress inoculation*, a form of cognitive restructuring that includes education, rehearsal, and implementation, can be used to minimize the hurt or annoyance such questions can elicit.

For biracial clients who have experienced racial discrimination, Koss (1990) makes several helpful suggestions for treating women who have experienced sexual harassment: (1) validate feelings; (2) provide information that places the experience within a larger U.S. sociopolitical context regarding race and power; (3) encourage the safe expression of anger; (4) monitor maladaptive coping patterns that might be adopted; (5) provide a place to mourn lost beliefs, build new ones, and develop support systems; and (6) offer hope and discuss actions that may empower and address the discrimination.

Counselors can assist their biracial clients in developing and affirming their racial/ethnic identity. A discussion of possible ethnic labels and a positive construction of how to describe oneself can help assist the client in formulating a sense of positive identity. It is important to affirm a "both/and" conceptualization of biracial identity (Fukuyama, 1999; Gillem et al., 2001). The specific term chosen does not matter as much as that it is positive and inclusive of the client's heritages. A label such as "half-Japanese" suggests a valuing of oneself as less than others (Fukuyama, 1999). In contrast, one schoolgirl described herself as "half-Japanese, half-Chinese, full American," a source of envy from peers who understood the connotation that biracial meant more than a single ethnicity (Lee, 2004). Wardle (1992) recommended the label of "brown" for young children ages 2–7 as it is based on skin color, a salient feature for children. Fukuyama (1999) self-reported the positive benefit of her counselor acknowledging and affirming her Asian American identity by both naming and welcoming it. Root (1994) recommends that counselors support a "situational identity," a multicultural/multiracial identity that can change from day to day.

Various techniques may be helpful in fostering positive biracial identity development at different ages. With younger children as well as adolescents, opportunities to experiment with different labels and ideas about race have been recommended (Root, 1994; Wardle, 1992). Dolls with different physical features, pictures of people from various ethnic backgrounds, and self-portraits (with counselor attention to facial features, hair, and skin tones) may all be helpful with younger children (Wardle, 1992).

With older children, an adolescent might consider changing or adding to her or his name or might begin to use a middle or more formal name (Root, 1994). An adolescent girl might select her hairstyle, clothing, and overall appearance to take on a certain ethnic look one day and a different look the next. The counselor can frame these variations as positive, adaptive, conscious choices about the messages the client wants to communicate with her appearance. In this way, the client can examine racial stereotypes for herself (Root, 1994). Another technique is for the counselor to ask the client to examine her or his answers to the question "Who am I?" and "Who do I want to be?" to build self-awareness and a more in-depth foundation for her or his biracial identity (Lee, 2004).

Increasing community connections can prevent or minimize the potentially isolating effects of our society on biracial children. Youth organizations and activities with multicultural goals and interracial social activities can be recommended (Gibbs & Moskowitz-Sweet, 1991). Counselors can develop a biracial peer support group with group discussion topics such as how to handle name-calling, being stared at, or being conspicuous; the stereotype regarding biracial attractiveness and sexuality; and the benefits of being biracial (Coleman, 2001; Gibbs & Moskowitz-Sweet, 1991; Root, 1994). The goals for the group would be to understand that differences are normal, not indicative of inferiority (Nishimura, 1995), and to develop pride in ethnic diversity.

Finally, parents can be educated in techniques that might help them in raising a biracial child as summarized by Lee (2004):

1. Be clear about their own racial feelings, attend to the child's racial feelings, and discuss cultural experiences, cultural differences, and ethnic identity issues within the family (Coleman, 2001; Gibbs & Hines, 1992; Gibbs & Moskowitz-Sweet, 1991; Jacobs, 1992).

2. Immerse the child in opportunities to learn about each of her or his heritage groups through attending cultural, artistic, social, and political events, eating ethnic foods, being involved with extended family on both sides, and developing friends from all family backgrounds (Herring, 1992; Wehrly, 1996).

3. Establish family rituals that promote family pride and uniqueness (Herring, 1992; Winn & Priest, 1993).

4. Carefully consider the presence of other biracial families in choosing where to live, schools, and religious organizations (Coleman, 2001; Harrison, 1997).

5. Expose the child to books and stories with multiracial protagonists and give her or him opportunities to interract with biracial adults who can serve as role models (Wehrly, 1996).

6. Teach children about racism and sexism and their interactions, discuss examples from television and magazines, and model the acceptance and celebration of cultural differences (Winn & Priest, 1993).

7. Teach girls about the attitudes of society toward women and women's physical appearance, how to deal with stereotypes regarding multiracial people, and how to be prepared to respond to racial or sexual slurs (Root, 1994).

☐ Case Vignette

Denise is a 25-year-old woman with a graduate degree in education. She has an African American father from New Orleans and a Japanese mother from Hawaii. She spent more time growing up with her father's family who embraced her since she was a baby. However, her mother's family has not always acknowledged her and her two sisters, by saying negative things about her father and making comments such as, "Those are you-know-who's children" when speaking about Denise or her siblings. Denise admitted that she mostly wore dark colors, that is, brown, black, and so on, cut her hair short, and wore African wraps and jewelry in order to "fit in" while growing up. She currently attends Alcohol and Narcotics Anonymous meetings and expresses that she is lonely and does not have any of the same friends anymore.

Questions

1. How are Denise's multiracial experiences related to her current concerns?

2. How might you work with Denise as her counselor?

3. What interventions outside of counseling sessions may be helpful for Denise?

Reflection 1

Denise's mother's family may have contributed to feelings of isolation and rejection, which Denise may have dealt with by turning to alcohol and drugs. Supportive therapy to help Denise discover and feel good about her own unique identity may be helpful. In terms of her feelings of loneliness, helping Denise find other groups in the community to join that she might feel more connected to is recommended. Some possible organizations are a biracial club or a church.

Reflection 2

Based on the information presented above, Denise appears to feel more connected to her father's family than to her mother's family. Growing up, the lack of warmth and acknowledgment from her mother's family may very well have been difficult for Denise to deal with; hence she may have turned to alcohol or drugs. I would consider using a Bowenian approach to working with Denise, perhaps helping her construct a genogram that represents her personal, familial, and environmental circumstances. She may be able to see patterns emerge with this information and maybe deal more directly with issues related to her extended family.

I also might utilize bibliotherapy, encouraging Denise to read stories of other biracial individuals and how they overcame family obstacles and difficulties. Depending on her community, it might be possible for her to find multicultural, interracial, or biracial support groups or social groups so that she and others could share activities and experiences.

☐ Recommended Cultural Resources

Print Media

Wehrly, B. (1996). *Interracial books and stories. Counseling interracial individuals and families.* Alexandria, VA: American Counseling Association. This book includes a resource list with good reading suggestions for biracial children and adolescents.

Multimedia

Feldman, E. S. (Producer). (1985). *Witness* [Film]. Hollywood: Paramount Pictures. Mainstream American and Amish cultures collide in this violent, suspenseful, and romantic drama.

Fulbeck, K. (n.d.). *The Hapa project.* Retrieved June 5, 2006, from http://www.thehapaproject.com/hapa/default.htm. Originally begun as a forum for Hapas to answer the question "What are you?" in their own words and photographic portraits, the project has become a book, traveling photo exhibit, and online community.

Organizations

Association of MultiEthnic Americans, PO Box 29223, Los Angeles, CA 90029-0223, info@AMEAsite.org. The Association of MultiEthnic Americans (AMEA), a nonprofit organization, is an international association of organizations dedicated to advocacy, education, and collaboration on behalf of the multiethnic, multiracial, and transracial adoption community.

Black Native American Association, http://www.bnaa.org/

Swirl, Inc., 244 Fifth Avenue, Suite J230, New York, NY 10001-7604. Swirl's main listserv: http://www.yahoogroups.com/group/SWIRLinc. Swirl's listserv for teens: http://www.yahoogroups.com/group/SwirlTeens. This is an organization for self-identified mixed heritage individuals and families.

REFERENCES

Abbitt, D., & Bennett, B. (1984). Being a lesbian mother. In B. Berzon (Ed.), *Positively gay* (pp. 123–129). Los Angeles: Mediamix Associates.

About. (n.d.). *Sexual harassment statistics.* Retrieved February 17, 2006, from http://womensissues.about.com/cs/governornews/a/sexharassstats.htm

Abraham, A., & Jacobs, W. R., Jr. (1999). *Diversity in college faculty.* Atlanta, GA: Southern Regional Education Board. Retrieved July 5, 2006, from http://www.sreb.org/programs/dsp/publications/Diversity.pdf

Abraham, N. (1995). Arab Americans. In R. J. Vecoli, J. Gadens, A. Sheets, & R. V. Young (Eds.), *Gale encyclopedia of multicultural America* (Vol. 1, pp. 84–98). New York: Gale Research.

Abreu, J. M. (2001). Theory and research on stereotypes and perceptual bias: A didactic resource for multicultural counseling trainers. *The Counseling Psychologist, 29*(4), 487–512.

Abudabbeh, N. (1996). Arab Families. In M. McGoldrick, J. Giodana, & J. K. Pearce (Eds.). *Ethnicity and family therapy* (2nd ed., pp. 333–346). New York: Guilford Press.

Acuña, R. (2000). *Occupied America: A history of Chicanos.* New York: Longman.

Adelman, M. (1990). Stigma, gay lifestyles, and adjustment to aging: A study of later life gay men and lesbians. *Journal of Homosexuality, 20*(3/4), 7–32.

Adler, N. J. (1981). Re-entry: Managing cross-cultural transitions. *Group & Organization Studies, 6*(3), 341–356.

Adler, P. (1975). The transitional experience: An alternative view of culture shock. *Journal of Humanistic Psychology, 15*(4), 13–23.

Adler, T. (1990, January). Causes, cure of PMS still elude researchers. *APA Monitor,* 10.

Administration on Aging. (2001). *Achieving cultural competence: A guidebook for providers of services to older Americans and their families.* Washington, DC: U.S. Department of Health and Human Services.

Administration on Aging. (2004). *A profile of older Americans: 2004.* Washington, DC: U.S. Department of Health and Human Services.

Administration on Aging. (2005). *Elder rights and resources: Elder abuse* [Online document]. Washington, DC: U.S. Department of Health and Human Services. Retrieved July 5, 2005, from http://www.aoa.gov/eldfam/Elder_Rights/Elder_Abuse/Elder_Abuse.asp

Ahmed, S., & Lemkau, J. (2001). Cultural issues in the primary care of South Asians. *Journal of Immigrant Health, 2*(2), 89–96.

Akbar, N. (2004). *Papers in African psychology*. Florida: Mind Productions and Associates.

Al-Deen, N. (1991). Understanding Arab Americans: A matter of diversities. In *cross-communications and aging in the US*. Mahwah, NJ: Erlbaum.

Alderete, E., Vega, W. A., Kolody, B., & Aguilar-Gaxiola, S. (2000). Lifetime prevalence of and risk factors for psychiatric disorders among Mexican migrant farm workers in California. *American Journal of Public Health, 90*(4), 608.

Al-Krenawi, A., & Graham, J. R. (2005). Mental health practice for the Muslim Arab population in Israel. In C. L. Rabin (Ed.), *Understanding gender and culture in the helping* process. Belmont, CA: Thomson Wadsworth.

Alliance for Aging Research (2003). *Ageism: How healthcare fails the elderly*. Washington, DC: Author.

Allison, K. W., Crawford, I., Echemendia, R., Robinson, L., & Knepp, D. (1994). Human diversity and professional competence. *American Psychologist, 49*, 792–796.

Allport, G. W. (1954). *The nature of prejudice*. Reading, MA: Addison-Wesley.

Alvarez, A. N., & Miville, M. L. (2003). Walking a tightrope: Strategies for teaching undergraduate multicultural counseling courses. In D. B. Pope-Davis, H. Coleman, W. M. Liu, & R. L. Toporek (Eds.), *Handbook of multicultural competencies in counseling & psychology* (pp. 528–545). Thousand Oaks, CA: Sage.

Alzheimer's Association (2005). *Statistics about Alzheimer's disease* [Online document]. Chicago, IL: Author. Retrieved, June 21, 2005, from www.alz.org/AboutAD/statistics.asp

American Academy of Family Physicians. (2004). *Premenstrual dysphoric disorder*. Retrieved July 20, 2006, from http://familydoctor.org/752.xml

American Association of Retired Persons (1986). *A portrait of older minorities*. Long Beach, CA: Author.

American Association of Retired Persons (1995). *A portrait of older minorities: Research report*. Washington, DC: Author. Retrieved October 24, 2005, from www.AARP.org/research/reference/minorities/aresearch-import-509.html

American Association of Retired Persons (2001, July). *In the middle: A report on multicultural boomers coping with family and aging issues*. Washington, DC: Author.

American Association of University Professors. (2004). *Faculty salary and faculty distribution fact sheet 2003–04*. Retrieved February 15, 2006, from http://www.aaup.org/research/sal&distribution.htm

American Association of University Professors, Committee on Women (2005, July/August). The AAUP's Committeee on Women responds to Lawrence Summers. *Academe, 91*(4), 59.

American Association of University Women (1991). *Shortchanging girls, shortchanging America*. Washington, DC: Author.

American Council on Education (2006). *Making the case for affirmative action in higher education*. Retrieved June 29, 2006 from http://www.acenet.edu/bookstore/descriptions/making_the_case/works/research.cfm#college_participation.

American Counseling Association (2005). *Code of ethics*. Retrieved June 15, 2006, from http://www.counseling.org/Counselors/

American Federation of Labor—Congress of Industrial Organizations (2006). *The global economy and women*. Retrieved July 24, 2006, from http://www.aflcio.org/issues/jobseconomy/women/global/

American Men's Studies Association (n.d.). Retrieved August 10, 2006, from http://www.mensstudies.org/ and http://www.mensstudies.org/newsletter.html

American Psychiatric Association. (1987). *Diagnostic and statistical manual of mental disorders* (3rd ed. Rev.). Washington, DC: Author.

American Psychiatric Association. (1994). *Diagnostic and statistical manual of mental disorders* (4th ed.). Washington, DC: Author.

American Psychiatric Association. (2000a). *Diagnostic and statistical manual of mental disorders (DSM–IV–TR)* (4th ed. Rev.). Washington, DC: Author.

American Psychiatric Association. (2000b). *Diagnostic and statistical manual of mental disorders DSM–IV–TR* (Text Revision). Arlington, VA: American Psychiatric Press.

American Psychological Association (2000). *Guidelines for psychotherapy with lesbian, gay, and bisexual clients*. Retrieved June 15, 2006, from http://www.apa.org/pi/lgbc/publications/guidelines.html

American Psychological Association (2002). Ethical principles and code of conduct [Electronic version]. *American Psychologist, 57*(12), 1060–1073.

American Psychological Association (2003a). Guidelines on multicultural education, training, research, practice, and organizational change for psychologists. *American Psychologist, 58*(5), 377–402.

American Psychological Association (2003b). *Guidelines for psychological practice with older adults*. Retrieved June 15, 2006, from http://www.apa.org/practice/Guidelines_for_Psychological_Practice_with_Older_Adults.pdf

American Psychological Association Presidential Task Force on Enhancing Diversity (2005). *Final report* [Electronic version]. Washington, DC: American Psychological Association.

Americans with Disabilities Act. (1990). Washington, DC: Office on the Americans with Disabilities Act, U.S. Department of Justice.

Amott, T. (1993). *Caught in the crisis, women and the U.S. economy today*. New York: Monthly Review Press.

Anderson, D. (1987). Family and peer relations of gay adolescents. *Adolescent Psychiatry, 14*, 162–178.

Anderson, M. J., & Ellis, R. (1995). On the reservation. In N. Vacc, S. DeVaney, & J. Wittmer (Eds.), *Experiencing and counseling multicultural and diverse populations* (pp. 179–198). Bristol, PA: Accelerated Development.

Anwar, M. S. (1995). Review of *The function of myth in Akan healing experience: A psychological inquiry into two traditional Akan healing communities. Journal of Cross-cultural Psychology, 26*(3), 442–443.

Ariel, J., & Stearns, S. M. (1992). Challenges facing gay and lesbian families. In S. H. Dworkin & F. J. Gutierrez (Eds.), *Counseling gay men and lesbians: Journey to the end of the rainbow* (pp. 95–112). Alexandria, VA: American Counseling Association.

Arizona's Child Abuse InfoCenter. (2006). *Child abuse and children with disabilities*. Phoenix, AZ: University of Arizona Health Sciences Center. Retrieved August 3, 2006, from www.acainfo.ahsc.arizona.edu/disabilities.htm

Arredondo, P. (1991). Counseling Latinas. In C. C. Lee & B. L. Richardson (Eds.), *Multicultural issues in counseling: New approaches to diversity* (pp. 143–156). Alexandria, VA: American Counseling Association.

Arredondo, P. (1999). Multicultural counseling competencies as tools to address oppression and racism. *Journal of Counseling & Development, 77*(1), 102–108.

Arredondo, P., & Arciniega, G. M. (2001). Strategies and techniques for counselor training based on the multicultural counseling competencies. *Journal of Multicultural Counseling and Development, 29*, 263–273.

Asante, M. K. (1987). *The Afrocentric idea*. Philadelphia: Temple University Press.

Ashby, M. R., Gilchrist, L. D., & Miramontez, A. (1987). Group treatment for sexually abused American Indian adolescents. *Social Work with Groups, 10*, 21–32.

AssistHers. (n.d.). Retrieved August 13, 2006, from http://www.assisthers.org/mainwebsite_html/about.htm

Association for Multicultural Counseling and Development. (1986). *Multicultural skill competencies*. Alexandria, VA: Author.

Astin, A. W. (1982). *Minorities in American higher education*. San Francisco: Jossey-Bass.

Atkinson, D. R. (1983). Ethnic minority representation in counselor education. *Counselor Education and Supervision, 23*, 7–19.

Atkinson, D.R. (2004). *Counseling American minorities* (6th ed.). New York: McGraw-Hill.

Atkinson, D.R., & Israel, T. (2003). The future of multicultural counseling competence. In D. B. Pope-Davis, H. Coleman, W. M. Liu, & R. L. Toporek (Eds.), *Handbook of multicultural competencies in counseling & psychology* (pp. 591–606). Thousand Oaks, CA: Sage.

Atkinson, D. R., Morten, G., & Sue, D. W. (1989). *Counseling American minorities: A cross-cultural perspective* (3rd ed.). Dubuque, IA: Wm. C. Brown.

Attneave, C. (1969). Therapy in tribal settings and urban network intervention. *Family Process, 8*, 192–210.

Attneave, C. (1982). American Indian and Alaskan native families: Emigrants in their own homeland. In M. McGoldrick, J. Pearce, & J. Giordano (Eds.), *Ethnicity and family therapy* (pp. 55–83). New York: Guilford Press.

Axelson, J. A. (1993). *Counseling and development in a multicultural society*. Pacific Grove, CA: Brooks/Cole.

Azar, B. (1996a, October). Intrusive thoughts proven to undermine our health. *APA Monitor*, 34.

Azar, B. (1996b, October). Model compares heterosexual women, lesbians. *APA Monitor, 27*(10), 59.

Azar, B. (1996c, October). More money is needed for AIDS prevention efforts. *APA Monitor, 27*(10), 55.

Babcock, L. & Laschever, S. (2003). *Women don't ask: Negotiation and the gender divide*. Princeton, NJ: Princeton University Press.

Bachman, S. L. (1996, June 22). California leads nation in mixed-race marriages. *San Jose Mercury News*, p. 20A.

Backover, A. (1992, August). Minority Ph.D.s: Some groups make gains, others fall. *Guidepost, 35*(2), 1, 14.

Baker, K. (1999). Acculturation and reacculturation influence: Multilayer contexts in therapy. *Clinical Psychology Review, 19*(8), 951–967.

Baldwin, J. A., & Bell, Y. R. (1985). The African Self-Consciousness Scale: An Africentric personality questionnaire. *The Western Journal of Black Studies, 9*(2), 65–68.

Ballou, M., & Gabalac, N. (1984). *A feminist position on mental health.* Springfield, IL: Thomas.

Baratz, S. S., & Baratz, J. C. (1970) Early childhood intervention: The social science base of institutional racism. *Harvard Educational Review, 40*(1), 29–50.

Barnes, J. S., & Bennett, C. E. (2002). *The Asian population: 2000.* Washington, DC: U.S. Census Bureau, Dept. of Commerce. Retrieved January 11, 2006, from http://www.census.gov/prod/2002pubs/c2kbr01-16

Bartholomew, C. G., & Schnorr, D. L. (1994). Gender equity: Suggestions for broadening career options of female students. *The School Counselor, 41,* 245–255.

Bartlett, J. (1992). *Familiar quotations* (16th ed.). Boston: Little, Brown.

Baruth, L. G., & Manning, M. L. (1991). *Multicultural counseling and psychotherapy.* New York: Merrill (Macmillan).

Baruth, L. G., & Manning, M. L. (2003). *Multicultural counseling and psychotherapy: A lifespan perspective* (3rd ed.). Upper Saddle River, NJ: Merrill Prentice Hall.

Bayer, R. (1987). *Homosexuality and American psychiatry.* Princeton, NJ: Princeton University Press.

Behrens, J. T. (1997). Does the White Racial Identity Attitude Scale measure racial identity? *Journal of Counseling Psychology, 44,* 3–12.

Behrens, J. T., & Rowe, W. (1997). Measuring White racial identity: A reply to Helms (1997). *Journal of Counseling Psychology, 44,* 17–19.

Bell, L. A., Washington, S., Weinstein, G., & Love, B. (1997). Knowing ourselves as instructors. In M. Adams, L. A. Bell, & P. Griffin (Eds.), *Teaching for diversity and social justice: A sourcebook* (pp. 299–310). New York: Routledge.

Belsky, J. K. (1999). *The psychology of aging: Theory, research, and interventions* (3rd ed.). Pacific Grove, CA: Brooks/Cole.

Berg, I. K., & Miller, S. D. (1992). Working with Asian American clients: One person at a time. *Families in Society: The Journal of Contemporary Human Services, 73,* 356–363.

Berger, R. M. (1990). Passing: Impact on the quality of same-sex couple relationships. *Social Work, 35,* 328–332.

Bernal, M. E. (1990). Ethnic minority mental health training: Trends and issues. In F. C. Sarafica, A. I. Schwebel, R. K. Russell, P. D. Isaac, & L. B. Myers (Eds.), *Mental health of ethnic minorities* (pp. 249–274). New York: Praeger.

Berry, J. W. (1969). On cross-cultural comparability. *International Journal of Psychology, 4,* 119–128.

Berry, J. W. (1997). Immigration, acculturation, and adaptation. *International Association of Applied Psychology, 46*(1), 5–35.

Berry, J. W., Kim, U., Minde, T., & Mok, D. (1987). Comparative studies of acculturative stress. *International Migration Review, 21,* 491–511.

Berry, J. W., Kim, U., Power, S., Young, M., & Bujaki, M. (1989). Acculturation attitudes in plural societies. *International Association of Applied Psychology, 38* (2), 185–206.

Berube, M. (1997, May 30). The cultural representation of people with disabilities affects us all. *Chronicle of Higher Education*, pp. B4–B5.

Betz, N., & Fitzgerald, L. (1987). *Career psychology of women*. Orlando, FL: Academic Press.

Bhatia, S. C., & Bhatia, S. K. (1999). Depression in women: Diagnostic and treatment considerations. *American Family Physician, 60*(1), 225–244. Retrieved February 17, 2006, from http://www.aafp.org/afp/990700ap/225.html

Bidell, M. P. (2005). The Sexual Orientation Counselor Competency Scale: Assessing attitudes, skills, and knowledge of counselors working with lesbian/gay/bisexual clients. *Counselor Education and Supervision, 44*, 267–279.

Bienvenue, M., & Colonomous, B. (1988). *An introduction to American deaf culture* [Videotape]. Silver Spring, MD: Sign Media Inc.

Biggs, M. (1996). *Women's words*. New York: Columbia University Press.

Billingsley, A. (1992). *Climbing Jacob's ladder*. New York: Simon & Schuster.

Birren, J. E., & Deutchman, D. E. (2005). Guided autobiography groups. In B. Haight & F. Gibson (Eds.), *Burnside's working with older adults: Group process and techniques* (4th ed.). Sudbury, MA: Jones & Bartlett.

Bishop, B. (1989, April). Great expectations: Cultural consultant Gay Tischbirek discusses intercultural marriages. *The Paris Free Voice, 12*(3), 3.

Block, C. B. (1981). Black Americans and the cross-cultural counseling and psychotherapy experience. In A. J. Marsella & P. B. Pedersen (Eds.), *Cross-cultural counseling and psychotherapy* (pp. 177–194). New York: Pergamon Press.

Boden, R. (1988). Countertransference responses to lesbians with physical disability and chronic illness. In M. Shernoff (Ed.), *The sourcebook on lesbian–gay health care* (p. 157). Washington, DC: National Lesbian/Gay Health Foundation.

Boden, R. (1992). Psychotherapy with physically disabled lesbians. In S. H. Dworkin & F. J. Gutierrez (Eds.), *Counseling gay men and lesbians: Journey to the end of the rainbow* (pp. 157–174). Alexandria, VA: American Counseling Association.

Bornstein, K. (1994). *Gender outlaw: On men, women, and the rest of us*. New York: Vintage.

Bosch, K. (2003). *Common stressors for aging adults* [Online document]. Nebraska Cooperative Extension NF03-575. Lincoln, NE: University of Nebraska. Retrieved Oct. 14, 2005, from http://ianrpubs.unl.edu/family/nf575.htm

Bowler, R.M. (1980). Expatriate in Saudi Arabia: Stress, social support, modernity & coping. *Dissertation Abstracts International, 41*, 405B.

Boyd-Franklin, N. (2003). *Black families in therapy: Understanding the African-American experience*. New York: Guilford Press.

Boyer, S. P., & Sedlacek, W. E. (1989). Noncognitive predictors of counseling center use by international students. *Journal of Counseling and Development, 67*, 404–407.

Bracken, B. A., & McCallum, R. S. (2001). Assessing intelligence in a population that speaks more than two hundred languages: A nonverbal solution. In L. A. Suzuki, J. G. Ponterotto, & P. J. Meller (Eds.), *Handbook of multicultural assessment: Clinical, psychological, and educational applications* (2nd ed., pp. 405–431). NetLibrary Version. San Francisco: Jossey-Bass.

Brandell, J. R. (1988). Treatment of the biracial child: Theoretical and clinical issues. *Journal of Multicultural Counseling and Development, 16*, 176–187.

Brantlinger, E. (2001, March). Poverty, class, and disability: A historical, social, and political perspective. *Focus on exceptional children (FindArticles Edition)*. Retrieved August 3, 2006, from www.findarticles.com/p/articles/mi_qa3813/is_200103/ai_n8935496

Braunstein, M. (1997, February). In search of disability culture. *New Mobility, 8*(41), 29–31.

Brazziel, W. F. (1987/1988, Fall/Winter). Road blocks to graduate school: Black Americans are not achieving parity. *Educational Record, 68*(4) & *69*(1), 108–115.

Brice, J. (1982). West Indian families. In M. McGoldrick, J. Pearce, & J. Giordano (Eds.), *Ethnicity & family therapy* (pp. 123–133). New York: Guilford Press.

Bridgewater, D. (1992). A gay male survivor of antigay violence. In S. H. Dworkin & F. J. Gutierrez (Eds.), *Counseling gay men and lesbians: Journey to the end of the rainbow* (pp. 219–230). Alexandria, VA: American Counseling Association.

Brittingham, A., & de la Cruz, G. P. (2005). *We the people of Arab ancestry in the United States*. Retrieved July 27, 2006, from http://www.census.gov/prod/2005pubs/censr-21.pdf

Bronski, M. (1998). The pleasure principle: Sex, backlash, and the struggle for gay freedom. New York: St. Martin's Press.

Brown, C., & Augusta-Scott, T. (Eds.). (2006). *Narrative therapy: Making meaning, making lives*. Thousand Oaks, CA: Sage.

Brown, D. (1996, Winter). Reply to Derald Wind (sic) Sue. *ACES Spectrum, 57*(2), 3, 6.

Brown, J. F. (1993). Helping Black women build high self-esteem. *American Counselor, 2*(1), 9–11.

Brown, L. S. (1989). New voices, new visions: Toward a lesbian/gay paradigm for psychology. *Psychology of Women Quarterly, 13*, 445–458.

Browning, R. (1864). Rabbi Ben Ezra. In I. Lancashire (Ed.), *Representative poetry online* [Online book]. Toronto, CA: University of Toronto. Retrieved June 21, 2005, from http://eir.library.utoronto.ca/rpo/display/poem295.html

Brunner, B. (2006). *Timeline of affirmative action milestones*. Retrieved August 21, 2006, from http://www.infoplease.com/spot/affirmativetimeline1.html

Burnette, E. (1995, September). The strengths of mixed-race relationships. *APA Monitor*, 41–42.

Burnette, E. (1996, October). Anger undercuts ethnic-minority women's health. *APA Monitor*, 53.

Butler, R. N. (1969). Age-ism: Another form of bigotry. *The Gerontologist, 9*, 243–246.

Butler, R. N., & Lewis, M. I. (1995). Late-life depression: When and how to intervene. *Geriatrics, 50*(8), 44–55.

Cabanatuan, M., Hendricks, T., & Johnson, J. B. (2006, May 2). A million say: Let us all stay, historic day: Across the nation, a rallying call for immigrants. *The San Francisco Chronicle*. pp. 1, 9.

Cahill, S., South, K., & Spade, J. (2000). *Outing age: Public policy issues affecting gay, lesbian, bisexual and transgender elders*. New York: The Policy Institute of the National Gay and Lesbian Task Force Foundation.

Caiazza, A., Shaw, A., & Werschkul, M. (2004). *Women's economic status in the states: Wide disparities by race, ethnicity, and region.* Washington, DC: Institute for Women's Policy Research.

California Tomorrow. (2004). *Bridging multiple worlds: Mandela High School advisory curriculum.* Oakland, CA: Author. Available at www.californiatomorrow.org

Capps, R., Passel, J. S., Perez-Lopez, D., & Fix, M. (2003). *The new neighbors: A user's guide to data on immigrants in U.S. communities.* Washington, DC: The Urban Institute.

Carney, C. G., & Kahn, K. B. (1984). Building competencies for effective cross-cultural counseling: A developmental view. *Counseling Psychologist, 12*(1), 111–119.

Carter, R. T. (1990). The relationship between racism and racial identity among White Americans: An exploratory investigation. *Journal of Counseling and Development, 69,* 46–50.

Carter, R. T., & Swanson, J. L. (1990). The validity of the Strong Interest Inventory with Black Americans: A review of the literature. *Journal of Vocational Behavior, 36,* 195–209.

Cass, V. C. (1979). Homosexual identity formation: A theoretical model. *Journal of Homosexuality, 4,* 219–235.

Cass, V. C. (1984). Homosexual identity formation: Testing a theoretical model. *Journal of Sex Research, 20,* 143–167.

Catalyst. (2005). *Women "take care," men "take charge": Stereotyping of U.S. business leaders exposed.* Retrieved February 15, 2006, from http://catalyst.org/files/fact/Stereotype%20factsheet.pdf

Center for American Women and Politics. (n.d.). *Women in elected office 2006.* Retrieved February 15, 2006, from http://www.cawp.rutgers.edu/Facts/Officeholders/cawpfs.html

Centers for Disease Control & Prevention. (2004). HIV/AIDS among women. Retrieved February 15, 2006, from http://www.cdc.gov/hiv/pubs/facts/women.pdf

Cerhan, J. U. (1990). The Hmong in the United States: An overview for mental health professionals. *Journal of Counseling & Development, 69,* 88–92.

Chan, C. S. (1989). Issues of identity development among Asian American lesbians and gay men. *Journal of Counseling and Development, 68,* 16–20.

Chan, C. S. (1992). Cultural considerations in counseling Asian American lesbians and gay men. In S. H. Dworkin & F. J. Gutierrez (Eds.), *Counseling gay men and lesbians: Journey to the end of the rainbow* (pp. 115–124). Alexandria, VA: American Counseling Association.

Chan, F., Lam, C. S., Wong, D., Leung, P., & Fang, X. (1988). Counseling Chinese Americans with disabilities. *Journal of Applied Rehabilitation Counseling, 19*(4), 21–25.

Chan, S. (1991). *Asian Americans, an interpretive history.* Boston: Twayne.

Chance, P. (1981, October). The remedial thinker. *Psychology Today, 15,* 62–73.

Chavez, S. (1986). Ethnic minorities in higher education adapting to a new social system. *International Journal for the Advancement of Counselling, 9,* 381–384.

Cheatham, H. (1990). Empowering Black families. In H. Cheatham & J. Stewart (Eds.), *Black families* (pp. 373–393). New Brunswick, NJ: Transaction Press.

Chen, S., Sullivan, N. Y., Lu, Y. E., & Shibusawa, T. (2003). Asian Americans and mental health services: A study of utilization patterns in the 1990s. *Journal of Ethnic and Cultural Diversity in Social Work, 12*(2), 19–42.

Chodorow, N. (1978). *The reproduction of mothering, psychoanalysis and the sociology of gender.* Berkeley and Los Angeles, CA: University of California Press.

Chojnacki, J. T., & Gelberg, S. (1995). The facilitation of a gay/lesbian/bisexual support-therapy group by heterosexual counselors. *Journal of Counseling and Development,* 73, 352–354.

Christensen, P. (1989). Cross-cultural awareness development: A conceptual model. *Counselor Education & Supervision, 28,* 270–289.

Chung, R. C., & Okazaki, S. (1991). Counseling Americans of Southeast Asian descent: The impact of the refugee experience. In C. C. Lee & B. L. Richardson (Eds.), *Multicultural issues in counseling: New approaches to diversity* (pp. 107–126). Alexandria, VA: American Counseling Association.

Church, A. (1982). Sojourner adjustment. *Psychological Bulletin, 91,* 540–572.

Cloninger, C. R., Reich, T., & Guze, S. B. (1975). The multifactorial model of disease transmission: II. Sex differences in the familial transmission of sociopathy (antisocial personality). *British Journal of Psychiatry, 127,* 11–22.

Cohen, P. N. (2002). Book review of *Glass ceilings and Asian Americans: The new face of workplace barriers. Review of Radical Political Economics, 34,* 499–518.

Coleman, N. L. (2001). Biracial identity development individuals of African-American and European-American parentage. *Dissertation Abstracts International, 61*(11), 6162B.

Comas-Diaz, L. (1996). LatiNegra: Mental health issues of African Latinas. In M. P. P. Root (Ed.), *The multiracial experience: Racial borders as the new frontier* (pp. 167–190). Thousand Oaks, CA: Sage.

Comas-Diaz, L., & Jacobsen, F. M. (1987). Ethnocultural identification in psychotherapy. *Psychiatry, 50,* 232–241.

Conti, K. (2001). *Medicine Wheel nutrition model.* Unpublished manuscript.

Corey, G., Corey, M., & Callanan, P. (1988). *Issues and ethics in the helping professions* (3rd ed.). Pacific Grove, CA: Brooks/Cole.

Corsini, R. J., & Wedding, D. (2004). *Current psychotherapies* (7th ed.). Belmont, CA: Wadsworth.

Costantino, G., Malgady, R., & Rogler, L. (1986). Cuento therapy: A culturally sensitive modality for Puerto Rican children. *Journal of Consulting and Clinical Psychology, 54*(5), 639–645.

Coulter, D. L. (2001). Recognition of spirituality in health care: Personal and universal implications. *Journal of Religion, Disability, and Health, 5*(2/3), 1–11. Retrieved August 3, 2006, from http://books.google.com/books?vid=ISBN 0789016850&id=IfT6AwMvWZ8C&pg=PA1&lpg=PR17&dq=spirituality+and+disability&sig=yLVb4patwIfF0o_6_6uPxcPWPX4

Council for Accreditation of Counseling and Related Educational Programs. (2006). *CACREP 2008 standards revision draft #2.* Retrieved June 15, 2006, from http://www.cacrep.org/draft2-5.23.doc

Courtois, C. A. (1988). *Healing the incest wound.* New York: Norton.

Cox, H. G. (1988). *Later life: The realities of aging* (2nd ed.). Englewood Cliffs, NJ: Prentice Hall.

Cross, W. E. (1995). The psychology of Nigrescence: Revising the Cross model. In J. G. Ponterotto, J. M. Casas, L. A. Suzuki, & C. M. Alexander (Eds.), *Handbook of multicultural counseling* (pp. 93–122). Thousand Oaks, CA: Sage.

Cuellar, I., Harris, I. C., & Jasso, R. (1980). An acculturation scale for Mexican American normal and clinical populations. *Hispanic Journal of Behavioral Science, 2,* 199–217.

Curry, G. D., & Spergel, I. A. (1992). Gang involvement and delinquency among Hispanic and African-American adolescent males. *Journal of Research in Crime and Delinquency, 29*(3), 273–291.

Dahlstrom, W. G., Lachar, D., & Dahlstrom, L. E. (1986). *MMPI patterns of American minorities.* Minneapolis: University of Minnesota Press.

Dana, R. (1988). Culturally diverse groups and MMPI interpretation. *Professional Psychology: Research and Practice, 19*(5), 490–495.

Dana, R. (1993). *Multicultural assessment perspectives for professional psychology.* Boston: Allyn & Bacon.

Dana, R. H. (2001). Clinical diagnosis of multicultural populations in the United States. In L. A. Suzuki, J. G. Ponterotto, & P. J. Meller (Eds.), *Handbook of multicultural assessment: Clinical, psychological, and educational applications* (2nd ed., pp. 101–131). NetLibrary Version. San Francisco, CA: Jossey-Bass.

D'Andrea, M., & Daniels, J. (1991). Exploring the different levels of multicultural counseling training in counselor education. *Journal of Counseling and Development, 70,* 78–85.

D'Andrea, M., Daniels, J., & Heck, R. (1991). Evaluating the impact of multicultural counseling training. *Journal of Counseling and Development, 70,* 143–150.

Darling, E. (1997, February 19). "We speak standard English." *Palo Alto Weekly,* pp. 28–31.

Das, A. K. (1987). Indigenous models of therapy in traditional Asian societies. *Journal of Multicultural Counseling and Development, 15,* 25–36.

Das, A. K. (1995). Rethinking multicultural counseling: Implications for counselor education. *Journal of Counseling & Development, 74,* 45–52.

D'Avanzo, C., Frye, B., & Froman, R. (1994). Stress in Cambodian refugee families. *IMAGE: Journal of Nursing Scholarship. 26*(2), 101–105.

Davenport, D. S., & Yurich, J. M. (1991). Multicultural gender issues. *Journal of Counseling and Development, 70*(1), 64–71.

Davidson, K. (1993, May 2). Doctors becoming versed in curses. *San Francisco Examiner,* pp. A1, A8.

Deaf culture. (1995, Fall). *The Source,* p. 1.

DeAngelis, T. (1992, November). Div. 38 conference explores ethnic-minority health issues. *APA Monitor, 23*(11), 32–33.

DeAngelis, T. (1994a, March). Mass. now requires multicultural training. *APA Monitor,* 41.

DeAngelis, T. (1994b, September). More research is needed on gay, lesbian concerns. *APA Monitor, 25*(9), 39.

DeFour, D. C., & Hirsch, B. J. (1990). The adaptation of Black graduate students: A social network approach. *American Journal of Community Psychology, 18,* 487–503.

DeLaGarza, D. V. (1996). Exploring the web: Hispanic women with visual impairments. In A. Leal-Idrogo, J. T. Gonzales-Calvo, & V. D. Krenz (Eds.), *Multicultural women: Health, disability, and rehabilitation* (pp. 259–292). Dubuque, IA: Kendall/Hunt.

Delgado, J. L. (1997). *¡Salud! A Latina's guide to total health—Body, mind, and spirit.* New York: HarperCollins.

DelVecchio, R. (1995, May 14). Showing their true colors. *San Francisco Examiner & Chronicle,* pp. Datebook 30–31.

DeNavas-Walt, C., Proctor, D. B., & Hill Lee, C. (2005). *Income, poverty, and health insurance coverage in the United States: 2004.* Washington, DC: U.S. Census Bureau.

Dent, H. E. (1995, December). Everything you thought was true about testing, but isn't. *Focus, 9*(2), 4–6.

Dillard, J. M. (1983). *Multicultural counseling.* Chicago: Nelson-Hall.

Dinges, N. G., Trimble, J. E., Manson, S. M., & Pasquale, F. L. (1981). Counseling and psychotherapy with American Indian and Alaskan Natives. In A. J. Marsella & P. B. Pedersen (Eds.), *Cross-cultural counseling and psychotherapy* (pp. 243–276). New York: Pergamon Press.

Disability from mental health problems. (1995, September). *Counseling Today,* p. 41.

Dobbins, J. E., & Skillings, J. H. (1991). The utility of race labeling in understanding cultural identity: A conceptual tool for the social science practitioner. *Journal of Counseling and Development, 70,* 37–44.

Donnelly, K. (1994, April 1). Living in America. *San Jose Mercury News,* pp. C1, 3.

Dougherty, P. (1990). A personal perspective on working with men in groups. In D. Moore & F. Leafgren (Eds.), *Men in conflict* (pp. 265–275). Alexandria, VA: American Association for Counseling and Development.

Downing, N. E., & Roush, K. L. (1985). From passive acceptance to active commitment: A model of feminist identity development for women. *The Counseling Psychologist, 13,* 695–709.

Dudley, J. I. E. (1992). *Choteau Creek: A Sioux reminiscence.* Lincoln: University of Nebraska Press.

Dunbar, E. (1993). Preparation of the international employee: Career and consultation needs. *Consulting Psychology Journal: Practice & Research, 45*(1), 18–24.

Dupuy, P. (1993). Women in intimate relationships. In E. P. Cook (Ed.), *Women, relationships, and power: Implications for counseling* (pp. 79–108). Alexandria, VA: American Counseling Association.

Edgerton, R. B., & Karno, M. (1971). Mexican-American bilingualism and the perception of mental illness. *Archives of General Psychiatry, 24,* 286–290.

Edwards, A., & Polite, C. K. (1992). *Children of the dream: The psychology of Black success.* New York: Doubleday.

Edwards, L. M., & Pedrotti, J. T. (2004). Utilizing the strengths of our cultures: Therapy with biracial women and girls. *Women in Therapy. 27*(1/2), 33–43.

Ehrlich, E., & DeBruhl, M. (1996). *International thesaurus of quotations.* New York: Harper Perennial.

Eichler, A., & Parron, D. L. (1987). *Women's mental health: Agenda for research.* Rockville, MD: National Institute for Mental Health.

Elman, M. R., & Gilbert, L. A. (1984). Coping strategies for role conflict in married professional women with children. *Family Relations, 33,* 317–337.

Emerson, G. (1985). *Some American men*. New York: Simon & Schuster.

Encyclopedia Britannica. (2006). Retrieved June 28, 2006, from Encyclopædia Britannica Premium Service: http://www.britannica.com/eb/article?tocId= 9362009

Enns, C. Z. (1992). Self-esteem groups: A synthesis of consciousness-raising and assertiveness training. *Journal of Counseling and Development, 71*(1), 7–13.

Enns, C. Z. (1993). Twenty years of feminist counseling and therapy: From naming biases to implementing multifaceted practice. *Counseling Psychologist, 21*(1), 3–87.

Enns, C. Z. (1994). Archetypes and gender: Goddesses, warriors, and psychological health. *Journal of Counseling and Development, 73*(2), 127–133.

Erickson, C., & Al-Timimi, N. (2001). Providing mental health services to Arab Americans: Recommendations and considerations. *Cultural Diversity and Ethnic Minority Psychology 7*(4), 308–327.

Erickson, M., Rossi, E., & Rossi, S. (1976). *Hypnotic realities*. New York: John Wiley & Sons.

Erikson, E. (1963). *Childhood and society*. New York: Norton.

Erikson, E. (1968). *Identity: Youth and crisis*. New York: Norton.

Erikson, E. (1985). *The life cycle completed: A review*. New York: Norton.

Fabrega, H., & Nutini, H. (1994). Tlaxcalan constructions of acute grief. *Culture, Medicine and Psychiatry, 18*, 405–431.

Falk, P. J. (1989). Lesbian mothers. *American Psychologist, 44*, 941–947.

Family Circle and Kaiser Family Foundation (2000, September). *The Family Circle/Kaiser Family Foundation national survey on health care and other elder care issues: Summary of findings and chart pack*. Menlo Park, CA: The Henry J. Kaiser Family Foundation.

Fears, D. (2006, July 14). Survey shows Latinos feel empowered. *The Contra Costa Times*, p. A8.

Federal Interagency Forum on Aging-Related Statistics. (2005). *Older Americans 2004: Key indicators of well-being* [Online document]. Washington, DC: Author. Retrieved May 17, 2005, from www.agingstats.gov/chartbook2004/ highlights.html

Femiano, S. (1990). Developing a contemporary men's studies curriculum. In D. Moore & F. Leafgren (Eds.), *Men in conflict* (pp. 237–248). Alexandria, VA: American Association for Counseling and Development.

Fendel, N., Hurtado, S., Long, J., & Giraldo, Z. (1996). Affirmative action: Who does it help? Who does it hurt? *CFA Professor, 28*(2), 13–17.

Fernandez, R. R. (1989). *Five cities high school dropout study: Characteristics of Hispanic high school students*. Washington, DC: Aspira Association Inc. (ERIC Document Reproduction Service No. ED 322 240).

Festinger, L. (1954). A theory of social comparison process. *Human Relations, 7*, 117–140.

Festinger, L. (1957). *A theory of cognitive dissonance*. Evanston, IL: Harper and Row.

Figueroa, A. (1996, October 23). Latinos at Silicon Graphics work to expand minority applicant pool. *San Jose Mercury News*, p. 1TCL.

Fisher, L. L. (May, 2005). *Sexuality at midlife: Recent research from AARP*. Paper presented to the National Advisory Council on Sexual Health and Sexual Responsibility, Morehouse School of Medicine, Atlanta, GA.

Foeman, A. K., & Nance, T. (1999). From miscegenation to multiculturalism: Perceptions and stages of interracial relationship development. *Journal of Black Studies, 29*(4), 540–557.

Folwarski, J., & Smolinsk, J. (2005). Polish families. In M. McGoldrick, J. Giordano, & N. Garcia-Preto (Eds.), *Ethnicity and family therapy,* (3rd ed., pp. 741–755). New York: Guilford Press.

Fontaine, C. M. (1983, March/April). International relocation: A comprehensive psychosocial approach. *EAP Digest, 3*(3), 27–31.

Foo, L. J. (2003). *Asian American women: Issues, concerns, and responsive human and civil rights advocacy.* New York: Ford Foundation.

Food and Drug Administration (2003). *Medications and older people.* Washington, DC: Author. Retrieved October 28, 2005, from http://www.fda.gov/fdac/features/1997/697_old.html

Forrester, D. A. (1986). Myths of masculinity. *Nursing Clinics of North America, 21*(1), 15–23.

Foster, S. (1995a, August). Bridging the counseling gap between Native Americans and mainstream America. *Counseling Today, 38*(2), 1, 26–27.

Foster, S. (1995b, September). Understanding Black rage. *Counseling Today, 38*(3), 10, 22.

Foster, S. (1996a, October). October is national disability employment awareness month. *Counseling Today, 39*(4), 18.

Foster, S. (1996b, March). Tension running high in higher education. *Counseling Today, 38*(9), 10, 16, 21.

Fouad, N. A., & Carter, R. T. (1992). Gender and racial issues for new counseling psychologists in academia. *Counseling Psychologist, 20*(1), 123–140.

Fouad, N. A., Manese, J., & Casas, J. M. (1992, August). Curricular and training approaches in implementing crosscultural counseling competencies. In D. W. Sue (Chair), *Cross-cultural counseling competencies: Revision, expansion and implementation.* Symposium conducted at the meeting of the American Psychological Association, Washington, DC.

Frankl, V. E. (1978). *The unheard cry for meaning: Psychotherapy and humanism.* New York: Simon & Schuster.

Freiberg, P. (1991a, March). Black men may act cool to advertise masculinity. *American Psychological Association Monitor,* 30.

Freiberg, P. (1991b, February). Hispanics lack knowledge about AIDS. *APA Monitor, 22*(2), 31.

Fukuyama, M. A. (1999). Personal narrative: Growing up biracial. *Journal of Counseling and Development, 77,* 12–14.

Fulbeck, K. (n.d.). *The Hapa project.* Retrieved June 5, 2006, from http://www.thehapaproject.com/hapa/default.htm

Furnham, A., & Bochner, S. (1986). *Culture shock: Psychological reactions to unfamiliar environments.* New York: Methuen.

Gallaudet Research Institute. (2006). *Can you tell me how many deaf people there are in the United States?* Washington, DC: Author. Retrieved August 3, 2006, from http://gri.gallaudet.edu/Demographics/deaf-US.php

Gallo, J. J., & Lebowitz, B. D. (1999). The epidemiology of common late-life mental disorders in the community: Themes for the new century. *Psychiatric Services, 50,* 1158–1166.

Gándara, P. (1995). *Over the ivy walls: The educational mobility of low-income Chicanos.* Albany: State University of New York Press.

Garcia, M., & Lega., L. I. (1979). Development of a Cuban Ethnic Identity Questionnaire. *Hispanic Journal of Behavioral Sciences, 1,* 247–261.

Garrett, J. T., & Garrett, M. W. (1994). The path of good medicine: Understanding and counseling Native American Indians. *Journal of Multicultural Counseling and Development, 22,* 134–144.

Gibbs, J. T. (1987). Identity and marginality: Issues in the treatment of biracial adolescents. *American Journal of Orthopsychiatry, 57,* 265–278.

Gibbs, J. T., & Hines, A. M. (1992). Negotiating ethnic identity: Issues for Black-White biracial adolescents. In M. P. P. Root (Ed.), *Racially mixed people in America* (pp. 223–238). Newbury Park, CA: Sage.

Gibbs, J. T., & Moskowitz-Sweet, G. (1991). Clinical and cultural issues in the treatment of biracial and bicultural adolescents. *Families in Society, 72*(10), 579–592.

Gibson, F., & Burnside, I. (2005). Reminiscence group work. In B. Haight & F. Gibson (Eds.), *Burnside's working with older adults: Group process and techniques* (4th ed.). Sudbury, MA: Jones & Bartlett.

Gil, R. M., & Vazquez, C. I. (1996). The Maria paradox: How Latinas can merge old world traditions with new world self-esteem. New York: G. P. Putnam's Sons.

Gillem, A. R., Cohn, L. R., & Thorne, C. (2001). Black identity in biracial Black/White people: A comparison of Jacqueline who refuses to be exclusively Black and Adolphus who wishes he were. *Cultural Diversity & Ethnic Minority Psychology, 7*(2), 182–196.

Gilligan, C. (1982). *In a different voice: Psychological theory and women's development.* Cambridge, MA: Harvard University Press.

Giordano, J., McGoldrick, M., & Guarino Klages, J. (2005). Italian families. In M. McGoldrick, J. Giordano, & N. Garcia-Preto (Eds.), *Ethnicity and family therapy,* (3rd ed., pp. 616–628). New York: Guilford Press.

Gloria, A. M., & Segura-Herrera, T. A. (2004). ¡Somos! Latinas and Latinos in the United States. In D. R. Atkinson (Ed.), *Counseling American minorities* (pp. 279–299). New York: McGraw-Hill.

GLSEN. (2005). *From teasing to torment: New national report on school bullying.* New York: Gay, Lesbian & Straight Education Network. Retrieved June 4, 2006, from http://www.glsen.org/cgi-bin/iowa/educator/library/record/1859.html

GLSEN. (2006). *Welcome to the students resource page.* New York: Gay, Lesbian & Straight Education Network. Retrieved June 4, 2006, from http://www.glsen.org/cgi-bin/iowa/student/student/index.html

Gong-Guy, E., Cravens, R. B., & Patterson, T. W. (1991). Clinical issues in mental health service delivery to refugees. *American Psychologist, 46*(6), 642–648.

Gonsiorek, J. C., Sell, R. L., and Weinrich, J. D. (1995). Definition and measurement of sexual orientation. *Suicide and Life-Threatening Behavior, 25* (Supplement), 40–51.

Gonzales, R., & Ruiz, A. (1995). *My first book of proverbs (Mi primer libro de dichos).* San Francisco: Children's Book Press.

Gonzales, S. A. (1979). The Chicano perspective: A design for self-awareness. In A. D. Trejo (Ed.), *The Chicanos* (pp. 81–98). Tucson: University of Arizona Press.

González Chévez, L. (2005). Latin American healers and healing: Healing as a redefinition process. In R. Moodley & W. West (Eds.), *Integrating traditional healing practices into counseling and psychotherapy* (pp. 85–99). Thousand Oaks, CA: Sage.

Good, B., & Good, M. D. (1985). The cultural context of diagnosis and therapy: A view from medical anthropology. In M. Miranda & H. H. L. Kitano (Eds.), *Mental health research in minority communities: Development of culturally sensitive training programs* (pp. 1–27). Rockville, MD: National Institute of Mental Health.

Gottfredson, L. S. (1994). The science and politics of race-norming. *American Psychologist, 49*(11), 955–963.

Grandin, T. (1996). *Making the transition from the world of school into the world of work.* Unpublished manuscript, Colorado State University, Fort Collins, CO.

Grieger, I., & Ponterotto, J. G. (1995). A framework for assessment in multicultural counseling. In J. G. Ponterotto, J. M. Casas, L. A. Suzuki, & C. M. Alexander (Eds.), *Handbook of multicultural counseling* (pp. 357–374). Thousand Oaks, CA: Sage.

Grusznski, R., & Bankovics, G. (1990). Treating men who batter: A group approach. In D. Moore & F. Leafgren (Eds.), *Men in conflict* (pp. 201–211). Alexandria, VA: American Association for Counseling and Development.

Gullahorn, J. E., & Gullahorn, J. T. (1963). An extension of the U-curve hypothesis. *Journal of Social Issues, 19*(3), 33–47.

Gutierrez, F. J. (1985). Bicultural personality development: A process model. In E. Garcia & R. Padilla (Eds.), *Advances in bilingual education research* (pp. 96–124). Tucson: University of Arizona Press.

Gutierrez, F. J., & Dworkin, S. H. (1992). Gay, lesbian and African American: Managing the integration of identities. In S. H. Dworkin & F. J. Gutierrez (Eds.), *Counseling gay men and lesbians: Journey to the end of the rainbow* (pp. 141–156). Alexandria, VA: American Counseling Association.

Gwyn, F., & Kilpatrick, A. (1981). Family therapy with low-income Blacks: A tool or turn-off? *Social Casework, 62,* 259–266.

Haight, B., & Burnside, I. (2005). History and overview of group work. In B. Haight & F. Gibson (Eds.), *Burnside's working with older adults: Group process and techniques* (4th ed., pp. 25–37). Sudbury, MA: Jones & Bartlett.

Haley, J. (1973). *Uncommon therapy.* New York: W. W. Norton.

Hall, C. C. I. (1980). *The ethnic identity of racially mixed people: A study of Black-Japanese.* Unpublished doctoral dissertation, University of California, Los Angeles.

Hall, C. C. I. (1992). Please choose one: The ethnic identity choices for biracial individuals. In M. P. P. Root (Ed.), *Racially mixed people in America* (pp. 250–264). Newbury Park, CA: Sage.

Hamilton, J. A., Alagna, S. W., King, L. S., & Lloyd, C. (1987). The emotional consequences of gender-based abuse in the workplace: New counseling programs for sex discrimination. *Women and Therapy, 6*(1–2), 155–182.

Hamilton, M. (1984, February 15). The "superwoman" syndrome. *San Francisco Examiner,* p. E5.

Hapas in the spotlight. (1999, May 20). *Asian Week, 20*(38). Retrieved June 8, 2006, from http://www.asianweek.com/052099/news_hapa.html

Harrison, P. M. (1997). Racial identification and self-concept issues in biracial. *Dissertation Abstracts International, 58*(04), 2123B.

Harsh, M. (1993). Women who are visually impaired or blind as psychotherapy client: A personal and professional perspective. *Women & Therapy, 14*(3/4), 55–64.

Harvey, D. F. (1970). Cross-cultural stress and adaptation in global organizations. *Dissertation Abstracts International, 31,* 2958B–2959B.

Haviland, W. (1975). *Cultural anthropology.* New York: Holt, Rinehart & Winston.

Havinghurst, R. J., & Neugarten, B. L. (1968). Social class differences. In E. M. Lloyd-Jones & N. Rosenau (Eds.), *Social & cultural foundations of guidance* (pp. 363–372). New York: Holt, Rinehart & Winston.

Hawkins, R. L. (1992). Therapy with the male couple. In S. H. Dworkin & F. J. Gutierrez (Eds.), *Counseling gay men and lesbians: Journey to the end of the rainbow* (pp. 81–94). Alexandria, VA: American Counseling Association.

Hayes-Bautista, D. E. (2004). *La nueva California: Latinos in the golden state.* Berkeley and Los Angeles: University of California Press.

Heesacker, M., & Prichard, S. (1992). In a different voice revisited: Men, women, and emotion. *Journal of Mental Health Counseling, 14*(3), 274–290.

Heinrich, R. K., Corbine, J. L., & Thomas, K. R. (1990). Counseling Native Americans. *Journal of Counseling & Development, 69,* 128–133.

Helms, J. E. (1984). Toward a theoretical explanation of the effects of race on counseling: A Black and White model. *The Counseling Psychologist, 12,* 153–165.

Helms, J. E. (1990). Three perspectives on counseling and psychotherapy with visible racial/ethnic group clients. In F. Serafica, A. Schwebel, R. Russell, P. Isaac, & L. Myers (Eds.), *Mental health of ethnic minorities* (pp. 171–201). New York: Praeger.

Helms, J. E. (1995). An update of Helms's White and people of color racial identity models. In J. G. Ponterotto, J. M. Casas, L. A. Suzuki, & C. M. Alexander (Eds.), *Handbook of multicultural counseling* (pp. 181–198). Thousand Oaks, CA: Sage.

Helms, J. E. (1997). Implications of Behrens (1997) for the Validity of the White Racial Identity Attitude Scale. *Journal of Counseling Psychology, 44,* 13–16.

Helms, J. E., & Carter, R. T. (1990). Development of the White racial identity inventory. In J. E. Helms (Ed.), *Black and White racial identity: Theory, research and practice* (pp. 67–80). Westport, CT: Greenwood.

Hendrix, L. R. (2001). *Curriculum in ethnogeriatrics: Ethnic specific modules: American Indian/Alaska Native.* Stanford, CA: Collaborative on Ethnogeriatric Eduation, Stanford Geriatric Education Center. Retrieved July 8, 2005, from www.stanford.edu/group/ethnoger

Henry J. Kaiser Family Foundation. (2001). *Latinos' views of the HIV/aids epidemic at 20 years: Findings from a national survey.* Menlo Park, CA: Henry J. Kaiser Family Foundation. Publication #3184 available at www.kff.org.

Herdt, G., & Kernzer, R. (2006). I do, but I can't: The impact of marriage denial on the mental health and sexual citizenship of lesbians and gay men in the United States. *Sexuality Research and Social Policy: Journal of the NSRC, 13*(1), 33–49.

Herek, G. M. (1989). Hate crimes against lesbians and gay men: Issues for research and policy. *American Psychologist, 44,* 948–955.

Hernandez Morales, A. (2005). Exploring and conceptualizing the negotiation of racial differences in counseling. *Dissertation Abstracts International Section A: Humanities & Social Sciences, 65*(8-A), 2907.

Herring, R. D. (1991). Counseling Native American youth. In C. C. Lee & B. L. Richardson (Eds.), *Multicultural issues in counseling: New approaches to diversity* (pp. 37–47). Alexandria, VA: American Counseling Association. Development of a Cuban Ethnic Identity Questionnaire. *Hispanic Journal of Behavioral Sciences, 1*, 247–261.

Herring, R. D. (1992). Biracial children: An increasing concern for elementary and middle school counselors. *Elementary School Guidance and Counseling, 27*, 123–130.

Herrnstein, R. J., & Murray, C. (1994). *The bell curve: Intelligence and class structure in American life*. New York: Free Press.

Hersch, P. (1991, January/February). Secret lives. *Family Therapy Networker, 15*(1), 37–43.

Herz, F. M., & Rosen, E. J. (1982). Jewish families. In M. McGoldrick, J. Pearce, & J. Giordano (Eds.), *Ethnicity and family therapy* (pp. 364–392). New York: Guilford Press.

Hetrick, E. S., & Martin, A. D. (1987). Developmental issues and their resolution for gay and lesbian adolescents. *Journal of Homosexuality, 14*, 25–43.

Hiegel, J. P. (1983). Collaboration with traditional healers: Experience in refugees' mental care. *International Journal of Mental Health, 12*(3), 30–43.

Hill, R. (1993). *Research on the African-American family*. Westport, CT: Auburn House.

Hills, H. I., & Strozier, A. L. (1992). Multicultural training in APA-approved counseling psychology programs: A survey. *Professional Psychology, 23*, 43–51.

Hines, P., & Boyd-Franklin, N. (1982). Black families. In M. McGoldrick, J. Pearce, & J. Giordano (Eds.), *Ethnicity & family therapy* (pp. 84–99). New York: Guilford Press.

Hines, P., & Boyd-Franklin, N. (2005). African American Families. In M. McGoldrick, J. Giordano, & N. Garcia-Preto (Eds.), Ethnicity & family therapy (3rd ed.) (pp. 87–100). New York: Guilford Press.

Ho, L. (1990). *Cross-cultural swinging: A handbook for self-awareness and multi-cultural living!* (Available from Liang Ho, 2238 Kaala Way, Honolulu, HI 96822).

Ho, M. K. (1987). *Family therapy with minorities*. Newbury Park, CA: Sage.

Hobbs, R. (2000). *Bridging borders in Silicon Valley: Summit on immigrant needs and contributions*. San Jose, CA: Santa Clara County Office of Human Relations, Citizenship and Immigrant Services Program.

Hoffman, L. (1991). A reflexive stance for family therapy. *Journal of Strategic and Systemic Therapies, 10*(3&4), 4–17.

Hoffman, T., Dana, R. H., & Bolton, B. (1985). Measured acculturation and MMPI-168 performance of Native American adults. *Journal of Cross-Cultural Psychology, 16*, 243–256.

Holmes, T. H., & Rahe, R. H. (1967). The Social Readjustment Rating Scale. *Journal of Psychosomatic Research, 11*, 213–218.

Homma-True, R. (1990). Psychotherapeutic issues with Asian American women. *Sex Roles, 22*(7/8), 477–486.

Hooks, B. (2003). *Rock my soul: Black people and self-esteem*. New York: Washington Square Press.

Hopkins, R. S. (1982). Defining and predicting overseas effectiveness for adolescent exchange students. *Dissertation Abstracts International, 42,* 5052A–5053A.

Horner, M. (1972). Toward an understanding of achievement-related conflicts in women. *Journal of Social Issues, 28,* 129–156.

How affirmative action should work. (1995, Spring). *Stanford Observer, 29*(3), pp. 1, 20.

Howe Chief, E. (1940). An assimilation study of Indian girls. *Journal of Social Psychology, 11,* 19–30.

Hoyert, D. L., Heron, M. P., Murphy, S. L., & Kung, H.-C. (2006). Deaths: Final data for 2003. *National Vital Statistics Reports, 54*(13). Hyattsville, MD: National Center for Health Statistics.

Hoyt, K. B. (1989). The career status of women and minority persons: A 20-year retrospective. *The Career Development Quarterly, 37,* 202–212.

Huang, L. (1994). An integrative approach to clinical assessment and intervention with Asian-American adolescents. *Journal of Clinical Child Psychology, 23*(1), 21–31.

Human Capital Initiative. (1993). *Vitality for life: Psychological research for productive aging*. Washington, DC: American Psychological Association.

Human Rights Campaign. (2006). Hate crimes. Washington, DC: Author. Retrieved May 24, 2006, from http://www.hrc.org/Template.cfm?Section=Hate_Crimes1

Hunter, J., & Schaecher, R. (1987). Stresses on lesbian and gay adolescents in schools. *Social Work in Education, 9,* 180–190.

Hwang, S. (2005, November 19). The new white flight. *Wall Street Journal,* p. A1.

Ibrahim, F. A., & Kahn, H. (1984). *Scale to assess world views (SAWV)*. Unpublished manuscript, University of Connecticut.

In-country refugees at record levels. (1995, November 15). *San Francisco Examiner,* p. C20.

Institute of International Education. (2006). *Open doors on the Web*. Retrieved June 26, 2006, from http://www.opendoors.iienetwork.org

Ipsaro, A. J. (1986). Male client–male therapist: Issues in a therapeutic alliance [Special Issue: Gender issues in psychotherapy]. *Psychotherapy, 23*(2), 257–266.

Ishiyama, F. I. (1990). A Japanese perspective on client inaction: Removing attitudinal blocks through Morita therapy. *Journal of Counseling and Development, 68,* 566–570.

Istar Lev, A. (2004). *Transgender emergence: Therapeutic guidelines for working with gender-variant people and their families*. Binghamton, NY: Haworth.

Ivey, A. E., & Ivey, M. B. (2007). *Intentional interviewing and counseling: Facilitating client development in a multicultural society*. Belmont, CA: Thomson-Brooks/Cole.

Ivey, A. E., Ivey, M. B., & Simek–Morgan, K. (1993). *Counseling and psychotherapy: A multicultural perspective*. Boston: Allyn & Bacon.

Jackson, M. (1997). Counseling Arab Americans. In C, Lee (Ed.), *Multicultural issues in counseling: New approaches in diversity* (2nd ed., pp. 333–349). Alexandria, VA: American Counseling Association.

Jackson, M. L. (1995). The demise of multiculturalism in America and the counseling profession. *Counseling Today, 37*(10), 30–31.

Jacobs, J. H. (1992). Identity development in biracial children. In M. P. Root (Ed.), *Racially mixed people in America* (pp. 190–206). Newbury Park, CA: Sage.

Jaynes, G. D., & Williams, R. M. (1989). *A common destiny: Blacks and American society*. Washington, DC: National Academic Press.

Jensen, A. (1969). How much can we boost IQ and school achievement? *Harvard Educational Review, 39*(1), 1–123.

Johnson, C. L. (1985a). *Growing up and growing old in Italian American families*. Rutgers, NJ: Rutgers University Press.

Johnson, C. L. (1985b). Socialization to family attachments. In *Growing up and growing old in Italian American families* (pp. 183–199). Rutgers, NJ: Rutgers University Press.

Johnson, D. (1994, July 3). In bleak area in South Dakota, Indians put hopes in classroom. *New York Times*, p. 19.

Johnson, F., Foxall, M., Kelleher, E., Kentopp, E., Mannlein, E., & Cook, E. (1988). Comparison of mental health and life satisfaction of five elderly ethnic groups. *Western Journal of Nursing Research, 10*, 613–628.

Johnson, F. A., & Marsella, A. J. (1978). Differential attitudes toward verbal behavior in students of Japanese and European ancestry. *Genetic Psychology Monographs, 97*, 43–76.

Johnson, R. P., & Riker, H. C. (1982). Counselors' goals and roles in assisting older persons. *Journal of Mental Health Counseling, 4*, 30–40.

Joint Committee on Testing Practices (2004). *Code of fair testing practices in education*. Washington, DC: Author. (Joint Committee on Testing Practices, Science Directorate, American Psychological Association [APA], 750 First Street, NE, Washington, DC 20002-4242; URL: www.apa.org/science/jctpweb.html)

Jones, A. C. (1985). Psychological functioning in Black Americans: A conceptual guide for use in psychotherapy. *Psychotherapy, 22*, 363–369.

Jones, C. P. (2000). Levels of racism: A theoretic framework and a gardener's tale. *American Journal of Public Health, 90*(8), 1212–1216.

Jones, J. E. (2000). Multiethnic identity development, psychological adjustment, and parental attachment in adolescence. *Dissertation Abstracts International, 60*(10), 5227B.

Jones, J. M. (1997). *Prejudice and racism* (2nd ed.). New York: McGraw-Hill.

Jones, R. L. (1975). Intercultural education for overseas managers of multinational corporations. *Dissertation Abstracts International, 36*, 1982A.

Jordan, M. B. (1993). Diversity issues concerning therapists: Diagnosis and training. *Independent Practitioner, 13*(5), 216–218.

Judell, B. (1997). *The gay quote book*. New York: Dutton.

Kamin, L. J. (1974). *The science & politics of I.Q.* New York: John Wiley & Sons.

Katz, J. H. (1989). *White awareness* (6th ed.). Norman: University of Oklahoma Press.

Katz, J. H. (2003). *White awareness: Handbook for anti-racism training* (2nd ed.). Norman: University of Oklahoma Press.

Katz, P. (1981). Psychotherapy with Native adolescents. *Canadian Journal of Psychiatry, 26*, 455–459.

Keerdoja, E. (1984, November 19). Children of the rainbow: New parent support groups help interracial kids cope. *Newsweek*, pp. 120–122.

Kemp, A. (1998). *Abuse in the family: An introduction.* Pacific Grove, CA: Brooks/Cole.

Kemp, A. D. (1990). From matriculation to graduation: Focusing beyond minority retention. *Journal of Multicultural Counseling and Development, 18*(3), 144–149.

Kerwin, C. (1991). Racial identity development in biracial children of Black/ White racial heritage. *Dissertation Abstracts International, 52*(7), 2469A.

Kerwin, C. (1993). Issues in biracial identity development. *Focus, 7*(2), 12.

Kerwin, C., & Ponterotto, J. G. (1995). Biracial identity development: Theory and research. In J. G. Ponterotto, J. M. Casas, L. A. Suzuki, & C. M. Alexander (Eds.), *Handbook of multicultural counseling* (pp. 199–217). Thousand Oaks, CA: Sage.

Kerwin, C., Ponterotto, J. G., Jackson, B. L., & Harris, A. (1993). Racial identity in biracial children: A qualitative investigation. *Journal of Counseling Psychology, 40*(2), 221–231.

Khoury, R. (2002). *Refugee mental health manual: Culturally competent practice with Arab Americans.* Retrieved July 27, 2006, from http://www.arabacc.org/ Refugee_Manual/body_refugee_manual.html

Killian, K. D. & Agathangelou, A. M. (2005). Greek families. In M. McGoldrick, J. Giordano, & N. Garcia-Preto (Eds.), *Ethnicity and family therapy* (3rd ed., pp. 573–585). New York: Guilford Press.

Kim, B. S. K., & Abreu, J. M. (2001). Acculturation measurement: Theory, current instruments, and future directions. In J. G. Ponterotto, J. M. Casas, L. A. Suzuki, & C. M. Alexander (Eds.), *Handbook of multicultural counseling* (2nd ed., pp. 394–424). Thousand Oaks, CA: Sage.

Kindschi Gosselin, D. (2003). *Heavy hands: An introduction to the crimes of famly violence* (2nd ed.). Upper Saddle River, NJ: Prentice Hall.

Kinsey, A., Pomeroy, W., & Martin, C. (1948). *Sexual behavior in the human male.* Philadelphia: W.B. Saunders.

Kinsey, A., Pomeroy, W., Martin, C., & Gebhard, P. (1953). *Sexual behavior in the human female.* Philadelphia: W.B. Saunders.

Kiselica, M. S. (1998). Preparing Anglos for the challenges and joys of multiculturalism. *The Counseling Psychologist, 26*, 5–21.

Kitano, H. H. L. (1981). Counseling and psychotherapy with Japanese Americans. In A. J. Marsella & P. B. Pedersen (Eds.), *Cross-cultural counseling and psychotherapy* (pp. 228–242). New York: Pergamon Press.

Kitano, H. H. L. (1989). A model for counseling Asian Americans. In P. B. Pedersen, J. G. Draguns, W. J. Lonner, & J. E. Trimble (Eds.), *Counseling across cultures* (3rd ed., pp. 139–151). Honolulu: University of Hawaii Press.

Kluckhohn, F. R., & Strodtbeck, F. L. (1961). *Variations in value orientation.* New York: Harper and Row.

Knight, B. G. (2004). *Psychotherapy with older adults* (3rd ed.). Thousand Oaks, CA: Sage.

Koehler, N. (1980). Re-entry shock. *Ladycom, 12*(3), 38–40.

Kohatsu, E. L. (1996, Winter). Identity and racism: Applying racial identity theory to research on Asian American psychology. *Variability, 15*(1), 8, 14.

Kohout, J., Wicherski, M., & Cooney, B. (1992). *Characteristic of graduate departments of psychology: 1989–1990.* Washington, DC: American Psychological Association.

Koss, M. P. (1985). The hidden rape victim: Personality, attitudinal, and situational characteristics. *Psychology of Women Quarterly, 9*, 193–212.

Koss, M. P. (1990). Changed lives: The psychological impact of sexual harassment. In M. A. Paludi (Ed.), *Ivory power: Sexual harassment on campus* (pp. 73–92). Albany: State University of New York Press.

Kristof, N. D. (1996, February 11). Family values, Japanese style. *San Jose Mercury News*, p. 17A.

Kroll, J., Habenicht, M., Mackenzie, T., Yang, M., Chan, S., Vang, T., et al. (1989). Depression and post-traumatic stress disorder in Southeast Asian refugees. *American Journal of Psychiatry, 146*(12), 1592–1597.

Kubler-Ross, E. (1969). *On death and dying.* New York: Macmillan.

Kulwicki, A. (2000). Arab women. In M. Julia (Ed.), *Constructing gender: Multicultural perspectives in working with women.* Belmont, CA: Brooks/Cole.

Kuypers, J. A., & Bengtson, V. L. (1973). Competence and social breakdown: A social-psychological view of aging. *Human Development, 16*, 37–49.

Lachs, M. S., & Pillemer, K. (2004). Elder abuse. *The Lancet, 364*, 1192–1263.

LaFromboise, T. D. (1988). American Indian mental health policy. *American Psychologist, 43*, 388–397.

LaFromboise, T. D., Berman, J. S., & Sohi, B. K. (1994). American Indian women. In L. Comas-Diaz & B. Greene (Eds.), *Women of color: Integrating ethnic and gender identities in psychotherapy.* New York: Guilford Press.

LaFromboise, T. D., Coleman, H. L. K., & Hernandez, A. (1991). Development and factor sturcture of the Cross-Cultural Counseling Inventory—Revised. *Professional Psychology: Research and Practice, 22*, 380–388. In *Psychotherapy* (pp. 30–71). New York: Guilford Press.

LaFromboise, T. D., Trimble, J., & Mohatt, G. (1990). Counseling intervention and American Indian tradition: An integrative approach. *Counseling Psychologist, 18*, 628–654.

Lai, E. W. M., & Sodowsky, G. R. (1992, August). *Acculturation: An examination of theory, measurement, and sociocultural, mental health, and counseling variables.* Paper presented at the meeting of the American Psychological Association, Washington, DC.

Lambert, N. M. (1981). Psychological evidence in *Larry P. v. Wilson Riles*: An evaluation by a witness for the defense. *American Psychologist, 36*, 937–952.

Landrine, H. (1989). The politics of personality disorder. *Psychology of Women Quarterly, 13*, 325–339.

Langelier, R., & Langelier, P. (2005). French Canadian families. In M. McGoldrick, J. Giordano, & N. Garcia-Preto (Eds.), *Ethnicity and family therapy* (3rd ed., pp. 545–554). New York: Guilford Press.

Langston, D. (1998). Tired of playing Monopoly? In M. L. Andersen & P. H. Collins (Eds.), *Race, class, and gender: An anthology* (3rd ed., pp. 126–136). Belmont, CA: Wadsworth.

Lappin, J., & Scott, S. (1982). Intervention in a Vietnamese refugee family. In M. McGoldrick, J. Pearce, & J. Giordano (Eds.), *Ethnicity & family therapy* (pp. 483–491). New York: Guilford Press.

Lark, J. S., & Paul, B. D. (1998). Beyond multicultural training: Mentoring stories from two White American doctoral students. *The Counseling Psychologist, 26*, 33–42.

Laster, L. T. (1993, July). Another mother, a different dad: Lesbian and gay parenting in the '90s. *Peninsula Parent, 15,* 62.

Lau, A., & Zane, N. (2000). Examining the effects of ethnic-specific services: An analysis of cost-utilization and treatment outcome for Asian American clients. *Journal of Community Psychology, 28,* 63–77.

Lazarus, P. (1982). Counseling the Native American child: A question of values. *Elementary School Guidance and Counseling, 17,* 83–88.

Le, C. N. (2006a). Asian-nation: The landscape of Asian America. *Religion, spirituality, and faith.* Retrieved July 10, 2006, from http://www.asian-nation. org/religion.shtml

Le, C. N. (2006b). Asian-nation: The landscape of Asian America. *Socioeconomic Statistics & Demographics.* Retrieved July 10, 2006, from http://www.asian-nation. org/demographics.shtml

Le, P. (1996, February 11). Students from Asia flock to Cupertino. *San Jose Mercury News,* pp. 1A, 6A.

Leafgren, F. (1990a). Being a man can be hazardous to your health: Life-style issues. In D. Moore & F. Leafgren (Eds.), *Men in conflict* (pp. 265–275). Alexandria, VA: American Association for Counseling and Development.

Leafgren, F. (1990b). Men on a journey. In D. Moore & F. Leafgren (Eds.), *Men in conflict* (pp. 3–10). Alexandria, VA: American Association for Counseling and Development.

Leal, A., & Menjivar, C. (1992). Xenophobia or xenophilia? Hispanic women in higher education. In L. B. Welch (Ed.), *Perspectives on minority women in higher education* (pp. 93–103). New York: Praeger.

Lee, C. (1990). Black male development: Counseling the "Native Son." In D. Moore & F. Leafgren (Eds.), *Men in conflict* (pp. 125–137). Alexandria, VA: American Association for Counseling and Development.

Lee, C. C. (1994). Pioneers of multicultural counseling: A conversation with Clemmont E. Vontress. *Journal of Multicultural Counseling and Development, 22,* 66–78.

Lee, C. C., & Armstrong, K. L. (1995). Indigenous models of mental health intervention: Lessons from traditional healers. In J. G. Ponterotto, J. M. Casas, L. A. Suzuki, & C. M. Alexander (Eds.), *Handbook of multicultural counseling* (pp. 441–456). Thousand Oaks, CA: Sage

Lee, C. C., & Richardson, B. L. (1991) *Multicultural issues in counseling: New approaches to diversity.* Alexandria, VA: American Counseling Association.

Lee, J. S., Koeske, G. F., & Sales, E. (2004). Social support buffering of acculturative stress: A study of mental health symptoms among Korean international students. *International Journal of Intercultural Relations, 28*(5), 399–414.

Lee, M. W. (Producer). (1994). *The color of fear* [Film]. Oakland, CA: Stir-Fry Productions.

Lee, W. M. (1995, April). *Counselors of color: Graduate school and early career experiences.* Presentation at the annual meeting of the American Counselors Association, Denver, CO.

Lee, W. M. (1996). New directions in multicultural counseling. *Counseling and Human Development, 29*(2), 1–11.

Lee, W. M. (2004). Therapeutic considerations in work with biracial girls. *Women in Therapy, 27*(1/2), 203–216.

Lee, W. M., & Mixson, R. J. (1995). Asian and Caucasian client perceptions of the effectiveness of counseling. *Journal of Multicultural Counseling and Development, 23*, 48–56.

Lee, W. M., & Nakagawa, J. Y. (1996). Ethnic and gender issues in making a work disability assessment for Southeast Asian women. In A. Leal-Idrogo, J. T. Gonzales-Calvo, & V. D. Krenz (Eds.), *Multicultural women: Health, disability, and rehabilitation* (pp. 319–329). Dubuque, IA: Kendall/Hunt.

Lefley, H. P. (1989). Counseling refugees: The North American experience. In P. Pedersen, J. G. Draguns, W. J. Lonner, & J. E. Trimble (Eds.), *Counseling across cultures* (3rd ed., pp. 205–241). Honolulu: University of Hawaii Press.

Lefrancois, G. R. (1993). *The lifespan* (4th ed.). Belmont, CA: Wadsworth.

Leong, F. T. (1991). Career development attributes and occupational values of Asian American and White American college students. *The Career Development Quarterly, 39*, 221–230.

Levant, R. F. (1990). Coping with the new father role. In D. Moore & F. Leafgren (Eds.), *Men in conflict* (pp. 81–94). Alexandria, VA: American Association for Counseling and Development.

LeVay, S., & Valente, S. M. (2006). *Human sexuality* (2nd ed.). Sunderland, MA: Sinauer.

Levers, L. L., & Maki, D. R. (1995). African indigenous healing and cosmology: Toward a philosophy of ethnorehabilitation. *Rehabilitation Education, 9*(2), 127–145.

Le Vine, P. (1993). Morita-based therapy and its use across cultures in the treatment of bulimia nervosa. *Journal of Counseling and Development, 72*, 82–90.

Levy, J. (1987). Psychological and social problems of epileptic children in four Southwestern Indian tribes. *Journal of Community Psychology, 15*(3), 307–315.

Lieberg, C. (1996). *Calling the Midwest home.* Berkeley, CA: Wildcat Canyon Press.

Lijtmaer, R. M. (1993). Bilingual-bicultural difficulties in the therapeutic process with the Hispanic patient. *Independent Practitioner, 13*(5), 215–216.

Liu, W. M. (2002). The social class-related experiences of men: Integrating theory and practice. *Professional Psychology: Research and Practice, 33*(4), 355–360.

Locke, D. C. (1995). Counseling interventions with African American youth. In C. C. Lee (Ed.), *Counseling for diversity: A guide for school counselors and related professionals* (pp. 21–40). Boston: Allyn and Bacon.

Logan, C. R. (1996). Homophobia? No, homoprejudice. *Journal of Homosexuality, 31*(3) 31–53.

Logan, C. R. (1997, March). It takes a village to care for a lesbian. *Counseling Today, 39*(9), pp. 29, 35, 55.

Loiacano, D. (1989). Gay identity issues among Black Americans: Racism, homophobia, and the need for validation. *Journal of Counseling and Development, 68*, 21–25.

Longley, R. (2006). *Why women still make less than men.* Retrieved February 17, 2006, from http://usgovinfo.about.com/cs/censusstatistic/a/womenspay.htm

Lopez, S. (1988). The empirical basis of ethnocultural and linguistic bias in mental health evaluations of Hispanics. *American Psychologist, 43*(12), 1095–1097.

Lorion, R. P. (1974). Patient and therapist variables in the treatment of low income patients. *Psychological Bulletin, 81*, 344–354.

Lowrey, L. (1983). Bridging a culture in counseling. *The Journal of Applied Rehabilitation Counseling, 14*(1), 69–73.

Lum, D. (1986). *Social work practice and people of color: A process–stage approach.* Monterey, CA: Brooks/Cole.

Lyon, J. M., Henggeler, S., & Hall, J. A. (1992). The family relations, peer relations, and criminal activities of Caucasian and Hispanic American gang members. *Journal of Abnormal Child Psychology, 29*(5), 439–449.

Lysgaard S. (1955). Adjustment in a foreign society: Norwegian Fulbright grantees visiting the United States. *International Social Science Bulletin, 7,* 45–51.

Macias, C. J. (1989). American Indian academic success: The role of indigenous learning strategies. *Journal of American Indian Education, 28*(special issue), 43–52.

Mahalik, J. R., Locke, B. D., Theodore, H., Cournoyer, R. J., & Lloyd, B. F. (2001, July). A cross-national and cross-sectional comparison of men's gender role conflict and its relationship to social intimacy and self-esteem. *Sex Roles: A Journal of Research.* Retrieved June 13, 2006 from www.findarticles.com/p/articles/mi_m2294/ is_2001_July/ai_81478071

Malde, S. (1988). Guided autobiography: A counseling tool for older adults. *Journal of Counseling and Development, 66,* 290–293.

Malgady, R. G., Rogler, L. H., & Costantino, G. (1990). Culturally sensitive psycho therapy for Puerto Rican children and adolescents: A program of treatment outcome research. *Journal of Consulting and Clinical Psychology, 58*(6), 704–712.

Malyon, A. K. (1982). Psychotherapeutic implications of internalized homophobia in gay men. *Journal of Homosexuality, 7*(2/3), 59–69.

Marcos, L. R. (1979). Effects of interpreters on the evaluation of psychopathology in non-English-speaking patients. *American Journal of Psychiatry, 136,* 171–174.

Marin, G., Sabogal, F., VanOss Marin, B., Otero-Sabogal, R., & Perez-Stable, E. J. (1987). Development of a short acculturation scale for Hispanics. *Hispanic Journal of Behavioral Science, 9,* 183–205.

Marino, T. (1996). Career counselor offers unique bilingual skills. *Counseling Today, 38*(9), 24–26.

Marino, T. W. (1995, December). Mixed couples get mixed reactions. *Counseling Today, 38*(6), 21, 26.

Marshall, C. A. (1996). The power of inquiry as regards American Indian women with disabilities: Divisive manipulation or clinical necessity? In A. Leal-Idrogo, J. T. Gonzales-Calvo, & V. D. Krenz (Eds.), *Multicultural women: Health, disability, and rehabilitation* (pp. 293–308). Dubuque, IA: Kendall/Hunt.

Martin, A. D., & Hetrick, E. S. (1988). The stigmatization of the gay and lesbian adolescent. *Journal of Homosexuality, 5*(1/2), 163–183.

Martin, E. P., & Martin, J. M. (2002). *Spirituality and the Black helping tradition in social work.* Washington, DC: National Association of Social Workers.

Martin, W. E., Jr., Frank, L. W., Minkler, S., & Johnson, M. (1988). A survey of vocational rehabilitation counselors who work with American Indians. *Journal of Applied Rehabilitation Counseling, 19*(4), 29–34.

Martinez, R., Norman, R. D., & Delaney, H. D. (1984). A Children's Hispanic Background Scale. *Hispanic Journal of Behavioral Sciences, 6,* 103–112.

Masuda, M., Matsumoto, G. H., & Meredith, G. M. (1970) Ethnic identity in three generations of Japanese Americans. *Journal of Social Psychology, 81,* 199–207.

Matheson, L. (1986). If you are not an Indian, how do you treat an Indian? In H. Lefley (Ed.), *Cross-cultural training for mental health professionals* (pp. 115–130). Springfield, IL: Charles C. Thomas.

Mattox, C., Sanchez, F., Ulsh, S., & Valero, M. (1982). *Repatriation: A study of dual viewpoints.* (Graduate Research Group Paper, GBM, 651). Unpublished manuscript, University of Miami.

Mattson, S. (1993). Mental health of Southeast Asian refugee women: An overview. *Health Care for Women International, 14*, 155–165.

May, R. (1990). Finding ourselves: Self-esteem, self-disclosure, and self-acceptance. In D. Moore & F. Leafgren (Eds.), *Men in conflict* (pp. 11–21). Alexandria, VA: American Association for Counseling and Development.

Mayo, J. (1974). The significance of soiciocultural variables in the psychiatric treatment of black outpatients. *Comprehensive Psychiatry, 15*, 471–482.

McCaulley, M. H., & Moody, R. A. (2001). Multicultural applications of the Myers–Briggs type indicator. In L. A. Suzuki, J. G. Ponterotto, & P. J. Meller (Eds.), *Handbook of multicultural assessment: Clinical, psychological, and educational applications* (2nd ed., pp. 279–305). NetLibrary Version. San Francisco: Jossey-Bass.

McDavis, R. J., Parker, W. M., & Parker, W. J. (1995). Counseling African Americans. In N. Vacc, S. DeVaney, & J. Wittmer (Eds.), *Experiencing and counseling multicultural and diverse populations* (pp. 217–250). Bristol, PA: Accelerated Development.

McDougall, J. G. (1993). Therapeutic issues with gay and lesbian elders. *Clinical Gerontologist, 14*, 45–57.

McGaraghan, N. (2006, July 5). Overcoming intolerance one story at a time. *Palo Alto Weekly*, p. 21.

McGill, D., & Pearce, J. K. (1982). British families. In M. McGoldrick, J. Pearce, & J. Giordano (Eds.), *Ethnicity and family therapy* (pp. 457–479). New York: Guilford Press.

McGill, D. W., & Pearce, J. K. (2005). American families with English ancestors from the colonial era: Anglo Americans. In M. McGoldrick, J. Giordano, & N. Garcia-Preto (Eds.), *Ethnicity and family therapy* (3rd ed., pp. 520–533). New York: Guilford Press.

McGoldrick, M. (1982). Irish families. In M. McGoldrick, J. Pearce, & J. Giordano (Eds.), *Ethnicity and family therapy* (pp. 370–339). New York: Guilford Press.

McGoldrick, M. (2005). Irish families. In M. McGoldrick, J. Giordano, & N. Garcia-Preto (Eds.), *Ethnicity and family therapy* (3rd ed., pp. 595–615). New York: Guilford Press.

McGoldrick, M., Giordano, J., & Garcia-Preto, N. (2005) *Ethnicity and family therapy* (3rd ed.). New York: Guilford Press.

McGoldrick, M., Pearce, J. K., & Giordano, J. (Eds.). (1982). *Ethnicity and family therapy.* New York: Guilford Press.

McGowan, S. (1993). Equal job, equal pay: Women and minorities just aren't getting it. *Guidepost, 35*(10), 13–14.

McGrath, E., Keita, G. P., Strickland, B. R., & Russo, N. F. (1990). *Women and depression: Risk factors and treatment issues* (Final Report of the American Psychological Association's Task Force on Women and Depression). Washington, DC: American Psychological Association.

McGrath, P., & Axelson, J. A. (1993). *Accessing awareness and developing knowledge: Foundations for skill in a multicultural society.* Pacific Grove, CA: Brooks/Cole.

McIntosh, P. (1988). *White privilege and male privilege* (Working Paper No. 189). Wellesley, MA: Wellesley College Center for Research on Women.

McNair, L. D. (1992). African American women in therapy: An Afrocentric and feminist synthesis. *Women and Therapy, 12*(1/2), 5–19.

McRae, M. B., & Johnson, S. D., Jr. (1991). Toward training for competence in multicultural counselor education. *Journal of Counseling & Development, 70,* 131–135.

McRoy, R. G., & Oglesby, Z. (1984). Group work with Black adoptive applicants. *Social Work with Groups, 7,* 125–134.

Mercer, J. R. (1979). *SOMPA: Technical and conceptual manual.* New York: Psychological Corporation.

Merriam-Webster. (2006). Retrieved June 27, 2006, from http://www.m-w.com/dictionary/culture

Midnight Sun. (1988). Sex/gender systems in native North America. In W. Roscoe (Ed.), *Living the spirit: A gay American Indian anthology* (pp. 32–47). New York: St. Martin's Press.

Miller, J. B. (1976). *Toward a new psychology of women.* New York: Beacon Press.

Milliones, J. (1980). Construction of a black consciousness measure: Psychotherapeutic implications. *Psychotherapy: Theory, Research and Practice, 17,* 175–182.

Mintz, L. B., & Wright, D. M. (1993). Women and their bodies: Eating disorders and addictions. In E. P. Cook (Ed.), *Women, relationships, and power: Implications for counseling* (pp. 211–246). Alexandria, VA: American Counseling Association.

Mollen, D., Ridley, C. R., & Hill, C. L. (2003). Models of multicultural counseling competence: A critical evaluation. In D. B. Pope-Davis, H. Coleman, W. M. Liu, & R. L. Toporek (Eds.), *Handbook of multicultural competencies in counseling & psychology* (pp. 21–37). Thousand Oaks, CA: Sage.

Mollica, R. F., Wyshak, G., & Lavelle, J. (1987). The psychosocial impact of war trauma and torture on Southeast Asian refugees. *American Journal of Psychiatry, 144*(12), 1567–1572.

Mondykowski, S. M. (1982). Polish families. In M. McGoldrick, J. Pearce, & J. Giordano (Eds.), *Ethnicity and family therapy* (pp. 393–411). New York: Guilford Press.

Moore, D., Parker, S., Thompson, T., & Dougherty, P. (1990). The journey continues. In D. Moore & F. Leafgren (Eds.), *Men in conflict* (pp. 277–283). Alexandria, VA: American Association for Counseling and Development.

Morales, E. S. (1992). Counseling Latino gays and Latina lesbians. In S. H. Dworkin & F. J. Gutierrez (Eds.), *Counseling gay men and lesbians: Journey to the end of the rainbow* (pp. 125–139). Alexandria, VA: American Counseling Association.

Mordkowitz, E. R., & Ginsburg, H. P. (1986, April). *The academic socialization of successful Asian American college students.* Paper presented at the meeting of the American Educational Research Association, San Francisco, CA. (ERIC Document Reproduction Service No. ED 273 219.)

Morganthau, T. (1994, October 24). IQ is it destiny? *Newsweek,* pp. 52–56.

Morrison, A. M., & Von Glinow, M.A. (1990). Women and minorities in management. *American Psychologist, 45,* 200–208.

Morrissey, M. (1995a, October). Rising number of immigrants means new challenges for counselors. *Counseling Today, 38*(4), 22, 28–29.

Morrissey, M. (1995b, August). Report on women and mental health hopes to call attention to women's unique needs. *Counseling Today, 38*(2), 22–23.

Moscicki, E. K., Rae, D. S., Regier, D. A., & Locke, B. Z. (1987). The Hispanic health and nutrition examination survey: Depression among Mexican Americans, Cuban Americans, Puerto Ricans. In M. Gaviria & J. D. Arana (Eds.), *Health and behavior: Research agenda for Hispanics* (pp. 145–159). Chicago: University of Illinois at Chicago.

Moser, N., & Rendon, M. E. (1992). Alcohol and drug services: A jigsaw puzzle. *Journal of the American Deafness and Rehabilitation Association, 26*(2), 18–21.

Moses, S. (1992, February). Minority scholarships at risk. *APA Monitor, 23*(2), 9.

Mosher, D. L. (1991). Scared straight: Homosexual threat in heterosexual therapists. In C. Silverstein (Ed.), *Gays, lesbians, and their therapists: Studies in psychotherapy* (pp. 187–200). New York: W. W. Norton.

Murphy, B. C. (1992). Counseling lesbian couples: Sexism, heterosexism, and homophobia. In S. H. Dworkin & F. J. Gutierrez (Eds.), *Counseling gay men and lesbians: Journey to the end of the rainbow* (pp. 63–79). Alexandria, VA: American Counseling Association.

Murphy, D. M., & Murphy, J. T. (1997). Enabling disabled students. *NEA Higher Education Journal, 13*(1), 41–52.

Murphy, D. S. (1994, Spring). From multicultural infusion theory to multicultural infusion practice in a weekend! *MEI Center Connection, 2*(2), 3–5.

Murphy, M. C., Wright, B. V., & Bellamy, D. E. (1995). Multicultural training in university counseling center predoctoral psychology internship programs: A survey. *Journal of Multicultural Counseling & Development, 23*, 170–180.

Murray, B. (1996, October). How does a couple cope when one partner is HIV+? *APA Monitor, 27*(10), 55.

Murray, B. (1998). Why are some minority faculty unhappy? *APA Monitor Online, 29*(6). Retrieved July 5, 2006, from http://www.apa.org/monitor/jun98/frus.html

Myers, J. E. (1983). A national survey of geriatric mental health services. *AMHCA Journal, 5*, 69–74.

Myers, J. E., & Schwiebert, V. L. (1996). *Competencies for gerontological counseling.* Alexandria, VA: American Counseling Association.

Myers, J. E., & Sweeney, T. J. (1990). *Gerontological competencies for counselors and human development professionals.* Alexandria, VA: American Association for Counseling and Development.

Nadler, A. (2001). The victim and the psychologist: Changing perceptions of Israeli Holocaust survivors by the mental health community in the past 50 years. *History of Psychology, 4*(2), 159–181.

Nagayama Hall, G. C., & Phung, A. H. (2001). Minnesota Multiphasic Personality Inventory and Millon Clinical Multiaxial Inventory. In L. A. Suzuki, J. G. Ponterotto, & P. J. Meller (Eds.), *Handbook of multicultural assessment: Clinical, psychological, and educational applications* (2nd ed., pp. 307–330). NetLibrary Version. San Francisco: Jossey-Bass.

Nakao, S., & Lum, C. (1977). *Yellow is not White and White is not right: Counseling techniques for Japanese and Chinese clients.* Master's thesis, University of California, Los Angeles.

Nakashima, C. L. (1992). An invisible monster: The creation and denial of mixed-race people in America. In M. P. P. Root (Ed.), *Racially mixed people in America* (pp. 162–178). Newbury Park, CA: Sage.

National Adoption Information Clearinghouse (2000). *Gay and lesbian adoptive parents: Resources for professionals and parents.* Washington, DC: Administration for Children and Families. Retrieved August 13, 2006, from http://www.childwelfare.gov/search/view_pub.cfm?recno=40973&simple=1&criteria=gay%20and%20lesbian%20adoptive%20parents&cb_website=1&rps=1&uberorgs=1&cb_express=1&calendar=1

National Alliance for Caregiving and American Association of Retired Persons (1997, June). *Family caregiving in the U.S.: Findings from a national survey.* Bethesda, MD and Washington, DC: Authors.

National Center for Educational Statistics. (2002). *Dropout rates in the U.S.: 1988.* Washington, DC: Author.

National Center for Injury Prevention and Control. (2006a). *Intimate Partner Violence: Fact Sheet.* Retrieved February 15, 2006, from http://www.cdc.gov/ncipc/factsheets/ipvfacts.htm

National Center for Injury Prevention and Control. (2006b). *Sexual Violence: Fact Sheet.* Retrieved February 15, 2006, from http://www.cdc.gov/ncipc/factsheets/svfacts.htm

National Center for Transgender Equality. (2006). *Hate crimes.* Washington, DC: Author. Retrieved May 24, 2006, from http://www.nctequality.org/Hate_Crimes.asp

National Center on Elder Abuse. (2005). *Frequently asked questions* [Online document]. Washington, DC: Author. Retrieved July 5, 2005, from www.elderabusecenter.org/default.cfm?p=faqs.cfm

National Coalition of Hispanic Health and Human Services Organizations. (1999). The *state of Hispanic girls.* Washington, DC: COSSMHO Press. (Available from National Alliance for Hispanic Health, 1501 16th St., NW, Washington, DC 20036.)

National Committee on Pay Equity (2001a). *African-American women in the workplace.* Retrieved Septermber 23, 2005, from http://www.pay-equity.org/PDFs/BLACKWMN2000d.pdf

National Committee on Pay Equity (2001b). *Profile of the gender wage gap by selected occupations for the year 2000.* Retrieved September 23, 2005, from http://www.pay-equity.org/PDFs/occupation2000.pdf

National Committee on Pay Equity (2004, August). *The wage gap over time.* Retrieved September 23, 2005, from http://www.pay-equity.org/info-time.html

National Federation of the Blind. (2006). *Blindness statistics.* Baltimore, MD: Author. Retrieved August 3, 2006, from http://www.nfb.org/nfb/blindness_statistics.asp?SnID=70363466

National Institute of Mental Health. (1999). *Frequently asked questions about suicide* [Online document]. Bethesda, MD: Author. Retrieved July 22, 2005, from www.nimh.nih.gov/suicideprevention/suicidefaq.cfm

National Institute of Mental Health. (2001). *The numbers count: Mental disorders in America* [Online document]. Bethesda, MD: Author. Retrieved July 16, 2005, from www.nimh.nih.gov/publicat/numbers.cfm

National Institute of Mental Health. (2003). *Older adults: Depression and suicide facts* [Online document]. Bethesda, MD: Author. Retrieved July 22, 2005, from www.nimh.nih.gov/publicat/elderlydepsuicide.cfm?textSize=L

National Institute on Aging. (2003). *National Institute on Aging AgePage: Crime and older people* [Online document]. Washington, DC: Author. Retrieved July 5, 2005, from www.niapublications.org/engagepages/crime.asp

National Mental Health Information Center. (2005). *How to deal with grief* [Online document]. Washington, DC: Author. Retrieved October 11, 2005, from www.mentalhealth.samhsa.gov/publications/allpubs/KEN-01-0104/default.asp

National Organization on Disability. (2006). Religion and disability program. Retrieved August 1, 2006, from www.nod.org/index.cfm?fuseaction=Page.viewPage&pageId=93

National Women's Health Information Center. (2003). *Health Problems in American Indian/Alaska Native Women*. Retrieved February 15, 2006, from http://womenshealth.gov/faq/american_indian.pdf

Neal, A. M., & Wilson, M. L. (1989). The role of skin color and features in the Black community: Implications for Black women and therapy. *Clinical Psychology Review, 9*, 323–333.

Ness, C. (1993, October 10). The corporate closet. *San Francisco Examiner,* pp. A1, A12.

Newsome, C. (2001). Multiple identities: The case of biracial children. In V. H. Milhouse & M. K. Asante (Eds.), *Transcultural realities: Interdisciplinary perspectives on cross-cultural relations* (pp. 145–159). Thousand Oaks, CA: Sage.

Nichols, M. (2000). Therapy with sexual minorities. In S. R. Leiblum & R. C. Rosen (Eds.), *Principles and practice of sex therapy* (3rd ed., pp. 335–367). New York: Guilford Press.

Niemann, Y. F. (2001). Stereotypes about Chicanas and Chicanos: Implications for counseling. *The Counseling Psychologist, 29*(1), 55–90.

Neimeyer, G. J., Fukuyama, M. A., Bingham, R. P., Hall, L. E., & Mussenden, M. E. (1986). Training cross-cultural counselors: A comparison of the pro-counselor and the anti-counselor triad models. *Journal of Counseling & Development, 64*, 437–439.

Nettles, M. (1987). *Financial aid and minority participation in graduate education: A research agenda for today.* Princeton, NJ: Graduate Record Examinations Board MGE Project. (ERIC Document Reproduction Service No. ED299905)

Neville, H. A., Worthington, R. L., & Spanierman, L. B. (2001). Race, power, and multicultural counseling psychology: Understanding White privilege and color-blind racial attitudes. In J. G. Ponterotto, J. M. Casas, L. A. Suzuki, & C. M. Alexander (Eds.), *Handbook of multicultural counseling* (2nd ed., pp. 257–288). Thousand Oaks, CA: Sage.

New Oxford American Dictionary (2nd ed.). (2005). New York: Oxford University Press.

Nishimura, N. J. (1995). Addressing the needs of biracial children: An issue for counselors in a multicultural school environment. *School Counselor, 43*(1), 52–57.

Nishioka, J. (1999, May 20). UC Berkeley hosts Hapa conference. *Asian Week, 20* (38). Retrieved June 8, 2006, from http://www.asianweek.com/052099/news_hapa.html

Nobles, W. W. (1974). African root and American fruit: The Black family. *The Journal of Social and Behavioral Sciences, 20,* 66–75.

Norcross, J. C., Hanych, J. M., & Terranova, R. D. (1996). Graduate study in psychology: 1992–1993. *American Psychologist, 51*(6), 631–643.

Nwachuku, U. T., & Ivey, A. E. (1991). Culture-specific counseling: An alternative training model. *Journal of Counseling and Development, 70,* 106–111.

Oberg, K. (1960). Culture shock: Adjustment to new cultural environments. *Practical Anthropology, 7,* 177–182.

O'Connor, M. F. (1992). Psychotherapy with gay and lesbian adolescents. In S. H. Dworkin & F. J. Gutierrez (Eds.), *Counseling gay men and lesbians: Journey to the end of the rainbow* (pp. 3–21). Alexandria, VA: American Counseling Association.

Okasha, A. (1999). Mental health in the Middle East: An Egyptian perspective. *Clinical Psychology Review, 19*(8), 917–933.

Okonogi, K. (1978). The Ajase complex of Japanese. *Japan Echo, 5*(4), 88–105.

O'Neil, J. M., & Egan, J. (1993). Abuses of power against women: Sexism, gender role conflict, and psychological violence. In E. P. Cook (Ed.), *Women, relationships, and power: Implications for counseling* (pp. 49–78). Alexandria, VA: American Counseling Association.

O'Neil, J. M., & Good, G. E. (1997). Men's gender role conflict: Personal reflections and overview of recent research (1994–1997). *SPSMM Bulletin, 3*(1), 10–15. Retrieved June 13, 2006, from http://www.ucc.uconn.edu/~oneil/newsltr2.htm

Ontario Consultants on Religious Tolerance. (2006). *Homosexuality and bisexuality: All sides to the issue.* Retrieved on August 17, 2006, from http://www.religioustolerance.org/homosexu.htm

Orzek, A. M. (1992). Career counseling for the gay and lesbian community. In S. H. Dworkin & F. J. Gutierrez (Eds.), *Counseling gay men and lesbians: Journey to the end of the rainbow* (pp. 23–33). Alexandria, VA: American Counseling Association.

Osgood, N. (1985). *Suicide in the elderly.* Rockville, MD: Aspen.

O'Toole, K. (1988, February). American culture appears to reduce school grades. *Stanford Observer,* Stanford Center for the Study of Families, Children, and Youth supplement.

Oxford, R., & Nuby, J. F. (1998, January). *Racial differences in learning styles grades 9–12.* Paper presented at the meeting of the Multicultural Research Conference for Psychological Type and Culture, Honolulu, HI.

Padilla, A. M. (1981). Pluralistic counseling and psychotherapy for Hispanic Americans. In A. J. Marsella & P. B. Pedersen (Eds.), *Cross-cultural counseling and psychotherapy* (pp. 195–227). Elmsford, NY: Pergamon.

Padilla, A. M. (2001). Issues in culturally appropriate assessment. In L. A. Suzuki, J. G. Ponterotto, & P. J. Meller (Eds.), *Handbook of multicultural assessment* (2nd ed., pp. 5–27). San Francisco: Jossey-Bass.

Page, R. C., Cheng, H., Pate, T. C., Mathus, B., Pryor, D., & Ko, J. (1987). The perceptions of spinal cord injured persons toward sex. *Sexuality and Disability, 8*(2), 112–132.

Palombo, J. (1979). Perceptual deficits and self-esteem in adolescence. *Clinical Social Work Journal, 7*(1), 34–61.

Pang, V. O., Mizokawa, D. T., Moishima, J. K., & Olstad, R. G. (1985). Self-concepts of Japanese-American children. *Journal of Cross-Cultural Psychology, 16*, 99–109.

Pania, T. (1992, May 10). Mother's Day brings no respite from worry about son. *San Jose Mercury News*, p. 17A.

Paniagua, F. A. (2005). Assessing and treating culturally diverse clients: A practical guide (3rd ed.). Thousand Oaks, CA: Sage.

Parham, T. A., & Helms, J. E. (1981). The influence of black students' racial identity attitudes on preference for counselor's race. *Journal of Counseling Psychology, 28*, 250–257.

Parham, T. A., & McDavis, R. J. (1987). Black men, an endangered species: Who's really pulled the trigger? *Journal of Counseling and Development, 66*(1), 24–27.

Parker, W. D. (1983). The disabled and clinical sexuality. In S. F. Pariser, S. B. Levine, & M. L. Gardner (Eds.), *Clinical sexuality* (pp. 185–202). New York: Marcel Dekker.

Paster, V. S. (1985). Adapting psychotherapy for the depressed, unacculturated, acting-out, Black male adolescent. *Psychotherapy, 22*, 408–417.

Pate, W. E. (2001). *Analyses of data from graduate study in psychology: 1999–2000.* Washington, DC: American Psychological Association.

Patterson, C. J. (1995). Summary of research findings. In American Psychological Association, *Lesbian and gay parenting: A resource for psychologists* (pp. 1–12). Washington, DC: Author.

Payer, L. (1989, March). Hell week. *Ms., 17*(9), 28, 30–31.

Payne, M. (2006). *Narrative therapy.* Thousand Oaks, CA: Sage.

Pedersen, P. (1978). Four dimensions of cross-cultural counselor skill in counselor training. *Personnel & Guidance Journal, 56*, 480–484.

Pedersen, P. (1991). Counseling international students. *Counseling Psychologist, 19*(1), 10–58.

Pedersen, P. (1995). *The five stages of culture shock.* Westport, CT: Greenwood Press.

Pedersen, P., Draguns, J. G., Lonner, W. J., & Trimble, J. E. (Eds.). (2002). *Counseling across cultures* (5th ed.). Thousand Oaks, CA: Sage.

Pedersen, P., Lonner, W. J., & Draguns, J. G. (Eds.). (1976). *Counseling across cultures.* Honolulu: University Press of Hawaii.

Pedersen, P. B. (1977). The triad model of cross-cultural counselor training. *Personnel and Guidance Journal, 56*, 94–100.

Pedersen, P. B. (1994). *A handbook for developing multicultural awareness* (2nd ed.). Alexandria, VA: American Counseling Association.

Pengra, L. M. (2000). *Your values, my values: Multicultural services in developmental disabilities.* Baltimore, MD: Paul H. Brookes.

Peterkin, A., & Rison, C. (2003). *Caring for lesbian and gay people: A clinical guide.* Toronto: University of Toronto Press.

Pew Hispanic Center. (2005). *Hispanics: A people in motion*. Washington, DC: The Pew Hispanic Center. Retrieved July 10, 2006, from www.pewhispanic.org.

Pew Hispanic Center. (2006). *Fact sheet: Hispanic attitudes toward learning English*. (June 7). Washington, DC. Retrieved June 30, 2006, from www.pewhispanic.org

Phinney, J. (1990). Ethnic identity in adolescence and adulthood: A review of research. *Psychological Bulletin, 108*, 499–514.

Phinney, J. S. (1992). The Multigroup Ethnic Identity Measure. *Journal of Adolescent Research, 7*(2), 156–176.

Pinderhughes, E. (1982). Afro-American families and the victim system. In M. McGoldrick, J. Pearce, & J. Giordano (Eds.), *Ethnicity & family therapy* (pp. 108–122). New York: Guilford Press.

Pine, G. J., & Hilliard, A. G. (1990). Rx for racism: Imperatives for America's schools. *Phi Delta Kappan, 71*(8), 593–600.

Pipher, M. (1999). *Another country: Navigating the emotional terrain of our elders*. New York: Riverhead.

Plas, J. M., & Bellet, W. (1983). Assessment of the value-attitude orientations of American Indian children. *Journal of School Psychology, 21*, 57–64.

PMS: A complex problem for many. (1989, Fall). *Health Scene*, p. 8.

Pollard, R. Q., Jr. (1996). Professional psychology and deaf people. *American Psychologist, 51*(4), 389–396.

Pomales, J., & Williams, V. (1989). Effects of level of acculturation and counseling style on Hispanic students' perceptions of counselor. *Journal of Counseling Psychology, 36*, 79–83.

Ponterotto, J. G. (1988). Racial consciousness development among White counselor trainees: A stage model. *Journal of Multicultural Counseling & Development, 16*, 146–156.

Ponterotto, J. G. (1997). Multicultural counseling training: A competency model and national survey. In D. B. Pope-Davis & H. L. K. Coleman (Eds.), *Multicultural counseling competencies: Assessment, education and training, and supervision* (pp. 111–130). Thousand Oaks, CA: Sage.

Ponterotto, J. G. (1998). Charting a course for research in multicultural counseling training. *The Counseling Psychologist, 26*, 43–68.

Ponterotto, J. G., & Casas, J. M. (1991). *Handbook of racial/ethnic minority counseling research*. Springfield, IL: Charles C Thomas.

Ponterotto, J. G., Gretchen, D., Utsey, S. O., Rieger, B. P., & Austin, R. (2002). A revision of the Multicultural Counseling Awareness Scale. *Journal of Multicultural Counseling and Development, 30*, 153–180.

Ponterotto, J. G., Rieger, B. P., Barrett, A., & Sparks, R. (1994). Assessing multicultural counseling competence: A review of instrumentation. *Journal of Counseling and Development, 72*, 316–322.

Pope-Davis, D. B., & Dings, J. G. (1995). The assessment of multicultural counseling competencies. In J. G. Ponterotto, J. M. Casas, L. A. Suzuki, & C. M. Alexander (Eds.), *Handbook of multicultural counseling* (pp. 287–311). Thousand Oaks, CA: Sage.

Pope-Davis, D. B., & Ottavi, T. M. (1994). The relationship between racism and racial identity among White Americans: A replication and extension. *Journal of Counseling and Development, 72*(3), 293–297.

Portes, A., & Rumbaut, R. G. (2001). *Legacies: The story of the immigrant second generation.* Berkeley and Los Angeles: University of California Press.

Poston, W. S. C. (1990). The biracial identity development model: A needed addition. *Journal of Counseling and Development, 69,* 152–155.

Pouliot, J. S. (1996, June). Diabetes: Are you its type? *Better Homes and Gardens, 74*(6), 74, 76, 79.

Preli, R., & Bernard, J. M. (1993). Making multiculturalism relevant for majority culture graduate students. *Journal of Marital and Family Therapy, 19*(1), 5–16.

Protective Order Project. (2006). *Domestic violence overview.* Bloomington: Indiana University School of Law. Retrieved June 12, 2006, from www.law.indiana.edu/pop/domestic_violence

Pruitt, A. S., & Isaac, P. D. (1985). Discrimination in recruitment, admission, and retention of minority students. *Journal of Negro Education, 54,* 526–535.

Quintana, S. M., & Bernal, M. E. (1995). Ethnic minority training in counseling psychology: Comparisons with clinical psychology and proposed standards. *Counseling Psychologist, 23*(1), 102–121.

Rahkonen, O., & Takala, P. (1998). Social class differences in health and functional disability among older men and women. *International Journal of Health Services, 28*(3), 511–524.

Ramirez, M., III. (1984). Assessing and understanding biculturalism-multiculturalism in Mexican-American adults. In J. L. Martinez, Jr., & R. H. Mendoza (Eds.), *Chicano psychology* (pp. 77–94). Orlando, FL: Academic Press.

Raspberry, W. (1990, February 10). Asian Americans—too successful? *The Washington Post,* p. A23.

Reeves, T., & Bennett, C. (2003). *The Asian and Pacific Islander population in the United States: March 2002.* Washington, DC: U.S. Census Bureau, Dept. of Commerce. Retrieved July 10, 2006, from http://www.census.gov/prod/2003pubs/p20-540.pdf

Reid, P. T. (1993). Women of color have no "place." *Focus, 7*(1), 2–3.

Reis, M., & Nahmiash, D. (1995). When seniors are abused: An intervention model. *The Gerontologist, 35,* 666–671.

Reis, M., Nahmiash, D., & Shrier, R. (1993). *A Brief Abuse Screen for the Elderly (BASE): Its validity and use.* Paper presented at the 22nd annual meeting of the Canadian Association on Gerontology, Montreal, Canada.

Remafedi, G. (1987). Homosexual youth: A challenge to contemporary society. *Journal of the American Medical Association, 258,* 222–225.

Reynolds, A. L. (1995). Challenges and strategies for teaching multicultural counseling courses. In J. G. Ponterotto, J. M. Casas, L. A. Suzuki, & C. M. Alexander (Eds.), *Handbook of multicultural counseling* (pp. 312–330). Thousand Oaks, CA: Sage.

Richardson, B. L. (1991). Utilizing the resources of the African American church: Strategies for counseling professionals. In C. C. Lee & B. L. Richardson (Eds.)., *Multicultural issues in counseling: New approaches to diversity* (pp. 65–75). Alexandria, VA: American Counseling Association.

Richardson, E. H. (1981). Cultural and historical perspectives in counseling Indians. In D. W. Sue, *Counseling the culturally different* (pp. 216–255). New York: John Wiley & Sons.

Ridley, C. R. (1989). Racism in counseling as an adversive behavioral process. In P. B. Pedersen, J. G. Draguns, W. J. Lonner, & J. E. Trimble (Eds.), *Counseling across cultures* (3rd ed., pp. 55–77). Honolulu: University of Hawaii Press.

Ridley, C. R. (2005). *Overcoming unintentional racism in counseling and therapy: A practitioner's guide to intentional intervention* (2nd ed.). Thousand Oaks, CA: Sage.

Ridley, C. R., Mendoza, D. W., & Kanitz, B. E. (1994). Multicultural training: Reexamination, operationalization, and integration. *Counseling Psychologist, 22*(2), 227–289.

Riger, A. L. (1992). Disability issues stance tests our ethical integrity. *APA Monitor, 23*(11), 4.

Riggs, M. (1989). *Tongues untied.* New York: P.V.O.

Ritter, K. Y. (1993). Depression in women. In E. P. Cook (Ed.), *Women, relationships, and power: Implications for counseling* (pp. 139–178). Alexandria, VA: American Counseling Association.

Robertson, J. M., & Fitzgerald, L. F. (1992). Overcoming the masculine mystique: Preferences for alternative forms of assistance among men who avoid counseling. *Journal of Counseling Psychology, 39*(2), 240–246.

Robins, L. N., Helzer, J. E., Weissman, M. M., Orvarechel, H., Gruenberg, E., Burke, J. D. et al. (1984). Lifetime prevalence of specific psychiatric disorders in three sites. *Archives of General Psychiatry, 41,* 949–958.

Robinson, T. L., & Howard-Hamilton, M. (1994). An Afrocentric paradigm: Foundation for a healthy self-image and healthy interpersonal relationships. *Journal of Mental Health Counseling, 16*(3), 327–339.

Rochlin, M. (1982, Spring). The language of sex: The heterosexual questionnaire. *Changing Men.*

Rodriguez-Nelson, M. (1993, Spring). Counseling Latino women. *Focus,* pp. 6, 16.

Rogers, C. R. (1951). *Client-centered therapy: Its current practice, implications, and theory.* Boston: Houghton Mifflin.

Rogers, M.R. (2006). Exemplary multicultural training in school psychology programs. *Cultural Diversity & Ethnic Minority Psychology, 12*(1), 115–133.

Rogers, M. R., Ponterotto, J. G., Conoley, J. C., & Wiese, M. J. (1992). Multicultural training in school psychology: A national survey. *School Psychology Review, 21,* 603–616.

Rogers-Dulan, J., & Blacher, J. (1995). African American families, religion, and disability: A conceptual framework. *Mental Retardation, 33*(4), 226–238.

Rogler, L. H., Cortes, D. E., & Malgady, R. G. (1991). Acculturation and mental health status among Hispanics. *American Psychologist, 46*(6), 585–597.

Rogoff, B., & Chavajzy, P. (1995). What's become of research on the cultural basis of cognitive development? *American Psychologist, 50*(10), 859–877.

Roland, J. (1994). *Families, illness & disability.* New York: Basic Books.

Romei, L. K. (1991, September). No handicap to hiring: How the new law affects you. *Modern Office Technology,* pp. 88–90.

Rooks, R. N., & Whitfield, K. E. (2004). Health disparities among older African Americans: Past, present, and future perspectives. In K. E. Whitfield (Ed.), *Closing the gap: Improving the health of minority elders.* Washington, DC: Gerontological Society of America.

Rooney, S. C., Flores, L. Y., & Mercier, C. A. (1998). Making multicultural education effective for everyone. *The Counseling Psychologist, 26,* 22–32.

Root, M. P. P. (1994). Mixed-race women. In L. Comas-Diaz & B. Greene (Eds.), *Women of color* (pp. 455–478). New York: Guilford Press.

Root, M. P. P. (2001). Bill of rights for racially mixed people. Retrieved June 5, 2006, from http://www.webcom.com/~intvoice/rights.html

Rosen, E. J. (2005). Men in transition: The "new man." In B. Carter & M. McGoldrick (Eds.), *The expanded family life cycle: Individual, family and social perspectives* (3rd ed., pp. 124–140). Boston, MA: Allyn & Bacon.

Rosen, E. J., & Weltman, S. F. (2005). Jewish families: An overview. In M. McGoldrick, J. Giordano, & N. Garcia-Preto (Eds.), *Ethnicity and family therapy* (3rd ed., pp. 667–679). New York: Guilford Press.

Rothblum, E. D. (1990). Depression among lesbians: An invisible and unresearched phenomenon. *Journal of Gay and Lesbian Psychotherapy, 1,* 67–87.

Rotunno, M., & McGoldrick, M. (1982). Italian families. In M. McGoldrick, J. Pearce, & J. Giordano (Eds.), *Ethnicity and family therapy* (pp. 340–363). New York: Guilford Press.

Row, W., Behrens, J. T., & Leach, M. M. (1995). Racial/ethnic identity and racial consciousness. In J. G. Ponterotto, J. M. Casas, L. A. Suzuki, & C. M. Alexander (Eds.), *Handbook of multicultural counseling* (pp. 218–235). Thousand Oaks, CA: Sage.

Rudacile, D. (2006). *The riddle of gender: Science, activism, and transgender rights.* New York: Anchor.

Ruiz, A. (1981). Cultural and historical perspectives in counseling Hispanics. In D. W. Sue (Ed.), *Counseling the culturally different: Theory & practice* (pp. 186–215). New York: John Wiley & Sons.

Ruiz, A. S. (1990). Ethnic identity: Crisis and resolution. *Journal of Multicultural Counseling and Development, 18,* 29–40.

Ruiz, R. A., & Padilla, A. M. (1977). Counseling Latinos. *Personnel and Guidance Journal, 55,* 401–408.

Rumbaut, R. (1985). Mental health and the refugee experience: A comparative study of Southeast Asian refugees. In T. Owan (Ed.), *Southeast Asian mental health: Treatment prevention, services, training, and research* (pp. 433–456). Washington, DC: U.S. Department of Health and Human Services.

Rumbaut, R. G. (1999). *Transformations: The post-immigrant generation in an age of diversity.* JSRI research report no. 30. East Lansing: Michigan State University, The Julian Samora Research Institute. Retrieved March 15, 2006, from http://www.jsri.msu.edu/RandS/research/irr/rr30.html

Russo, N. F. (1990). Forging research priorities for women's mental health. *American Psychologist, 45*(3), 368–373.

Saakvitne, K. W., & Pearlman, L. A. (1993). The impact of internalized misogyny and violence against women on feminine identity. In E. P. Cook (Ed.), *Women, relationships, and power: Implications for counseling* (pp. 247–274). Alexandria, VA: American Counseling Association.

Sabnani, H. B., Ponterotto, J. G., & Borodovsky, L. G. (1991). White racial identity development and cross-cultural counselor training: A stage model. *Counseling Psychologist, 19,* 76–102.

Sabogal, F., Marin, G., Otero-Sabogal, R., Marin, B. V., & Perez-Stable, E. J. (1987). Hispanic familism and acculturation: What changes and what doesn't? *Hispanic Journal of Behavioral Sciences, 9,* 397–412.

Sackett, P. R., & Wilk, S. L. (1994). Within-group norming and other forms of score adjustment in preemployment testing. *American Psychologist, 49*(11), 929–954.

Sage, G. P. (1991). Counseling American Indian adults. In C. C. Lee & B. L. Richardson (Eds.), *Multicultural issues in counseling: New approaches to diversity* (pp. 23–35). Alexandria, VA: American Counseling Association.

Salgado de Snyder, V. N. (1987). Factors associated with acculturative stress and depressive symptomatology among married Mexican immigrant women. *Psychology of Women Quarterly, 11*, 475–488.

Salgado de Snyder, V. N., Cervantes, R. C., & Padilla, A. M. (1990). Gender and ethnic differences in psychosocial stress and generalized distress among Hispanics. *Sex Roles, 22*, 441–453.

Samovar, L. A., Porter, R. F., & Jain, N. C. (1981). Understanding intercultural communication. Belmont, CA: Wadsworth.

Samuda, R. J. (1975). *Psychological testing of American minorities.* New York: Dodd, Mead.

Sanders, D. (1987). Cultural conflicts: An important factor in the academic failures of American Indian students. *Journal of Multicultural Counseling and Development, 15*, 81–90.

Sandhu, D. S. (1993). Making the foreign familiar. *American Counselor, 2*(2), 22–25.

Sandoval, M. C. (1979). *Santeria* as a mental health care system: An historical overview. *Social Science and Medicine, 13B*(2), 137–151.

Sang, B. E. (1992). Counseling and psychotherapy with midlife and older lesbians. In S. H. Dworkin & F. J. Gutierrez (Eds.), *Counseling gay men and lesbians: Journey to the end of the rainbow* (pp. 35–48). Alexandria, VA: American Counseling Association.

Santiago-Rivera, A. L. (1995). Developing a culturally sensitive treatment modality for bilingual Spanish-speaking clients: Incorporating language and culture in counseling. *Journal of Counseling & Development, 74*, 12–17.

Scales-Trent, J. (1995). *Notes of a White Black woman: Race, color, community.* University Park, PA: Pennsylvania State University Press.

Scarr, S., Phillips, D., & McCartney, K. (1989). Working mothers and their families. *American Psychologist, 44*(11), 1402–1409.

Scher, M. (1979). On counseling men. *Personnel and Guidance Journal, 57*, 252–254.

Schoenfeld, P., Halevy-Martini, J., Hemley-Van der Velden, E., & Ruhf, L. (1985). Network therapy: An outcome study of twelve social networks. *Journal of Community Psychology, 13*, 281–287.

Schulz, E. K. (2005). Spirituality and disability: An analysis of select themes. *Occupational Therapy in Healthcare, 18*(4), 57–83. Retrieved August 3, 2006, from http://www.haworthpress.com/store/ArticleAbstract.asp?sid= VEQDEPW7WKEG8GTPXBU44A43NWR17FF8&ID=51551

Scott, A. (1984, August 5). Prejudice awaits Japanese children returning from abroad. *San Francisco Examiner*, p. A14.

Scott-Blair, M. (1986, December 28). Ethnic background results in added pressure to do well. *The San Diego Union*, p. A10.

Scott-Jones, D. (1995). The bell curve critique. *Focus, 9*(2), 14–16.

Sex survey finds fewer gays and lesbians than many thought. (1994, October 19). *San Francisco Chronicle*, p. E3.

Shackford, K. (1984). Interracial children: Growing up healthy in an unhealthy society. *Interracial Books for Children Bulletin, 15*, 4–6.

Shepard, D. (2005). Male development and the journey toward disconnection. In D. Comstock (Ed.), *Diversity and development: Critical contexts that shape our lives and relationships* (pp. 133–160). Pacific Grove, CA: Brooks/Cole.

Shi, Y. (2005). *Suicide in Chinese and Chinese American elders: A review of the literature.* San Francisco: Author. Unpublished manuscript.

Shibutani, T., & Kwan, K. M. (1965). *Ethnic stratification.* New York: Macmillan.

Shih, M., & Sanchez, D. T. (2005). Perspectives and research on the positive and negative implications of having multiple racial identities. *Psychological Bulletin, 131*(4), 569–591.

Shockley, W. (1971). Models, mathematics, and the moral obligation to diagnose the origin of Negro IQ deficits. *Review of Educational Research, 41*, 369–377.

Shore, J. (1975). American Indian suicide: Fact and fantasy. *Psychiatry, 8*, 86–91.

Siegel, A. (1992, February). Black professionals: A progress report. *Working Woman, 17*(2), 24.

Silverberg, R. A. (1986). *Psychotherapy for men.* Springfield, IL: Charles C. Thomas.

Sjogren, E. (1988, November). Growing up abroad. *TWA Ambassador*, pp. 52, 78, 81–82.

Skodol, A. E., Oldham, J. M., Gallear, P. E., & Bezirganian, S. (1994). Validity of self-defeating personality disorder. *American Journal of Psychiatry, 151*, 560–567.

Slater, B. R. (1988). Essential issues in working with lesbian and gay male youths. *Professional Psychology: Research and Practice, 19*, 226–235.

Sleek, S. (1995, September). Religion can play hidden role in relationships. *APA Monitor*, 41.

Sleek, S. (1996, October). Research identifies causes of internal homophobia. *APA Monitor, 27*(10), p. 57.

Smart, J. F., & Smart, D. W. (1995). Acculturative stress of Hispanics: Loss and challenge. *Journal of Counseling and Development, 73*, 390–396.

Smith, T. B., Constantine, M. G., Dunn, T., Dinehart, J., & Montoya, J. A. (2006). Multicultural education in the mental health professions: A meta-analytic review. *Journal of Counseling Psychology, 53*, 132–145.

Smith, T. W. (1991). Adult sexual behavior in 1989: Number of partners, frequency of intercourse and risk of AIDS. *Family Planning Perspectives 23*(3), 102–107.

Snyder, F. (1990, May). Women's health. *Ladies' Home Journal*, pp. 112, 114.

Sobie, J. (1986). The culture shock of coming home again. In C. N. Austin (Ed.), *Cross cultural re-entry: A book of readings* (pp. 95–101). Abilene, TX: Abilene Christian University.

Sodowsky, G. R., Taffe, R. C., Gutkin, T. B., & Wise, S. L. (1994). Development of the Multicultural Counseling Inventory: A self-report measure of multicultural competencies. *Journal of Counseling Psychology, 41*, 137–148.

Soissons-Segal, A. (2004). *The disability experience: A healing journey.* Haverford, PA: Infinity.

Special Committee on Aging. (1983). *Developments in aging: 1983* (Vol. I). Washington, DC: U.S. Government Printing Office.

Spector, W., Fleishman, J., Pezzin, L., & Spillman, B. (2000). *The characteristics of long-term care users.* Rockville, MD: Agency for Healthcare Research and Policy (AHRQ Publication No. 00-0049).

Srole, L., Langner, T., Michael, S., Opler, M. K., & Rennies, T. A. (1962). *Mental health in the metropolis: Midtown Manhattan study* (Vol. 1). New York: McGraw-Hill.

Starr, T. (1991). *The "natural inferiority" of women.* New York: Poseidon Press.

State of California, Department of Mental Health (1981a). *Asian/Pacific islander cultural strengths and stresses: Samoans in America.* Oakland, CA: Author.

State of California, Department of Mental Health (1981b). *Asian/Pacific islander cultural strengths and stresses: Vietnamese in America.* Oakland, CA: Author.

Stave, B. M., Sutherland, J. F., with (Salerno, A.) (1994). *From the Old Country.* New York: Twayne.

Stokoe, W. C., Casterline, D. C., & Croneberg, C. G. (1965). *A dictionary of American Sign Language on linguistic principles.* Washington, DC: Gallaudet College Press.

Stoltz-Loike, M. (1992). The working family: Helping women balance the roles of wife, mother, and career woman. *Career Development Quarterly, 40,* 244–256.

Streeter, C. A. (1996). Ambiguous bodies: Locating Black/White women in cultural representations. In M. P. P. Root (Ed.), *The multiracial experience: Racial borders as the new frontier* (pp. 305–320). Thousand Oaks, CA: Sage.

Sturm, R., & Wells, K. B. (1995). How can care for depression become more cost-effective? *Journal of the American Medical Association, 273,* 51–58.

Suárez-Orozco, M. S., & Suárez-Orozco, C. (1995). *Transformations: Immigration, family life, and achievement motivation among Latino adolescents.* Stanford, CA: Stanford University Press.

Sudbury, M.A. (1993). Cross cultural psychotherapy with deaf persons: A hearing, White, middle class, middle aged, non-gay, Jewish, male therapist's perspective. *Journal of the American Deafness and Rehabilitation Association, 26*(4), 43–55.

Sue, D. (1990). Culture in transition: Counseling Asian-American men. In D. Moore & F. Leafgren (Eds.), *Men in conflict* (pp. 153–165). Alexandria, VA: American Association for Counseling and Development.

Sue, D., & Sue, D. M. (1995). Asian Americans. In N. Vacc, S. DeVaney, & J. Wittmer (Eds.), *Experiencing and counseling multicultural and diverse populations* (pp. 63–89). Bristol, PA: Accelerated Development.

Sue, D., & Sue, S. (1987). Cultural factors in the clinical assessment of Asian Americans. *Journal of Consulting and Clinical Psychology, 55,* 479–487.

Sue, D. W. (1973). Asians are ... . *Personnel and Guidance Journal, 51,* 397–399.

Sue, D. W. (2001). Multidimensional facets of cultural competence. *The Counseling Psychologist, 29,* 790–821.

Sue, D. W., Arredondo, P., & McDavis, R. J. (1992a). Multicultural counseling competencies and standards: A call to the profession. *Journal of Multicultural Counseling & Development, 20*(2), 64–89.

Sue. D. W., Arredondo, P., & McDavis, R. J. (1992b). Multicultural counseling competencies and standards: A call to the profession. *Journal of Counseling and Development, 70,* 477–486.

Sue, D. W., Bernier, J. E., Durran, D., Feinberg, L., Pedersen, P. B., Smith, E. J., et al. (1982). Position paper: Cross-cultural counseling competencies. *Counseling Psychologist, 10*, 45–52.

Sue, D. W., Ivey, A. E., & Pedersen, P. B. (Eds.). (1996). *A theory of multicultural counseling and therapy.* Pacific Grove, CA: Brooks/Cole.

Sue, D. W., & Sue, D. (1990). *Counseling the culturally different: Theory & practice* (2nd ed.). New York: John Wiley & Sons.

Sue, D. W., & Sue, D. (2003). *Counseling the culturally diverse: Theory & practice* (4th ed.). New York: John Wiley & Sons.

Sue, S. (1998). In search of cultural competence in psychotherapy and counseling. *American Psychologist, 53*(4), 440–448.

Sue, S., & Sue, D. W. (1974). MMPI comparisons between Asian-American and non-Asian students utilizing a student health psychiatric clinic. *Journal of Counseling Psychology, 21*, 423–427.

Suinn, R. M., Rickard-Figueroa, K., Lew, S., & Vigil, S. (1987). The Suinn-Lew Asian Self-Identity Acculturation Scale: An initial report. *Educational and Psychological Measurement, 47*, 401–407.

Summit results in formation of spirituality competencies. (1995, December). *Counseling Today, 38*(6), p. 30.

Sutton, C. T., & Broken Nose, M. A. (1996). American Indian families: An overview. In M. McGoldrick, J. Giordano, & J. K. Pearce (Eds.), *Ethnicity and family therapy* (2nd ed., pp. 31–44). New York: Guilford Press.

Suzuki, L. A., & Kugler, J. F. (1995). Intelligence and personality assessment: Multicultural perspectives. In J. G. Ponterotto, J. M. Casas, L. A. Suzuki, & C. M. Alexander (Eds.), *Handbook of multicultural counseling* (pp. 493–515). Thousand Oaks, CA: Sage.

Suzuki, L. A., Ponterotto, J. G., & Meller, P. J. (Eds.). (2001). *Handbook of multicultural assessment: Clinical, psychological, and educational applications* (2nd ed.). NetLibrary Version. San Francisco: Jossey-Bass.

Swanson, J. L., & Tokar, D. M. (1991). Development and initial validation of the Career Barriers Inventory. *Journal of Vocational Behavior, 39*, 344–361.

Sweeney, T. J., & Myers, J. E. (1991). Early recollections: An Adlerian technique with older people. *The Clinical Gerontologist, 4*(4), 3–12.

Sweetland, R. C., & Keyser, D. J. (Eds.). (1983). *Tests.* Kansas City, MO: Test Corporation of America.

Taffel, R. (1991). Bringing the job home. *Family Therapy Networker, 15*(6), 46–54.

Tafoya, N., & Del Vecchio, A. D. (1996). Back to the future: An examination of the Native American holocaust experience. In M. McGoldrick, J. Giordano, & J. K. Pearce (Eds.), *Ethnicity and family therapy* (2nd ed., pp. 45–54). New York: Guilford Press.

Tainter, B., Compisi, C., & Richards, C. (1995). Embracing cultural diversity in the rehabilitation system. In *Disability and diversity: New leadership for a new era* (pp. 28–32). Washington, DC: President's Committee on Employment of People with Disabilities and the Howard University Research and Training Center.

Tajfel, H. (1981). *Human groups and social categories.* New York: Cambridge University Press.

Takeuchi, D. T., Sue, S., & Yeh, M. (1995). Return rates and outcomes from ethnicity-specific mental health programs in Los Angeles. *American Journal of Public Health, 85,* 638–643.

Takushi, R., & Uomoto, J. M. (2001). The clinical interview from a multicultural perspective. In L. A. Suzuki, J. G. Ponterotto, & P. J. Meller (Eds.), *Handbook of multicultural assessment: Clinical, psychological, and educational applications* (2nd ed., pp. 47–66). NetLibrary Version. San Francisco: Jossey-Bass.

Tannen, D. (1990). *You just don't understand: Women and men in conversation.* New York: William Morrow.

Tatum, B. D. (1993). Coming of age: Black youth in White communities. *Focus, 7*(2), 15–16.

Taylor, S. E., Wood, J. V., & Lichtman, R. R. (1983). It could be worse: Selective evaluation as a response to victimization. *Journal of Social Issues, 39,* 19–40.

Tefft, S. K. (1967). Anomy, values and culture change among teen-age Indians: An exploratory study. *Sociology of Education, 40*(2), 145–157.

Texeira, E. (2005, November 13). *Asian youths suffer harrassment in schools.* Associated Press. Retrieved January 11, 2006, from http://www.boston.com/news/nation/articles/2005/11/13/asian_youths_suffer_harrassment_in_schools/

Thomas, K., & Althen, G. (1989). Counseling foreign students. In P. Pedersen, J. G. Draguns, W. J. Lonner, & J. E. Trimble (Eds.), *Counseling across cultures* (3rd ed., pp. 205–241). Honolulu: University of Hawaii Press.

Thomas, M. B., & Dansby, P. G. (1985). Black clients: Family structures, therapeutic issues, and strengths. *Psychotherapy, 22,* 398–407.

Thomason, T. C. (1995). Counseling Native American students. In C. C. Lee (Ed.), *Counseling for diversity: A guide for school counselors and related professionals* (pp. 109–126). Boston: Allyn and Bacon.

TIAA-CREF. (1996, August). Born to retire. *The Participant,* 8–13.

Tien, L. (1994). Southeast Asian American refugee women. In L. Comas-Diaz & B. Greene (Eds.), *Women of color: Integrating ethnic and gender identities in psychotherapy* (pp. 479–503). New York: Guilford Press.

Tomes, H. (1992). Disabilities are major public interest issue. *APA Monitor, 23*(3), 26.

Tomine, S. I. (1991). Counseling Japanese Americans: From internment to reparation. In C. C. Lee & B. L. Richardson (Eds.), *Multicultural issues in counseling: New approaches to diversity* (pp. 91–105). Alexandria, VA: American Counseling Association.

Tornstam, L. (2003). *Gerotranscendence from young old age to old old age* [Online publication]. Uppsala, Sweden: The Social Gerontology Group. Retrieved May 8, 2005, from www.soc.uu.se/publications/fulltext/gtransoldold.pdf

Trimble, J. E., & Fleming, C. M. (1989). Providing counseling services for Native American Indians: Client, counselor, and community characteristics. In P. B. Pedersen, J. G. Draguns, W. J. Lonner, & J. E. Trimble (Eds.), *Counseling across cultures* (3rd ed., pp. 177–204). Honolulu: University of Hawaii Press.

Troiden, R. R. (1989). The formation of homosexual identities. *Journal of Homosexuality, 17*(1/2), 43–73.

Trueba, E. T. (1999). *Latinos unidos: From cultural diversity to the politics of solidarity.* Lanham, MD: Rowman & Littlefield.

Tucker, M. B., & Mitchell-Kernan, C. (1990). New trends in Black-American interracial marriage: The social structural context. *Journal of Marriage and the Family, 52*, 209–218.

Uba, L. (1994). *Asian Americans: Personality patterns, identity, & mental health*. New York: Guilford Press.

U.S. Census Bureau. (1985). *American Indians, Eskimos and Aleuts on identified reservations and in the historic areas of Oklahoma (excluding urbanized areas): 1980 census of population*. (Subject Report PC80–2–1D, Part 1). Washington, DC: U.S. Department of Commerce.

U.S. Census Bureau (1986). *Statistical abstract of the United States: 1987*. (107th ed.). Washington, DC: U.S. Department of Commerce.

U.S. Census Bureau (1990). *Marital status and living arrangements: March, 1990*. (Current Population Reports, Series P-20, No. 450). Washington, DC: U.S. Government Printing Office.

U.S. Census Bureau. (1993, September). *We the first Americans*. Washington, DC: U.S. Department of Commerce, Economics and Statistics Administration.

U.S. Census Bureau (2000). *Statistical abstracts of the United States* (120th ed.). Washington, DC: Author.

U.S. Census Bureau. (2001). *Current population reports: Series P23-205, Population profile of the United States: 1999*. Washington, DC: U.S. Government Printing Office.

U.S. Census Bureau (2001, March 14). *Questions and answers for Census 2000 data on race*. Retrieved June 2, 2006, from http://www.census.gov/Press-Release/www/2001/raceqandas.html

U.S. Census Bureau. (2001a). *Current population reports, series P23-205, population profile of the United States: 1999*. Washington, DC: U.S. Government Printing Office.

U.S. Census Bureau. (2001b). *Population by race and Hispanic or Latino origin for the United States*. Retrieved June 14, 2006, from http://www.census.gov/population/www/cen2000/phc-t1.html

U.S. Census Bureau (2003, January 21). *Census Bureau releases population estimates by age, sex, race and Hispanic origin*. Retrieved July 12, 2006, from http://www.census.gov/Press-Release/www/2003/cb03-16.html

U.S. Census Bureau (2004). *Digest of education statistics: 2004*. Washington, DC: U.S. Government Printing Office.

U.S. Census Bureau. (2004). *Population profile of the United States: 2004*. Washington, DC: U.S. Government Printing Office.

U.S. Census Bureau (2004, August 27). *Women's earnings fall*. U.S. Census Bureau press release.

U.S. Census Bureau (2005, April). *We the people of more than one race in the United States*. Retrieved June 2, 2006, from http://www.censusgov/prod/2005pubs/censr-22.pdf

U.S. Census Bureau. (2005a). *U.S. interim projections by age, sex, race, and Hispanic origin: Table 2b. Projected population change in the United States, by age and sex: 2000 to 2050* [Online document]. Washington, DC: Author. Retrieved June 21, 2005, from www.census.gov/ipc/www/usinterimproj

U.S. Census Bureau. (2005b). *Statistical abstract of the United States: Section 1. Population, 2004–2005*. [Online document]. Washington, DC: Author. Retrieved July 22, 2005, from www.census.gov/prod/2004pubs/04statab/pop.pdf

U.S. Census Bureau. (2006). *American factfinder: Population finder: Fact sheet.* Washington, DC: Author. Retrieved June 6, 2006, from http://factfinder.census.gov

U.S. Census Bureau. (2006). *Resident population estimates of the United States by sex, race, and hispanic origin: April 1, 1990 to July 1, 1999, with short-term projection to November 1, 2000.* Washington, DC: Author. Retrieved June 9, 2006, from www.census.gov/population/estimates/nation/intfile3-1.txt

U.S. Census Bureau. (2006a). More than 50 million Americans Report some level of disability. U.S. Census Bureau News, May 12. Washington, DC: Author. Retrieved August 3, 2006, from http://www.census.gov/Press-Release/www/releases/archives/ aging_population/006809.html

U.S. Census Bureau. (2006b). Americans with disabilities act, July 26. Facts for Features, July 19, 2006. Washington, DC: Author. Retrieved August 3, 2006, from http://www.census.gov/Press-Release/www/releases/archives/facts_for_features_special_editions/006841.html

U.S. Census Bureau. (2006c). *B18005. Sex by age by mental disability for the civilian noninstitutionalized population 5 years and over—Universe: Civilian noninstituionalized population 5 years and over.* Washington, DC: Author. Retrieved August 3, 2006, from http://factfinder.census.gov/servlet/DTTable?_bm=y&-state=dt&-ds_name=ACS_2004_EST_G00_&-_geoSkip=0&-mt_name=ACS_2004_EST_G2000_B18005&-redoLog=false&-_skip=0&-geo_id=01000US&-geo_id=NBSP&-_showChild=N&-format=&-_lang=en

U.S. Department of Health and Human Services (1998). *Informal caregiving: Compassion in action.* Washington, DC: Author.

U.S. Department of Labor (1982). *Accommodation can be reasonable: A study of accommodations provided to handicapped employees be federal contractors.* Washington, DC: Author.

United States Equal Employment Opportunity Commission (2005). *Sexual harassment.* Retrieved October 14, 2005, from http://www.eeoc.gov/types/sexual_harassment.html

United States Senate Select Committee on Indian Affairs. (1985). *Indian juvenile alcoholism and eligibility for BIA schools* (Senate Hearing 99-286). Washington, DC: U.S. Government Printing Office.

Useem, R. H. (1966). The American family in India. *The Annals, 368,* 132–145.

Vacc, N. A., & Clifford, K. (1995). Individuals with a physical disability. In N. Vacc, S. DeVaney, & J. Wittmer, *Experiencing and counseling multicultural and diverse populations* (pp. 251–271). Bristol, PA: Accelerated Development.

Van Meter, M. J. S., & Agronow, S. J. (1982). The stress of multiple roles: The case for role strain among married college women. *Family Relations, 31,* 131–138.

Vasquez, M. J. T. (1982). Confronting barriers to participation of Mexican American women in higher education. *Hispanic Journal of Behavioral Sciences, 4,* 147–165.

Vazquez, L. A., & Garcia-Vasquez, E. (2003). Teaching multicultural competence in the counseling curriculum. In D. B. Pope-Davis, H. Coleman, W. M. Liu, & R. L. Toporek (Eds.), *Handbook of multicultural competencies in counseling & psychology* (pp. 546–561). Thousand Oaks, CA: Sage.

Vedantam, S. (2005, June 27). Social network's healing power is borne out in poorer nations. *Washington Post,* p. A1.

Vedantam, S. (2005, December 10). Psychiatry ponders whether extreme bias can be an illness. *Washington Post*, p. A01.

Vega, W. A., Kolody, B., Aguilar-Gaxiola, S., & Catalano, R. (1999). Gaps in service utilization by Mexican Americans with mental health problems. *American Journal of Psychiatry, 156*(6), 928–934.

Vernon, J. (1995). An historical perspective on psychology and deafness. *Journal of the American Deafness and Rehabilitation Association, 29*(2), 8–13.

Vernon, M., & Andrews, J. F. (1989). *The psychology of deafness: Understanding deaf and hard of hearing people*. New York: Longman.

Voices of diversity. (1993, March 7). *San Jose Mercury News West Magazine*, pp. 8–23.

Vontress, C. E. (1976). Counseling middle-aged and aging cultural minorities. *Personnel and Guidance Journal, 55*, 132–135.

Vontress, C. E. (1981). Racial and ethnic barriers in counseling. In P. B. Pedersen, J. G. Draguns, W. J. Lonner, & J. E. Trimble (Eds.), *Counseling across cultures* (2nd ed., pp. 87–107). Honolulu: University of Hawaii Press.

Waking up to a nightmare: Hispanics confront the growing threat of AIDS. (1988, December 5). *Newsweek*, pp. 24, 29.

Walker, L. (1984). *The battered woman syndrome*. New York: Springer.

Wampold, B. E., Casas, J. M., & Atkinson, D. R. (1981). Ethnic bias in counseling: An information processing approach. *Journal of Counseling Psychology, 28*, 498–503.

Wardle, F. (1987). Are you sensitive to interracial children's special identity needs? *Young Children, 42*(2), 53–59.

Wardle, F. (1992). Supporting biracial children in the school setting. *Education and Treatment of Children, 15*, 163–172.

Warren, L. W. (1983). Male intolerance of depression: A review with implications for psychotherapy. *Clinical Psychology Review, 3*, 147–156.

Watanabe, T. (2005, August 6). Muslim woman crosses a line. *San Jose Mercury News*, p. 5D.

Watters, E. (1995, September 17). Claude Steele has scores to settle. *New York Times Magazine*. pp. 45–47.

Waxman, H. M., Carner, E. A., & Klein, M. A. (1984). Underutilization of mental health professionals by community elders. *The Gerontologist, 24*, 23–30.

Wehrly, B. (1991). Preparing multicultural counselors. *Counseling and Human Development, 24*(3), 1–24.

Wehrly, B. (1996). *Counseling interracial individuals and families*. Alexandria, VA: American Counseling Association.

Weinberg, G. (1972). *Society and the healthy homosexual.* Garden City, NY: Anchor.

Weiss, D. E. (1991, March 31). Long and short of the division between the sexes. *San Jose Mercury News*, pp. 1L, 8L.

Whealin, J. (2006). *Child sexual abuse: A National Center for PTSD fact sheet.* Retrieved July 20, 2006, from http://www.ncptsd.va.gov/facts/specific/fs_child_sexual_abuse.html

Whitbourne, S. K. (2005). *Adult development and aging: Biopsychosocial perspectives* (2nd ed.). Somerset, NJ: John Wiley & Sons.

White, J. (1984). *The psychology of Blacks*. Englewood Cliffs, NJ: Prentice Hall.

White, J., & Parham, T. (1990). *The psychology of Blacks: An African-American perspective* (2nd ed.). Englewood Cliffs, NJ: Prentice Hall.

Wilcox, D. W., & Forrest, L. (1992). The problems of men and counseling: Gender bias or gender truth? *Journal of Mental Health Counseling, 14*(3), 291–304.

Wilkins, R. (1995, March 27). Racism has its privileges. *Nation, 260*(12), 409–410, 412, 414–416.

Williams, C. (1987). Issues surrounding psychological testing of minority patients. *Hospital and Community Psychiatry, 38*(2), 184–189.

Williams, C. L., & Berry, J. W. (1991). Primary prevention of acculturative stress among refugees. *American Psychologist, 46*(6), 632–641.

Willms, G. (1990). The application of Morita's principle to work with HIV-infected clients. *Journal of Morita Therapy, 1*(2), 233–235.

Wilson, L. L., & Stith, S. M. (1991). Culturally sensitive therapy with Black clients. *Journal of Multicultural Counseling and Development, 19*, 32–43.

Winawer, H., & Wetzel, N. A. (2005). German families. In M. McGoldrick, J. Giordano, & N. Garcia-Preto (Eds.). *Ethnicity and family therapy* (3rd ed., pp. 555–572). New York: Guilford Press.

Winn, N. N., & Priest, R. (1993). Counseling biracial children: A forgotten component of multicultural counseling. *Family Therapy, 20*(1), 29–36.

Wolf, T. J. (1992). Bisexuality: A counseling perspective. In S. H. Dworkin & F. J. Gutierrez (Eds.), *Counseling gay men and lesbians: Journey to the end of the rainbow* (pp. 175–187). Alexandria, VA: American Counseling Association.

Wolfe, H. B. (1995). Women entering or reentering the work force. In N. Vacc, S. DeVaney, & J. Wittmer (Eds.), *Experiencing and counseling multicultural and diverse populations* (3rd ed., pp. 317–337). Bristol, PA: Accelerated Development.

Women narrow the paycheck gap. (1996, January 16). *San Jose Mercury News*, p. 3E.

Wong, J. (2006, April 1). Coming clean. *The Globe and Mail*, pp. A12–A13.

Woodlief, B., Thomas, C., & Orozco, G. (2003). *California's gold: Claiming the promise of diversity in our community colleges*. Oakland: California Tomorrow.

Wrenn, G. (1962). The encapsulated counselor. *Harvard Educational Review, 32*(4), 444–449.

Wright, B. A. (1983). *Physical disability—A psychosocial approach* (2nd ed.). New York: Harper & Row.

Yamaguchi, S. (1995). [Review of *Japanese sense of self*]. *Journal of Cross-cultural Psychology, 26*(3), 441–442.

Yamamoto, J., & Acosta, F. X. (1982). Treatment of Asian Americans and Hispanic Americans: Similarities and differences. *American Academy of Psychoanalysis, 10*, 585–607.

Yang, K. Y. (2004). Southeast Asian American children: Not the "model minority." From *The Future of Children, 14*(2). Retrieved January 11, 2006, from http://www.futureofchildren.org/information2827/information_show.htm?doc_id=240866

Yee, D. (2004). Aging Asian Americans and health disparities. In K. Whitfield (Ed.), *Closing the gap: Improving the health of minority elders in the new millennium*. Washington, DC: The Gerontological Society of America.

Yeh, C. J., & Inose, M. (2003). International students' reported English fluency, social support satisfaction, and social connectedness as predictors of acculturative stress. *Counseling Psychology Quarterly, 16*(1), 15–28.

Yeh, M., Takeuchi, D. T., & Sue, S. (1994). Asian American children in the mental health system: A comparison of parallel and mainstream outpatient service centers. *Journal of Clinical Child Psychology, 23,* 5–12.

Yeo, G., & Hikoyeda, N. (2000). Asian and Pacific Island American elders. In G. Maddox (Ed.), *Encyclopedia of aging* (3rd ed.). New York: Springer.

Yeskel & Leondar-Wright, (1997). Classism curriculum design. In M. Adams, L. A. Bell, & P. Griffin (Eds.), *Teaching for diversity and social justice* (pp. 231–260). New York: Routledge.

Young, J. J., & Gu, N. (1995). *Demographic and socio-economic characteristics of elderly Asian and Pacific Island Americans.* Seattle, WA: National Asian Pacific Center on Aging.

Youngstrom, N. (1992). ADA is super advocate for those with disabilities. *APA Monitor, 23*(7), 26.

Youngstrom, N. (1992a, February). Adapt to diversity or risk irrelevance, field warned. *APA Monitor, 23*(2), 44.

Zack, N. (1996). On being and not-being Black and Jewish. In M. P. P. Root (Ed.), *The multiracial experience: Racial borders as the new frontier* (pp. 140–151). Thousand Oaks, CA: Sage.

Zapata, J. T. (1995). Counseling Hispanic children and youth. In C. C. Lee (Ed.), *Counseling for diversity: A guide for school counselors and related professionals* (pp. 85–108). Boston: Allyn and Bacon.

Zera, D. (1992). Coming of age in a heterosexist world: The development of gay and lesbian adolescents. *Adolescence, 27*(108), 849–854.

Ziegler, J. (1986, February 5). Doctors talk about race and mental illness. *San Francisco Examiner,* p. E2.

Zinick, G. (1985). Identity conflict or adaptive flexibility? Bisexuality reconsidered. *Journal of Homosexuality,* 11, 7–19.

Zuckerman, M. (1990). Some dubious premises in research and theory on racial differences. *American Psychologist, 45*(12), 1297–1303.

Zuniga, M. E. (1988), Assessment issues with Chicanas: Practice implications. *Psychotherapy, 25*(2), 288–293.

Zuniga, M. E. (1991). "Dichos" as metaphorical tools for Latino clients. *Psychotherapy, 28,* 480–483.

ABOUT THE AUTHORS

Wanda M. L. Lee is a professor of counseling and associate dean of the College of Health and Human Services at San Francisco State University. An Asian American woman who earned her PhD in clinical psychology, she has more than two decades of experience in the field as a college counselor, private practitioner, counselor educator, and university administrator. Dr. Lee taught for many years in a practitioner-oriented graduate program and her specialty is multicultural counseling training. She has published journal articles and book chapters on topics such as counseling biracial girls, multicultural competency in faculty hiring, ethnic and gender issues in assessment, and counseling effectiveness with Asian Americans. She was raised in Hawaii, traveled extensively around the world and in the United States, and now resides in California.

John A. Blando is an associate professor in the Department of Counseling at San Francisco State University. He received his PhD in educational psychology from Stanford University and is licensed as a psychologist, with a specialty in clinical psychology. Dr. Blando has written a number of articles and book chapters on counseling, aging, and gay and lesbian issues. He has a particular interest in the intersection of spirituality, culture, and counseling. He currently resides in San Francisco with his husband and his beloved animal companion.

Nathalie D. Mizelle is currently an assistant professor in the Department of Rehabilitation Studies at East Carolina University in Greenville, North Carolina. Dr. Mizelle was an assistant professor and the past coordinator of the Rehabilitation Counseling Training Program in the Department of Counseling at San Francisco State University. She received her doctorate in rehabilitation psychology from the University of Wisconsin-Madison and holds degrees in psychology and rehabilitation studies with emphases on rehabilitation counseling and vocational evaluation from both

North Carolina Central University and East Carolina University. Her past employment has included working as a rehabilitation counselor and vocational evaluator in both the public and private sectors. Her chosen fields of interest include utilization of the construct of resiliency with individuals with disabilities and their families and multicultural issues in rehabilitation counseling.

Graciela León Orozco is an assistant professor and coordinator of the School Counseling Program at San Francisco State University, where her vision is to prepare school counselors to work with the diverse populations in today's schools. She holds a doctoral degree in educational psychology with an emphasis in multicultural studies from University of the Pacific in Stockton, California. Graciela León Orozco previously worked as a long-time bilingual educator and counselor in the K–12 schools in underserved communities. For over 15 years, she served as a volunteer producer/programmer and development associate for Radio Bilingüe, the national Latino public radio network, where she was instrumental in developing educational programming for Mixtec, Hmong, and Latino audiences. Dr. Orozco is Chicana of Purépecha Indian ancestry and grew up in a farmworker family in the Central Valley of California.

INDEX